THE CAMBRIDGE GUIDE TO WORLD THEATRE HISTORY

Presenting a panoramic, world-ranging view of history, *The Cambridge Guide to World Theatre History* identifies theatre's most important moments of widespread change from 50,000 BCE to modernity, across Eurasia, Africa, the Americas, and Australasia. It explains why those moments came about and examines how they found expression in distinctive theatre practices. Its global perspective complements more localized perspectives and foregrounds the importance of sometimes trivialized and overlooked traditions. The *Guide* provides students, scholars, and all who are interested in theatre with a fresh, lively, and compelling understanding of world theatre history.

STEVE TILLIS is the author of *The Challenge of World Theatre History* (2020), *Rethinking Folk Drama* (1999), and *Toward an Aesthetics of the Puppet* (1992). He has taught theatre at Stanford University and the University of California, Berkeley, and currently teaches at Saint Mary's College of California.

THE CAMBRIDGE GUIDE TO WORLD THEATRE HISTORY

STEVE TILLIS

Saint Mary's College of California

Shaftesbury Road, Cambridge CB2 8EA, United Kingdom

One Liberty Plaza, 20th Floor, New York, NY 10006, USA

477 Williamstown Road, Port Melbourne, VIC 3207, Australia

314–321, 3rd Floor, Plot 3, Splendor Forum, Jasola District Centre, New Delhi – 110025, India

103 Penang Road, #05–06/07, Visioncrest Commercial, Singapore 238467

Cambridge University Press is part of Cambridge University Press & Assessment, a department of the University of Cambridge.

We share the University's mission to contribute to society through the pursuit of education, learning and research at the highest international levels of excellence.

www.cambridge.org
Information on this title: www.cambridge.org/9781009703451
DOI: 10.1017/9781009703475

© Steve Tillis 2026

This publication is in copyright. Subject to statutory exception and to the provisions of relevant collective licensing agreements, no reproduction of any part may take place without the written permission of Cambridge University Press & Assessment.

When citing this work, please include a reference to the DOI 10.1017/9781009703475

First published 2026

Cover image: Kamal-ol-molk, *Tekiyeh Dowlat [Dawlat Hall]*, 1892. The Picture Art Collection / Alamy.

A catalogue record for this publication is available from the British Library

A Cataloging-in-Publication data record for this book is available from the Library of Congress

ISBN 978-1-009-70344-4 Hardback
ISBN 978-1-009-70345-1 Paperback

Cambridge University Press & Assessment has no responsibility for the persistence or accuracy of URLs for external or third-party internet websites referred to in this publication and does not guarantee that any content on such websites is, or will remain, accurate or appropriate.

For EU product safety concerns, contact us at Calle de José Abascal, 56, 1°, 28003 Madrid, Spain, or email eugpsr@cambridge.org

To my children, Sam Tillis and Annie Tillis

Contents

List of Figures — page ix
Acknowledgments — xi
Note on Orthography — xiii

Introduction: Shaping World Theatre History — 1

PART I   THE DEEP HISTORY OF THEATRE
(STARTING C. 50,000 BCE)

1 The Wellspring of Theatre — 31
2 The Social Uses of Theatre — 45

PART II   THE EURASIAN BREAKTHROUGHS
(STARTING C. 500 BCE)

3 Inventing Literary Theatre — 59
4 Silences and Successes — 74

PART III   THE EURASIAN CONVERGENCE
(STARTING C. 900 CE)

5 The Engine of Convergence — 93
6 Along the Sea Route — 102
7 On the Margins of Eurasia — 115

PART IV   THE EURASIAN RESURGENCE
         (STARTING C. 1500 CE)

8   Okuni's Crucifix   137
9   Islamic Empires   145
10 Across the South China Sea   162
11 Erasmus's Prophecy   176

PART V   THE GLOBAL TRANSFORMATION
         (STARTING C. 1800 CE)

12 The Dynamo of Transformation   195
13 The Neo-Europes   207
14 Colonial Experiences   226
15 Pacific Lands   251
    Conclusion   270

Notes   278
Index   334

Figures

1.1	The emergence of theatre forms since 900 CE.	page 19
3.1	*Bhava* and *rasa* in Sanskrit theatre.	71
4.1	Ancient Mediterranean theatre region.	81
5.1	Role categories of *nanxi* and Yuan *zaju*.	100
6.1	*Muá rôi nuoc* (Vietnamese water puppetry): a scene from a contemporary production in Ho Chi Minh City.	106
6.2	*Kutiyattam*: Guru Ammanur Madhava Chakkyar performs the role of the demon Ravana in a contemporary production in Irinjalakuda.	110
7.1	*Nō*: a scene from *Matsukaze*, a play begun by Kan'ami and expanded by Zeami. Artwork by Kogyo Tsukioka.	127
8.1	*Kabuki*: an early performer, often claimed to be Okuni. Detail from a seventeenth-century painting (artist unknown).	139
9.1	*Ta'ziyeh*: a contemporary performance at an arena theatre in Yazd, enacting the burning of the tents during the Battle of Karbala.	151
9.2	*Ramlila*: an actor portrays the monkey-god Hanuman (model of courageous devotion to Rama) in a contemporary performance in Ramnagar.	158
10.1	*Kunqu*: a scene from a contemporary performance of Kong Shangren's *The Peach Blossom Fan*, in Beijing.	167
10.2	*Wayang kulit purwa*: a pair of shadow puppets.	172
11.1	*Commedia dell'arte*: the Gelosi troupe in performance.	181
PV.1	Theatre regions of the world, circa nineteenth and twentieth centuries.	194
12.1	Ballet: Marie Taglioni in *La Sylphide*, as performed in Vienna in 1833.	198
12.2	Spoken theatre: Hedvig Winterhjelm and August Lindberg in a scene from the first German production (1883) of Henrik Ibsen's *Ghosts*.	204

13.1	*Sainete criollo*: a scene from Alberto Vacarezza's 1929 play *El conventillo de la Paloma* (*The LaPaloma Tenement*), as remounted in 2013 by The Teatro Nacional Cervantes in Buenos Aires.	213
13.2	Tom show: a color lithograph poster by W. J. Morgan & Co. for an 1881 stage production of *Uncle Tom's Cabin*.	221
14.1	Conceptualizing multiple theatrical paths.	228
14.2	*Gelede* masquerade: a performer in Cove, Benin, wearing a female mask and costume.	231
14.3	Masquerade traditions and language phyla of Africa.	232
14.4	*Nautanki*: Devendra Sharma and Palak Joshi in a contemporary production of *Sultana Daku*.	241
14.5	*Bangsawan*: a scene from an unidentified play mounted in Penang, circa 1895.	248
15.1	*Ch'anggŭk*: a scene from a contemporary production in Seoul of the traditional *p'ansori* story-song *Sugungga*.	259
15.2	*Jingju*: a scene from a contemporary production of *Hegemon King Says Farewell to His Queen*.	261

Acknowledgments

I began imagining a book that offered a history of world theatre more than three decades ago. For English-language theatre studies at the time, the "world" consisted of little more than the ancient Mediterranean, post-tenth-century Europe, and the United States. But my reading of world historians had convinced me that a global perspective on the long expanse of theatre history was not only possible but necessary, for the simple reason that theatre is an enduring global phenomenon.

The book that I originally imagined has turned into a pair of books. The first was *The Challenge of World Theatre History* (Palgrave Macmillan, 2020), which sought to explain and justify the global perspective as well as to develop methodologies appropriate to that perspective; as such, it was a work of historiography. The second book, which you are now reading, is a work of history that takes up that perspective and applies those methodologies. I encourage readers interested in historiography to consult the earlier book; the endnotes in this book will point to where the relevant discussions can be found.

I am happy to observe that the study of world theatre history has made significant strides since I first imagined writing about it, thanks especially to scholars working outside of the Eurocentric theatrical context. This book would not have been possible without their labors, as even a quick glance at its endnotes will make plain. But I would especially like to acknowledge the personal encouragement given to me, in various ways, by theatre scholars committed to the global perspective: Arnab Banerji, John Bell, James R. Brandon, Marvin Carlson, Margaret "Jiggs" Coldiron, Jennifer Goodlander, Samuel Leiter, Glen Odom, Claudia Orenstein, Susan Pertel Jain, Leonard Pronko, E. J. Westlake, and Kevin J. Wetmore. I could not have written this book without their wisdom and kind words.

I am very grateful for the assistance of George Paul Laver and Nicola Maclean at Cambridge University Press; I especially want to thank the commissioning editor, Emily Hockley, whose faith in this project was unshakeable. I would also like to thank Swati Kumari and Polly Chester for their editorial work on the book. I also deeply appreciate the efforts of the anonymous outside readers who made valuable suggestions and corrections to earlier drafts of this book. And I am grateful to John McLain for his help in producing the original graphics and maps included herein.

Finally, I want to thank my family. I can merely acknowledge, but never repay, the debt I owe my wife, Adrienne Baker, for her boundless love and encouragement. And I cannot overstate the joy that our children, Sam and Annie Tillis, have brought to our lives. It is with the greatest pleasure that I dedicate this book to them.

As I trust will be clear, many people deserve credit for whatever value this book might have. I alone am responsible for its factual errors and foolish ideas.

Note on Orthography

Any book about theatre from around the world confronts its writer with an insoluble problem: How is one to refer to (and, in many cases, transliterate) the various words and names that one will need to use? Rather than attempting to determine the "correct" terms or transliterations (if such things even exist) on a case-by-case basis, I have generally defaulted to the usages given in *The Cambridge Guide to Theatre*, edited by Martin Banham (Cambridge University Press, 2000). I have also followed *The Cambridge Guide* in italicizing non-English terms (and avoiding initial capitalization, except for proper names), even if those terms have become familiar in English (e.g., *kabuki* rather than Kabuki). I have, however, retained alternative transliterations, italicizations, and capitalizations when given in quotations, and so (for example) while my text will refer to the Indian theatre form known as *raslila*, quoted sources might refer to rāslīlā or rās līlā (with or without italicization or initial capitalization).

The main exception to my default ruling is with the Chinese form sometimes called Peking (or Beijing) opera (or theatre). *The Cambridge Guide* refers to this form as *jingxi*, but I follow most contemporary scholars in calling it *jingju*. Note also that *The Cambridge Guide* avoids diacritical marks in African and Indian languages. I must ask for the forbearance of specialists who are accustomed to (and understand the meaning of) such marks, as well as the forbearance of all readers for the occasional orthographic inconsistencies that will result from the choices I have made.

Introduction
Shaping World Theatre History

Here is how the story has long been told: The history of theatre begins with its birth in Dionysian ritual and the literary brilliance of ancient Athens and Rome. It resumes, long after the fall of the Roman Empire, with theatre's rebirth in Christian ritual, from where it spills out into the streets of Western Europe and becomes the popular medieval theatre. It continues with Europe's national theatre traditions from the Renaissance onward, up through spoken theatre's intellectually challenging realism and avant-garde formulations. And it culminates with modern Western theatre flowing out into the broader world, where it readily displaces primitive and Eastern theatrical traditions that for centuries had failed to show meaningful progress.

Thus runs, in brief, the confection of false assumptions, unjustifiable exclusions, and cultural self-aggrandizements that for more than a century has been understood as the arc of theatre history. It is the theatre-history version (as historically minded readers might recognize) of what has been called the "Whig" (or "whiggish") interpretation of history, in which world history is seen as the story of freedom's progress that finds its ultimate expression in modern Western democracies. That interpretation has been discredited by generations of historians, but its counterpart in theatre history lingers on, zombie-like, in many classrooms, textbooks, and scholarly works. This book presents a different way to look at theatre history. Above all, it refuses to accept that theatre history consists of little more than the history of theatre in Europe and its cultural descendants. Instead, it views theatre as a global phenomenon and offers a new understanding of the arc of theatre history – one that integrates the world's great diversity of theatrical traditions without making any presumptions about progress.

While the global perspective presented here is intended to replace what I will call the Standard Western Approach to theatre history, it in no way discounts more tightly focused historical studies, whether of theatre regions (e.g., South Asia and Europe), states (Kerala and France), theatre forms (*kathakali* and opera), or specific locales, troupes, theatre artists, or theatrical events. The global perspective can in fact offer fresh insights on each of these levels by showing how they fit into a larger picture. But this book presents a global overview of theatre across what the historian Fernand Braudel has famously called the *longue durée* – a scale of time that can span centuries, even millennia. It identifies theatre history's most important inflection points, explains why those inflection points came about, and examines how they found expression in the world's various theatre traditions. My hope is to offer the overarching context for world theatre history that the Standard Western Approach so manifestly fails to provide.

The Fallacies of the Standard Western Approach

What, specifically, is wrong with the Standard Western Approach? The approach is, of course, a metanarrative (or, as some say, a master narrative), and metanarratives are now often viewed with suspicion. The theorist Jean-François Lyotard suggests that the defining characteristic of postmodernism is an "incredulity toward metanarratives"; along the same lines, the philosopher Michel Foucault argues that "the traditional devices for constructing a comprehensive view of history and for retracing the past as a patient and continuous development must be systematically dismantled."[1] Lyotard and Foucault (along with many others) have sought primarily to dismantle the Eurocentric "Whig" interpretation of history – along with other such metanarratives that assume some teleological necessity drives historical development – although their rhetoric extends far beyond that reasonable goal.

The fundamental problem with the metanarrative of the Standard Western Approach is *not* that it is a metanarrative, per se, but that it is a grossly misleading one that glorifies "Western" theatre as the standard for and inevitable endpoint of theatre history. As with any historical narrative, a metanarrative must be judged on the soundness of its historical reasoning and its adherence to the available evidence. The Standard Western Approach patently fails on both counts, and so its endurance as the default metanarrative in theatre studies – especially in the United States – is disturbing. I am willing to assume, for the sake of argument, that it endures largely as a matter of unreflective habit, although its glorification of "Western" theatre has no doubt made it a comfortable habit for "Westerners." But whatever ethical or political objections can be raised against it, the Standard Western Approach is most immediately objectionable because it is bad history.

Three fallacies of historical reasoning undermine the Standard Western Approach.[2] The first is its profound ethnocentrism, which allows its proponents to contend that the mainstream of world theatre history runs through Europe. A prime support for this mainstreaming of European theatre is the second fallacy: a dichotomy drawn between "East" and "West" that divides the world into a pair of ostensibly equivalent units and allows for the "othering" of all "Eastern" theatre as a single alien entity. The third fallacy is the approach's progressivist thesis, which holds that the "West" alone has shown true historical progress as its theatre has evolved from ritual to realism and beyond, thereby allowing proponents of the Standard Western Approach to spuriously justify mainstreaming European theatre while offering minimal attention to all other theatres.

Ethnocentrism is by no means unique to Europe, but European ethnocentrism (or, more succinctly, Eurocentrism) has been especially pernicious for the past few centuries because of its globalist aspirations. Not only does it seek to subsume all the world into the history of Europe, its proponents also insist that the rest of the world accept it as the only valid historical account.[3] But as the cultural critic Edward W. Said has noted, it is no longer tenable to believe that "European culture could be viewed coherently and importantly as unquestionably central to human history." Instead, "new cultures, new societies, and emerging visions of social, political, and aesthetic order now lay claim to the humanist's attention, with an insistence that cannot long be denied."[4] To be clear, the idea that Europe (or any other place) might be (or might have been) the center of the theatrical world is not necessarily fallacious. China was, after all, for centuries the incontestable center of the porcelain trade throughout Eurasia – by which term I mean not only the Eurasian landmass itself but also the islands that flank that landmass, along with North Africa. If one place or another is to be recognized as the center of the theatrical world, it must be shown that the theatre of other regions has in some way been dependent on or derived from it. But this cannot be shown of the relationship between European theatre and theatre anywhere else in the world (aside from a few European colonies in the Americas) before the eighteenth century.

No matter, though, because proponents of the Standard Western Approach have employed the simple expedient of minimizing or outright ignoring the evidence of theatrical traditions unrelated to that of Europe. Consider the textbook *Living Theatre: A History of Theatre*, by Edwin Wilson and Alvin Goldfarb. After a short introductory section and a detailed examination of theatre in ancient Greece and Rome, these authors confront an obvious problem: the disconnection between the collapse of ancient

Mediterranean theatre and the theatre that emerged in Europe some 500 years later. To plug this gap, Wilson and Goldfarb shift their attention to Asia, jamming a perfunctory account of almost the entire theatre history of the various Asian regions into fewer than thirty pages. With that chore accomplished, they can return exclusively to the European mainstream until they reach the twentieth century. Only then do they expand their focus, but their interest remains entirely on the spread of European-style theatre.[5]

The *dichotomy between East and West* is a critical prop for the mainstreaming of European theatre. Identifying an actual boundary between East and West has always been a problem for European geographers because the Eurasian landmass runs without meaningful interruption all the way from the Atlantic to the Pacific. But logical geography was never the point of the East–West dichotomy. Of more importance was the desire to distinguish Europe from everything to its east while also putting it on an equal footing with the entirety of that geographically vast and culturally varied expanse. Europeans were not willing to accept that (as the historian Marshall G. S. Hodgson points out) Europe is "historically simply one among several regions of the Eastern Hemisphere, each of the same order as itself in size, populousness, and cultural wealth."[6] And the "cultural wealth" of those regions includes theatrical traditions at least as long-lived and complex as that of Europe. Moreover, "Eastern" theatrical traditions are as different from one another as they are from European theatre. James R. Brandon writes, "There is no single Asian-Oceanic aesthetic of theatre nor is there a single structural pattern, but rather numerous, even opposing, aesthetics and structures."[7] And Leonard C. Pronko observes, "The abyss that separates Kathakali, for example, from Noh, or Peking opera from Kabuki, is as deep as that which distinguishes a Balinese dance from *Oedipus*."[8] There is, in brief, no single *thing* as "Eastern" theatre, just as there is no single *thing* as the "East."

But again, no matter. Viewed from a distance, and with sufficient disregard for the evidence, one could deploy familiar stereotypes to convince oneself that all "Eastern" theatre is the alien other to "Western" theatre. Brander Matthews, the first American exponent of the Standard Western Approach, wrote that "the orientals have no vital drama because they are fatalists, because they do not believe in the free will without which drama cannot exist."[9] But this is demonstrably false. *Orphan of Zhao*, written by Ji Junxiang, shares a central characteristic with many other plays of China's Yuan-era *zaju* theatre: According to the scholar Wang Guowei, "Courageous actions are … performed through the heroes' assertion of will."[10] Similarly, Kalidasa's *Sakuntala and the Ring of Recognition*, written for ancient India's Sanskrit theatre, conforms to the *Natyasastra*, which holds (in Farley P. Richmond's gloss) that "the principle objective of the plot is to show the hero struggling for and finally attaining his object of desire."[11] I mention these particular plays because both were available to Matthews in English translation,[12] but he apparently preferred to make up his mind about "oriental" theatre on the basis of a crude stereotype.

The *progressivist thesis* is similarly predicated on a long-standing European conceit, this time about historical teleology. According to the historian Peter Burke, "That 'history' is going somewhere, that it is guided by destiny or Providence ... is an old [and] widespread assumption in the West," being "deeply embedded in the Jewish and the Christian traditions"; more "modern concepts of historical development may be viewed as secular forms of these religious ideas."[13] These "modern concepts" were most famously enunciated first by the *philosophes* of the French Enlightenment and then in the 1820s by the German philosopher G. W. F. Hegel. "The history of the world," Hegel famously proclaimed, "is none other than the progress of the consciousness of freedom"; whatever is not, or has ceased to be, part of that progress is therefore irrelevant to history.

The Whig historians of Great Britain were equally progressivist. The historian William H. McNeill notes that they were the first to see "British, American, and Continental European history as a common whole" (i.e., as a unified "West"); they argued "that all mankind has been toiling onward and upward through time toward the pinnacle of English (and/or American) constitutional liberty."[14] In the United States, the whiggish version of the progressivist thesis was promulgated in surveys of "Western Civilization" that became popular in academia around the start of the twentieth century. Their progressivist story, writes the historian Lawrence W. Levine, "pictured 'Western Civilization' as the end product of all world history, or at least the world history that mattered, since entire continents, whole peoples, and complete historical epochs were ignored as if they had not existed."[15] Not coincidentally, it was just as "Western Civ" surveys were becoming widespread that the earliest academic theatre programs were created in the United States. Shannon Jackson points out that these programs bore the stigma of academic illegitimacy: "Dramatic literature, especially drama performed, risked association with the feminine, the primitive, and the commercial." To erase (or at least obscure) this stigma, Jackson suggests, theatre scholars introduced modes of discourse that were broadly accepted in academia for their "manifest rigor."[16]

The progressivist thesis was one of those modes: Theatre scholars sought to "reproduce turn-of-the-century conventions of historical singularity and progressive continuity." A hallmark of this thesis was "the evolutionary paradigm of 'from ritual to theatre.'"[17] Sheldon Cheney, author of an influential theatre history textbook first published in 1929, stated: "From being a [ritualistic] convention, [theatre] had progressed through all the stages of part-artificial-part-imitational portrayal until it had arrived at photographic representation of familiar men and women."[18] As late as the 1990s, Glynne Wickham could offer a related version of the thesis: "As society achieves greater stability and coherence ... it turns increasingly away from [ritualistic] dance and toward [natural] language as a more flexible medium through which to formulate and express its views of itself in action."[19] I will withhold further comment on the ritual-to-theatre paradigm until Part I of this book, when discussing the origins of theatre. It is notable, however, that a significant realm of twentieth-century European and American theatre belies the notion that theatre's progress culminated in the realism of spoken theatre. But once more, no matter, for the century's parade of avant-garde movements could itself be construed as a progressive development. Alan Woods observes, "The very term 'avant-garde' ... defines the process of progress,"[20] although what the avant-garde might be progressing toward remains very much an open question.

Another hallmark of the Standard Western Approach is its willingness to ignore entire realms of evidence from around the world – a propensity it shares with the progressivism of Hegel, the Whig historians, and the World Civ surveys. But even for the supposedly progressive "West," it turns out that demonstrating progress requires ad hoc justifications and the exclusion of contrary evidence. An obvious problem is the aforementioned discontinuity between the end of ancient Mediterranean theatre and the tenth-century emergence of European theatre, which needs to be rationalized away with the notion that theatre was reborn in the Church. But if this is the case, it undercuts Cheney's claim that "from Greek times to [the] twentieth century, there has been a wider and wider deviation from *conventional* methods toward *naturalism*." Cheney's modest proviso that "the progression has not been direct" can scarcely account for a complete reset after a lapse of some 500 years.[21]

To gain at least a superficial plausibility, the progressivist thesis would need to be confined to the post-tenth-century "West" – but even that cannot salvage it. Consider that just after Shakespeare's *Macbeth* (1606) hit the boards, Monteverdi's *Orfeo* (1607) signaled the emergence of European opera. This presents a problem for the progressivist thesis, for opera is obviously based in song and has long included highly conventionalized dance. So where is the inevitable progress "toward *naturalism*"?

One widely adopted solution is simply to ignore opera, implicitly denying that it even is dramatic theatre. But this is surely a case of special pleading. After all, Greek tragedy also included ample amounts of song and dance, and no one in their right mind would argue that *it* is not dramatic theatre. Another solution is to claim, with Wickham, that opera (and presumably the Broadway musical as well) is a "reversion" to "the primacy of song and dance within primitive dramatic ritual."[22] But if such "reversions" are possible as late as the seventeenth and twentieth centuries – and for theatre forms that might be considered among the greatest or most popular of Euro-American theatre arts – how can one retain the claim of continuous progress? In light of all this, it is understandable that explicit restatements of the progressivist thesis have become more rare in recent years. It is far less understandable why that thesis continues to provide the underlying rationale of most theatre history classrooms and textbooks.

Two additional problems with the Standard Western Approach deserve mention. First is its reliance on nationhood as its basic unit of geographic analysis. Studies of theatre in Europe invariably track national theatres as if they have not been intimately connected since the emergence of liturgical theatre a millennium ago and as if, over the past four centuries, opera, ballet, and spoken theatre have not become virtually pan-European. But the emphasis on nationhood should come as no surprise. The historian Pamela Crossley writes, "Well into the twentieth century the structure of all [European] historical narrative was dominated by the archetypical story of each nation's cultural evolution and political emancipation, sometimes followed by its ability to expand and dominate other peoples."[23] But what is a "nation"? The word is often used in reference to nation-states, which can be defined as "a single people [i.e., an *ethnos*] in a single territory constituting itself as a unique political community."[24] The existence of such states, however, is usually a polite fiction, for the large majority of self-proclaimed nation-states plainly fail to conform to this definition.[25] Moreover, the very existence of nation-states is a historical novelty in most of the world, with other kinds of polities (ranging from tribal formations to multiethnic empires) having long been far more common.

"Nationhood" might alternatively be construed simply in terms of an *ethnos*. But any stable sense of ethnicity is also little more than fiction. The geneticist David Reich observes that with the advent of DNA analysis "we know now that nearly every group living today is the product of repeated population mixtures that have occurred over thousands and tens of thousands of years."[26] A further difficulty is presented by the fact that people claiming one or another ethnicity have migrated (willingly or unwillingly) to lands near and far and often live together cheek by jowl. Another alternative is to construe "nationhood" in terms of a shared language. Indeed, an excellent book on German theatre takes this approach, stating that its subject is "all of German-speaking Europe and the German-language theatre that was performed in this large area."[27] Perhaps this linguistic focus is useful for German theatre (given the absence of a unified German nation-state before the mid nineteenth century), but its general lack of utility becomes obvious when one contemplates the prospect of identifying most theatre in North America and Australasia, as well as a fair amount of theatre in Africa and South Asia, as *English* theatre.[28] However useful it might sometimes be to define nations in terms of ethnicity or language, such definitions fail to function as units of geographical analysis.

The second additional problem is the Standard Western Approach's inability to identify its periods – that is, its units of *temporal* analysis – with any taxonomic clarity. Thomas Postlewait has compiled a list of twenty-two different taxonomic categories on which theatre periods have been based, noting that although "these categorical riches are no doubt a measure of the complexity of the field of theatre history," they are also "a measure of its confusion."[29] The most frequently encountered period designations are in the category Postlewait calls "traditional eras": ancient, medieval, and modern. But Marshall G. S. Hodgson observes that this familiar tripartite division of history "has been attacked by innumerable historians as inadequate for a fair long-run view even of European history" while being "still more distortive of the world scene."[30]

Also commonly used for identifying theatre's periods are Postlewait's overlapping categories of "art and literary movements" and "styles of visual art and architecture." Period designations in these categories, however, are notoriously vague as temporal units. It is disconcerting that multiple period designations can be applied to the same historical moment, even if limited to a single theatre form in a single place. Spoken theatre in seventeenth-century France, for example, can plausibly be characterized as Renaissance or Neoclassical or Baroque. But if one is to use such terms as period designations, one needs to be able to distinguish between them temporally. Also (and no small matter), while period designations based on European arts might have at least a modest utility for European theatre, they are useless for making sense of theatre periods globally: Can the concept of, say, the Baroque period possibly have meaning for theatre in South Asia?

The Standard Western Approach, in brief, is intellectually bankrupt. Supplementing its account with tokenistic forays into theatre from beyond the European tradition might salve one's conscience but offers little challenge to the false shape that the approach gives to theatre history. Nor is a challenge offered by refusing *any* sort of integrated perspective, taking recourse instead to a semirandom variety of localized theatre studies. However satisfying each of these studies might individually be, their cumulative incoherence can scarcely overcome the deeply entrenched Eurocentric metanarrative.

World History and World Theatre History

Can the field of world history help us to make sense of how to study world *theatre* history?[31] We can begin by noting, with the historian Jerry H. Bentley, that "the term *world history* has never been a clear signifier with a stable referent." Indeed, "it shares a semantic and analytic terrain with several alternative approaches … includ[ing] universal history, comparative history, global history, big history, transnational history, connected history, entangled history, shared history, and others."[32] Historians debate the differences between these terms, defining them in various and sometimes contradictory ways, but the two most oft-used terms are "world" and "global" history, which many historians employ interchangeably.[33] I will generally refer to "world" theatre history because it is less likely to imply that this history is necessarily connected to colonial and postcolonial processes of globalization. But given the awkwardness of using "world" as an adjective – with "worldly" having its own distinct connotations – I will not hesitate to refer to a "global" approach to theatre history.

As one might gather from the multiplicity of names associated with it, this approach "is no unitary and monolithic discourse." The historian Jürgen Osterhammel comments that "practicing Global Historians are likely to find it difficult to agree on a definition that goes beyond the claim that Global History is an approach to the past that is non-Eurocentric and focussed on long-distance connectivity across national and cultural boundaries. Under such a spacious roof, several different historiographical styles live in peaceful coexistence."[34] The two claims on which these historians agree, however, are sufficient markers for a global approach to theatre history, which similarly need not be restricted to any single manner of analysis. I therefore hold that *world theatre history strives for an integrated view of theatre history in two or more regions of the world, or in a single region within the context of the world itself.*[35]

By emphasizing an "integrated view," I mean to suggest that an account of, say, Chinese theatre history (whether of that whole tradition or some aspect thereof) is no more world theatre history than a similarly focused account of European theatre; to argue otherwise would be to accept the odious premise that somehow Europe stands apart from the "world." Indeed, even if one were to place accounts of Chinese and European theatre within the covers of a single book, that would still not quite be what I mean. To speak of this pairing as world theatre history, one would need to focus on some points of connection between the two traditions, even if only to show how they were impacted by a shared larger context. But when taking a global approach, according to the historians James Belich, John Darwin, and Chris Wickham, attempts to identify connections need to be done "reciprocally"; that is, "one side should not be considered the 'norm' and the other the 'deviation,'"[36] as has been a recurring practice of the Standard Western Approach when it has deigned to acknowledge theatre beyond Europe.

The connections with which world theatre histories might be concerned are quite various. They might arise from direct contact between theatre forms of two or more regions, whether brought about by the transference of whole theatre forms or of specific theatrical traits thereof. In such cases the connection is *homological*. The transfer of European spoken theatre to many other world regions in the past two centuries, whence it has been domesticated in various ways, is an obvious example of homology; a far more limited homology is the transfer of the particular trait of blackface performance from American minstrel shows to the Ghanian Concert Party theatre.[37]

Conversely, connections between theatre forms of different regions might reside in similarities that have arisen in the absence of any direct theatrical contact. These *analogical* connections might be either similar theatrical responses to similar societal contexts (i.e., convergent analogies) or pure happenstance (coincidental analogies). Stock characters of the wily servant/slave type, for example, are a convergent analogical trait in many theatre forms, including ancient Roman comedy and Indonesia's *wayang kulit purwa*. There has been no direct contact between these two forms (nor between forms that are homological with them), but such characters are common in the theatre of societies with well-developed systems of servitude. Coincidental analogies arise with even greater frequency. Masked actors, for example, can be found in theatre forms ranging from Greek tragedy to Japan's *nō* to the various masquerade traditions of sub-Saharan Africa. These forms have not directly interacted, nor do they share a common ancestor, and so the similarity is analogical rather than homological. But neither does there seem to be any shared societal context that would have led these theatre forms to converge on this trait, so the analogy is simply coincidental.

One can examine world theatre history on a variety of temporal and spatial scales, from a fully global view of the *longue durée* right down to matters that are purely local in time and space. While it might seem counterintuitive, there is no inherent contradiction between world history and what is often called microhistory. Giovanni Levi (a microhistorian) writes, "Even the apparently minutest action of, say, somebody going to buy a loaf of bread, actually encompasses the far wider system of the whole world's grain markets."[38] There is, to be sure, "a radicalized form" of microhistory that "essentializes the uniqueness of each place to the extent that it denies the very possibility of any historical narrative of exchanges and connections."[39] But microhistory need not be so extreme. John Darwin (a world historian) comments that for many historians "the appeal of global history will lie in its capacity to enhance our knowledge of the 'local'. ... To an extent that would astonish historians of a generation or two ago, the global and the local have converged – to the intellectual benefit of both."[40]

Given the many temporal and spatial scales on which world history – and likewise, world theatre history – can be written, a key asset is the ability to move *between* those scales. According to the historian Douglas Northrop, "World historians do not see the simple expansion of scale – including to the globe as a whole – as the only story worth telling." History exists simultaneously on multiple temporal and spatial scales, and all scales "work together, [with] each lend[ing] structure and composition to the others."[41] It is axiomatic, for example, that every theatrical event is unique and, as such, is susceptible to microhistorical study. But there are connections between these unique events that can be illuminated by a shift of scale. While shifting to a larger scale necessitates the loss of detail about individual events, it also allows for consideration of different sorts of detail that are impossible to see on a microhistorical scale. William H. McNeill therefore argues that no historical scale is more "true" than any other; instead, each has its own "appropriate conceptualization and amount of detail, just as each scale of a map has an appropriate projection and amount of detail."[42]

Although this book will not hesitate to dive into localized scales, its basic perspective is large scale. To the historian Janet L. Abu-Lughod, the chief value of such a perspective "lies in its search for explanations beyond the narrow confines of historical specialization in a given time and place," providing "a vision that gives depth of perspective to historical (re)construction."[43] Such a "search for explanations" benefits studies on more localized scales as well. Northrop argues, "Grand perspectives give new meaning to national (and local) developments, and cross-regional or global developments shape local-to-national stories. The basic idea is that none of these histories, at whatever level, exist in isolation."[44]

I seek, in sum, to offer a panoramic view of world theatre history that avoids Eurocentrism and emphasizes the various connections that bind together the world's theatres. I reject any sense of an East–West dichotomy (or of the more recent and extreme formulation of a dichotomy between "the West" and "the Rest") because I see Europe as a part *of* the world, not apart *from* the world; I also reject the teleology of the progressivist thesis because historical evidence does not support the claim that all the world's theatre is moving in a single and inevitable direction. The Standard Western Approach that continues to dominate the field cannot provide even the facsimile of a creditable account of theatre history. Theatre is, and always has been, a global phenomenon, and that fact must be at the basis of any work that claims to treat the general history of theatre.

Dramatic Theatre as the Enactment of Make-Believe Narratives

What do I mean when I refer to *theatre*? Beyond its root meaning of a place to see performance, the word has accrued multiple (and often contradictory) meanings.[45] Without rehearsing those meanings, let me say that my concern is specifically with dramatic theatre, although for the sake of convenience I will usually refer to this as theatre. But I recognize that, strictly speaking, dramatic theatre is a subset of the broader field of theatre, per se, which also includes performances of music, dance, circus, and variety acts and at least some nondramatic rituals. The folklorist Richard Bauman notes that all theatrical performance is offered in the presence of a live audience and is "aesthetically marked and heightened."[46] Further, in all such performance there is a "frame," as the sociologist Erving Goffman puts it, that "transforms an individual into a stage performer who may be 'looked at' and 'looked to' by persons in the 'audience' role."[47] All theatrical performance, in other words, is an intentional artistic communication between performers and their audiences.

Dramatic theatre adds to this its own defining pair of traits. First, its performers enact characters in a narrative that is not really occurring at the time and place of the performance; second, its audience willingly assents to engage imaginatively in the performers' enactment. As P. E. Easterling observes, dramatic theatre "depends on the paradox that everything presented to an audience is *both* real, in the sense that flesh-and-blood people are taking part in the enacting and witnessing of the event, *and* make-believe, in that the characters and situations presented to the audience are feigned," adding that "audiences are generally capable of dealing with this paradox."[48]

This understanding of dramatic theatre does not privilege dramatic literature, as has long been common in European and American scholarship. It recognizes instead that a given theatrical event might employ a verbal text that is written, orally transmitted, or improvised (either from a scenario or as a whole) or that it might eschew a verbal text altogether in presenting its narrative. It also recognizes the variety of means available to the performers of that event, including spoken dialogue and monologue, music, song, chant, gesture, movement, dance, acrobatics, martial arts, and more. This understanding of dramatic theatre also accepts that performers can carry their own individual roles, or carry multiple roles, or share roles between them, or perform their roles through puppets, or even be meta-dramatic figures. They might wear any manner of makeup and costume, and their performance might involve any manner of prop, scenography, and staging.

One consequence of this understanding is that it effaces the line between dramatic theatre and storytelling. Some performances might readily be identifiable as one or the other, but the enactment of characters typical of dramatic theatre is actually quite common in storytelling. Eli Rozik points out that "the moment oral storytellers perform dialogue 'in character' there is acting."[49] In the words of Yellowman, a Navajo storyteller, "Tales should not be viewed as narratives but as dramatic presentations performed within certain cultural contexts for moral and philosophical reasons."[50] Conversely, the oral narration typical of storytelling is often an important element in dramatic theatre. Most notable, perhaps, is Japan's *bunraku* puppet theatre, in which the narrator sits to one side of the stage and visibly delivers third-person narration as well as the play's dialogue, while puppets embody the characters "speaking" that dialogue. It is best to say that rather than there being a clear boundary between dramatic theatre and storytelling, the two exist on a continuum of performed make-believe narrative.

Despite the breadth of this understanding of dramatic theatre, it is possible that some might see in it a lurking Eurocentrism, which I would like to forestall. Bharata (the early theorist of Sanskrit theatre) had the god Brahma say, "The drama I have devised, is a mimicry of actions and conducts of people, which is rich in various emotions, and which depicts different situations."[51] According to Zeami (the cofounder and theorist of *nō*), "Role playing ... forms the fundamental basis of our art"; it involves "an imitation, in every particular, with nothing left out," though "depending on the circumstances, one must know how to vary the degree of imitation involved."[52] Chinese theatre has no theorist of quite the stature of Bharata or Zeami, but the great sixteenth-century playwright Tang Xianzu commented that "theater creates heaven and earth, ghosts and deities. Theater can exhaust ten thousand possibilities of human characters and present a thousand changes in human history. Several actors on a stage ... may show spectators the illusion of a people a thousand years from now or scenes from any dream."[53]

We can also look beyond these Eurasian testimonies. Amerindians not only have storytelling that is distinctly dramatic, as already noted, but also performance that is more obviously toward the dramatic theatre end of the continuum. Among the Maya, traditional practices included "dialogues [that] were sung or chanted by choruses while the actors danced [the roles] silently."[54] Farther north, the Aztecs created "a deeply theatrical" culture that included "mock combats, masked dancing, puppetry, and other dramas."[55] Yet farther north, we find the "Wolf Ritual" of the Makah, which includes a special evening known as the "Night of Dancing" that combines music, dance, and pantomime – of which an early European observer wrote that he "never saw acting more to the life; the performers would be the making of a minor theatre in London."[56] In Australia, according to Maryrose Casey, "formal Aboriginal performance practices historically include the alternating of a number of elements within the framework of the performance; these elements include story telling through narrative, poetry, dance, mime, song, music and visual art. The interaction and integration of art forms is commonplace; the story has many ways of being told."[57]

Sub-Saharan Africa, meanwhile, has been something of an intellectual wrestling match over the existence of indigenous dramatic theatre. But Osita Okagbue notes that in forms such as the *kote-tlon* of the Bamana people, the Ekong comic plays of the Ibibio, and various sketches in other masquerade traditions, "drama is well developed, and there is nothing 'quasi' or 'pre-drama' about them."[58] And of course there are numerous sub-Saharan African storytelling traditions as well, many of which involve "impersonation and masking and comic costuming."[59] Such traditions also have a long history in North Africa and Southwest Asia, where Arab storytellers present their tales "with a strong theatrical element including improvised dramatic action, impersonation of a variety of characters, singing and dancing, usually accompanied by a tambourine and a flute."[60] And despite the common presumption that Islam forbids dramatic theatre, such theatre has nonetheless been a constant presence in Islamic lands for at least a thousand years, as we will see.

All of this suggests that the enactment of make-believe narratives is a virtually universal human activity. This book will focus on it because despite its familiarity it is a remarkably strange activity. One can readily understand why people like to perform and to watch feats of talent and artistry, as in dance, music, circus acts, and so on. But while dramatic theatre certainly avails itself of that attraction by incorporating such feats into its performances, it also asks its audience to participate in what everyone involved recognizes to be, in effect, falsehoods. As the philosopher Ludwig Wittgenstein wisely cautions: "Don't take it as a matter of course, but as a remarkable fact, that pictures and fictitious narratives [such as dramatic theatre] give us pleasure [and] occupy our minds."[61] This book seeks to make sense of the history of this "remarkable fact."

The Inflection Points of World Theatre History

Does world theatre history have a discernable shape?[62] I contend that there are a handful of moments – extended though they might be – during which theatre in multiple regions of the world saw unusual and impressive degrees of change in rough synchronicity, thereby shaping theatre's course through time. Identifying these inflection points, as I will call them, makes it possible to comprehend the general development of world theatre by identifying its broadest historical periods.

One might reasonably object that any such set of periods reimposes a metanarrative onto theatre history. But as I have suggested, the real problem is not with metanarratives; it is with teleological metanarratives such as theatre's Standard Western Approach. Without *some* sort of metanarrative, we would be left with what John Russell Brown fears would be nothing more than a nightmarish "compendium of local reports" and "disparate narratives."[63] Humans create metanarratives for a simple reason: "Coherence," writes the historian David Carr, "seems to be imposed on us whether we seek it or not. Things need to make sense."[64] The lack of a well-considered metanarrative is an invitation to default to the Standard Western Approach. That said, there can be no doubt that "all periodizations are in some measure biased, arbitrary, and illusory"; nevertheless, the historian Ross E. Dunn continues, they "are also absolutely essential tools for making sense of the constructable past."[65] The historian Adam McKeown refers to these tools as "heuristic" and suggests that the "frameworks" they provide are created precisely so that others might "elaborate, modify, rethink, challenge, and even undermine" them.⁶⁶ Such is certainly the case with this book.

But how is one to identify the moments of widespread theatrical change on which a scheme of periods must depend? Theatrical events are, quite literally, not only beyond counting but beyond even approximating. We need to simplify matters by categorizing the events in a way that can, at least in theory, be universally applicable, even absent specific knowledge about the overwhelming majority of them. The categories should group together theatrical events whose interactions have bred demonstrable similarities, even if those events are separated by hundreds of years or thousands of miles; conversely, they should avoid grouping together events that exhibit substantial differences, even if those events are offered in close proximity of time and/or space. Any sort of categorization for theatrical events will necessarily be blurry around the edges, with some events being outliers and others arguably fitting into multiple categories at once – but such is the case, writes the cognitive psychologist Steven Pinker, with categories "in any realm in which history plays a role," such as biology or linguistics. Despite this blurriness, Pinker argues, categorization "works because things come in clusters."⁶⁷

One kind of categorization that accords with these criteria, and which is regularly used in Asian theatre scholarship, is the *theatre form*.⁶⁸ When writing of Japanese theatre, for example, one does not hesitate to distinguish between forms such as *nō*, *kabuki*, and *bunraku*, among yet others, despite these forms having coexisted in the same society for some four hundred years. But because spoken theatre has been so dominant in Euro-American theatre studies, it can be difficult to see that it too is merely a single theatre form among many. This difficulty is apparent in a comment by the director Ariane Mnouchkine: "We Westerners have only created realistic forms. That is to say, we haven't created a form at all, in the true sense." But as M. Cody Poulton responds, "Standing inside the tradition of realism, it may be difficult to see the form that the mimetic takes"; nonetheless, "all artistic expression, even the realistic kind, takes some form or other."⁶⁹ I might add that Mnouchkine is plainly incorrect in saying that "Westerners have only created realistic forms," as the existence of opera and ballet (as well of avant-garde works such as her own) clearly demonstrates.

I define a theatre form as *a population of associated theatrical events with a distinctive system of performance and reception*. The theatrical events that make up a form are, to return to Steven Pinker's term, a "cluster" of events whose palpable similarities are the result of a web of associations among the people and institutions that have created them. There will always be variation within a theatre form, and when a distinctive cluster of events within the form becomes especially evident, we can speak of it as a *subform*. Subforms can eventually become forms in their own right if they become sufficiently distinctive, so it can sometimes be difficult to decide whether one is looking at a form or a subform – but this is usually an issue for specialists to hash out. If all of this seems abstract, consider someone in, say, Paris, Berlin, or New York who decides to attend a theatrical event. She likely has some idea of what sort of event she wants to see, and an even clearer idea of what she does not want to see, because she has learned to distinguish between the theatre forms available to her. Pity the person who fancies attending a play with lots of music but does not know the difference between a musical and an opera.

The concept of the theatre form provides a way to identify when theatre history has seen its most widespread change – that is, the inflection points that have given it its shape. Most importantly, using theatre forms to categorize events allows us to avoid basing theatrical periods on matters that are external to theatre itself. The historian David Hackett Fischer states, "The logic of any narrative scheme must conform to the logic of the problem at hand and not to some extraneous structure."[70] The "problem at hand" in theatre history is *theatre* – and so theatre itself must be the basis for determining its periods. This is not to suggest that theatre history is autonomous from the world around it, but to avoid forcing theatre history into one or another Procrustean bed, we need to look first to theatre itself for clues about its historical shape and only then expand our view.

I will focus on the *emergence* of theatre forms to identify the most significant moments of theatrical change. New forms have, of course, come into being throughout theatre history, and each introduces change. One might imagine that these forms have emerged more or less independently and sporadically over the centuries. But what if the emergence of multiple theatre forms occurs at a few specific moments – and not just in one region, but across multiple regions of the world, all at once? It would then be plausible to see those moments of widespread change as the major inflection points in theatre history and therefore as the start of new historical periods.

There are obvious methodological problems with using the emergence of theatre forms as the basis for periodization. The most immediate is the gross unevenness of the available evidence. Little is known about the history (or even the existence) of many theatre forms in sub-Saharan Africa, the pre-Columbian Americas, and the South Pacific, while historical information about the history of at least some Eurasian forms is frustratingly slight. And even when substantial information is available, emergence can be difficult to date, for fifty years or more might pass between the first evidence of a form and its full establishment as an ongoing way of creating theatre. These problems are serious but not fatal. We cannot hope to offer a truly global periodicity for any time before the nineteenth century, but we can hope for a pan-Eurasian scheme of periods going back about a thousand years from now. And given the temporal scale on which we are working, the fifty or so years it might take for a form to emerge is little more than a rounding error that should have limited impact on delineating the inflection points in the *longue durée* of theatre history.

The basic method for identifying interregional or global inflection points is what the historian Joseph Fletcher calls "integrative history." Fletcher comments that this method "is conceptually simple," if not easy to put into practice: "First one searches for historical parallels (roughly contemporaneous similar developments in the world's various societies), and then one determines whether they are causally interrelated."[71] I propose that we can track the emergence of a sufficient number of theatre forms to allow for a tentative periodization of theatre history over the past 1,000 years. Further, upon discovering *when* theatre forms in multiple regions emerged in rough synchronicity, we can then seek to understand *why* and *how* each theatrical efflorescence has occurred.

To those ends, I compiled a roster of theatre forms from as many regions as possible, listing the forms in the chronological order of their emergence. My main sources were standard reference works such as *The Cambridge Guide to Theatre*, *The Oxford Encyclopedia of Theatre & Performance*, *The Cambridge Guide to Asian Theatre*, *The Encyclopedia of Asian Theatre*, and *The Dictionary of Southeast Asia Theatre*, supplemented by more locally focused histories. The full roster is available on the webpage associated with this book.[72] It includes more than 150 theatre forms for which some period of emergence is given in the sources.

Let me be clear about the limitations of this roster. First, it is not comprehensive. It does not include forms for which no date of emergence is suggested by my sources, even as it also excludes the countless forms for which virtually no historical information is available. Second, it is not authoritative in its dating. The sources themselves sometimes disagree; where they do, I have used what seem the more likely dates but claim only that these dates are defensible. Third, the roster is not chronologically precise. It dates the emergence of theatre forms in fifty-year increments, but no doubt a form might have emerged in the previous fifty-year period than the one in which I have included it or become fully established

The Inflection Points of World Theatre History   19

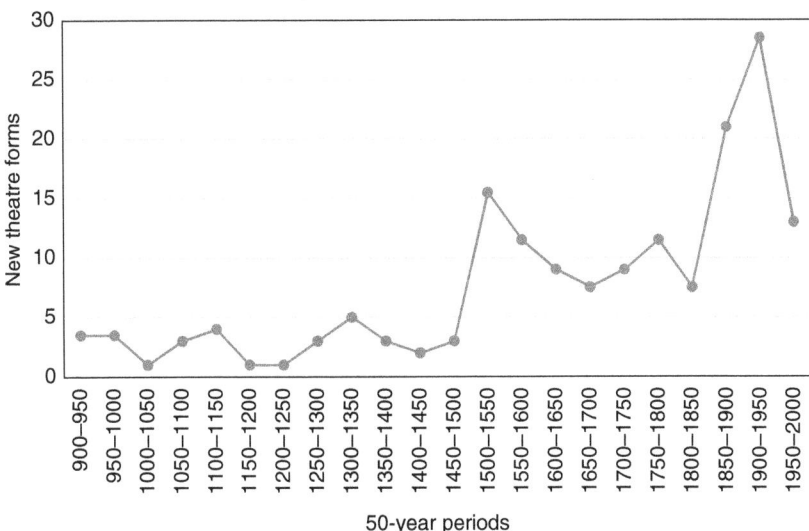

Figure I.1   The emergence of theatre forms since 900 CE. Note that for forms whose emergence is identified by a century (e.g., "dates from the fourteenth century") or a period spanning two half-centuries (e.g., "dates from mid fourteenth century"), I have given half-value to each half-century.

only in the subsequent period. My goal with this roster, however, is to be neither comprehensive, authoritative, nor precise. It is merely to discover if, indeed, theatre forms have tended to emerge at identifiable moments across multiple regions, thereby giving theatre history a discernable shape. And indeed, when the data from the roster is presented in graph form, a shape most certainly presents itself (Figure I.1).

The graph begins in the year 900 CE because information about theatre in earlier centuries is far too spotty for historical analysis, with the obvious exceptions of the breakthroughs to literary theatre in ancient Greece (and its follow-up in Rome) and India. Through the centuries before and after those breakthroughs, the emergence of new forms seems to show no pattern – perhaps owing to the paucity of information or perhaps because the forms emerged for purely local reasons. As best one can tell, though, there is no interregional shape to theatre history before the tenth century.

But in the centuries immediately after 900 CE, the roster shows something unprecedented: There is now not a single fifty-year span without at least one new form, and the few fifty-year periods without multiple new forms might well be statistical artifacts. For a region such as Europe, one might suspect that increasing literacy starting in the tenth century is responsible for the emergence of new forms (or at least for the recording of their emergence), but the new forms are not limited to Europe; they are emerging all across Eurasia. The strong impression one gets is that theatre has entered a new period of creativity and that we are seeing a pan-Eurasian rising tide of theatrical change. And as the graph clearly shows, a true wave of theatrical change arose suddenly in the sixteenth century, extending across Eurasia and now touching the Americas and the South Pacific as well. Again, one might suspect that Europe's new print technology played a role in this change, but the efflorescence of new theatre forms takes place both in regions to which print had not yet been introduced (e.g., South Asia) and in regions where it had long existed (e.g., East Asia). Moreover, while the sixteenth-century wave seems to come out of nowhere, the late seventeenth and eighteenth centuries show a relatively steady state of emergence at a significantly lower level than the sixteenth century, which suggests a waning in the impetus behind the wave. In the mid nineteenth century, however, comes another wave of theatrical change, which grows into a virtual tsunami by the early twentieth century, washing over the entire world before it drains away in the aftermath of the Second World War.

The upshot of all this is that theatre forms over the past millennium do tend to emerge in rough synchronicity, rather than being random and independent occurrences. Although the forms in each efflorescence were shaped by their local theatrical and societal contexts, the global perspective allows us to see that each efflorescence was interregional, with the first two extending across Eurasia and the third encompassing the globe.

But it is not sufficient merely to identify these inflection points in theatre history. There remain the critical issues of considering why these inflections took place when they did and how they did. The historian William A. Green observes, "Ideally, all periodizations should be rooted in disciplined concepts of continuity and change …. We must identify how powerful historical forces interacted to generate particular forms of change at particular velocities."[73] The "historical forces" that might stimulate interregional moments of theatrical change can of course be quite various, and the same forces might impact the theatre of different societies (and also the various theatre forms of a given society) in differing ways. Still, the most powerful of these forces are not entirely unknowable.

The inflection points I have identified are based on nothing more than the emergence of theatre forms, but as it happens, these same points are widely recognized by world historians as moments of significant change in *general* history.[74] Most striking, perhaps, is an account of Eurasian history by Victor Lieberman. His "central thesis," argued through two volumes totaling more than 1,300 pages, "is that over at least a thousand years, vast stretches of Eurasia, including Southeast Asia, Europe, Japan, China, and South Asia, responded in broadly comparable ways to coordinated economic, climatic, and military stimuli. Most regions, for example, saw a great upsurge in economic and political vitality in the late first and early second millennia, and again for much of the 16th and 17th centuries."[75] I need to add that Lieberman's volumes cover only until 1830, at which point European empires were gaining temporary mastery over much of Eurasia, bringing about yet another moment of synchronized sociopolitical change.

The congruence of our theatrical inflection points with the period-markers identified by Lieberman and many other world historians explains why the moments of theatrical efflorescence took place in multiple regions: The relevant historical forces came from beyond theatre and were interregional in their impact. Societies undergoing certain kinds of change create opportunities for the emergence of new forms of theatre. This is not to say that theatre is a "mirror" that "reflects" the world, as the now-hackneyed metaphor has it, but it does suggest that theatre exists *in* the world and that its history is not separable *from* it. This should not be surprising, because theatre is both created and attended by people *of* that world. And so, over the past 1,000 years, as societies across Eurasia have changed in rough synchronicity, the theatres of those societies give the impression of having danced in their own various ways to a common historical rhythm.

But all of this takes us back "only" a thousand years. The centuries immediately before that are (as I have noted) difficult to parse, but the earlier emergence of literary forms of theatre in Greece and India is undoubtedly another inflection point needing examination. And even that fails to take us back far enough, for it is evident that Greece's tragedy and comedy and India's Sanskrit theatre were preceded by nonliterary forms of theatre. And so to begin examining the shape of theatre history, we need to go back to the earliest inflection point in theatre history: the emergence of dramatic theatre itself.

The inflection points I will discuss set off new periods of world theatre history – but they do not necessarily mark the end of the previous periods. As I conceive them, the periods of theatre history are open-ended, for with the onset of a new period, the theatre of previous periods does not suddenly cease. Continuity, after all, is as much a part of history as is change. Established theatre forms often remain in performance well into subsequent periods, and even if the forms might cease being performed, their plays and performance practices will often be taken up by the artists of successor theatre forms, modified as necessary to fit their needs. And so rather than see each period as a discrete entity, I see the periods as a set of layers, with each new period being, in effect, placed atop the existing ones. In this way, one can recognize the theatrical efflorescence that marks the start of a new period while still acknowledging the ongoing vitality of at least some aspects of previous periods.

I use theatre history's major inflection points to structure this book. Part I delves into the "deep history" of dramatic theatre: Chapter 1 offers a Darwinian explanation for the development of theatrical behavior, and Chapter 2 contemplates what we can say about early forms of theatre for which there is virtually no evidence. Part II explores the theatrical breakthroughs that took place in ancient Greece and India: Chapter 3 analyzes the societal conditions that allowed for the invention of those lands' literary theatres, and Chapter 4 considers why other ancient societies did not then invent their own literary theatre forms, while also showing how the Greek and Indian breakthroughs created the legacies of long-enduring theatre regions.

Part III of this book takes up the rising tide of theatrical change that began in the tenth century, when the various parts of Eurasia grew increasingly interconnected even as they crystalized their own societal identities. Chapter 5 explains how China served as the engine of the Eurasian convergence while developing a pair of theatre forms that would influence the East Asian theatre region for centuries to come. Chapter 6 follows the most important sea route outward from China, making stops in Southeast Asia, South Asia, and North Africa to show how each of these regions was stimulated to create its own new forms of theatre. Chapter 7 then turns to the lands on the margins of Eurasia – Europe to the west, Japan to the east – to see how each developed its own distinctive societal identity and theatre forms.

Part IV of the book considers the sixteenth-century resurgence of Eurasia in the wake of the bubonic plague and the post-Mongol collapse of commerce, noting how each region was reconfigured in ways that opened numerous opportunities for theatrical innovation. Chapter 8 examines the emergence of urban-based theatre forms in Japan after it suffered from its own profound internal disruptions. Chapter 9 looks to the Islamic empires of the Ottomans, the Safavids, and the Mughals, alike in sharing a common tradition of improvisatory comic theatre but otherwise notably different in their theatrical directions. Chapter 10 takes on the lands bordering the South China Sea and charts the disparate theatrical courses of East Asia, Southeast Asia, and the Philippines. Chapter 11 focuses on Europe, noting how humanistic studies and the growing importance of the Atlantic Ocean spurred theatrical change.

Part V surveys the global transformation that began in the nineteenth century with the onset of industrialization and the challenge, virtually everywhere in the world, of confronting the modernity that ensued. Chapter 12 tells of Europe, with its new working- and middle-class audiences and its new ideologies of romanticism and realism. Chapter 13 discusses the "Neo-Europes" of the Americas and Australasia that had been created by European colonization and that continued to be influenced by European theatre even as they went their own ways. Chapter 14 turns to three regions directly subjected to European imperialism – sub-Saharan Africa, South Asia, and Southeast Asia – and to the diversity of theatrical paths taken in each region. Chapter 15 considers Japan, Korea, and East Asia, which were less directly subjected to European imperialism but nonetheless compelled to create their own versions of modernity.

Finally, the Conclusion will take a closer look at three aspects of world theatre history that are recurring themes in this book. First is the immense impact of nontheatrical historical forces, especially at theatre history's major inflection points; second is the frequency with which theatre forms have been influenced by syncretism, whether *intra*cultural or *inter*cultural; and third is the depth of attraction that dramatic theatre has exerted upon people everywhere. World theatre history, one might say, has been shaped by general history, but it has also been shaped by the transmission of theatrical ideas as well as by the intrinsically human desire to participate in dramatic theatre.

A Personal Note

Allow me to conclude this Introduction on a personal note. Who am I to write about world theatre history? Everyone comes from somewhere or (for some people) a set of somewheres. I come from the United States, a fact that has undoubtedly influenced my thinking, sometimes in ways I will have failed to recognize. But the same is true, mutatis mutandis, of everyone. All claims about history come from one or another person (or group of people) hailing from one or another place (or set of places). Because we are all inescapably positioned *in* the world, no one automatically has a greater or lesser authority to write *about* the world. But as the historian David Hackett Fischer notes, "The fact that historical knowledge is itself historically caused by the situation of the historian does not in any degree imply that it is false."[76] The validity of a historical claim is conditional not on who or where it comes from but on the quality of its historical reasoning and on its adherence to the available evidence.

I am aware, though, that I bring a set of presuppositions to this book. I presuppose that the world *matters*, for we all share a common humanity, however much our individual lives might be embedded in one or another society. I also presuppose that historical evidence allows for the making of meaningful historical claims, even if those claims cannot be granted absolute certainty. Regarding theatre history, I have already suggested that I reject the view that it should focus on dramatic literature. But I also reject A. M. Nagler's view that theatre historians should focus on "styles of performance and their more or less plausible reconstructions," while engaging "neither in historical philology nor in the study of literature, neither in folklore nor in sociology."[77] My presupposition, rather, is that everything associated with theatrical events is legitimate territory for theatre historians. Further, while I reject the view that theatre exists in an aesthetic universe of its own, I also reject the contrary view that it merely reflects or expresses the society in which it is performed. My presupposition, instead, is that dramatic theatre is a constituent part *of* society, at once affecting and being affected by it – but that societal forces do not compel theatre to develop in any particular direction. I believe that theatre artists, while working within specific theatrical and societal contexts, are the primary agents of theatrical continuity and change.

But I am only one person. A strong argument can be made that a book on world theatre history should be written by a team of scholars, each an expert on the place of which they write. The offsetting advantage that can be offered by a single author (whoever he or she might be) is a unity of vision that provides a clear thesis and a coherent argument in support of that thesis. Works by teams of experts present multiple perspectives and differing points of emphasis, sometimes leading to contradictions, repetitions, and/or gaps in the overall discussion; they also tend to be quite unwieldy.[78] No single author can claim anything like the depth of knowledge that a team of experts will have, but such an author *can* hope to offer a cogent and concise line of thought.

I make no claim to expertise in the theatre (or general) history of any particular time and/or place. Because this book is based on the expertise of others, it should be understood as a work of synthesis. But it is a fundamentally different synthesis than can be found elsewhere, for its discussion of the *longue durée* of theatre history is based on the premise that all the places of the world are in the world, together, and that none is intrinsically more or less worthy of consideration than any other place. Starting from this premise, the following pages seek to make sense of the enduring continuities and the most important moments of change that have given world theatre history its shape.

PART I

The Deep History of Theatre (starting c. 50,000 BCE)

A short story by Jorge Luis Borges tells of the renowned Islamic philosopher Averroës (Abu'l-Walid Ibn Rushd) and his struggle to write a commentary on Aristotle's *Poetics*. It is the twelfth century, in Islamic Spain's cosmopolitan city of Córdoba; Averroës's immediate problem is that Arabic has no words commensurate to *tragedy* and *comedy*. In the courtyard outside the scholar's study, "half-naked children" are at play in make-believe; Averroës notes their activity but muses only about the dialect in which they speak. Later that day, guests arrive, among them a friend recently returned from China who reports on a curiosity he saw there: Twenty people presented a story by singing, dancing, and pretending to be persons other than themselves. No one hearing this report can make sense of it: What need is there for twenty people when "a single speaker could *tell* anything, no matter how complex it might be"? Averroës (both in Borges's story and in real life) ends up translating *tragedy* as "panegyrics" and *comedy* as "satires and anathemas," noting that the Quran includes examples of both. In a concluding comment, Borges writes that he has "tried to narrate the process of failure": "Bounded within the circle of Islam, [Averroës] could never have known the meaning of the words *tragedy* and *comedy*" and was committing an absurdity by "trying to imagine what a play is without ever having suspected what a theater is."[1]

A notable irony lurks in this tale, no doubt intentionally. Those half-naked children might not have been acting out anything that one would want to call tragedy or comedy, but they were certainly engaged in theatrical behavior, albeit without the audience that the Chinese performance had (and that dramatic theatre, properly speaking, requires). But the tale also holds a second irony, most likely unintentional. For as Shmuel Moreh points out, "There were certainly many kinds of dramatic entertainment" in Islamic Spain in the twelfth century. Indeed, Averroës's translation of *tragedy* and *comedy* might well have been born of "a desire to apply Aristotle's methodology to Arabic poetry, not due to ignorance of the

27

theatrical arts and their terminology."[2] If Averroës wanted to experience theatre, he would have needed to do little more than to step out from the pages of Borges's story and into the teeming streets of Córdoba.

People throughout the world have the ability to partake of dramatic theatre. This claim for the universality of theatre does not mean that everyone regularly participates in theatre, nor that every society hosts organized theatre forms.[3] It means that the overwhelming majority of people, regardless of the society in which they live, have a natural (though highly variable) capacity for theatrical behavior, which I understand to be the ability to participate in dramatic theatre, whether as a performer or an audience member. The sheer ubiquity of theatrical behavior compels one to wonder: How did all of this *begin*?

As I noted in the Introduction, the theory that theatre originated in ritual is baked into the progressivism of the Standard Western Approach. The most immediate problem with that theory is the ambiguity of the word *ritual* itself. Richard Schechner comments that "even to say it in one word, ritual, is asking for trouble. Ritual has been so variously defined – as concept, praxis, process, ideology, yearning, religious experience, function – that it means very little because it can mean too much."[4] Most often, though, ritual-origins theory appeals specifically to *religious* ritual. Brander Matthews wrote in his seminal 1916 survey of theatre history, "It is from religious exercises, set off always with music and often dancing, that the drama has evolved in almost every literature."[5] This emphasis on religious ritual accords with the definition given by the anthropologist Victor Turner, who sees ritual as "prescribed formal behavior for occasions not given over to technological routine, having reference to beliefs in invisible beings or powers regarded as the first and final causes of all effects."[6]

There are two basic versions of the theory that theatre "evolved" from religious ritual. The first, which itself comes in many flavors, derives from the nineteenth-century myth-ritual theorizing of the anthropologist James G. Frazer. Members of the so-called Cambridge School claimed that one or another kind of ritual was the point of origin for Greek theatre: F. M. Cornford suggested the ritual killing and revival (or replacement) of a king;[7] Gilbert Murray suggested rituals associated with a dying-and-reviving vegetation god;[8] Jane Ellen Harrison suggested both a dying-and-reviving vegetation god and a primitive initiation ritual.[9] To further complicate matters, others (such as William Ridgeway) suggested rituals involving the worship of the dead.[10] Myth-ritualists, however, were never able to demonstrate an evolutionary line from any specific rituals to either Greek tragedy or comedy; recent scholarship, under the banner of "New Ritualism," has therefore preferred to emphasize "synchronic relations between Greek drama and ritual, not diachronic or historic" ones.[11]

More generally, it is unclear why theories about the origins of Greek theatre should necessarily have significance for theatre elsewhere. Sometimes it seems assumed that once theatre was born of ritual in ancient Greece, it then spread to other places and so bore the same ritual ancestry. At other times, it seems assumed that the birth of theatre from ritual in Greece is the model for theatre's origins elsewhere – an assumption ostensibly confirmed by theatre's supposed rebirth from ritual in tenth-century Europe. It is telling, however, that in a collection of essays entitled *The Origins of Theater in Ancient Greece and Beyond: From Ritual to Drama*, the penultimate essay argues that in the three non-Greek cases examined in the book, "what we might call 'theater' did not in fact emerge from ritual, or else did not emerge and differentiate itself [from ritual] in a way that developmentalist theory would predict."[12]

The second basic version of ritual-origins theory was most fully articulated in the 1970s by E. T. Kirby. Starting from the premise that shamanism was once the universal religion, Kirby suggests that the shaman was the original performer and that shamanistic ritual was "'the great unitarian artwork' that fragmented into numerous performance arts," including "dialogue, enactments, ventriloquism, incantations, music, dance, and song."[13] But as Eli Rozik points out, Kirby's "model of shamanism ... does not correspond to any real shamanistic culture in the world but is constructed of features from various cultures."[14] Indeed, shamanism might well not have been as universal as Kirby assumes. In its most precise sense, it was limited to Northeast Asia, although many scholars accept that shamanism (or something related to it) has also existed in parts of East Asia and perhaps also in the Americas (which were originally settled via Northeast Asia). Shamanism's existence anywhere else depends on one's willingness to accept that anything *like* shamanism *is* shamanism. But even beyond haggling over the definition and extent of shamanism, it beggars the imagination to think that music and dance did not preexist shamanism, as these might well have been practiced as far back as the time of Neanderthals.[15] It also is evident that children around the world regularly manage to sing, dance, and even create rudimentary theatre without the slightest knowledge of or involvement with shamans.

There can be no doubt that at least some forms of theatre are associated in some way with religious ritual, but that is a far cry from asserting that *all* theatre has necessarily evolved from ritual. The literary scholar Brian Boyd argues that ritual-origins theories get the matter backwards, as religion "needs art as a precursor [and itself] depends on the power of story."¹⁶ Bruce McConachie similarly suggests, "There is some evidence to reverse the assumption of many theorists that performance and the arts grew out of religion. Rather, rituals tied to religious beliefs are the evolutionary offspring of play and performance."¹⁷

We are thus returned to the question of theatre's origins, the most revealing clue of which is the fact that wherever people exist, theatrical behavior exists. This raises the possibility that such behavior is an inborn capacity in humans, explainable through Darwinian evolution. And although the theatre of early human history is accessible neither through direct observation nor through the examination of artifacts, one can still get a sense of what it might have involved by using the process of inference from what we *do* know about theatre history. The "deep history" I will discuss in Part I of this book, therefore, has a pair of connotations. It is "deep" because it refers to a virtually timeless sort of history buried within the human psyche, but it is also "deep" in that it refers to the continuities that exist between the theatre of the far-distant past and the theatre created to this day.

CHAPTER I

The Wellspring of Theatre

The Role of Human Evolution

Recall those half-naked children in the tale by Borges. Their behavior is so common that the fictional Averroës scarcely acknowledges that they are pretending to be other than who they are as they enact their make-believe scene. But why would they do this? Indeed, why would children around the world regularly engage in that same sort of behavior? And why, no less curiously, would the adults at the Chinese performance reported to the fictional Averroës willingly attend and enjoy the make-believe of *that* performance, just as adults in the Córdoba of the historical Averroës would have attended and enjoyed performances of make-believe?

There can be no doubt that theatrical behavior expresses itself in ways that are shaped by one or another society. The children in Borges's tale play at being a minaret, a muezzin who stands atop it while making the call to daily prayers, and a one-boy "congregation of the faithful";[1] their playing, in other words, is embedded in their Islamic culture. Indeed, the psychologists Sabine Doebel and Angeline S. Lillard suggest that children's pretend play "may be a key way that ... cultural knowledge is rapidly acquired. By freely exploring their environment and the objects and affordances within it, children not only quickly gain rich knowledge about the world ..., they also gain cultural knowledge that can then be applied in goal-directed activities."[2] "Cultural knowledge" was presumably also acquired by the audiences in the Chinese performance reported to the fictional Averroës. But although societies undoubtedly *shape* theatrical behavior, that does not imply that the behavior itself is the *product* of society. One must seek an explanation that accounts for the universality of children's pretend play – as well as for adults' willing participation in the make-believe of dramatic theatre, whether as actors or audience members, long after childhood pretending has ceased.

That explanation can begin with the realization, strongly hinted at in many languages, that pretend play and the plays of dramatic theatre are related phenomena. The semantic range of the English word "play" implies that relationship, as do the similar semantic ranges of the French *jeu* and the German *spiel*.[3] In India, meanwhile, the Marathi term *khel* "refers to many things – from children's 'play,' to 'entertainment' and 'sport,' in addition to 'performance,'" but the term is associated only with human play, for when divinities play, or are the characters *in* a play, the relevant term is *lila*.[4] In various Dravidian languages of southern India, which are linguistically distinct from Marathi or other Indo-Aryan languages, *attam* has the semantic range to encompass childhood play, games, sports, and dramatic performance.[5] Similarly, in the Yoruba language (spoken mostly in what is now Nigeria), "the semantic scope of *eré* … covers drama, theatre, games, singing, chanting, drumming, dancing, miming, acrobatics, storytelling, masquerading, regatta, shows, riddles and jokes," while in China, the term "*xiju* was long used for both 'child's play' or 'game' and 'live performance.'"[6] The evolutionary development of humans, I will argue, has endowed us with the ability to engage in the theatrical behavior that connects the semantically related phenomena of pretend play and theatrical play. The wellspring of theatre can be found in that ability, and it is a wellspring that has continued to flow throughout human history.[7]

There are two main ways that a physical or behavioral characteristic (such as theatrical behavior) might be the product of evolution. The first is that the characteristic is an *adaptation*, which the evolutionary psychologists David M. Buss et al. define as "an inherited and reliably developing characteristic that came into existence as a feature of a species through natural selection because it helped to directly or indirectly facilitate reproduction during the period of its evolution."[8] But not all characteristics (whether physical or behavioral) have an adaptive function, so the second main way a characteristic might arise from evolution is as the *by-product* of an adaptive characteristic. Buss et al. write, "By-products are characteristics that do not solve adaptive problems and do not have to have functional design. They are carried along with characteristics that do have functional design because they happen to be coupled with those adaptations." An example of an evolutionary by-product is the whiteness of bones, a color that serves no adaptive purpose but is simply the result of bones being made of calcium.[9]

This is still, however, a bit too simple, for in addition to adaptations and by-products it is now generally accepted that there are also two kinds of *exaptations*.[10] Buss et al. explain that the first kind are "adaptations that initially arose through natural selection and were subsequently co-opted for another function." A famous example is the feathers that certain species of dinosaurs evolved, probably to regulate their internal temperature.

Feathers, however, also proved very useful for flight, so the evolutionary function of feathers was "co-opted" in some species (and in the birds that descended from them) to serve the different evolutionary function of enabling flight. The second kind of exaptation pertains to "features that did not arise as adaptations through natural selection but rather as [by-products] of adaptive processes and that have [subsequently] been co-opted for a biological function," thereby becoming adaptations in their own right.[11] For example, the sutures in the skulls of young mammals were originally a by-product of the way that bones grow, but that by-product has been co-opted by evolution to aid the birthing process in some abnormally large-headed mammals, including humans. In the first kind of exaptation, then, a new evolutionary function is given to an existing adaptation; in the second kind, a previously nonfunctional by-product gains an evolutionary function.[12]

Whether theatrical behavior is an evolutionary adaptation, a by-product of some such adaptation, or one or the other kind of exaptation, we would be justified in viewing it as an innate characteristic of the human psyche. But any such explanation comes hard against the problem that theatrical behavior would appear, in terms of evolution, to be strikingly counterproductive. The evolutionary psychologists John Tooby and Leda Cosmides observe that quite a few aspects of human behavior "are puzzling anomalies from an evolutionary perspective" and that "chief among these are [sic] the human attraction to fictional experience (in all media and genres)"; yet "involvement in fictional, imagined worlds appears to be a cross-culturally universal, species-typical phenomenon."[13]

The nub of the problem is that "organisms should have an appetite for obtaining accurate information, and the distinction between true information or false information should be important in determining whether the information is absorbed or disregarded"; but in fact, humans obviously desire and become deeply immersed in the "'false information' of stories, plays, movies, and so on."[14] An adaptation or exaptation will be passed through generations only if it benefits survival and reproductive success; a by-product will be tolerated only if its costs do not outweigh the benefits of the adaptation from which it is derived. But how can survival and reproductive success benefit when the vitally important "distinction between true information and false information" is compromised? This problem presents itself most immediately in the pretend play of young children, for as the psychologists Caren Walker and Alison Gopnik write: "Children need to learn so much about the real world" if they are to survive. "So why do they spend such a large amount of time and energy engaging with unreal worlds? How could exploring manifestly false worlds improve their understanding of the real one?"[15]

One widely accepted definition of this apparently counterproductive pretend play is offered by the psychologists Angeline S. Lillard et al.: "Pretend play activities are the subset of play activities characterized by an 'as-if' stance …. Beyond being simply nonliteral, in pretend play a 'pretense' is layered over reality …; specifically, a pretender knowingly and intentionally projects some mentally represented alternative onto the present situation in the spirit of play."[16] These activities typically start before two years of age and develop sequentially through the next four years, beginning with "object substitutions (using an object as if it is something different than what its properties suggest it to be)" and leading eventually to "role enactment" and then "pretense-related metacommunication (planning, negotiation, or role assignments to organize role play into complex scenarios)."[17] Borges's half-naked children have reached that highest level of pretend play, for Borges tells us the children must negotiate who plays which role, as "they all wanted to be the muezzin."[18] I have referred to this level of pretend play as theatrical behavior, for these children clearly have the ability to partake in dramatic theatre. But their playing is not yet theatre itself because it has no audience; Averroës alone observes them, but with obvious disinterest in their playing. The natural development of pretend play leads children to the brink of theatre itself, but it awaits an audience to truly *be* theatre.

Almost all researchers agree that pretend play "is a universal, cross cultural, and central aspect of child development."[19] As Lillard summarizes: "Pretend play is a signature behavior of early childhood …. Although the frequency and content of pretend play vary across cultures, its occurrence and basic schedule do not. Pretend play occurs even in settings where parents discourage it, although its schedule is slightly delayed." She goes on to observe that "these two features – a predictable developmental sequence and universality – suggest an evolved behavior."[20] But what adaptive purpose, if any, might the "evolved behavior" of pretend play have served?

Psychologists have not reached a consensus in answering that question. In their extensive review of the experimental literature (as of 2013), Lillard et al. examine evidence that pretend play might be crucial for the development of cognitive aptitudes (specifically, for creativity, intelligence, problem solving, reasoning, and conservation), theory of mind (i.e., the ability to understand that others have their own thoughts), social skills, language/symbolic understanding, narrative skills, and self-regulation. As they judge the evidence, "The causal account is most plausible for language, as pretend play is quite consistently related to it," but they note that "correlation is not causation, and reverse causality (from language to play) is shown in some studies." It might well be, these authors suggest, that "the domains" of pretend play and language "are related due to an underlying symbolic function," in which case they would both be manifestations of that "symbolic function."[21]

In her solo article, Lillard develops the idea that an advanced capacity for symbolic thinking, per se, is the relevant adaptive characteristic. Newer research, she writes, shows evidence for "a symbolic component underlying pretending itself, language, and specific symbol understanding tasks at 2.5 and 3 years of age [that] predicted social understanding at ages 4 and 5 years"; moreover, "what was key about pretense comprehension for later theory of mind was the symbolic component."[22] The evolutionary value of symbolic thinking is clear enough: The ability to deploy and understand complex symbols (such as words and pictures) greatly expands the human facility to exchange ideas and information, thereby advancing the prospects for survival and reproduction among those who have that ability. In the far-distant past, when symbolic thinking would have been evolving, a family or clan that shared even a rudimentary capacity for complex symbols would have had a distinct evolutionary advantage over those who lacked it. Owing to this advantage, the capacity for advanced symbolic thinking would become dominant in what was then a small and geographically confined human population. By this account, pretend play, language, and theory of mind are all manifestations of an advanced capacity for symbolic thinking. In young children they develop roughly in tandem, with increasing and mutually supportive interactions. Together, they establish the fundamental abilities on which human social life is based.

But let me return to pretend play itself. Its defining characteristic, as we have seen, is its symbolic "'as-if' stance" in which "a 'pretense' is layered over reality" by a child, "knowingly and intentionally." Knowledge and intentionality are at the heart of pretend play. The child is aware that what she represents in her play is *just* a representation. She knows that the banana she uses as a pretend "telephone" is really just a banana, however much she enjoys using it for a pretend "conversation" with a grandparent; likewise, she knows that the mud she shapes into a "chocolate pie" is really just mud, however much she pretends to savor its "taste."

This understanding of the symbolic "'as-if' stance" of pretend play solves the basic conundrum for an evolutionary explanation of pretend play. People (indeed, all sentient organisms) need to be able to distinguish between true and false information, but even when very young, children develop their native ability with symbols to understand pretense *as* pretense and so can avoid confusing it *with* reality. The pretense is knowing and intentional, and so while the "telephone" banana might eventually be eaten, the "chocolate pie" mudpie will not.

Precisely how children can distinguish between pretense and reality, especially when someone else is doing the pretending, is a matter of much debate. Behavioralist psychologists argue that pretense is a learned behavior,[23] but many other psychologists hold that children naturally develop their evolved ability to understand the symbolic aspect of pretense. If, as I have suggested with Lillard, the capacity for advanced symbolic thinking is indeed an evolutionary adaptation, one would not need to be taught to think symbolically, any more than one needs to be taught to develop sexual interests during adolescence. Symbolic thinking, including the ability to adopt the "'as-if' stance" of pretend play, would develop naturally in children; when confronted with another person engaging in pretense, children would at most need reminding to take the pretense as such. The psychologists Ori Friedman and Alan M. Leslie argue: "The young child possesses the concept PRETEND by virtue of possessing the requisite neurocognitive mechanisms that deploy the necessary symbolic structures. These mechanisms allow other systems to plan and undertake actions under the description I PRETEND P, and empower the child to recognize that someone else is pretending P."[24]

From early childhood we develop our natural ability to engage in pretense ourselves and (as pretend play develops) to understand it in others. The knowing and intentional "'as-if' stance" of pretend play allows children to "decouple" pretense from reality so that reality is "quarantined" from any possible confusion with the pretense of play. The winks, knowing looks, and exaggerated movements often associated with pretend play are not teaching children to behave as if something were real; they simply remind children to decouple the pretense from reality and to understand it *as* symbolic. Decoupling markers, argue Friedman and Leslie, serve to communicate "that one is 'only' pretending. At the same time, [these markers] further the communicative aim by drawing attention to what is being pretended."[25]

Decoupling markers of one sort or another are common not only in childhood pretend play but in the performance of all sorts of fictional narratives. In storytelling around the world, decoupling markers include well-established opening formulae such as the "Once upon a time …" that sets fairytales in a make-believe world. Decoupling markers are also ubiquitous in dramatic theatre and include fantastical makeup, as in *kathakali*; carefully delineated playing areas, such as the circle of sanctified oil inscribed on the ground for *bhavai*; clear indicators of the fictionality of the performance, such as the holding of scripts along with the onstage presence of the director in *taʿziyeh*; and the nonliteral uses of props, such as a whip held in a certain way to symbolize the presence of a horse, as in many Chinese theatre forms. Even the most realistic performances of European spoken theatre have conventional decoupling markers, most typically a dimming of the houselights and/or a rising curtain at the start of the show. In all forms of dramatic theatre, that is to say, reality is quarantined from the pretend world of the play, however much that play might engage with or mimic the affairs of the real world.

I should also point out, though, that quarantining occasionally fails. Children might respond to scary pretend play (involving, say, a monster attack) with true fright. This does not mean they are generally susceptible to quarantine failure, "but because physiological reactions to real and imagined scary events are similar … children might interpret the physiological signs of fear as a cue to reality," not realizing "that the source of fear is purely their own imagination."[26] Quarantine failures are similarly possible in theatre. Audience members might interpret their own physiological responses to powerful emotions such as fear, anger, or lust "as a cue to reality," overriding whatever decoupling markers have been put in place. It is presumably rare for audience members to forget entirely that they are watching a play, but the emotions inspired by the play can surely be powerful emotions.

Bringing in the Audience

Childhood pretend play, having attained its full development when a child is around six years old, typically draws to a close at around eleven years of age;[27] the ability to engage in pretense is by then well developed, along with the related symbolic abilities of using language and applying theory of mind. All three are subsequently carried into adulthood and put to more adult purposes. Our ability to "respond deeply and passionately" to fiction of all sorts, suggests the psychologist Henry M. Wellman (writing with Karen Lind), is an "extension of our childhood powers of imaginary play."[28] But even sophisticated pretend play, such as that engaged in by the children whom Averroës casually observes, falls short of dramatic theatre, per se. The fundamental difference is that while the make-believe of pretend play is restricted to the players themselves, the make-believe of theatre is directed to an audience and is an intentional artistic communication *between* the performers and their audience. Paul Hernadi refers to audiences as participating in a "co-creation": Theatre is a "transaction [that] should be viewed not so much as production leading to consumption, but as seduction leading to consummation – to gratifying intercourse with someone else's imagination."[29]

Kendall L. Walton, a philosopher of aesthetics, offers an influential account of how audiences become active participants in fictional narratives (such as dramatic theatre and storytelling) as well as in other kinds of representational art. Walton writes: "What all representations have in common is a role in *make-believe*."[30] His central point is that those who make representations, including the performers of a show, are playing a complex sort of "game" in which they "make-believe" a fiction, just as the children do in Borges's tale. The basic role of audience members "consists, in a word, in *participating* in [that] game of make-believe" by using the performance as "a prop" for their own imaginative involvement in it.[31] Audience members "don't just observe fictional worlds from without" but imaginatively "live in them" with the fictional characters, "sharing their joys and sorrows, rejoicing and commiserating with them, admiring and detesting them. True, the worlds are merely fictional, and we are well aware that they are, but *from inside* they seem actual." Our imaginative participation in these worlds "gives us a sense of intimacy with characters and their other contents. It is this experience that underlies much of the fascination representations have for us and their power over us."[32] But while imaginative participation is central for an audience member, one must also recognize that "his perspective is a dual one. He observes fictional worlds as well as living in them; he discovers what is fictional as well as fictionally learning about and responding to characters and their situations."[33] Imaginative participation in make-believe, in other words, does not necessitate that audience members lose their sense of reality: Unless there is a failure of quarantining, audiences know they are imaginatively participating in what amounts to a game of make-believe.[34]

Every such game, Walton argues, requires establishing "a fictional truth ..., a prescription or mandate in some context to imagine something." These "truths" are "proposition[s] that are *to be* imagined" if one is to participate in the game.[35] The "fictional truths" in childhood pretend play are the implicit or explicit rules of the game in which the players are engaged. Dramatic theatre proposes the same sort of "fictional truths," but its "truths" bind not only the players but also the audience that chooses to play along with them. According to Walton, "a minimal condition" for the audience's imaginative participation is that they "consider the rules or principles of generation to apply to themselves"; conversely, mere onlookers (such as Borges's Averroës) do not accept the "fictional truths" of the make-believe and so cannot enter imaginatively into it.[36] The fundamental fictional truth for the audience of a theatrical performance is that the action being performed has a spurious reality, although everyone involved knows it is distinct *from* reality. Beyond that, theatre's fictional truths are governed both by the theatre form of the show and by the individual show itself. Theatre forms such as China's *jingju*, Japan's *kabuki*, and the British Mummers' Play, among many others, traditionally called for the men playing female roles to be fictionally accepted as women; other forms require the converse, as with the "trouser roles" (male roles performed by women) in European opera and *otokoyaku* (literally, "male roles") in the all-female Takarazuka theatre companies of contemporary Japan.[37] Similarly, in many theatre forms it must be accepted as perfectly normal for characters to "speak" in sung monologues, dialogues, and choruses, even though they are not "singing" within the fiction. Such outbursts of non-diegetic song would be shockingly inappropriate if they were to occur in certain other forms, such as European spoken theatre.

Fictional truths are also created by individual shows, whether on a textual or performative basis. *Peter Pan* and *Sweeney Todd* are both American musicals set in London, but while the make-believe of *Peter Pan* contains the fictional truth that some of its characters can fly, such flight would grossly violate the fictional truth of *Sweeney Todd*. In terms of performance, the fictional truth of a show might require its audience to imagine that a particular character is young and attractive, even if the actor playing that character is in fact middle-aged and dumpy. If audience members are unable to accept these fictional truths, their imaginative participation in the make-believe inevitably falters.

The fictional truths required by childhood pretend play and dramatic theatre make it possible for them to present counterfactual "realities": The "'as-if' stance" becomes sufficiently well-developed to present *what*-if scenarios that contemplate how events might follow from certain premises. Consider a child with her doll, thinking "If I were mommy, this is how I would treat my baby." Walker and Gopnik propose that pretend play "enables children to exercise the cognitive abilities that are necessary for counterfactual reasoning – setting false premises … and following the effects of [these] counterfactual premise[s] downstream." They contend that "the very act of engaging in pretend play promotes the development of causal learning" by giving "children a chance to practice and perfect the distinctive cognitive operations involved in counterfactual thinking."

Walker and Gopnik stop short of suggesting that the development of causal learning is *the* basic evolutionary function of pretend play but hold that imagining counterfactuals is critical to children's development of causal thinking.[38]

Something very interesting occurs when we bring in an adult audience that is not engaged in creating the counterfactual scenario of the play – but presumably is perfectly capable of understanding causation and therefore has little need to practice it. Why would adults *want* to imaginatively participate in the make-believe of others, taking pleasure even when the enactment might be deeply tragic or unsettling? Pleasure, after all, is an evolved response that motivates an organism to act in ways that enhance its prospects for survival and reproduction. Why would attending theatre be inherently pleasurable for adults?[39]

A good part of that pleasure might derive from continuing to exercise the capacity for symbolic pretense first expressed in childhood play; as such, it would be a lingering by-product that serves no adaptive function but is not so costly in an evolutionary sense as to present a problem. It is also possible, however, that adult engagement with counterfactuals does indeed serve an adaptive function. It might, in other words, be an *exaptation*, in which our evolved ability to engage in the symbolic expression of childhood pretend play has been co-opted for a new function.

It is not hard to imagine what this function might be, although it is no more than a hypothesis at this point. Steven Pinker suggests that the ability to engage with fiction (including dramatic theatre) might well serve an adaptive function because fictions "supply us with a mental catalogue of the fatal conundrums we might face someday and the outcomes of strategies we could deploy in them."[40] This suggestion is notable because Pinker also argues that the arts in general are "biologically functionless activities" that are mere by-products of the evolved mind.[41] Michelle Scalise Sugiyama, an evolutionary psychologist, makes the related argument that fiction (again, including dramatic theatre) offers "the representation of problems humans encounter in their lives and the constraints individuals struggle against in the efforts to solve them." In this way it "offers a low-cost, readily available means of amplifying our social experience by enabling us to witness a variety of adaptively momentous moments ... from multiple perspectives."[42]

This line of reasoning suggests that the counterfactual aspect of symbolic pretend play has been co-opted for a new adaptive function: By adding an audience, the make-believe scenarios of pretend play gain a *social* value. Making a point especially relevant to theatre, the literary scholar Joseph Carroll contends that stories are "indispensable ... for the organization of shared experience that makes cultural collective life possible."[43] It is by no means coincidental, Carroll observes, that "there is a fundamental parallel between the structure of human motivations and concerns and the organizing principles of literary representation," with our fictional characters motivated by such basic human concerns as survival, mating and reproduction, parenting and kinship, social interactions, and relations with supernatural power.[44] We create counterfactuals about the issues that matter to us – and these counterfactuals are so useful for our survival and reproductive success that we have evolved an appetite to continue participating in them, whether as their creators or as their audiences, even after childhood play has ceased. But for counterfactuals to be effective, Carroll writes, they "must be emotionally saturated [and] imaginatively vivid."[45] Dramatic theatre does not simply lay out its counterfactual narratives for thoughtful contemplation; it presents them in a way that is pleasurable enough to stimulate our desire *for* them and to focus our attention *on* them.

According to an analysis of "the theatrical event" by Jacqueline Martin and Willmar Sauter, dramatic theatre involves three kinds of communication between audiences and actors that provide this sense of pleasure. The first kind is between the audience and the actors-as-*fellow humans*, to whom the audience responds with varying degrees of affection, expectation, and recognition.[46] In *kabuki*, such responses are formalized in the practice of *kakegoe*: "Words of praise shouted impromptu by playgoers when stimulated by a fine piece of acting … or to encourage an actor on his entrance."[47] In many other forms, the first appearance of a beloved actor will unleash a round of applause that has nothing to do with the fictional action itself. By offering themselves as people whom others are allowed to unguardedly examine, actors can exert a strong sense of personal *presence* that attracts the attention of the audience and offers an immediate human connection with them.

The second kind of communication is between the audience and the actors-as-*artists*. The actors are expected to know the appropriate artistic conventions of their theatre form and to perform them effectively; in return, the audience is expected to understand those conventions and judge the artistry with which they are deployed.[48] What counts as "good singing" differs greatly between theatre forms, but when the audience for a play in a given form hears what it considers an excellent voice, the artistic impact is at the very least pleasing, and can be quite riveting. But there can be no such impact when artistry and audience expectations are mismatched. A witness to a late nineteenth-century performance of

Italian opera in Japan commented that after the Japanese audience members "had recovered from the first shock of surprise [they] were seized with a wild fit of hilarity at the high notes of the *prima donna*," laughing "at the absurdities of European singing till their sides shook and the tears rolled down their faces."[49] There was nothing wrong with either the singers or the audience, but the mismatch of artistry and expectations undermined the artistic communication, making the performance memorable for all the wrong reasons.

The third kind of communication identified by Martin and Souter is between the audience and the actors-as-*fictional-characters*.[50] This is the kind of communication with which Walton is most concerned in his analysis of the make-believe in representational arts, as when he writes of the audience sharing the characters' "joys and sorrows, rejoicing and commiserating with them, admiring and detesting them."[51] There is an intellectual component to this sort of communication (as the audience tries to understand the plot), just as there is an interpretive component (as it tries to understand the motives of a complex character) and an evaluative component (as it contemplates whether a play's fiction is plausible or well-plotted). But fundamentally, this third kind of communication is predicated on the *empathy* that the audience feels for one or more of the characters. Without that empathy, audiences might well not care enough to sort out a plot, develop an interpretation, or render an evaluation. Empathy motivates the audience's imaginative engagement with the characters of dramatic theatre, giving it a personal stake in the play's make-believe "reality."

Although the word empathy can be used in multiple ways, the most common usage refers to the ability to take another's perspective – or, more colloquially, to put oneself in another's shoes. This common usage, however, lacks psychological nuance, for it fails to consider why a person might empathize with some fictional characters (or, for that matter, with some people in real life) but not with others or why that empathy might shift between characters as a play progresses. It seems, however, that we are inclined to empathize especially with characters with whom we believe we share an identity (e.g., gender, race, social status, or nationality), situational characteristic (e.g., a difficult childhood, a desire for revenge, or the vicissitudes of old age), mood or disposition (e.g., happiness, depression, or rebelliousness), or some other personal trait, belief, or desire. If this is indeed the case, then characters attract our empathy less because we place ourselves in their situation than because we recognize at least something of ourselves in them.[52] The difference between these two perspectives might seem subtle. Consider, though, how often we come across a character with whom we think we *should* empathize (if only because the play centers around that character) but cannot bring ourselves to care about because the character seems alien to us. But when audience members see meaningful aspects of themselves in a play's characters, they are most compellingly drawn into the play's imaginary world.

In sum, then, dramatic theatre is not merely the presentation of counterfactual "what-if" scenarios. Taking advantage of the audience–actor communications associated with presence, artistry, and empathy, theatre's counterfactuals are rendered pleasurable in multiple ways to stimulate our desire *for* them and focus our attention *on* them. The same can be said of storytelling – and although the artistic devices available to it are more limited (including its typical reliance on a single performer), these limitations allow it to be presented at little cost almost anywhere. But whether in dramatic theatre or storytelling, the performance of these counterfactual scenarios might well be an exaptation that serves the evolutionary function of preparing people for the seemingly limitless range of contingencies they might confront in the real world.

We have come a long way from childhood pretend play. Such play, as we have seen, is likely associated with an evolutionary adaptation for advanced symbolic thinking. Dramatic theatre might merely be a by-product of pretend play, carried over into adult life, but it might be an exaptation in which the childhood development of pretense has been co-opted for a new evolutionary purpose. At this point, psychological research does not firmly justify making that claim. But one way or the other, the evidence suggests that the wellspring of theatre is childhood pretend play, a universal human phenomenon that leaves us all capable of theatrical behavior, whether as performers who enact make-believe "realities" or as audience members who imaginatively engage in the make-believe of others. Throughout human history and around the world, theatre has allowed performers and audiences to explore "what-if" situations in ways that compel attention through presence, artistry, and empathy.

There remains the question of *when* advanced symbolic thinking (and, by implication, pretend play, theatrical behavior, and perhaps the earliest dramatic theatre) evolved in humans. No sure answer can be given because ongoing archaeological and genetic research continually modifies or overturns previously accepted chronologies. But it is possible to gain a sense of the latest possible time by which symbolic thinking had evolved to the point of being essentially the same as ours.

The hominin lineage that would come to include *Homo sapiens* dates back more than a million years and it is now usually accepted that what are called "anatomically modern humans" had evolved by about 200,000 years ago.[53] This evolution took place in East Africa, with some dispersals perhaps 100,000 years ago to other parts of Africa as well as into Eurasia. But it was only between about 70,000 and 50,000 years ago that humans began an expansion that would eventually take their descendants throughout the world in what the archeologist Clive Gamble calls "one breathless rush."[54] Some scholars argue that this expansion was the result of a revolutionary genetic change that enabled advanced symbolic thinking, but this argument is no longer widely accepted. Gamble writes, "Instead of a human revolution, we see a long drawn-out affair" that stretched back hundreds of thousands of years into the prehuman past.[55] The paleoanthropologists Julia Galway-Witham, James Cole, and Chris Stringer concur, suggesting that it is now "clear that the origins of complex modern human behaviours associated with *H. sapiens* originated as an older, more gradual behavioural package [deep in the hominin lineage] in Africa."[56]

Whether the relevant genetic changes were a uniquely human revolution or part of "a long drawn-out affair" that became especially advanced in humans, it is generally accepted that "fully modern [human] behaviour [is] detectable in the archeological record beginning 50,000–40,000 years ago." Notably, this evidence includes the "earliest appearance of incontrovertible art," as well as the "earliest secure evidence for ceremony or ritual, expressed both in art and in relatively elaborate graves."[57] The clear implication is that by this time, the humans who were spreading out across the world already had a well-developed capacity for symbolic thinking – and with it, the symbolic behavior of pretend play. It seems reasonable to suggest, therefore, that theatre's origin can plausibly be said to be carried within all of us. The unceasingly renewed variety of theatrical expression around the world is the direct result of that origin.

CHAPTER 2

The Social Uses of Theatre

History, Anthropology, and Inference

What can one say about early theatre in the absence of virtually any evidence? Legend has it that in ancient Athens, a little more than 2,500 years ago, Thespis stepped out from the dithyrambic chorus to become the first actor of tragedy. But from 50,000 years ago to Thespis is an exceedingly long time. It is tempting to simplify the problem, if just a bit, by dividing that time at the emergence of complex urbanized societies in Mesopotamia and Egypt some 5,000 years ago.[1] But no unequivocal evidence justifies such a split for the history of dramatic theatre, a point I will discuss in Chapter 4. And even if we *were* to find clear evidence of theatre in those early urbanized societies, that would still say nothing about the theatre that might have existed for the preceding 45,000 years. Can we simply exclude all these millennia from history?

Historians have often been willing to do precisely that, designating them as *pre*history. Andrew Shyrock (an anthropologist) and Daniel Lord Smail (a historian) note that in the early nineteenth century, the "proud new [academic] discipline" of history justified itself by adopting "as its signature methodology the analysis of written documents," but of course, humanity's far-distant past had no such documents, which "made a deep history of humanity methodologically unthinkable."[2] The preoccupation with written documents fit quite nicely with the contemporaneous preoccupation with national histories (as mentioned in the Introduction), for nowhere were written documents more available than in national archives. As a result, everything outside the universe of documents was understood to be the provenance of fields such as archeology and anthropology – which had their own distinctive methodologies and preoccupations.

Theatre historians have likewise been willing to mark off everything before the invention of literary theatre as a sort of prehistory of theatre.

Almost all textbooks on theatre history begin with an uncertain slog through theories of ritual origins (and perhaps an acknowledgment of the possibility of ancient Mesopotamian and/or Egyptian theatre) before moving quickly to the terra firma of ancient Greece, where the existence of dramatic literature at last provides a solid footing. An immediate consequence of identifying dramatic theatre in terms of literature is the ease with which it also allows for discounting nonliterary forms that to the present day have existed alongside literary ones; in this way, numerous performance forms, most notably in Africa, the Americas, and the South Pacific, are relegated to what is essentially the realm of prehistory.

Where historians (and theatre historians) feared to tread, however, early exponents of anthropology happily rushed in, developing a theory known as unilinear (or sometimes, unilineal) cultural evolution that claimed to make sense of prehistory through the study of still-existing nonliterate societies. First propounded in the nineteenth century by Edward Burnett Tylor (in Great Britain) and Lewis Morgan (in the United States), this theory holds that all human cultures pass through the same basic stages, evolving from "savagery" (sometimes called "primitivism") to "barbarism" to "civilization."[3] As Morgan explained: "Since mankind were one in origin, their career has been essentially one, running in different but uniform channels upon all continents, and very similarly in all the tribes and nations of mankind down to the same status of advancement."[4] This claimed similarity allowed cultural evolutionists to combine traits from different "savage" societies to create a composite picture that ostensibly applied to them all. No less usefully, they could also look for aspects of "savage" life that might still linger in "civilized" cultures. Such "survivals" (identified primarily in folklore) allowed cultural evolutionists to "fill in the cultural blanks and reconstruct the life of bygone eras."[5]

If unilinear cultural evolution were a valid theory, it would be possible to see what theatre looked like in the millennia before 500 BCE by examining, say, theatre forms of contemporary "savage" peoples in New Guinea, Nigeria, and the American Southwest, along with the folkloric "survival" of the Mummers' Play in Great Britain. I have not chosen these examples at random. They are all mentioned in the opening section of Glynne Wickham's *History of Theatre*, wherein the author claims, in words that Tylor and Morgan might themselves have written, that these forms "were broadly the same and represent the start of the story of theatre throughout the world."[6]

The theory of unilinear cultural evolution, however, is ahistorical nonsense.[7] The idea that all cultures evolve through a single and unvarying set of stages has been undermined by more than a century of ethnography; the intellectual construct of a uniform "savage" stage of culture has likewise been demolished; and the promiscuous joining together of cultural traits from different "savage" societies, without reference to the societal and historical contexts of those traits, has long been condemned as methodologically absurd. Moreover, the idea of folklore as "survivals" is intrinsically flawed, failing to account for either the transmission of folklore between societies or the creation of new folkloric materials within a given society.[8] As we have seen with Wickham's invocation of tribal and folk theatre, however, the theory of unilinear cultural evolution has had a distressingly long half-life. The anthropologist William Bascom lamented generations ago that it is "disturbing to anthropologists to find folklorists, or economists, or anyone else repeating an anthropological theory which anthropologists themselves have rejected."[9]

But if we cannot rely on the theory of unilinear cultural evolution, what *can* one say about theatre before 500 BCE? The most important thing to suggest is that it was likely surprisingly varied, if only because societies before that time (along with nonliterate societies for the past 2,500 years) were themselves surprisingly diverse, including hunter-gatherers, nomads, semi- or fully sedentary populations, semi- or fully urbanized populations, pastoralists, horticulturalists, agriculturalists, practitioners of transhumance – and almost any combination thereof. Moreover, the way that any given society created theatre was affected by the society's particular history, cultural practices, spiritual beliefs, and interactions with neighboring societies; it was also affected by the society's degree of approval for organized theatre, the amount of time that could be taken from productive labor for rehearsal, performance, and attendance, the social organizations that might be interested in creating or sponsoring theatre, the kinds of occasions that the society provided for performance, and (not to be overlooked) the theatrical imagination of its people.

We *can* at least get a sense of the variety of early theatre, however, even if we know nothing directly about it. I argued in Chapter 1 that about 50,000 years ago, humans not only were apparently anatomically the same as now but also had the same well-developed capacity for symbolic thinking. Some genetic changes have certainly taken place since then (such as the change in certain populations that makes it possible for them to digest cow's milk), but we are all the direct heirs of the *Homo sapiens* who settled throughout Africa and around the world.

Dipesh Chakrabarty notes that "biological-sounding talk of species" can be worrying to historians, who might "feel concerned about their finely honed sense of contingency and freedom in human affairs having to cede ground to a more deterministic view of the world." Moreover, not only are there "dangerous historical examples of the political use of biology" but there is also the fear that talk of species "may introduce a powerful degree of essentialism in our understanding of humans."[10] But our species-wide similarities neither rule out contingency nor restrict our freedom to make choices, nor does the political (mis)use of biology invalidate biology itself. The fear of essentialism is also misguided, for as Smail points out, "natural selection does not homogenize the individuals of a species";[11] to identify species-wide similarities says nothing about any person's particular abilities or interests, including the ability and/or interest to be *dis*similar in some ways. Nor, for that matter, does it say anything about the abilities and/or interests of any social groups.

If, therefore, we refuse to draw a line between prehistory and history, we can use a process of *inference* to help us get a sense of the variety of theatre that likely existed before 500 BCE. More specifically, because we know that *Homo sapiens*' capacity for advanced symbolic thinking allowed them to be deeply social creatures, we can look at the various social uses to which we know dramatic theatre has regularly been put and infer that at least some early theatre, of which we know nothing, was put to similar uses.

It will be helpful here to return to the relationship between ritual and theatre. The usual understanding of this relationship, as we have seen, is that theatre evolved out of religious ritual, with ritual being concerned with efficacy (making things happen through appeal to supernatural power) and theatre with entertainment. But surely efficacious action can be entertaining, just as entertainment can serve efficacious purposes, muddying this neat distinction between the two. A more useful way to understand the relationship between ritual and theatre, suggests Eli Rozik, is to recognize that they "are entities on different ontological levels." Rozik sees ritual as "a mode of action" that reflects social "intentions and purposes," whereas theatre is "a kind of medium" that "can be employed for any sort of [social] action," including (but not limited to) ritual.[12] If, as is evident throughout *known* theatre history, the action of ritual has sometimes used the medium of theatre, it is safe to infer that ritual sometimes used this same medium during theatre's deeper unknown history. But we can also look at *other* modes of social action that we know to have regularly used the medium of theatre and infer that at least some of the theatre before 500 BCE was similarly used as a medium for those activities.

Theatre as a Medium for Social Activities

I will look at five social activities that we know to have regularly used the medium of theatre, then more briefly at three others. As will be apparent, these activities somewhat overlap, and no doubt others can be added to the ones I discuss. But these should be sufficient to suggest at least some of the activities that have used the medium of theatre long in the past.

The first activity is *entertainment*, which is a mode of action in its own right but which plays into other activities as well. As the entertainment theorists Stephen Bates and Anthony J. Ferri observe, "Entertainment often does more than entertain – or, put differently, entertainment functions are often intertwined with nonentertainment functions."[13] Subjectively, "entertainment" can refer to any activity that evokes feelings of pleasure and/or amusement; no less subjectively, an activity that one person finds "entertaining" might well bore another to tears. Bates and Ferri therefore argue the need for an objective definition and suggest that entertainment involves a text (which, in theatre, should be construed as the performance as a whole) that is communicated to an audience (which, as we have seen, is actually a three-part communication between actors and audience) and that aims to provide pleasure (though no performance can hope to satisfy everyone) while perhaps being used by other social activities to advance their own purposes.[14] But even in the absence of other purposes, a performance that seeks *only* to give pleasure should not be trivialized as "mere" entertainment, for it is still efficacious in elevating the mood or altering the disposition of its audience, if only by providing a respite from real-world concerns.

One complication to Bates and Ferri's definition of entertainment is that they also argue for the "passivity" of the audience, seeking to distinguish entertainment from "leisure or play." But they note that passivity "does not exclude emotional involvement" and recognize that it "is the most problematic" aspect of their definition.[15] In their effort to differentiate between entertainment and play, they have missed the point that even their objectively defined entertainment can involve a kind of playing – a "game," as we have seen with Kendall Walton, in which the players make-believe and the audience imaginatively plays along. There is no reason why those who play along cannot become active participants in the making-believe if the "rules" of the game allow it. Audience passivity is by no means a requirement of theatre; indeed, the relative passivity of contemporary audiences for European spoken theatre is, if anything, more the historical exception than the norm.

The second social activity to consider is *ritual*. As I noted earlier, definitions of ritual vary widely, but the rituals with which I am concerned are in line with Victor Turner's definition, being appeals of one sort or another to a supernatural power in hopes of an efficacious response. We can identify at least three ways in which the medium of theatre has been associated with ritual activity, leaving aside those moments when a play might fictionally reference a ritual for dramatic or symbolic effect rather than truly offering an appeal to the supernatural.

First, ritual can exist in the context of theatre. Phillip B. Zarrilli observes, "Within every traditional Indian performance genre … there exist specific rituals which serve to punctuate, set off, and frame the performance."[16] This includes even theatre forms whose narrative content is primarily secular, such as *bhavai* and *tamasha*.[17] In such cases, it is probably the inclusion of ritual that needs explaining, not the medium of theatre. That explanation seems, above all, to derive from a native religiosity that, in many societies, calls for community activities to be sanctified appropriately; Indian theatre's long-standing tradition of using such rituals, which began at least as early as Sanskrit theatre, has no doubt influenced the practice in subsequent Indian theatre forms.

Second, theatre can exist in the context of ritual, often by enacting a particular event addressed in the ritual. The *Quem queritis* trope, widely performed in medieval European religious institutions, is a famous instance of this. According to Grace Frank, a "trope" introduces, adds to, or interpolates what "may be considered … commentaries upon the genuine liturgical text." At first this particular trope was a mere "lyrical embellishment," but when (in the tenth century) it was transferred to the Matins service on Easter, the singers began "impersonat[ing] the characters of the [three] Marys and the angels" at the tomb of the risen Christ, "with appropriate gestures and voice changes"; moreover, "definite stage-directions in the manuscripts told them how to speak and act [and] the costumes and properties they were to employ."[18] As the "lyrical embellishment" was itself embellished, dramatic theatre became part of the efficacious ritual liturgy, drawing attention to, and amplifying the impact of, the event by dramatically enacting it.

Third, theatre can serve as a ritual offering to a supernatural power. One example can be found in Hahoe Village, South Korea, where *pyŏlsin-gut* has been performed (in a festival of the same name) for what the villagers claim to have been 500 years.[19] The name of the form is highly suggestive. According to Oh-Kon Cho, its first word "broadly means an exorcism or an incantation practiced by shamans or by fishermen," while its second "denotes a spectacle or show."[20] Choe Sang-Su writes that "the villagers believe and fear their goddess's displeasure and the consequent divine punishment … if they fail to carry out the regular ceremony."²¹ Given its ritual significance, however, the standard *pyŏlsin-gut* show is strikingly nonreligious. It consists of five independent scenes, "tenuously held together by means of [its] themes: ridicule of transgressing Buddhist monks, the corruption of the upper class, and mockery of insensitive local officials."²² Even divinities, it seems, can savor an entertaining show.

The third social activity that has used the medium of theatre is *devotion*. Devotional theatre is related to ritual theatre in being concerned with religion – but differs because its focus is not on stimulating efficacious action by a supernatural power. Instead, the focus is on the participants themselves (whether actors or audience members), who hope to enhance their personal and/or communal connection to the supernatural power or a cultural hero associated with that power. The medieval Passion plays of mainland Europe and Corpus Christi cycle plays of England are well-known examples of devotional theatre, as are *raslila* and *ramlila* in India, which seek to enhance devotion to Krishna and Rama, respectively.

A less well-known devotional theatre form is the Iranian *taʻziyeh*, performed as a series of short plays centered on (but not limited to) the martyrdom of the Imam Husain at the Battle of Karbala in 680 CE (AH 61, according to the Islamic calendar). Husain's martyrdom is the defining moment for the Shiite branch of Islam, which holds that the Caliphate was stolen from him, just as it had been stolen from his brother and father.²³ As with many other devotional forms, there are secular and comical moments in the plays of *taʻziyeh*, but the name of the form literally means "expressions of sympathy, mourning, and consolation,"²⁴ and most of its plays seek to move the audience to enhance their devotion. At critical moments, audience members beat their breasts in anguish and cry "tears of personal sorrow" that evidence their "oneness with the historical events being portrayed."²⁵ The value of theatre for devotional activity should be obvious. By allowing for the fictional embodiment of the supernatural and/or an associated cultural hero, it draws on the power of theatre to enhance a profoundly empathetic relationship.

The fourth social activity to note is *social commentary*, by which I mean the offering of observations about the world in which the performers and audiences live. A vast amount of theatre is associated with this activity, ranging from children reenacting the foibles of others for an audience of friends to ancient Greece's Old Comedy (as with Aristophanes's skewering of philosophy in *The Clouds*) and to European spoken theatre (as with Molière's mockery of religious pretension in *Tartuffe*). Social commentary is often focused on contemporary life, but it can reach into the past to understand how the current world has come about (as in Shakespeare's English history plays). It can also use the past (whether legendary or real) as a way of commenting, however obliquely, on the present. This was a common practice in Greek tragedy (as in Euripides's implicit criticism of the Peloponnesian War in *Trojan Women*) and Japan's *bunraku* and *kabuki* (as in *Chūshingura*, in which a near-contemporary vendetta was retrojected by the play's multiple authors into the more distant past as a way of avoiding political censorship).[26]

Another form used for social commentary can be found in Mali. There, festivals of the Bamana people often include a theatrical performance known as *kote-tlon*, put on by the community's young men's association. These performances are satires that deal with "contemporary life and situations."[27] Adults are frequently the butts of the humor; conversely, youthful characters are presented as competent and strong.[28] According to Osita Okagbue, these performances "provide a context for conflict management between two generations," with "the sketches provid[ing] the youth with the only avenue for dissent and an instrument with which to challenge or speak back" to their elders.[29] One particular sketch captures this intergenerational dynamic quite plainly. In it, a youth "draws upon the vital force of his *daliluw*, his instruments of power (which in this example are represented by a long stick and two small calabashes), to crush … [an] elder's testicles by magic."[30] Freud, of course, would have been most intrigued by the symbolism here. But the relevant point for us is that sketches such as this are "situational comedies in which a range of social themes are explored."[31]

The fifth of our social activities that use the medium of dramatic theatre is *pedagogy*, which in some instances might be referred to as education, in others as propaganda, depending largely on one's attitude toward what is being taught. Though clearly related to social commentary, the emphasis in pedagogical theatre is explicitly on shaping the audience's thoughts on matters such as sociopolitical issues, cultural heritage, or appropriate behaviors. Bertolt Brecht, whose early *lehrstücke* ("learning plays") had the specific purpose of "pedagogics," long retained an interest in pedagogical theatre. But in arguing that "theatre remains theatre even when it is instructive theatre," he added that "and in so far as it is good theatre it will amuse."[32] On the opposite end of the political spectrum, the Nazi German government organized the production of *Thingspiele* ("plays of judgement") that contained "a ritualistic element that bordered on the cultic, suggesting a mystical bond of German blood"; these plays both "celebrated the new Reich" and "condemned the 'degeneracy' of the

Weimar republic."³³ Governmentally sanctioned pedagogical theatre also had a brief heyday in Communist China with the establishment of "model operas" during the Cultural Revolution (1966–1976). Regarding perhaps the most famous of these, *Taking Tiger Mountain by Strategy*, Colin Mackerras comments, "There is hardly a line … without conscious ideological content: politics carried to the final degree."³⁴

Beyond these (and many other) modern instances of pedagogical theatre – among them, Theatre for Development programs in Africa and Theatre for Education programs in the United Kingdom – extends a lineage that reaches far back in time. In nonliterate societies, cultural myths are regularly performed via storytelling and dramatic enactment. According to the anthropologist Bronislaw Malinowski, the performance of myth fulfills "an indispensable function: It expresses, enhances and codifies belief; it safeguards and enforces morality; [and] it vouches for the efficacy of ritual and contains practical rules for the guidance of man. Myth is … a pragmatic charter of primitive faith and moral wisdom."³⁵ One need not accept the proposition that *all* myths are "charters" to recognize the importance of Malinowski's insight. Ronald and Catherine Berndt say of Aboriginal Australian performance: "Apart from the matter of aesthetic appeal, all art – songs and poetic expression, oral literature, dancing and dramatic performances, visual manifestations – is a medium through which messages and ideas are communicated." When myth is being performed, its "messages and ideas" teach how a member of the society should live.³⁶

I also want to briefly note three other social activities that have long made use of dramatic theatre. First is *celebration*. Among indigenous communities in the Philippines, for example, "mimetic customs" are often "associated with courtship, wedding, and death."³⁷ While such personal celebrations can sometimes involve a large part of the community, other celebrations that make use of theatre are more explicitly celebrations of the community itself. Johann Friedrich Schiller's *Wilhelm Tell*, for example, has become the de facto national play of Switzerland and is annually produced both there (most famously, in Interlaken) and in heavily Swiss communities overseas (as in New Glarus, Wisconsin).³⁸ Second is *commemoration*, in which actual events involving the community are reenacted as a means of remembering and honoring them. In parts of Spain, for example, the so-called *Reconquista* has long been annually recalled in the folk theatre form *Moros y Cristianos*, performances of which generally conclude with the surrender and conversion of Muslims to Christians.³⁹ In nineteenth-century London, meanwhile, naval reenactments had some popularity: In 1804, Charles Dibden set a water tank some 90 feet by

25 feet large on the stage of Sadler's Wells Theatre for his *Siege of Gibraltar*, a commemoration (with scaled-down ships) of a famous British naval victory.[40] And third is the too-easily overlooked activity of *fund-raising*. The funds might be raised for the performing troupe, for a sponsor (perhaps a religious or civic institution or a commercial producer), or for any specific "cause" looking for support. Strictly speaking, fund-raising could not have existed before coinage was invented, but one can imagine that its functional equivalent was gifts-in-kind, such as food and drink.

Because these various social activities (along with others unmentioned here) have regularly used the medium of dramatic theatre all through *known* theatre history, and because the human capacity for symbolic thinking extends back far beyond that known history, we can reasonably infer that theatre was likely used in similar activities in the unknown past. When we also recall the many kinds of societal organization that existed in the long expanse of human time before 500 BCE, it seems safe to suggest that whatever the details of those unknown theatre forms might have been, theatre as a whole would have been far more varied and interesting than the speculations of unilinear cultural evolution would have us believe.

We have been investigating the deep history of theatre in Part I of this book, but the depth of that history, although measured in tens of thousands of years, does not indicate that we are removed from it. On the contrary, contemporary theatre throughout the world is merely its continuation through changing times and into different societies. To draw a single and fundamental dividing line at the invention of literary theatre, circa 500 BCE, would be as misguided as drawing a line between prehistory (that is, history before the availability of written documents) and history proper. And yet precisely that sort of dividing line is the heritage of the Standard Western Approach, which has often (though not universally) defined "drama" as literary texts intended for performance and "theatre" as the performance of those texts. Tracy C. Davis and Peter W. Marx report,

> At the beginning of the academic life of theatre, its subject and history seemed to be self-evident. Emerging from a scholarly system that privileged literary forms, such as drama, and that acknowledged performance only to the extent that it was part of the literary culture, theatre history was defined through its neighbouring disciplines: thus, theatre and its history were a sub-category of art and art history (as practices), and literature and literary history (as texts).[41]

The idea that "drama" means a certain kind of literature and "theatre" means the performance of dramatic literature has had profound implications. Obviously it entails an absolute dividing line at around 500 BCE, with everything before then being set apart as belonging to the prehistory of theatre. It also implicitly casts all nonliterary theatre forms *since* 500 BCE outside the bounds of theatre history, per se, associating them with theatre's prehistory and relegating their study to disciplines such as folklore (for European forms such as the British Mummers' Play) or anthropology (for the wide range of nonliterary African, Amerindian, and South Pacific forms). The idea also calls into question the status of countless popular theatre forms that rely on improvisation or whose written texts might be considered more as prompts for entertainment than as "literature."

Seeking to sidestep these various exclusionary implications, some American theatre scholars in the late twentieth century created the field of performance studies, whose fundamental appeal is its radical *inclusivity*. Richard Schechner, one of the field's pioneers, lists nine "kinds or categories" of "performance": everyday life; art (including theatre, music, dance, performance art, painting, and so on); sports and other popular entertainments; medicine, business, law, and other professions and occupations; politics; technology (including social media and mobile communication); sex; ritual; and play.[42] With such a breadth of material in hand, performance studies raises the exciting prospect of analytically crossing between wildly diverse domains. But how much breadth is *too* much breadth? Davis and Marx comment that "it is sometimes hard to imagine what is left out of Performance Studies' purview, and indeed it has been critiqued for this universalising tendency, for in practice it is as much a sensibility as a rationale."[43] That sensibility is, above all, oppositional to theatre studies as conducted along the lines of the Standard Western Approach, with its pronounced Eurocentric and literary biases.[44]

One can, however, oppose those biases without opposing theatre studies, per se. The exclusionary implications of the conventional distinction between "drama" and "theatre" need not be maintained; one can, instead, construe theatre studies in a way that readily incorporates the deep history of dramatic theatre as well as the numerous nonliterary and popular forms of theatre that exist to this day. Such has been the task of Part I of this book. If theatrical behavior is an evolved human trait, as I have argued, then dramatic theatre is part of our universal heritage, regardless of when or where we live and whether or not our theatres enact literary works; actors everywhere can rely (in their various ways) on the powers of presence, artistry, and empathy to communicate with their audiences.

And although the medium of dramatic theatre has undergone endless permutations across time and space, it has everywhere been a social art, serving social activities such as entertainment, ritual, devotion, social commentary, and pedagogy. Long before the first written word, dramatic theatre was using its make-believe narratives to bind communities together, just as it binds them together today. Although the specific theatre forms from before 2,500 years ago have long since fallen out of performance, the wellspring of theatre that streamed into those forms has continued to flow. The deep history of theatre carries on, within us and all around us.

PART II

The Eurasian Breakthroughs (starting c. 500 BCE)

We can imagine, albeit with little certainty about the details, the actors of Greek tragedy and Sanskrit theatre in performance: wearing costumes, masks, and/or makeup of one sort or another, moving about their performance spaces (perhaps dancing or symbolically gesturing), and delivering words (perhaps speaking, chanting, or singing). None of this necessarily differed from earlier forms of performance. But something about the words the actors delivered *was* different, for they had intentionally been written for theatrical performance.

Although we can say very little about any specific theatre forms that preexisted Greek tragedy and Sanskrit theatre, there is no evidence that any of them regularly used scripts written in advance of their first performances. Unless such evidence comes to light, the emergence of Greek tragedy (around 500 BCE) and Sanskrit theatre (a few hundred years later) must together be understood as a landmark in theatre history. The historical problem that needs confronting here can be stated simply: Why did the invention of literary theatre first take place in Greece and India? Or to look at the reverse side of the problem, why did it *not* take place elsewhere?

What makes this problem especially intriguing is that after the emergence of Sanskrit theatre, many hundreds of years would pass before the next literary theatre forms independently emerged (I say "independently" to acknowledge that some forms of Roman theatre were literary but were based on Greek models). There were certainly new theatre forms during these centuries; we can identify at least a few of them, specify some of their traits, and loosely date when they emerged. But for a thousand years or so, none followed Greek and Indian theatre in being literary. This is an astonishing length of time, and it throws the Greek and Indian accomplishments – and the problem of explaining them – into even greater relief.

The invention of literary theatre has usually been discussed in terms of Greece alone, with such discussions all too easily digressing into paeans to what is sometimes called "the Greek miracle." Literary theatre was almost certainly created first in Greece, but the fact that it was also created early on in India – and nowhere else for a very long time – undermines any claim that Greece was somehow uniquely blessed. Instead, our attention is turned to the Greek and Indian societies themselves: Were there any commonalities between them that might help explain their early invention of literary theatre forms?

Let me be clear about what I mean by "literary theatre." No simple dichotomy exists between literary and nonliterary theatre. In some forms, only important speeches are scripted, with lesser speeches and dialogue being orally transmitted or left to improvisation. In other forms, only a scenario might be scripted, and all the speech improvised, perhaps according to well-worn conventions. Sometimes a script that merely records a performance will be treated in subsequent productions as if it were a literary script, while literary scripts themselves can be transmitted orally and/or subjected in subsequent performance to improvisation. The single trait with which I am concerned here is the regular use of scripts written (in whole or significant part) in advance of their first production. I do not mean to imply that literary theatre forms are intrinsically superior to other forms, for scripted plays can be quite miserable, while oral transmission and improvisation can yield thrilling shows. But the use of prewritten scripts, first pioneered in Greece and India, presents a striking change from all that preceded it.

Indeed, the use of those scripts was not the only change introduced in Greece and India. Before the emergence of their literary theatre forms, theatre there seems to have been more or less of a piece with theatre most everywhere else in the world, being an assortment of local or semilocal traditions serving one or another of the various social activities discussed in Chapter 2. Such would apparently remain the case elsewhere in the world for many hundreds of years to come, although the paucity of historical information makes it impossible to assert this with any certainty. But in the hundreds of years following the emergence of Greek tragedy and Sanskrit theatre, these two forms vastly expanded their domains and influenced the emergence of homologous forms wherever they spread, thereby creating a pair of clearly identifiable theatre regions in the ancient Mediterranean and South Asia. This too was a breakthrough, and it offers further reason to recognize the invention of literary theatre as one of the major inflection points in world theatre history.

CHAPTER 3

Inventing Literary Theatre

The Historical Contexts

The emergence of tragedy in Greece – or, more precisely, in the single city-state of Athens – has traditionally been dated to about 534 BCE, when the City (or Great) Dionysia festival was established by the tyrant Pisistratus "to celebrate the common man's god, Dionysus" and yoke that celebration to Athenian patriotism.[1] The first tragic performance (led, according to legend, by Thespis) is said to have occurred at this festival; no one knows what it might have entailed. Recent scholarship, however, suggests that the City Dionysia "did not become formalized as a theatre festival of tragic (and satyric) drama" until Cleisthenes's political reforms in 508/7 BCE instituted Athenian democracy.[2] By this view, argues Paul Cartledge, "tragedy as we know it ... may have differed considerably from that pioneered by Thespis [and] could plausibly have come into being as a consequence of the re-scrutiny of traditional myth through the new democratic lens."[3] Whatever the precise date of its founding, the City Dionysia was both a religious and patriotic festival. Its celebration was highlighted by the performance of (and competition between) three sets of tragedies (each accompanied by a satyr play) – but it also involved sundry other activities, some religious (including a ritual purification of the theatre, an offering to the gods, and the performance of dithyrambs in honor of Dionysus), others patriotic (including public recognition of the city's benefactors and a display of tribute collected from states that were subjects or allies of Athens).[4]

The emergence of Sanskrit theatre is more difficult to place in time and space. Ananda Lal notes that dating the form's most acclaimed playwright, Kalidasa, "is one of the most discussed problems in Indian literary history."[5] Aparna Dharwadker suggests that his possible dates range from 150 BCE to 600 CE, with "most Indian scholars placing him among the 'nine gems' at the court of King Vikramaditya" in Ujjain (also known as

Ujjayini), in the mid first century BCE, while "most Western scholars prefer to link him with the court of Chandragupta II in the same city," circa 375–414 CE.[6] But this is not entirely an Indian versus "Western" issue, for many Indian scholars also place Kalidasa in Chandragupta II's court.[7] It is also relevant that King Vikramaditya (the possible early host of Kalidasa) might be a figure of legend rather than of history,[8] and that the name "Vikramaditya" might have been a title adopted by Chandragupta II (the possible late host of Kalidasa).[9] For these reasons, the late fourth century to early fifth century dating for Kalidasa seems more likely to be accurate.

But whichever dates one assigns to Kalidasa, he apparently lived at least a few generations after the *emergence* of Sanskrit theatre. The prologues to some of Kalidasa's plays mention earlier playwrights, the most notable of whom is Bhasa. According to Lal, if Kalidasa belonged to the court of Chandragupta II, the likely dating for Bhasa would be no later than the second century CE. Bhasa is especially important because his plays are the earliest to survive.[10] Although there is no reason to assume that Bhasa was the founding playwright of Sanskrit theatre, it seems plausible to accept the second century CE as the likely period for the emergence of the form.[11]

Slightly less uncertain is the location where Sanskrit theatre emerged. The place name most associated with the form's early centuries is Ujjain, a city in north-central India that was one of five regional capitals during the Maurya Empire (c. 322–185 BCE) and that dominated the trade route between the Arabian Sea and the regions served by the upper Ganges River.[12] Ujjain is associated with Kalidasa not only for his possible place in the court of Vikramaditya but also because of references to the city in some of his works. More significantly, perhaps, some scholars believe it was also the home of Bhasa,[13] and it is a locale in some of his plays as well. These recurring mentions of Ujjain encourage one to think of it as the place (or at least one of the primary places) where Sanskrit theatre emerged.

Beyond the time and place of the origins for tragedy and Sanskrit theatre, we must also look to the various forms of organized theatrical performance that existed in Greece and India *before* their emergence. I will not presume to offer full accounts of how the literary forms emerged, a problem still passionately debated among specialists. Instead, I want to emphasize that both Greek tragedy and Sanskrit theatre apparently incorporated elements of earlier kinds of performance, blending them in new ways for new purposes. These forms were, in a word, syncretic, although the syncretism was entirely intracultural. We will be seeing much more of theatrical syncretism – whether *intra*cultural or *inter*cultural – as we move along, because the adaptation of theatrical traits from existing performance traditions (whatever their place of origin) is an important way in which new theatre forms are created and existing forms are modified.

Three kinds of pretragic performance are most relevant in ancient Greece. First is the dithyramb, a narrative choral song apparently associated with a procession and/or dance. Many scholars insist that dithyrambs were at first ritualistic; Peter Levi neatly calls them "a kind of poetry in which narrative brilliance ... overwhelmed ritual meaning."[14] Aristotle, in the fourth chapter of his *Poetics*, suggested that tragedy originated when the leader of the dithyrambic chorus stepped out of that chorus to become the first tragic actor. In that same chapter, he mentioned a second kind of theatrical performance, satyr-like mimetic plays, which are also said to have originally been ritualistic; Aristotle's language about these plays is ambiguous, but there is little reason to doubt their existence.[15] A third kind of theatrical performance was the public recitation of Homeric epics, which transformed Attica (the region that includes Athens) from "a culture-poor backward land" to "suddenly becom[ing] *the* repository of Homeric heritage."[16]

Whatever the precise relationships between these three forms and tragedy, it seems that each of them had some bearing on tragedy's emergence – for tragedy includes ample choral singing (as in the dithyrambs), mimetic action (as in the satyr-like plays), and an emphasis on narratives derived from Homer. It may or may not be the case that dithyrambs and satyr-like plays were originally ritualistic, but it seems less urgent here to argue over that point than to recognize that the earliest tragedians were willing to draw from wherever they could to create something that was at once syncretic and new.

The situation is even less clear for Sanskrit theatre, but the *Rig Veda*, a collection of sacred hymns that likely dates back at least 3,000 years, contains numerous passages that are drama-like, sometimes being monologues, at other times dialogues.[17] Also, the existence of some sorts of organized performance before the emergence of Sanskrit theatre is beyond doubt. Gargi Bhattacharya observes that "the most significant claim to be the source of Indian drama, supported by the etymological evidence, is of the dance. All the words like *nātya*, *nātaka*, *nāta* (actor) have their origin in root *nāt*, which seems to be the Prakrit progeny of the Sanskrit root *nrt* carrying the meaning 'to dance.'"[18] Nothing specific can be said of this dance, which may or may not have been mimetic, but clearly Sanskrit theatre drew upon it. V. Raghavan comments, "The word '*natya*' means and comprises both dance and drama"; the dual meaning signifies that dramatic theatre, as conceived by Bharata, the great early theorist of Sanskrit theatre, "is an integrated art of music, dance, action, and poetry."[19]

It is highly likely that in addition to existing forms of dance there was also acting, per se. In the fifth century BCE, the grammarian Panini made apparent reference to "several acting manuals, all of which indicate that at least from the point of view of the performer, acting had developed into a sophisticated practice, with standards for actor training and enacting."[20] In the second century BCE, the grammarian Patanjali offered a list of "methods" by which events from the two great epics (*The Mahabharata* and *The Ramayana*) could be presented, one of which is through "pantomimic action."[21] Patanjali also seems to suggest a familiarity with *rasa* theory, which would become central to Sanskrit theatre, as we will see.[22] Evidence for acting also exists in early Buddhist sources, most notably when "drama is described as 'true-*cum*-false' ... referring to the nature of stage reality."[23] None of this points specifically to Sanskrit theatre, but just as Greek tragedy was built from existing performance, it is likely that creators of Sanskrit theatre took advantage of their own existing traditions.

One final aspect of the historical situations of Greek tragedy and Sanskrit theatre needs to be addressed. Several scholars have argued that the ancient Greek and Indian theatres were not independent developments, as I am assuming, but that the latter was derived from the former. M. L. Varadpande offers an extensive discussion of historical relations between ancient Greece and India but shows little evidence of a Greek influence on Indian theatre.[24] Perhaps the most important claim is that a satyr play was presented in 326 BCE in the military camp of Alexander the Great, just at the outset of his abortive invasion of India. It is entirely unclear, though, how the single performance of a Greek-language play might have impressed Alexander's few Indian allies sufficiently to have an impact on Indian theatre history. A different line of argument suggests that Greek theatre was introduced to India by a Central Asian people known as Sakas (sometimes transliterated as Shakas or referred to as Indo-Scythians), to whom we will return shortly. For now, it is sufficient to note that while there was undoubtedly a Greek influence in the Saka kingdoms in India (most notably in aspects of their artwork and coinage), the same can be said of native-ruled kingdoms through much of India and even into the western sections of China.[25] But not a shred of evidence suggests that Greek theatre was known to the Sakas.[26]

The arguments *against* a Greek derivation of Sanskrit theatre are powerful, for as Īndū Shekhar contends, there are "basic difference[s]" that "preclude the possibility" of one being derived from the other. Among the most significant is that Sanskrit theatre "aims at imitating the [emotional] state or condition while Greek drama imitates the action."[27] No less significant is that while the chorus is an integral part of all Greek theatre forms, there is no chorus in Sanskrit theatre.[28] Additionally, the plays of the two forms have radically different structures. Greek plays are generally concentrated in time, place, and action (even though they only occasionally adhere to the three "unities" that Aristotle is mistakenly said to have demanded), whereas the plays of Sanskrit theatre tend to sprawl temporally, geographically, and in the focus of their action.[29]

Bhattacharya's summary is apt: "No doubt … the origin and the development of ancient Indian drama carries multiple theories, but most of the scholars hold the view that Indian drama developed independently, without any Greek influence. Some features could be similar between these two … but the similarities can be considered as the basic requirement for the development of dramatic art in any country/culture."[30] The argument for Greek origins of Sanskrit theatre seems predicated on a pair of a priori assumptions: first, that theatre (or perhaps literary theatre) could have been invented only once; and second, that it required the genius of Greece to stimulate theatre's emergence in India. Both assumptions are unsupportable. Far more likely is that the emergence of literary theatre itself in these two lands is a convergent analogy.

Societal Conditions for Literary Theatre

Convergent analogies in theatre, as I noted in the Introduction, are similar theatrical traits that arise independently in response to similarities in their societal contexts. One should not assume that such convergences occur automatically: They are the result of choices made by artists of varying backgrounds, tastes, and abilities. But societies might present similar opportunities to those artists, leading them to respond with some similar choices. Greek tragedy and Sanskrit theatre differ in numerous and significant ways, a few of which I have already noted. Other differences will soon become apparent, but the issue here concerns the single trait of employing prewritten dramatic texts. My suggestion is that a particular set of societal conditions in Greece and India presented new opportunities for theatre artists, making possible the two independent inventions of literary theatre. As we will see in subsequent chapters, when this same set of conditions came to exist in other societies, literary theatre forms emerged in them as well.

The first of these societal conditions is the most obvious: the presence of a *literate class*. The extent of literacy in fifth-century Greece is difficult to determine, Rosalind Thomas writes, because "there are many different levels of literacy …. We might define literacy as the ability to read and write, but read and write *what?*"³¹ Being able to decipher a few words or sign one's name is a far cry from the ability to read or write literature. Thomas suggests that "in cities like Athens … most citizens had some basic ability [to read] and perhaps 'phonetic literacy' was pretty widespread; but the written texts of poetry and literary prose had a reading audience confined to the highly educated and wealthy elite, and their secretaries."³² The texts themselves would present difficulties even to the literate, being "without word-division, accents or much punctuation," and so Thomas suggests they were primarily "mnemonic aids" for people already familiar with their contents.³³ And at any rate, there were precious few of those written texts, at least early on. According to Eric Csapo and William J. Slater, "The Greek book trade did not exist when Aeschylus produced his plays" between 499 and 458 BCE, "and it seems not to have become profitable until just a few years before [Euripides'] death" in 406 BCE.³⁴ Widespread literacy was therefore not likely a factor in the emergence of Greek theatre, but there certainly existed a literate class capable of writing plays.

Ancient India saw a similar coexistence of limited literacy amid a generally oral society. Sanskrit was already a language for the learned when first used for the *Vedas*. These sacred materials were transmitted orally for many generations, but at some uncertain time they were put into writing; subsequently, "an extensive scholarly and practical literature" about the *Vedas* was "often transmitted in written form."³⁵ What is called Classical Sanskrit was then regularized by a series of scholars, most notably the aforementioned grammarians Panini and Patanjali. By around 400 BCE, the earliest elements of *The Mahabharata* and *The Ramayana* had apparently been committed to writing after a long existence as oral narratives. These epics were popular works whose texts would continue to be expanded for hundreds of years to come, even as they lived on in the oral tradition. The number of people capable of reading them was undoubtedly very limited, but as in Greece, even that limited number would have been sufficient to have an appreciable cultural impact.

There was, notably, a significant difference in the linguistic structures of ancient Greek and Indian societies, which is reflected in their theatre forms. All the city-states of Greece spoke the same language, albeit with differences in dialect (as evidenced by the speech of Spartan characters in Aristophanes's *Lysistrata*). India, however, was multilingual. The root word for "Sanskrit" means "the tongue perfected," and in its perfection, Classical Sanskrit was an "artificial" language.³⁶ The Sanskrit scholar J. A. B. Van Buitenen suggests that "to speak Sanskrit was the sign of a civilized man" and "spelt literacy" – but it was not a language for everyday living and was "always a second language" for the educated elite. Other languages, collectively known as Prakrits, were the vernaculars throughout India and were not merely spoken languages but served as literary and official languages as well.[37] The plays of Sanskrit theatre took advantage of this linguistic diversity to indicate the social status of their characters. Generally, male characters of the two highest castes (Brahmin and Kshatriya) "have the right to speak in Sanskrit"; men of the lower castes and women of all castes generally speak one or another vernacular language.[38] Though the presence of a literary class in both Greece and India was necessary for the emergence of each land's literary theatre, the way that those theatres used language suggests the profound linguistic differences in their societies.

Here, though, a question arises. Whether one is writing in a single language or multiple ones, why *write* plays at all? Given contemporary practices, it might seem only natural that plays would be written, but as already noted, playwrighting seems to have been unique to the ancient Mediterranean and South Asia until at least the tenth century CE. The answer is apparently that in Athens and Ujjain there was a premium on the creation of *new* plays. Such plays are a major investment of time and effort on the part of theatre troupes. The cost of this investment can never be eliminated, but it can be mitigated if part of the burden is borne by a single person (or small group of people). A new play is also a speculative risk, for one cannot be sure if it will satisfy its audience – or even if the relevant authorities will allow its performance. Again, the risk is most easily limited by off-loading the task of preparing the script in advance. In a society with limited literacy, that responsibility would best be handled by someone with a facility for words and a knowledge of existing literature. No one else in the troupe needs to even be literate, for the various roles could be orally transmitted to the actors. One cannot say whether this took place in Sanskrit theatre, but it was likely the case in Greece. There, David Wiles suggests, "the dramatists taught the roles to their actors face to face … and there is no evidence that actors ever received a script."[39]

The second societal condition for the breakthroughs to literary theatre is the opening or expansion of a *niche* capable of supporting the new theatre form.[40] In any given location, multiple forms of theatre can coexist; often, each form has its own niche within the larger complex of available theatre forms. Niches might be occasion-based (e.g., theatre performed in conjunction with specific holidays, festivals, or celebrations); class-based (e.g., theatre for the elite, for middling classes, or for the peasantry); gender- or age-based (e.g., theatre exclusively for men, women, or children), and so on. Some forms might occupy multiple niches, just as multiple forms might sometimes compete for a single niche. New niches themselves are generally created when societal disruption generates potential new audiences (and/or sponsors), although the disruption must not be so great as to cause societal chaos. The possible causes of generative disruptions are legion, and include socioeconomic change, demographic change, political or ideological change, and changing modes of communication. Although generative disruptions might shrink the niches for some existing forms of theatre, they present new opportunities for theatre artists with the talent and luck to exploit them.

What Jean Pierre Vernant and Pierre Vidal-Naquet call "the historical moment of tragedy" was the fifth century BCE, when the form was "born, flourish[ed], and degenerat[ed] in Athens, and all almost within the space of a hundred years."[41] The reference here to Athens, and not to Greece as a whole, is significant. Through most of the fifth century BCE, the niche that tragedy would occupy existed solely in Athens and its outlying territories.[42] At the start of tragedy's "moment," a pair of societal disruptions are especially relevant.

First is the onset of Athenian democracy. We have seen that tragedy's place in the City Dionysia festival might well have been directly associated with the institution of democracy just before 500 BCE; through the following century, the association between tragedy and democracy is clear. Simon Goldhill argues that "a discussion of the audience of Greek tragedy must take as its frame ... both the pervasiveness of the values of performance in Greek culture and in particular the special context of democracy and its institutions, where to be in an audience is above all *to play the role of democratic citizen.*"[43] By participating in the City Dionysia festival, Goldhill continues, "the Athenian citizen demonstrated his citizenship, and by its staging [of] the festival ... the city promoted and projected itself as a city."[44] Vernant and Vidal-Naquet similarly suggest, "Tragedy was one of the forms through which the new democratic city established its identity," paraphrasing Walter Nestle to the effect that "tragedy is born when myth starts to be considered from the point of view of the citizen."[45]

By modern standards, Athenian democracy was quite limited, for it excluded women, slaves, and resident aliens – in other words, a large majority of the city's adult population. Although it is generally believed that many (or perhaps most) citizens attended the plays presented during the festival, attendance by noncitizens is uncertain, with the question of women's attendance being especially controversial. After reviewing the evidence, Goldhill concludes that the question "cannot be securely answered" but suggests that "whether women are to be thought of as a silenced presence … or an absent sign, the audience represents the [male] body politic."[46] This seems a judicious conclusion. Greek tragedy was written and performed by men for men; the niche it filled for democratic discourse in a thoroughly male-dominated society was strictly gendered. Although female characters are often central to tragic narratives, Edith Hall notes that "play after play … portrays the disastrous effects on households and the larger community of divinely inspired madness, anger, sexual desire, or jealousy in women unsupervised by men."[47] Helen P. Foley observes that tragedy, conversely, "offers approval to female characters who, without abandoning their female character, voluntarily choose to sacrifice themselves for city or nation," while also "celebrat[ing] wives who … make choices that, even in the absence of their husbands, heroically serve the interests of their marital family."[48]

The second societal disruption in Athens was the Persian War and its aftermath. In 490 BCE, the Persian army invaded the Greek mainland but was repulsed at Marathon, primarily by Athenian forces. About a decade later, the Persians returned in even greater numbers, only to be stymied again. When the fighting was largely concluded, the city-state "best fitted to draw profit from the Greek triumph" was Athens, thanks to the wartime expansion of its navy. It "eagerly took up leadership of the Delian League" of city-states and within a few years had "converted [its] voluntary allies into involuntary subjects" as it turned itself into "the commercial hub of the Aegean."[49] Although the niche provided by the City Dionysia had been filled by whatever might have been performed before the Persian War, that niche was transformed by the suddenly increased wealth of postwar Athens. The city could now easily support the high degree of organization that tragedy would require, both directly (e.g., through constructing the Theatre of Dionysus) and indirectly (e.g., through the state's assigning to each playwright a wealthy citizen who would fund the playwright's set of plays).[50]

One characteristic of tragedy's festival niche is especially worth emphasizing: From its start, the festival included a competition between the sets of plays. Playwrights had to compete even to get their plays mounted, for only three sets of tragedies were selected each year; the festival itself had ten citizens rendering the official judgment in the competition between the selected sets.[51] Competition created an incessant demand for plays that could offer new considerations of legendary materials. At some point after the death of Aeschylus (in 456 BCE), a formal decree allowed for the remounting of his plays, but there is no reason to believe they were part of the main competition itself.⁵² Competition was also undoubtedly a critical motor for the form's rapid development. In the seventy or so years separating Aeschylus's *Persians* from the final plays of Sophocles and Euripides, tragedy saw increases in the number and professionalism of its actors, a growing emphasis on dramatic conflict, a decrease in the significance of the chorus, and alterations in its musical styles.⁵³

Turning now to India, the collapse of the Maurya Empire (in the second century BCE) was the most obvious disruption heading into the period under consideration. The Indologist Harry Falk discerns three phases in the roughly five centuries between the fall of the Maurya Empire and the rise of the Gupta Empire. The first phase was primarily indigenous in nature – many native rulers clawing their way to local power – and lasted until the mid-first century BCE. The second phase, which lasted until the mid third century CE, "was dominated by intruding Westerners, be they of Iranian, Scythian, or Kushana stock." This was followed by a third phase, which saw "the dispersal of foreign rule and the return of traditional values" that "culminat[ed] in the accession of the Guptas" around 320 CE.⁵⁴

If we work from the fourth century CE dating of Kalidasa and therefore the second century CE dating of Bhasa, the period of origins for Sanskrit theatre would fall midway into Falk's second phase. The key dynasty here seems to be the Sakas, in particular the Saka line that settled around Ujjain; its greatest ruler was Rudradaman I, who reigned in the mid second century CE. The Sakas were ethnically Iranian, but Rudradaman's throne name – "garland of Rudra" (i.e., Shiva) – suggests an openness to Hinduism. Significantly, a stone inscription from his rule "is well known as the first long inscription in classical Sanskrit …. This was a clear break with the tradition of writing in various [Prakrit languages] that went back some 400 years."⁵⁵ The inscription itself offers the striking claim that Rudradaman "has caused the strong attachment of *dharma*" and that (among his many other accomplishments) he composed "prose and verse which are clear, agreeable and sweet, charming, [and] beautiful."⁵⁶ No doubt the inscription is boastful, but as the historian John Keay notes, "clearly [Rudradaman] aspired to what he took to be an essentially Indian ideal of kingship."⁵⁷

In addition to the Sakas' deep interest in Indian culture, this was also a time of significantly increasing trade. The historian Shonaleeka Kaul writes, "If the sixth century BCE was the 'take-off' stage, the post-Mauryan period saw trade activity, both internal and external, overland and maritime, acquire full-blown proportions."⁵⁸ The Sakas' capital at Ujjain, located on one of India's most lucrative internal trade routes, would have been well-situated to participate in such trade, and Harry Falk writes that the Sakas "made a living through intensive trade relations with East and West." He also offers the highly suggestive point that they built a "center of learning" in Ujjain.[59] Although he does not mention precisely when this occurred, such a center would presumably have attracted and retained many men literate in Sanskrit. Taking all this together, one can easily imagine that the growing capital of a relatively new dynasty – engaged in and enriched by a thriving trade – would be undergoing precisely the sort of generative disruption that can open a new theatre niche. When we also note the Sakas' demonstrable interest in Indian culture and the Sanskrit language, it is not difficult to see this period as highly plausible for the emergence of a literary theatre form that employed not only Prakrit languages but Sanskrit as well, albeit for unprecedented purposes.

It is impossible to say with certainty what niche Sanskrit theatre might have filled. The *Natyasastra* (which might be dated to either before or after the playwright Bhasa) suggests that the form had "dramatic contests at which prizes were awarded by judges";[60] if these contests existed early in the form's history, one can see them functioning as they did in Athens, creating a demand for new material even as they drove the form's development. The *Natyasastra* also says (in Shekhar's gloss) that the form "was intended to provide entertainment to all the Varnas [castes] including the common folk who had no access to the Vedas." Shekhar argues that it was therefore "appropriate that the dialogues should be carried out in the local dialects."[61] But this seems implausible, because the most important passages of dialogue required an understanding of Sanskrit, which was limited to the educated elite.

More likely is that the primary audiences for the plays consisted of those who could understand vernacular languages *and* Sanskrit, and who were able to appreciate the literary merits of the plays' poetry. Shekhar himself suggests that from the "very inception" of the form, the playwrights "never cared for the thrill of popular admiration" but "produced highly cultivated literary drama with an eye to seek recognition of the learned … who dominated court life." Further, "in the prologues of various dramas, only the assembly of the learned and cultured is admired, but nowhere have the poets left any description of plebeians enjoying a show in some spacious hall."[62] Given the need to understand Sanskrit and the evidence of the plays' prologues, it is likely that the primary niche for the form was as an elite entertainment, perhaps performed primarily in the increasingly wealthy royal court.[63]

The fine psychological nuance of Sanskrit theatre also suggests an elite audience. Whereas Greek tragedy and Old Comedy staged what were, in effect, debates of public life, Sanskrit theatre staged the aestheticized display of human emotion. Vinay Dharwadker writes that in the *Natyasastra*, the word *bhava* refers to "emotions and emotional states in their existential manifestation – as we experience them in the raw in everyday life"; *rasa* had the original meaning of "juice, extract, essence, flavour, or taste," but the word "functions as a metaphor in the discourse of aesthetics and performance," where it "refers to emotional states, passions and feelings as we experience them" when represented in the arts.[64] As can be seen in Figure 3.1, the *Natyasastra* identifies eight stable *bhavas* that are modified by one or more of thirty-three possible "ancillary emotions" (*vyabhicaribhava*) and augmented by eight psychosomatic symptoms (*sattvika*).[65] The result is eight *rasas* that correspond to the eight stable *bhavas* but that have been exquisitely seasoned for aesthetic expression. In Sanskrit theatre, one might say, the raw emotional ingredients of life are expertly prepared and offered for the delectation of connoisseurs.

The third societal condition for the breakthroughs to literary theatre is an authoritative corpus of *popular narratives*, along with authorial freedom to *reimagine* those narratives on stage. Playwrights need stories to dramatize. They can, of course, draw them from contemporary life or sheer imagination. But Greek tragedians (after Aeschylus's *Persians*, in 472 BCE) and Sanskrit playwrights preferred narratives that were widely known and centered on heroic human characters and/or anthropomorphic deities. In both lands, such narratives could be found in their great epics, supplemented by other legendary materials. Given the cultural significance of the epics, however, it is noteworthy that playwrights in both Greece and India treated their sources with a free hand, shaping the materials to suit their dramaturgical purposes.

The reliance of Greek tragedians on Homer's *Iliad* and *Odyssey*, along with other (now lost) narratives, is well known. Aeschylus himself is said to have referred to his own works as "slices (portions) from Homer's great feasts."[66] But the freedom with which the tragedians treated their sources is evident in almost every surviving play, including those of Aeschylus's *Oresteia* trilogy. As originally related in *The Odyssey*, the basic story is that Aegisthus (paramour of Clytemnestra) kills Agamemnon (Clytemnestra's husband) upon Agamemnon's return to Mycenae after fighting in the Trojan War; some years later, Agamemnon's son, Orestes, gains triumphant revenge by killing Aegisthus.[67] Aeschylus radically recenters the narrative on Clytemnestra as both the killer of Agamemnon and the primary

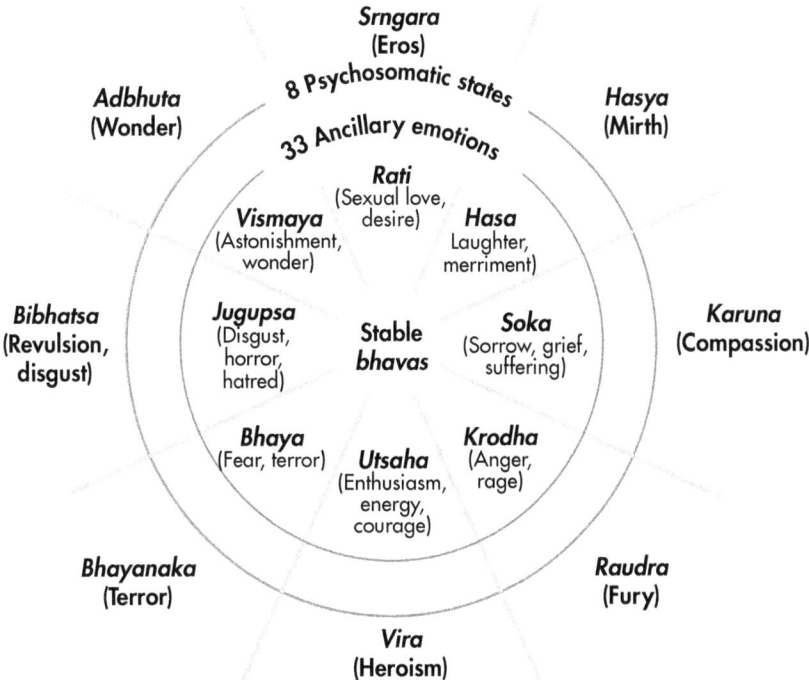

Figure 3.1 *Bhava* and *rasa* in Sanskrit theatre. The thirty-three ancillary emotions are despondency, weakness, apprehension, envy, intoxication, weariness, indolence, depression, anxiety, distraction, recollection, contentment, shame, inconsistency, joy, agitation, stupor, arrogance, despair, impotence, sleep, epilepsy, dreaming, awakening, indignation, dissimulation, cruelty, assurance, sickness, insanity, death, fright, and deliberation. The eight psychosomatic symptoms are paralysis, perspiration, horripilation, vocal change, trembling, color change, weeping, and fainting. The lists of ancillary emotions and psychosomatic states come from Farley P. Richmond, "Characteristics of Sanskrit Theatre and Drama," in *Indian Theatre: Traditions of Performance*, eds. Farley P. Richmond, Darius L. Swann, and Phillip B. Zarrilli (University of Hawaii Press, 1990), 81.

victim of Orestes, who himself is made to undergo a trial (in democratic Athens!) for his actions. Surviving plays by Sophocles and Euripides also treat portions of the same source material, with each playwright reshaping it in his own way.

This ongoing reimagining of a story from Homer is typical of Greek tragedy. Peter Burian observes that there are "close to six hundred works attributed by title to all known tragic poets" but that they draw from a surprisingly limited set of subjects. "The history of Greek tragedy," Burian writes, "is one of continuously recasting tales already known to the audience." This amounted to "a system of tragic discourse" in which "plot stood open to invention, most obviously in the areas of motivation and characterization, but also in such features as location and sequence of events."[68] Interpretive freedom followed from the tragedians' interest not in simply retelling the popular narratives but in what Vernant and Vidal-Naquet call their desire to place the legendary heroes "under examination before the public," where they become "problem[s]" for the democratic city's consideration.[69]

Sanskrit playwrights also largely relied on epic narratives, while occasionally looking to other legendary sources. Six of the thirteen surviving plays of Bhasa are based on *The Mahabharata*, with another based on the Krishna lore found in something of an appendix to that epic; two other plays are based on *The Ramayana*, while the remaining four relate legendary narratives, three of which are associated with Ujjain.[70] As with the Greek tragedians, Bhasa did not feel constrained in his use of the narrative sources. In his *Five Nights*, the "dramatist has taken enormous liberties with the epic material" drawn from *The Mahabharata*; similarly, while his *Statue Play* is based on an episode in *The Ramayana*, Bhasa freely invented the play's central scene.[71]

Kalidasa was no less willing to ring changes on his sources. In *Sakuntala and the Ring of Recognition*, he "remoulded a well-known story to the extent that it became unusual and changed the essential mood of the narrative"; he also altered the story by introducing the key plot point of a token ring by which the heroine will be recognized.[72] In general, suggests V. Raghavan, the theme for a given Sanskrit play "may be taken from well-known epics or invented or mixed; even when the story is well known, the dramatist could make innovations to suit his dramatic idea and purpose." This freedom arose because "what the Sanskrit drama endeavours to present is a harmonious character and harmonious emotional impression in the spectators' hearts," not an enactment of the epics themselves. "With these ends in view, the dramatist handled the factors of his theme, the story, the character and sentiment [*rasa*] according to the idea he had taken on hand. Those incidents in the story which were not necessary for his plot, or those which were in conflict with his main idea, he eschewed or remodelled."[73]

Given the freedom with which Greek and Indian playwrights treated their sources, one might reasonably ask: Why base their plays on popular narratives in the first place? For the Greek tragedians, it was, at least in part, a retreat to safety. Three of the earliest plays of which we know (Phyrnicus's *Capture of Miletus* and *Phoenician Women*, along with Aeschylus's *Persians*) dealt with contemporary matters, and Phyrnicus is said to have been punished for portraying in *Capture of Miletus* the Athenians' shameful betrayal of that city. After Aeschylus's *Persians*, suggest Csapo and Slater, "tragedy on sensitive current events then disappears," with such events apparently being considered "too hot to handle."[74] The social commentary in tragedy would henceforth be dressed in legendary garb. Greek comedy would show a similar (though later) retreat to safety. The licentious and politically charged Old Comedy associated most famously with Aristophanes would give way to New Comedy's more anodyne comedies of manners and character, usually set on the contemporary streets of everyday life but absent anything that might provoke serious controversy.

Sanskrit theatre, however, shows no evidence of a similar retreat. And in any case, this explanation for a Greek retreat overlooks a basic fact of theatre history, observable almost everywhere: Plays strongly tend to favor narratives (or at least the characters thereof) that their audiences already *know*. Often this means restaging plays that have a proven track record of success. In the absence of such plays (as at the start of regional traditions of theatre, especially) other familiar narratives must be pressed into service. The epics and legends of Greece and India provided cornucopias of well-known narratives. When success depends on audience approval, as with the competitions that were part of the City Dionysia and are said to have existed for Sanskrit theatre, reimagining these narratives allowed the playwrights to build on their established appeal in original ways. This offered a satisfying blend of familiarity *and* surprise. Aristophanes's Old Comedy gained that same blend by placing well-known contemporaries (such as Aeschylus and Euripides, in *The Frogs*) in novel situations.

It is likely that other societal conditions might be added to the three I have discussed, but it is worth emphasizing that these are merely *conditions*. However auspicious they might have been for the emergence of literary theatre forms, they did not in themselves create the forms. That creation must be credited to the artists who found a way to take advantage of those conditions: Aeschylus and his competitors in Athens and perhaps Bhasa (or some earlier artists) in the kingdom of the Sakas in Ujjain.

CHAPTER 4

Silences and Successes

The Greek and Indian inventions of literary theatre stand out for their uniqueness in world theatre until the tenth century CE; they also stand out for the way they helped to establish long-enduring theatre regions. A consideration of two other ancient societies can help to explain why the rest of the world apparently remained silent when it came to literary theatre, while a look at the theatre regions created in the wake of Greek tragedy and Sanskrit theatre can suggest the legacies of these literary forms.

The Silences of Ancient Egypt and China

Egypt would seem to have had the potential for literary theatre long before it emerged in Greece and India, while China surely seems a candidate for such theatre at roughly the same time as them. But in neither society did literary theatre develop until many centuries later. Let me consider ancient Egypt first. The most immediate question is, did it even have what we would call *dramatic* theatre? According to the Egyptologist Ronald J. Leprohon, "The question of dramatic performances in ancient Egypt has long been debated,"[1] but if the arguments I have made in Part I of this book are correct, it is likely that there *was* dramatic theatre in the service of various social activities, even if it was unknown to or beneath the notice of the few people able to make a record of it. Performance in the service of ritual, however, *was* recorded, though whether any of it can properly be called dramatic theatre is uncertain at best, given the present state of evidence.

Three Egyptian works have drawn the most scholarly attention. First is what is anachronistically called the "Abydos Passion Play." No text exists of this "play"; the surviving evidence comes from a commemorative stela (circa nineteenth century BCE) in which a treasury official records his participation in the ritual procession of a statue of Osiris. Leprohon comments that this text (as with others associated with it) implies that "festivals in ancient Egypt contained [performance] elements that were shared by drama in later cultures" but that these "do not coalesce into what can be termed a dramatic performance."[2]

The second relevant work is usually called the "Ramesseum Dramatic Papyrus" (circa eighteenth century BCE). It was found among a cache of materials that lead the Egyptologist Christina Geisen to suggest it was owned by (and buried with) a priest who "played a decisive role in rituals as well as in the temple cult of gods or deceased kings."[3] The text records a series of ritual actions performed in association with mythology about Osiris. But Geisen notes that the connections between the ritual actions and the mythology are based on little more than verbal puns,[4] and so the papyrus scarcely appears to be evidence of a ritual enactment or mimetic reimagining of the mythology. Again, it seems that some characteristics common to dramatic theatre are present, but Geisen concludes that "these characteristics do not suffice to categorize the manuscript as a liturgical or sacred drama or a festival play"; instead, the text records a ritual that might well have been recited and that was apparently performed without a human audience.[5]

The third work, known as *The Triumph of Horus*, is said by the Egyptologist H. W. Fairman to be (as his book's cover proclaims) "the oldest play in the world."[6] There are, however, difficulties with this claim. Briefly, the text was engraved on the walls of the Temple of Horus in Edfu, circa 110 BCE. Because some of its lines had also been engraved in earlier-constructed portions of the temple, Fairman contends the "complete text of the play must have existed, and the play [been] performed," since 237 BCE, when the older portions of the temple were constructed.[7] And because the surviving text is largely archaic in language, Fairman suggests that it must be based on a (currently unknown) text from the New Kingdom, about a thousand years earlier. And beyond even that, Fairman comments that the "harpoon ritual," a central and recurring motif in the text, dates back at least to the early Middle Kingdom, perhaps indicating an even earlier origin for the play.[8]

The existing text seems to give evidence that it was intended for performance (e.g., apparent stage directions), but no evidence suggests that this performance involved a human audience, despite Fairman's speculation about "an audience of privileged persons and local notables."[9] Nor is there any evidence that the hypothetical text from a thousand years earlier had anything like stage directions, or was even intended for performance, rather than being a narrative or a set of directions for conducting a nondramatic ritual. What then are we to make of this "oldest play in the world," which dates from 110 BCE, or 237 BCE, or 1200 BCE, or perhaps thousands of years earlier? As with the "Abydos Passion Play" and the "Ramesseum Dramatic Papyrus," the answer must be equivocal. Given the way I have defined dramatic theatre, we need not discount these texts on the grounds that they were associated with ritual. But it is entirely unclear if any of them involved performance that called for a frame of make-believe action shared by the performers and their audience.[10]

All that said, the problem at hand is not whether ancient Egypt had *any* dramatic theatre but whether it had dramatic theatre that made regular use of prewritten scripts. And here one need not equivocate, for nothing indicates that this was the case. Even if the aforementioned texts are accepted as evidence of dramatic theatre, they are almost certainly formal records of what *was* performed, not scripts written in advance of their first performances, alongside other (now-unknown) scripts. Why then did Egypt apparently not develop a form of literary theatre?

Pharaonic Egypt was a literate society, but literacy was limited to an extremely thin veneer of priest and scribes. The Egyptologist John Baines suggests that through the centuries of the New Kingdom (1549–1069 BCE), the number of literate people was probably not more than 1 percent of the population – and was likely smaller both before and after that period. Moreover, he observes that the literate few were mainly employed for "administration" (both religious and political) and "monumental display." The society's religious texts – mostly hymns, prayers, and instructions for the dead – were generally "not narrative" and could be considered neither "oral epic nor scriptures,"[11] nor could the various (auto)biographies, didactic writings, magical texts, private letters, love poems, or occasional short tales that are also part of ancient Egyptian literature.[12]

There was undoubtedly a well-known cycle of sacred myths about the death and resurrection of Osiris and the struggles between Horus and Seth. The existing literature sometimes refers to elements of this cycle, but they do not seem to have cohered into a popular narrative with a stabilizing written version, along the lines of the Greek and Indian epics. Ancient Egypt, in sum, lacked two of the three societal conditions we have identified in Greece and India. It is easy enough to find disruptions in ancient Egypt's long history that might have created new niches for emerging theatre forms, but it seems that severe limitations of literacy and the absence of an authoritative corpus of popular narrative worked against the possibility of those forms being literary.

The absence of literary theatre in ancient China is more perplexing. China has long been one of the most sophisticated societies in the world, with thriving cities and ample internal and external trade; it has also had a substantial literate class, especially after the Confucian exam system for governmental service was introduced in 178 BCE.[13] There was also no shortage of performance traditions to draw upon. Ancient China had its traveling players, court performances, and folk theatres: William Dolby finds hints of theatre in what were probably the later years of the Zhou Dynasty (1027–256 BCE) and clear evidence of short sketches during the Han years (206 BCE–220 CE), including a comic sketch called *Mr. Huang of the Eastern Ocean*.[14]

According to Tao-Ching Hsü, a survey of court pageants and spectacles from 221 BCE to 607 CE shows all manner of singing and dancing (including female and animal impersonations), a wide range of circus and magic acts, display puppetry (including a whale that transforms into a dragon some sixty feet in length), and so on.[15] Hsü's reported "animal impersonations" apparently include what was called the "horn-butting game," a staged combat between two performers, one of whom impersonates an animal. William Dolby suggests that the combat was probably "a comic sketch" that "easily could have grown into more elaborate plays or dramas,"[16] but there is no evidence that this growth took place. Toward the end of that period there was also an indistinct sort of urban theatre apparently performed once a month. This theatre, whatever it might have entailed, was popular enough to raise the ire of a contemporary court historian who objected to its "obscenity and vulgarity" as well as to the audience that drew no distinction "between the noble and the lowly, between men and women, or between monks and laymen."[17]

By the eighth century, two newer theatre forms had emerged: *canjun xi* ("Adjutant Plays") and *tayao niang* ("Stepping and Singing Woman"). The former was a comic sketch form that mocked officialdom and seems to have gained a relatively wide distribution.[18] The latter was a sort of musical "slapstick show." According to one account, the show centered on the dancing of a wife (played by a cross-dressed man) who offers a series of complaints against her husband, followed by the appearance of the husband who beats his wife for complaining – a beating "taken as the occasion for laughter and merriment."[19] Although these two forms might have been new, they do not seem to have been meaningfully *different* than the sketch-based comic forms that already existed. Given all this performance, along with China's wealth and literacy, the stage seems to have long been set, as it were, for the emergence of literary theatre – but it did not yet happen.

The glorious literary tradition of China might, paradoxically, be at least partially responsible for the lack of literary theatre until after the tenth century CE. China had a long-lived hierarchy of literary forms: "Ranked at the top … were history (which recorded the affairs of the rulers and their officials), moral disquisitions (which reinforced the sociopolitical order), and lyric verse (which expressed the deepest aspirations of the literati)."[20] What was *not* in this hierarchy were epic narratives. According to the Sinologist Victor H. Mair, "Historians of Chinese literature have often been puzzled by the fragmentary state of ancient Chinese myth and the lack of great epics" such as those found in Greece and India. The reason for this lack, Mair suggests, is that "myths and epics are essentially [oral] narratives" that were "originally the preserve of oral 'singers of tales'"; as such they "were naturally ranked low on the scale of genres in ancient China."[21] This low status apparently disinclined Chinese writers from creating the sort of literary versions that could stabilize and help to transmit them. But once Chinese literature began supplying the functional equivalent of epics with *chuanqi* novels and other popular fiction, two distinct forms of literary theatre would emerge almost simultaneously, as we will see.[22]

I do not think it necessary to examine other societies during the many millennia leading up to the tenth century CE. Throughout the world we can assume that dramatic theatre was being performed – perhaps as a medium for ritual or devotion or social commentary or pedagogy or just for entertainment, per se – but the development of *literary* forms of theatre seems to have required a particular set of societal conditions that existed first in Greece and India. This does not mean, I hasten to add, that these two societies were superior to other societies. It means merely that they were different enough to present theatre artists with a new sort of opportunity and that those artists were talented enough to make the most of it.

The Successes of the Mediterranean and South Asian Theatre Regions

In both Greece and India, the breakthroughs to literary theatre were enormously consequential. However geographically limited the breakthroughs might at first have been – to Athens and its environs for tragedy and then comedy, and to north-central India (likely centered on Ujjain) for Sanskrit theatre – each eventually created an extensive and long-enduring theatre region. By "theatre region" I mean a geographical area that is home to a widespread theatre form or to multiple forms that have significant interactions between their texts, performance traits, artists, or audiences; over time, theatre regions show continuities through unbroken chains of transmission as emerging theatre forms make syncretic use of various traits of existing forms. The theatre region instigated by Greek tragedy would come to include more than a dozen theatre forms; the region created by Sanskrit theatre would eventually prove to be even more prolific.

Even before the end of the fifth century BCE, Athenian tragedy had begun to spread from its home city.[23] Athenian comedy also flourished, at first with Old Comedy, later with the more anodyne New Comedy whose most famous playwright was Menander. As early as 400 BCE, writes Alan H. Sommerstein, "comedy of the Athenian type was probably already on the way to becoming a popular form of entertainment over most of the Greek world."[24] The fall of Athens in 404 BCE, at the end of the Peloponnesian War, did nothing to arrest the expansion of the theatre region. Oliver Taplin expresses the

> hope that it can now be taken as a well-grounded hypothesis that over the period 450 to 300 [BCE] tragedies – predominantly though not necessarily exclusively Athenian tragedies – were being performed widely and regularly throughout the scattered Greek world, with the audiences in Sicily and Magna Graecia [i.e., Greek colonies in southern Italy] probably among the keenest promoters of the hugely popular new art-form.[25]

The Hellenistic period, brought on by the conquests of Alexander of Macedonia (and conventionally dated from his death in 323 BCE), further extended Greek influence. Sarah Miles observes that there is "truly a mammoth expanse of cultures to place under the singular label 'Hellenistic,' and yet they do share common features, including Greek language, a common city model, and a wide-ranging engagement with Greek drama." To satisfy this engagement, the period saw "the rise of the Artists of Dionysus," professional actors who worked throughout the Greek-speaking world.[26] There was also an unprecedented engagement with the literature of theatre. P. E. Easterling comments that "an unbroken history of scholarly interest in tragedy can be traced from the time of Aristotle and his pupils at Athens [in the fourth century BCE] to the Alexandrian researchers" of the ensuing centuries, who "collected, emended, classified and analysed texts on a heroic scale."[27]

Greek theatre first reached Rome in the third century BCE, and eventually became domesticated there, most notably in the works of the playwrights Terence and Plautus, who based their Latin plays on Greek New Comedy. Other Roman playwrights continued the domestication by creating homologous theatre forms (such as *fabula togata*) that set their plays in Italy and portrayed Italian characters.[28] Gesine Manuwald notes that Greek tragedy was also domesticated and, until the early first century BCE, Roman versions of the Greek classics were not infrequent. An indigenous form of tragedy also emerged, the *fabula praetexta*, which Manuwald calls "a genuine Roman dramatic genre, namely serious plays on events from Roman history" that were "based on Greek exemplars." But neither of these tragic forms was any more long-lived than the comic ones, and by the early first century BCE, "only very few notices and fragments of tragedies have been preserved," aside from the plays of Seneca, which likely were intended for reading or reciting, not staged performance.[29]

In the wake of pre-Imperial Roman comedy and tragedy came coarser and more successful forms of theatre: mime and pantomime. Mime "was noted for its obscenity and license (including female nudity) and, consequently, was perennially popular." It was concerned primarily with "dramatic caricature, sensationalized enactments from everyday life … as well as more exotic subjects such as kidnappings, shipwrecks, and, occasionally, plots from mythology"; it also sometimes made use of "acrobatics, song and dance, and jokes," strung on a scenario so flimsy that it presented little more than "a variety show."[30] Pantomime, meanwhile, came in two varieties: comic pantomime, which was popular for only a short time (having to compete with mime for public favor), and tragic pantomime, which was performed for centuries. The latter was "evidently fashioned from sensational moments from Greek mythology, and from the tragedies in particular." In tragic pantomime, the central performer was a silent dancer who "impersonated all the characters … in a series of interlinked solos"; the dancer was backed by a musical ensemble and accompanied by either a single singer or chorus to "provide narrative continuity."[31]

The extent of the ancient Mediterranean theatre region can roughly be assessed by looking at the geographic distribution of theatres in which this mélange of related theatre forms was performed, as shown in Figure 4.1. Some of the theatres date from the classical or Hellenistic eras, but most were constructed (or reconstructed) during Roman times.[32] The numbers, compiled from a massive study by Frank Sear, probably understate the actual total, for not all theatres would have left physical remains or been mentioned in the surviving literature. The theatre region clearly encompassed the entire Mediterranean basin but was not "European" in the sense that the term is currently used. Instead, it centered on the three shores of the Mediterranean and almost entirely excluded anything east of the Rhine and north of the Danube.

Following the emergence of Athenian tragedy, circa 500 BCE, the ancient Mediterranean region lasted for roughly a millennium. According to Carol Symes, the "standard narrative" about theatre in the late Roman Empire holds that "the establishment of Christianity as the dominant religion …

The Successes of the Mediterranean and South Asia

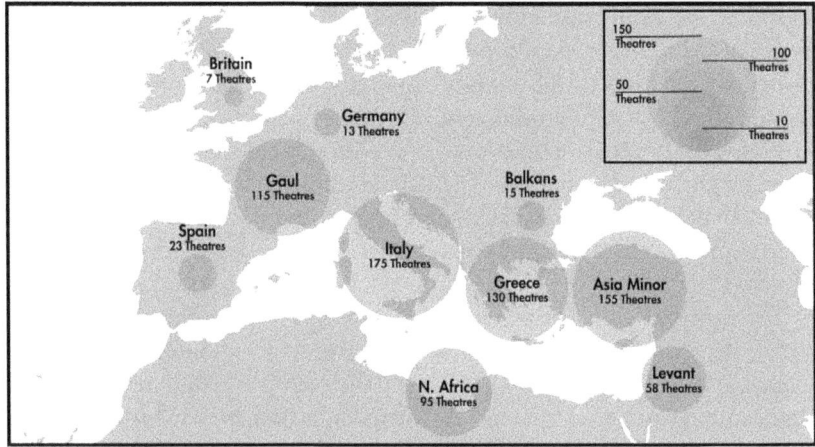

Figure 4.1 Ancient Mediterranean theatre region. Proportional circle map, Flannery scale. Data and place names from Frank Sear, *Roman Theatres: An Architectural Study* (Oxford University Press, 2006), 96–115. Sear includes Crete (fourteen theatres) with North Africa and Cyprus (five theatres) with Asia Minor.

quickly resulted in the eradication of Classical arts and learning," including dramatic theatre.[33] But this narrative is not quite accurate, for although Christianity was formally established as the official Roman religion in 380 CE, "imperial patronage [of the stage] remained very strong" for more than a century after.[34] And so, writes Richard C. Beacham, "despite the systematic suppression of paganism … and massive social and political upheaval, at the end of antiquity we find similar genres, [with] the same mixture of sophistication and vulgarity," being performed in Rome as had been performed centuries earlier.[35] Through the fifth and into the sixth century, even with the series of "barbarian" invasions that were now conquering and reconquering Rome itself, the public games (with their attendant theatrical performances) continued, until the last recorded games were given by King Totila, in 549 CE, "to celebrate his brief success in restoring Ostragothic power."[36]

The situation in the provinces of the west was far more dire than in Rome, but here again, Christianity does not deserve the full blame. Even before the reign of Constantine I (r. 306–337 CE), these provinces had become unstable and provincial citizens could no longer "finance the entertainments or … provide for maintaining their venues"; support was then "further eroded by the disapproval of the Church." By the start of the fifth century, provincial games "were infrequent and restricted to a few towns" as the empire fragmented.[37] The medievalist Chris Wickham supports the dominant view among historians that "the invasions and occupations of the western provinces" by the *barbari* "must be at the heart of our explanations of the period." The undoubted "religious and cultural continuities" in the collapsing empire "cannot mask the importance of the breakdown of state structures" as the provinces went their own ways under alien pressure and conquest. The organizational structures and material means that had supported theatre for a thousand years were failing – and what remained of organized theatre in the western provinces could not survive that failure.[38]

The Eastern Roman Empire fared somewhat better through the fifth and sixth centuries, not having suffered the repeated conquest of its capital, Constantinople. But by 650 CE (roughly the date at which many historians begin to refer to the empire as "Byzantine"), it had already lost control of some of its own provinces.[39] The literature of ancient Greek theatre, however, was not lost. Carol Symes suggests that "every minimally educated person in Byzantium" would have encountered in his schooling the four "Triads": selected plays of the three great tragedians and Aristophanes.[40] But it is not clear that these or any other plays were actually mounted after Justinian I (r. 527–565) ordered the closing of the theatres.[41] Although "we have no evidence that they were not" being performed, Symes notes that "overtly mimetic (realistic) dramatic representations were unacceptable in the Orthodox Church." Virtually all that remained of theatrical performance were "highly competitive rhetorical displays" and "religious homilies" that featured "the direct speech of holy characters."[42] And yet, Andrew Walker White comments, "perhaps because of Constantinople's role in preserving the dramatic literature of Antiquity, generations of Western scholars have maintained (despite a lack of evidence) that the Orthodox Church developed a taste for sacred plays. Western assumptions about the universality of our modern theatrical impulses have led to the creation of what Walter Puchner calls a 'ghost chapter' on Byzantine sacred drama."[43]

The second identifiable world theatre region took shape in South Asia – an area that includes present-day Pakistan, India, and Bangladesh – with the spread of Sanskrit theatre. It is, unfortunately, impossible to trace the early history of this theatre region in any detail, owing to extremely limited information. Aparna Dharwadker observes, "No work of 'theatre history' in Sanskrit places authors and performances in time or retrieves the historical specificity of an actual theatre event in relation to its vital constituents: author, work, date, performance space, performer, and audience";[44] nor do we have substantial information about any theatre forms that might have been performed alongside Sanskrit theatre. Nonetheless, at least a few comments can be made about the first thousand or so years of a theatre region that, in contrast to the ancient Mediterranean, continues to exist to the present day.

After the back and forth of indigenous and nonindigenous phases in the post-Mauryan centuries, a third phase (as noted earlier) saw "the dispersal of foreign rule and the return of traditional values" culminating "in the accession of the Guptas around 320 CE."[45] The empire of the Guptas grew, within a hundred years, to encompass (through direct rule or tributary states) most of South Asia, inaugurating one of the most glorious periods of Indian history.

If, as I have suggested, Sanskrit theatre itself emerged in the second century CE, the rise of the Guptas can only have redounded to the form's benefit, for it is evident that the Gupta Empire treasured Sanskrit theatre. As will be recalled, Kalidasa is said by many historians to have been associated with the royal court of Chandragupta II, and although little can be said with certainty about the playwright Visakhadatta, some scholars believe he was a "high courtier" in that same court.[46] It is also likely that just as the theatre of a single Greek city was transmitted throughout the Mediterranean basin by the Hellenistic and Roman Empires, so the Gupta Empire transmitted Sanskrit theatre throughout South Asia. The strongest evidence for this is the collection of Bhasa's plays discovered in Trivandrum, on the southwestern Malabar coast,[47] an area far beyond direct Gupta control. But by the late fifth century, the Gupta Empire came under military pressure from invading Huns.[48] The immediate impact of this assault was much like that suffered by the Western Roman Empire, with the empire collapsing by the mid sixth century.[49] What followed were centuries of renewed political fragmentation. The Huns themselves would eventually be repulsed, but the Gupta Empire was by then a thing of the past.

The historian Brajadulal Chattopadhyaya reports that after the sixth century, "the formation of local states and the transformation of some of them into major, regional states structures became much more historically significant" throughout South Asia.[50] These numerous states, each with its own royal court, were based on "a new agrarian structure [that] created a leisurely class of landed magnates."[51] The courts and the magnates that supported them apparently continued to embrace Sanskrit theatre as a way of maintaining their cultural credentials. The form had sufficient status that at least one king is certain to have been a playwright: The seventh-century King Harsha, to whom three plays are ascribed, was the subject of an account by an international traveler who explicitly noted the king's authorship of one of these plays.[52] In the early eighth century, meanwhile, the playwright Bhavabhuti is reported to have served in the court of a northern Indian king.[53]

The survival of Sanskrit theatre through the post-Gupta centuries stands in contrast to the collapse of organized theatre after the fall of the Western Roman Empire; it would make possible the continuity of the South Asian theatre region even after the decline of Sanskrit theatre itself around the tenth century. One critical factor in the form's long survival was likely that the Huns had indeed been repulsed. Despite centuries of post-Gupta fragmentation, numerous royal courts of Indian descent controlled the still-wealthy land and carried on the theatrical tradition spread during the Gupta years. All this contrasts with the more complete socioeconomic breakdown of the Western Roman Empire and its settlement by alien peoples who, however much they might have sought Roman wealth, had little investment in its theatrical traditions. Another contributing factor to the survival of Sanskrit theatre was undoubtedly the greater religious continuity in South Asia. Hinduism survived the onslaught of the Huns, albeit not without change, whereas the paganism of the Roman Empire succumbed completely to Christianity, which had scarce tolerance for dramatic theatre and the festivals at which it was performed.

The upshot of all this is that the niche in which Sanskrit theatre flourished was kept open by the native Hindu kingdoms that succeeded the Guptas, whereas the niche for Roman theatre was squeezed shut. What had once been the ancient Mediterranean theatre region would be "dismembered," writes the historian Richard Smith, as its provinces and districts "broke off and drifted apart."[54] Before long it would be split between a pair of mutually antagonistic societies: one Christian, the other Islamic, both of which at least sometimes professed an opposition to dramatic theatre. Eventually the ancient Mediterranean theatrical tradition would gain renewed attention and play a vital role in the development of European theatre, but that would occur roughly a thousand years after the ancient tradition's demise. The South Asian region, however, would maintain at least a modicum of continuity, for even after the decline of Sanskrit theatre, successor theatre forms would continue to draw upon its texts and performance practices for inspiration.

As we conclude Part II of this book, I want to emphasize the importance of *context* in making sense of world theatre history.[55] All theatrical events are created in specific contexts: Even the sophisticated pretend play of the half-naked children in the short story by Jorge Luis Borges was shaped (as we have seen) by the Islamic context in which they lived. When we bring in an audience that imaginatively shares in the make-believe of pretend play, the resulting theatrical event inescapably becomes a social event, filled with multiple kinds of communication between the actors and their audience that depend on shared contextual understandings. For that reason, suggests Willmar Sauter, the context of a theatrical event "is not something that exists outside or apart from the event itself; it is fully present in the Theatrical Event."[56]

"Context," however, is such a broad term that it is useful to distinguish between three different kinds of context: societal, theatrical, and formal. *Societal* context pertains to the relationship between a theatrical event (or, more broadly, a theatre form) and the structures that give its host society an enduring historical shape, including its language(s), religion(s), oral and/or literary traditions, demography, economy, and political organization. We have seen how these structures were embedded in the invention of literary theatres in ancient Greece and India, as well as in the subsequent establishment of expansive theatre regions. In Athens, the Greek language (along with the literary heritage that had begun with Homer) was shared by all citizens, making possible the public discourse of tragedy and Old Comedy, both of which were presented during festivals that were at once political and religious celebrations funded by the economic might of the democratic city. Old Comedy could not survive the fall of Athens, but theatre artists of the subsequent Hellenistic and Roman Empires spread tragedy and New Comedy throughout the Mediterranean even as they adapted them to new political and economic circumstances and (in the case of Rome) a new language as well. The social structures that supported the ancient Mediterranean theatre region failed only with the decline of Roman political and economic organization and the collapse of Greco-Roman polytheism.

In India, meanwhile, the very different societal context led to the emergence of a theatre form that took advantage of its own long-standing literary tradition but that employed the many vernacular languages of northern India alongside the sacred language of Sanskrit. As a form apparently based in wealthy royal courts (first perhaps of the Sakas in Ujjain, then certainly in the court of the imperial Guptas), the concerns of Sanskrit theatre were of a more intimate nature than those of tragedy and Old Comedy, even as its performance was predicated on Hindu belief and permeated with Hindu ritual. The expansion of the Gupta Empire spread Sanskrit theatre throughout South Asia, but even that empire's fall did not bring an end to the South Asian theatre region because ensuing native courts maintained Hindu traditions and used Sanskrit theatre to connect themselves to the remembered glory of the Guptas.

The second kind of context is *theatrical*: It pertains to the relationship between a theatrical event (or theatre form as a whole) and other kinds of theatre and performance known to its host society. In Athens, as we have seen, the most relevant kinds of performance that preexisted tragedy were dithyrambic song and dance, satyr-like mimetic plays, and the public recitation of Homeric epics. Tragedians readily took advantage of each, combining choral singing and dancing with the mimesis of actors in the enactment of narratives often drawn from *The Iliad* and *The Odyssey*. In India, meanwhile, there were the drama-like monologues and dialogues of the *Rig Veda*, the "pantomimic action" used for relating the narratives of the great epics, and various forms of dance, some of which might have enacted narratives. The theatrical context of a given event or form, I should add, includes not only preexisting kinds of theatre and performance but also ones that are concurrent with the event or form within the complex of theatre forms that make up each world region of theatre. Not enough is known about early South Asian theatre to comment on how Sanskrit theatre might have interacted with contemporaneous theatre forms, but the interactions of various forms in Roman times suggests the facility with which theatrical events or entire forms will readily adapt any textual or performance traits that might prove useful to them. These traits can themselves become structures of the theatrical context to which multiple forms can have access.

The third kind of context is *formal*: It pertains to the relationship between a given theatrical event and other events of the same theatre form. Theatre forms themselves can be understood as structures that, despite inevitable changes, maintain important continuities across time and space. The support provided by a theatre form is vital to the success of its individual events. It makes available to them a living tradition that includes dramatic texts that can be used as models, adapted, or fully appropriated; performance venues that can be modified, replicated, or directly inhabited; and a well-developed set of performance traits that can be varied to fit the interests and the abilities of the performers. Theatre forms also offer their individual events what amounts to a built-in audience (or at least *potential* audience) already trained to understand the form and inclined to attend its performances. To create theatre beyond the supporting structure of a theatre form is an inherently risky enterprise, so it comes as no surprise that once a theatre form is fully established it will develop a self-sustaining momentum. The breakup of the Western Roman Empire, in association with the collapse of its polytheism, spelt the end for the theatre forms of the ancient Mediterranean. Sanskrit theatre, by contrast, was able to survive the breakup of the Gupta Empire thanks to the cultural continuity provided by its Hindu successor states.

PART III

The Eurasian Convergence (starting c. 900 CE)

In the tenth century CE, something remarkable happened across Eurasia, both in general history and theatre history. After hundreds of years in which its various parts had largely gone their separate ways under the pressure of military and/or demographic incursions by alien peoples (leading, as we have seen, to the decline of empires in the ancient Mediterranean and South Asia) there began a period of intersocietal convergence. The historian David Northrup goes so far as to see this as the central dividing line in human history, arguing for an extremely broad historical periodization whose first period extends from human beginnings until around 1000 CE; he calls this an age of "divergence" in which societies existed in "relative isolation from each other." Northrup knows perfectly well that long before 1000 CE there were trade links spanning much of Eurasia; he also recognizes cultural transmissions such as the spread of Hinduism and Buddhism from India, Christianity from the Levant, and Islam from Arabia. But in the extended period of "divergence" up until the tenth century, he argues, intersocietal contact was mostly limited and irregular. That situation began to change around 1000 CE, when increasing interconnections mark the start of the second period of human history, which Northrup calls "the Great Convergence"; from that time forward, he argues, the central theme of history becomes the interactions of diverse societies.[1]

Although other world historians might not agree that the tenth century was the *single* decisive moment in human history, its importance is widely recognized (albeit with the date sometimes rounded up, as by Northrup). Both Jerry H. Bentley and William H. McNeill identify 1000 CE as one of the most significant period-markers in human history.[2] Broadening the temporal scope, Björn Wittrock writes that the period from the tenth to thirteenth centuries "stands out as highly significant," for "even if global interactions were limited by the standards of the twentieth and twenty-first centuries, there was ... an amazing array of long-distance connections across a number of different fields of human activity."[3] And Janet

L. Abu-Lughod suggests, "By the eleventh and, even more, the twelfth century, many parts of the Old World began to be integrated into a system of exchange from which all apparently benefitted." Integration then continued to escalate, with "the apogee of this cycle [coming] between the end of the thirteenth and the first decades of the fourteenth century."[4]

This apogee of Eurasian convergence was the result, above all, of an empire whose base was in Mongolia. Starting in the early thirteenth century, writes the historian Michal Biran, "Chinggis Khan and his heirs built the largest contiguous empire the world has ever seen, an empire that at its height stretched from Korea to Hungary, from Burma and Iraq to Siberia." The conquest of this vast empire was often brutal, but the "Mongol legacy" was more than mere ruthlessness. By "integrat[ing] Eurasia on an unprecedented scale," Biran observes, the Mongols "also triggered a long-lasting cultural effervescence; a thriving artistic and scientific exchange; booming international trade; new and abiding forms of legitimacy, jurisprudence and imperial culture; and a host of religious, ethnic and political changes."[5]

It should be no surprise that *theatre* history was profoundly affected by the convergence that began in the tenth century and peaked at the height of the Mongol Empire in the early fourteenth century, even if the effect was indirect. According to Abu-Lughod, "Increased economic integration and cultural efflorescence ... were not unrelated. Technological and social innovations produced surpluses, which were, in turn, traded internationally to further intensify development. Parallel advances in navigation and statecraft facilitated contact among distant societies, which generated even greater surpluses. In all areas, prosperity – at least at the top – yielded high culture."[6]

But there is a paradoxical aspect to the convergence that demands consideration. Increasing integration did not lead to a loss of difference between the various parts of Eurasia, as one might expect; instead, it gave each part the wherewithal to grow in its own distinctive way. Wittrock explains that agricultural expansion promoted substantial population increases and "the emergence of new cities and new types of urban life"; new urbanized elites were "closely related to the emergence of new types of institutions," such as universities in Islamic lands and Europe, as well as neo-Confucian academies in China. The rise of these new elites "had important implications for the overall social order" and instigated the rise "of what might even be termed a civil society."[7] With these developments of the tenth through early fourteenth centuries, "the [individual] trajectories of different civilizations became more clearly discernible." Wittrock refers to this as a process of "cultural crystallization" in which "the major civilizations of agro-literate societies were distinctly formed and became clearly demarcated from each other"; over the course of these centuries, "cultural and institutional patterns emerged that were seminal for shaping the later characteristically modern societies."[8]

This process of cultural crystallization is particularly relevant to theatre history. Outside of the ancient Mediterranean and South Asian regions, new theatre forms undoubtedly had arisen intermittently over the previous 1,000 years, but as best one can currently say, they were largely of the same amorphous variety not only as earlier forms but also as those being performed elsewhere. We have already seen that Chinese theatre before the tenth century consisted mainly of variety acts interlarded with comic sketches.[9] In Islamdom, a list of performers who appeared before the Caliph, his court, and the public in 983 CE includes "comic actors," "mimes and impersonators," and "masked actors," with "similar entertainments" being offered in other Islamic cities for their New Year celebrations.[10] In Europe, itinerant performers (sometimes referred to as jongleurs) were sketch-comedy actors, musicians, dancers, storytellers, acrobats, clowns, jugglers, and more; no single performer would likely have had all these skills, but "the professional entertainer's livelihood depended on his willingness to be all things to all people."[11] There were also undoubtedly many local or semilocal forms of folk and ritual performance traditions whose existence at the time went unrecorded. With the Eurasian convergence that began in the tenth century, and the cultural crystallizations that followed from it, these sorts of performances would all continue. But as numerous societies experienced generative disruptions, culturally distinctive forms of theatre would emerge to fill newly created niches, leading to the establishment of identifiable and enduring theatre regions throughout Eurasia. For this reason, the tenth century marks a major inflection point in world theatre history.

CHAPTER 5

The Engine of Convergence

China Leads the Way

The economic vitality of China powered the convergence that started in the tenth century, stimulating commerce through most of Eurasia.[1] After half a century of contention following the fall of the Tang Dynasty, the newly established Song Dynasty (960–1126 CE) not only restored order but brought on what the historian Philip Curtain calls a "phase of economic growth that was unprecedented in earlier Chinese history, perhaps in world history up to this time. It depended on a combination of commercialization, urbanization, and industrialization that has led some authorities to compare [it] with the development of early modern Europe six centuries later."[2] With its substantial population increasingly drawn together through the construction of roads and canals, Song Dynasty China established a vigorous internal market for all manner of goods; beyond that, it also conducted an interregional overland and sea-based trade. The historian Valerie Hansen notes: "The Chinese had more extensive trade ties to foreign countries than any other people in the world in 1000"; Chinese manufacturers and consumers, especially those who lived in the major trading cities, would reasonably have considered themselves to "live in a globalized world."[3]

Agricultural expansion was at the root of China's dynamism. As early as the eighth century, rice production in the relatively underdeveloped Yangtze basin (as well as in more southerly China) had begun to increase. Around the start of the eleventh century, a fast-growing strain of rice imported from Champa (in what is now Vietnam) was systematically distributed by the Chinese government; this new strain allowed for two or more harvests per year while also doubling the amount of land under cultivation.[4] Chinese agriculturalists were at the same time developing new hydraulic technologies for irrigating their rice paddies.[5] A changing climate might also be implicated in China's agricultural expansion, for the mid tenth century saw the start of the Medieval Climate Anomaly, during which temperatures rose sharply in much of the northern hemisphere. One needs to be careful about overgeneralizing the impact of climate change because ongoing research points to distinct regional differences. But this tenth-century warming apparently was evident in most of China, as well as in Southeast Asia, South Asia, and northern Europe.[6]

According to the historian Jacques Gernet, the "agricultural upsurge in China" was "the foundation of its economic expansion" because it "made a large fraction of the population available for other tasks than the production of food." Among those tasks were mining and iron production, which "increased rapidly in the eleventh century," and the production of porcelain, which "experienced an unprecedented expansion" and achieved technical "perfection" by the twelfth century; the mass production of silk was also of great importance.[7] To this already impressive list one can add world-leading advances in "paper making, printing, gunpowder, and the first mechanical processing of textiles."[8] Internal Chinese trade in all these goods was abetted by an expansion of coinage as well as the world's first paper currency, used throughout the empire by the late twelfth century.[9] China, in brief, was "radically change[d] in comparison with earlier ages." It was not simply a change of scale, writes Gernet, but also "a change of character. Political habits, society, the relations between the classes, the armies, the relations between town and country, and economic patterns [became] quite different from what they had been."[10]

The rapidly growing population and increasing commercial opportunities spurred what the historian Peter Burke calls "an urban revolution."[11] China had long had substantial cities, but now their much-increased populations were changed in character as well. What had been "largely centers of political administration" became centers of production and "great emporiums of trade."[12] Along with a wealthy and educated elite, the cities were becoming populated by substantial middling classes of shopkeepers, craftsmen, casual laborers, clerks, servants, and shop assistants.[13] These middling classes made possible new niches for theatre in a way that we will often see repeated. The immediate result was that Chinese cities "became permanent centers of entertainment [with] amusement districts" where pleasure – theatrical and otherwise – could easily be purchased for a coin or two.[14]

A New Theatre Region Takes Shape

The efflorescence of Chinese theatre began in this milieu of generative disruption, with the *zaju* ("miscellany/variety plays") of the Song Dynasty being its earliest known instance. Song *zaju* performances usually centered on comic sketches, but they also included song-and-dance performances, puppet acts, and acrobatics.[15] Closely related to the Song *zaju* was a form known as *yuanben* (the meaning of which is uncertain). By and large, these forms do not seem terribly different from the sorts of theatre already mentioned as having existed in pre-Song China, Islamdom (in the tenth century), and early Europe. Notable, however, is evidence that these forms' comic sketches pioneered the use of role categories, which would become characteristic of numerous Chinese theatre forms for hundreds of years to come.[16] It also seems that the sketches of both forms were sometimes composed by amateur "writing societies" (*shuhui*), preparing the way for fully literary theatre forms.[17] The purpose-built theatres in which *zaju* and *yuanben* were most frequently mounted were located in dedicated amusement districts of the bustling cities and were fully commercial enterprises, even while shows were also offered at the imperial palace.[18] It is with these forms, William Dolby writes, "that we can first be sure of the existence of a thriving, enduring theater as part of a booming entertainment world" in China.[19]

But in the early twelfth century, China was split asunder when its northern half was conquered by nomadic peoples from Central Asia who established the Jin Dynasty; the Song dynasts fled southward, and their reduced empire is now known as the Southern Song. Neither of these dynasties would last terribly long. The Mongols began chipping away at the Jin within a century of that dynasty's founding, eventually establishing the Yuan Dynasty in 1234; in 1279, the Mongols conquered the Southern Song as well. But by the time the Southern Song fell, China's north and south had each created its own fully literary and commercial form of theatre.

The first of the new forms, *nanxi* ("southern plays"), was originally known as Wenzhou *zaju*, after its city of origin. This name suggests that the form was in some way related to Song *zaju*; Mei Sun argues that it grew out of a folk theatre form that adapted certain traits of the established variety form.[20] *Nanxi* seems to have emerged just before the split of China, but it became especially popular toward the end of the twelfth century, after the Southern Song Dynasty had established its capital in Hangzhou.[21] Already a substantial city, Hangzhou quickly grew into what the historian Morris Rossabi calls "the greatest capital city in the world." With a population that might have reached as high as two million people, its "bountiful agriculture and … seaborne trade fostered prosperity for the elite and the merchants." After paying a visit, Marco Polo pronounced Hangzhou a place "where so many pleasures may be found that one fancies himself to be in Paradise."²² It was there that *nanxi* established itself.

Relatively little is known about *nanxi*. Sun explains that owing to "its coarse language, rough prosody, and unsophisticated writing style, it was disdained for a long time and was not written down in any official historiography or other formal records."²³ It is intriguing, though, that the heroes of the two twelfth-century plays that popularized the form were scholars "who proved unfaithful to their virtuous wives and were in the end destroyed, in the one case by thunder and lightning, and in the other by ghostly retribution." The earliest full text to survive, *Top Graduate Zhang Xie* (author unknown), comes from the mid or late thirteenth century; it too has a scholar as its hero, though it is "more in a comic style" than its melodramatic predecessors.²⁴ This recurrence of scholar-heroes might seem strange outside of a Chinese context. It is, however, explained by China's reliance on the Confucian exam system to populate its political offices: Especially after the Song Dynasty's neo-Confucian reforms, having a successful scholar in one's family meant social advancement and financial security.²⁵

The second new theatre form, known as Yuan *zaju*, emerged shortly after the Mongols took over northern China from the Jin Dynasty in 1234. Again, the form's establishment is associated with a new capital city – in this case, Dadu (now Beijing), which the Mongols began constructing in 1267 on the site of the former Jin capital. The extraordinary growth of Dadu rendered it, by 1300, the second most populous city in the world, behind only Hangzhou.²⁶ As was the case with *nanxi*, the urban milieu proved critical to the northern form. Colin Mackerras writes that although the plays of Yuan *zaju* "later found their way into the Chinese literary canon … they were definitely popular entertainments in their own day. The audiences were peasants, artisans, and traders on the one hand, the literati and educated on the other."²⁷ William Dolby points out that after the Mongol conquest of the north, the plays of Yuan *zaju* apparently "provided not only [a] more palatable diversion for the lusty, rough conquerors than the traditional formal court entertainment, but also more immediate and enjoyable instruction in Chinese culture than did formal education and written materials." The form, he suggests, "was welcomed high and low because it brought pleasure, edification, and colour to life."²⁸

Yuan *zaju* was, by all accounts, a more polished theatre form than *nanxi*, both in its writing and its music. Playwrights such as Guan Hanqing (c. 1220–c. 1300), often credited as the father of Yuan *zaju*, used a simple but flexible four-act structure, sometimes adding one or two short "wedge acts" before or between the acts. They were capable "of treating any topic, old or new, in great depth," including "love, war, religious conversion, devotion to learning, political scheming, diplomatic intrigue, criminal investigation, brigand adventures, [and] tales of the supernatural." The result, suggests Dolby, was a body of work with plots "at least as tightly and superbly constructed as those of any large body of drama anywhere in the world."[29] The polish of the plays was enhanced by their use of music. In each act there would be but a single singing role, with all the songs therein being in a single musical mode and containing a single dominant rhyme; the tunes themselves were generally drawn from a body of well-known songs, of which 335 are listed in one Yuan source.[30]

Three shared characteristics of *nanxi* and Yuan *zaju* warrant further consideration. First is the fact that both were literary theatre forms. This turn to the literary is usually discussed with regard only to Yuan *zaju*. Thus, Richard F. S. Yang notes that one explanation advanced in Chinese theatre historiography is that the literary turn was "a direct result of the examinations which required skill in composing songs"; a contradictory explanation is that "what gave stimulus to the drama was not the examination system but rather the suspension of it during the early years" of the Yuan Dynasty, which drove writers to the theatre; a third explanation holds that "drama was stimulated by three factors: unrestricted freedom of thought [under the Mongols], frustration of the people under foreign rule, and encouragement from the Yüan court."[31] Yang himself argues that when Chinese writers "found themselves ruled by a culturally inferior people, barred from government service, [and] shorn of respect and prestige …, the humiliation and frustration of the writers were almost more than they could bear. Then the song and drama were introduced, and writers seized upon them as a new medium to express their thought and feelings."[32] The obvious problem with all these explanations is that they fail to account for the slightly earlier emergence of *nanxi* in the portion of China that had not yet been conquered by the Mongols and where the Southern Song Dynasty maintained the exam system and still honored writers.

A more comprehensive explanation for the emergence of China's first literary theatre forms is therefore desirable. As I noted in Chapter 4, China had long had the necessary literate class to produce such theatre – and a niche for commercial theatre had already opened in the larger cities and was being filled by Song *zaju* and *yuanben*. But it apparently took the extraordinary growth of Hangzhou and Dadu to create the expansive urban niches that *nanxi* and Yuan *zaju* would come to dominate. Writing specifically of Yuan *zaju* (but implicitly of *nanxi* as well), Wilt T. Idema suggests that "the constant demand of the burgeoning commercial theatre for new plays contributed to the rise of the playwright."[33] Whether or not they were chafing under Mongol domination, writers sought to reap the benefits of the demand for new plays and so turned to the sort of "popular" work that had previously been "considered by the *literati* as unworthy of the name of literature."[34] As with ancient Greece and India, a critical spur to the emergence of the Chinese literary theatre forms was a niche (or rather, a pair of similar niches in China's north and south) that demanded a constant flow of new plays.

No less relevant than Chinese literacy and the expanding niche for urban commercial theatre, however, is the third of the societal conditions that seem necessary for literary theatre: a body of well-known narratives from which playwrights could creatively draw. As we have seen, China had long been without such narratives, but that began to change during the Tang Dynasty (618–907 CE). The new narratives of what is called *chuanqi* literature were likely to have been stimulated by the arrival from India of Buddhist popular sermons (often referred to as "transformation texts") that "narrated stories through a combination of spoken and sung elements."[35] The ensuing *chuanqi* narratives were popular fiction rather than epics (as in Greece and India), but "the better and longer stories," suggests Tao-Ching Hsü, "were soon recited in the same way as [the] religious stories," with storytelling as "a completely secularized form of entertainment."[36] The combination of literary and oral transmission widely disseminated and popularized these narratives.

Little can be said about the sources of *nanxi* plays, most of which apparently were centered on "love, marriage or other domestic situations." But Sun suggests that "many of these types of stories appear in popular and folk arts," and so the plays' plots might have been borrowed from well-known ballads and/or tales.[37] Yuan *zaju*, however, clearly drew on the now-popularized written narratives, albeit treating their sources "with great freedom and fantasy."[38] These narratives included early versions of *Romance of the Three Kingdoms* and *Water Margin*; another popular source was a well-known cycle of stories revolving around the eleventh-century judge Bao Zheng.[39] With narratives such as these, Hsü suggests, "audiences do not come to the theatre to learn the story …. What interests them is not the plot, but the treatment of the plot; not how the events turn out, but how they are presented; not the subsequent fate of the characters, but the present virtuosity of the actors."[40] This parallels the way that the great epics were used in

Greek and Indian theatre. Along with the commercial competition that created an incessant demand for new plays, the use of these well-known but reimagined narratives spurred the development and popularity of *nanxi* and Yuan *zaju*.

The second characteristic shared by *nanxi* and Yuan *zaju* is their use of role categories (known in Chinese as *hangdang*). Tian Mansha explains that "the concept of *hangdang* … has two connotations: firstly, it refers to a highly complex system of grouping or categorizing of dramatic characters, each group or category being defined by a set of shared traits and features. Secondly, it means the performing conventions that have been developed to (visually, acoustically, corporeally, etc.) express and emphasize these defining traits and features."[41] *Hangdang* serves multiple functions in Chinese theatre forms, facilitating actor-training while also imbuing audiences with "a feeling of familiarity and connoisseurship, in that they would to a considerable degree come to know what to look for and expect of the actor[s]."[42] The role categories, however, were not straightjackets, for once an actor gained mastery of a category's conventions, he or she could shape them to individualize the character and the performance thereof.[43]

Compared to later Chinese theatre forms, the role categories of *nanxi* and Yuan *zaju* were rather simple, being "mainly based on the character's sex, age and the importance the role takes in the play";[44] they were also relatively similar, as can be seen in Figure 5.1. Some of the similarities probably exist because the forms emerged in a theatrical context dominated by the Song *zaju*, whose "paired comic roles of *fujing* and *fumo*" were "transmuted into the *jing* and *mo* of *nanxi*" while also being taken up by Yuan *zaju*.[45] The differences in the forms' role categories, however, are intriguing, especially those of the male roles. *Nanxi*'s leading men were typically serious young scholars (thereby relegating its *mo* category to a variety of secondary roles), whereas the leading men in Yuan *zaju* could range "from young to old, from a peddler to a minister," and might even be comic.[46] This variety reflects the greater range of subject matter in Yuan *zaju*, just as the more careful elaboration of the form's role categories suggests a more fully developed performance tradition. One last point worth noting is that although it seems that both men and women might perform female roles in *nanxi*,[47] it is clear that Yuan *zaju* paid surprisingly little regard to the sex of the performers of male roles as well. "If anything," writes Dolby, "it was the actresses who predominated in Yuan *zaju*," though part of that appeal could be found in oft-salacious accounts of their love affairs.[48] Because the theatrical roles were molded by the conventions of

	Male roles	Female roles	Villain/comic roles
Nanxi	**Sheng:** Lead male (typically noncomic young scholar) **Wai:** Secondary males (typically older) **Mo:** Secondary males (sometimes comic)	**Dan:** Lead female (typically noncomic and young) **Tai** (or **Hou**): **Secondary females**	**Jing & Chou** (overlapping comic categories, male or female, sometimes painted-face)
Yuan zaju	**Mo** **Shengmo:** Lead Mo (young or old, singing role) **Waimo:** "Outer" Mo (secondary male roles) **Xiomo:** "Young" Mo (secondary male roles)	**Dan** **Shengdan:** Lead Dan (typically young, singing role) **Waidan:** "Outer" Dan (secondary female roles) **Xiodan:** "Young" Dan (age-based secondary female roles) **Laodan:** "Old" Dan (age-based secondary female roles)	**Jing** (Villain and/or comic categories, male or female at any social level, sometimes painted-face)

Figure 5.1   Role categories of *nanxi* and Yuan *zaju*.

hangdang, the actual sex of the actors was relatively unimportant to the presentation of their dramatic characters.

The third shared characteristic of *nanxi* and Yuan *zaju* was their extensive use of song. Indeed, the term now used to encompass virtually all "traditional" Chinese theatre forms is *xiqu*, which literally means "theatre of song."[49] But the two early forms took very different approaches to song, despite both typically drawing on familiar melodies. In *nanxi*, many musical modes could be mixed together in a single act and all of the role categories were allowed to sing – and not only in solos but also in "duets, songs with three or more people singing separately and in chorus."[50] This all contrasts with Yuan *zaju*, where (as we have seen) only a single musical mode would be used in each act, and only a single character (either the lead male or female) could sing in that act. Moreover, *nanxi* also incorporated a "helping chorus" (probably situated offstage) to heighten "the atmosphere of scenes" and enhance "the artistic appeal of their plays" by compensating for the limited number of instrumentalists in the troupes.[51] Although *nanxi* presented its songs in a greater variety of ways, its "lack of [musical] organization and musical consistency" kept it from being "accorded high esteem by the orthodox literati," even while lending it "a charm of its own."[52]

These two theatre forms set Chinese theatre on the course it would maintain for centuries to come. Over that time, hundreds of theatre forms would emerge to adapt their plays, modify their role categories, and follow their lead in relying on songs to enact dramatic narratives. Together, they created a template that would serve as the basis for a distinctively East Asian theatre region.

CHAPTER 6

Along the Sea Route

Beginning around 1000 CE, commerce with China stimulated economies across most of Eurasia, with the belated exception only of far-off Europe. One land route and two sea routes had historically connected Eurasia's various portions. The land route (sometimes referred to as the Silk Roads system) ran from China through Central Asia to the Black Sea, across which merchandise could be sailed to Constantinople. The two sea routes ran from China's port cities to Southeast Asia and onward to India; after that, the sea routes split. One of these routes led through the Persian Gulf to Basra (from where merchandise would be hauled overland to Baghdad), while the other headed up the Red Sea until a short overland haul brought merchandise to Cairo, whence it could be sailed down the Nile for transshipment throughout the Mediterranean. Each route had its vicissitudes over the centuries, but the sea routes were highly active from near the start of the Song Dynasty. When the land route gained renewed prominence after the Mongol conquests in China, all three worked together. "The economic vitality" of the areas they connected, Janet L. Abu-Lughod suggests, "was the result, at least in part, of the [commercial] system in which they participated," which "made prosperity endemic."[1] This prosperity, and the cultural crystallizations it helped make possible, created new niches for theatre through most of Eurasia.

Southeast Asia

We will follow the second of the sea routes, beginning with Southeast Asia. The historian Victor Lieberman sets the scene: "Lying in areas without indigenous writing and open to the seduction of literate arts and world religions" from India and China, Southeast Asian societies were engaged in "a process of cultural borrowing and localization that was well underway by the mid-first millennium CE, but that intensified toward the close of the first and the start of the second millennium."[2] Of particular note for theatre history is the mid first millennium transmission of Hinduism and Buddhism into Southeast Asia, where they mixed with indigenous animistic religions to create unique local syntheses.[3] The epics and lore of these Indian religions would eventually become the source material for numerous Southeast Asian theatre forms.

By the tenth century, the same "agricultural revolution" that would stimulate growth in Song Dynasty China was already taking place in Southeast Asia thanks to the spread of the quick-ripening Champa rice.[4] Concurrently, the Strait of Malacca was fast becoming one of the world's preeminent seaways because it offered the most direct passage between China and India. The historian Anthony Reid observes that "the expansion of civilizational cores [in Southeast Asia] coincided largely with the prosperous Song dynasty" and the vast increase in trade that it stimulated. Each core area of Southeast Asia quickly "established a vernacular civilization that survived subsequent vicissitudes as a sense of collective identity."[5] The "cultural crystallization" to which Björn Wittrock referred was largely a process that, in Southeast Asia, began in the tenth century.

At this point, it will be useful to distinguish between the mainland and maritime regions of Southeast Asia, with the Malay peninsula conventionally being included in the maritime region (along with the islands) because it is largely surrounded by the sea and its language belongs to the same Austronesian family as those of the islands.[6] The major physical differences between mainland and maritime Southeast Asia are topographical (the mainland having limited ports but vast upcountry areas teeming with wildlife) and climatic (the mainland having somewhat cooler temperatures and a well-defined dry season); these differences allowed the mainland to host "denser and wealthier populations" than maritime Southeast Asia.[7] Meanwhile, the maritime lands' "position athwart the chief east-west trade routes, their extraordinary high ratio of coast to interior, and their fine spices and pepper rendered [them] more dependent on international commercial rhythms" than most mainland areas.[8] As those "commercial rhythms" picked up, so did theatrical innovation.

Maritime Southeast Asia is home to the entire *wayang* tradition of puppetry, which originated on the island of Java. There, "the two great Indian epics [had been] 'Javanized' into a poetic form of old Javanese" by the tenth century, and "the economy was commercialized and monetized in a trade boom of the tenth to thirteenth centuries."[9] Shadow puppets in Java are first hinted at in a royal charter dated 840 CE, but the clearest early mention comes from a court poet of King Airlangga (r. 1035–1049): "There are people who weep, are sad and aroused watching the puppets, though they know they are merely carved pieces of leather manipulated and made to speak. These people are like men who, thirsting for sensuous pleasures, live in a world of illusion; they do not realize the magic hallucinations they see are not real."[10]

It is unknown whether, or to what degree, the emergence of *wayang kulit purwa* – generally considered the oldest *wayang* theatre form – was an indigenous development.[11] Its plays were (and largely remain) based on the "Javanized" Indian epics; similarly, its puppets bear a resemblance to those of an Indian puppet form, although those Indian puppets date from later than the Javanese ones.[12] It seems likely that the Indian-originated source material was at some point grafted onto an existing Javanese tradition of village-based shadow puppetry,[13] helping to elevate it into a form that could also fill a niche for elite performance in the royal court. The fact that the technical terms used in the form are in Old Javanese rather than an Indian language lends support to this theory.[14]

The form name *wayang kulit purwa* roughly translates to "performance with shadow puppets of ancient material." In this *wayang*, a single puppet master (the *dalang*) manipulates and speaks for some forty to sixty characters per show, accompanied by a musical ensemble (known as a *gamelan*) in a performance that runs from sundown until dawn.[15] It is difficult to say how closely the contemporary form approximates that of a thousand years ago, but clearly the design of the puppets has been modified over the centuries. At some uncertain point *dalangs* began painting their leather puppets while also incising them with elaborate cutouts, allowing for more complexity in their shadows; they also introduced new animal figures and types of ogres.[16] Individual *dalangs* usually created their own texts, albeit without writing them out in advance of performance. Some of these texts proved popular enough to be "passed on to following generations within the oral tradition" but were always subject to modification by later *dalangs*.[17]

In the centuries following its emergence, *wayang kulit purwa* would exert a profound influence throughout maritime Southeast Asia, spawning other *wayang* forms that drew upon its traits in one way or another. Ghulam-Sarwar Yousof offers descriptions of more than fifty forms of *wayang* that have been (and often still are) performed in the region. Some use leather shadow puppets, others wooden rod puppets, and yet others live actors (in some cases masked, in others unmasked); an additional *wayang* form is little more than storytelling associated with pictures on a scroll. The source materials for these many forms include not only the "Javanized" Indian epics used in *wayang kulit purwa* but also stories from a cycle of Javanese heroic romances as well as (in specifically Islamic forms that would later emerge) legends of Amir Hamza, the Prophet Muhammad's uncle.[18] These fifty or more theatre forms are best understood as a large family of homologous forms, though the details of the family's history are only spottily known.

Javanese shadow theatre also crossed into the lands that are now Cambodia and Thailand, each of which has long hosted a pair of shadow-puppet forms. In both lands one of these forms uses small puppets operated by puppet masters working from behind (and beneath) the shadow screen; these are almost certainly descended from the Javanese *wayang kulit purwa*, although it is unclear how early this transference took place. Both lands also have a form that uses very large puppets, each of which portrays multiple characters. The operators of these large puppets are usually fully visible to the audience, with "puppeteer and puppet blend[ing] into one dancing image."[19] These large-puppet forms might have been transferred from either Java or India;[20] it is also possible they are indigenous to Cambodia and were introduced into Thailand in the mid fifteenth century, having been brought there following a Thai invasion.[21] For Cambodia, both the small and large puppets "are known to have existed" during the Khmer Empire (802–1432 CE), with the theatre using the large puppets apparently having emerged there before the one using small puppets.[22]

From even before the tenth century CE, the Khmer Empire also hosted *lakon kabach boran*. Details of this early form are scarce, especially because it seems to have significantly changed after the fall of the empire to the Thais in the fifteenth century, but apparently it was primarily dance, perhaps accompanied by a sung narration that offered a storyline.[23] This too seems to have originated in Java, having been introduced to the mainland in 802 CE, when Jayavarman II arrived from Java and founded the Khmer Empire.[24] According to Beth Osnes, "The Cambodians themselves say that 'it was in fact Java that provided the great inspiration for Cambodian dancing and drama, in spite of themes borrowed from other sources'" such as India.[25]

In addition to maritime Southeast Asia and India, China is the third major theatrical influence on mainland Southeast Asia, with its impact being most noticeable in what is now Vietnam. A dubious legend has it that the musical theatre form *hat cheo* (sometimes called *cheo*) was introduced from China at the start of the eleventh century,[26] but Trinh Nguyen writes that it "has its roots in village festivals in northern Vietnam along the Red River Delta." Its orally transmitted narratives are drawn from "Vietnamese legends, poetry, history and daily life" and "are basically satirical in intent, often commenting on the peasant classes, farmers, monks, rich people, intellectuals, students, monks and so on." Performances are given in the vernacular and combine "poetry, song, dance and pantomime" while making little use of "elaborate scenery, costume, makeup or gesture."[27] Another eleventh-century form, *muá rôi nuoc* (usually called Vietnamese water puppetry), was apparently related in some way to a similar form of southern Chinese puppetry.[28] For the Vietnamese form, the communal ponds of towns and villages were turned into puppet stages, with the puppets performing on the surface of the water while being controlled from a distance via underwater rods (see Figure 6.1). The plays of *muá rôi nuoc*, Nguyen writes, generally focus on "the daily life of rural people, with folklores [sic], Vietnamese legends and history that are passed down through many generations." But these plays were not just for the human audience that attended them, for they "were thought to keep the spirits entertained enough so that they would not cause mischief."[29]

The relationship to Chinese theatre is clearer with the Vietnamese *tuông*, which as it spread southward would become known as *hat bôi* (literally, "to sing and to gesture"). According to a plausible legend, the form was introduced to Vietnam in 1285, when (during an invasion from China) a troupe of Chinese performers was captured and the troupe leader ordered to train Vietnamese actors in exchange for his life.[30] Chinese theatre would continue to influence the Vietnamese version of the form; as late as the

Figure 6.1 *Muá rôi nuoc* (Vietnamese water puppetry): a scene from a contemporary production in Ho Chi Minh City. (Photo by Mahaux Photography via Getty Images)

nineteenth century, Chinese performers and scholars were invited to train the troupe that performed for the Vietnamese emperor.[31] Tran Van Khe points out, though, that however much the form has transferred from Chinese theatre, it has "been able to retain and develop its own originality, to adapt the text of the plays, the stage effects and the songs and elocution to the tastes of its public."[32]

The same can be said of virtually all the theatre forms of mainland Southeast Asia. Despite influences from Java, India, and China, each of its forms "develop[ed] its own originality" as traits transferred from one place or another were brought together and domesticated in original ways. What ultimately matters in theatrical syncretism is less the source of a theatre form's materials than what the form's artists can make of them in the context of their own society.

South Asia

The two sea routes from China made their next major landfall at one or another of India's port cities, most often those in Gujarat (in the northwest) or on the Malabar coast (in the southwest). These latter ports, especially Quilon (now Kollam) and Calicut (now Kozhikode), were particularly valuable for long-distance trade, being near the junction of the separate monsoon systems of the Arabian Sea and the Bay of Bengal; as early as the ninth century they were regularly visited by Arab ships from the west and Chinese junks from the east.[33] India was also linked into the land route that ran across Eurasia, via spurs from Afghanistan and western China. Janet L. Abu-Lughod therefore observes that India was very much "on the way to everywhere."[34] That was, in a sense, both its blessing and its curse, for its wealth and accessibility made it an irresistible target.

As we saw in Chapter 4, after the invading Huns brought down the Gupta Empire in the sixth century CE, India fell into an extended period of political turmoil. But the empire had "developed a pattern of statehood that could be adopted by later rulers, albeit on a smaller scale and in mutual contest" with each other.[35] As Victor Lieberman puts it, "The dissemination of North Indian Sanskrit norms drew strength from competition among kingdoms eager to partake of Gupta glory."[36] Thanks to that shared heritage, as well as to the continuity of Hindu observance in these kingdoms, Sanskrit theatre was long maintained in their courts. This situation began to collapse at the start of the tenth century, when Mahmud of Ghazni brought his cavalry down from the mountain passes of Afghanistan, looting cities and razing Hindu temples. Mahmud was little more than a raider, but over the ensuing 500 years he would be followed by a series of Muslim invaders who "shatter[ed] autonomous Hindu power" and established numerous Islamic sultanates.[37] Relations between Muslims and Hindus in these centuries are controversial because for every instance of outright oppression one can find another of toleration.[38] But clearly it was at about the time the Muslim invasions began that Sanskrit theatre seriously faltered. Farley P. Richmond notes that "it is generally believed that the tenth century marks [its end] as a creative force," though its terminal decline was a drawn-out process.[39]

Indū Shekhar recognizes the impact of the Muslim invasions as a possible explanation for the decline of Sanskrit theatre, noting that the Muslims were "said to have been deadly opposed to all dramatic performances."[40] Islamic disapproval of dramatic theatre is often overstated, but in all likelihood the havoc wreaked by these invaders was a significant factor in Sanskrit theatre's decline, if only because they conquered numerous Indian kingdoms that had previously supported the theatre form. Even the surviving Hindu dynasties were often short on cash and long on enemies, stressing the societal structures on which Sanskrit theatre relied. Shekhar also notes another contributing factor: "The development of [modern] Indian languages … is alleged to have shifted general interest away from Sanskrit." And not only was interest in Sanskrit apparently declining, but the vernacular languages were changing as well, with the old Prakrits giving way to more modern vernaculars. The multiple languages of Sanskrit theatre were in most places all becoming archaic.[41]

That said, however, Shekhar places a greater share of the blame for the decline of Sanskrit theatre on factors within the form itself, such as its "abject surrender to literary conventions and injunctions" and its lack of "situation[s] full of fun and gaiety, sparkling with wit and juicy humour." He also blames the apparent practice of composing plays for "recitation" instead of full dramatic staging.[42] It seems, though, that whatever might have been the (extremely) long-term detrimental effect of these factors, they likely had helped it to *succeed* in its niche through the post-Gupta centuries, lending it the sort of dignified gravitas that would be desirable in royal courts seeking to bask in reflected Gupta glory. As long as that courtly niche remained well supported, the pressure would have been for artists to maintain continuity in the form, with an ever-greater emphasis on the very traits that marked it as being for elite audiences. But in the radically altered environment beginning in the tenth century – with many Hindu monarchies being destroyed, threatened, or impoverished – the niche that supported this highly refined theatre would have slowly shut down.

Relatively little can be said about what Govardhan Panchal calls India's "second generation" of theatre forms, which emerged as Sanskrit theatre declined. For the area around Gujarat, Panchal mentions six forms that existed between the tenth and sixteenth centuries.[43] The few available details suggest that they maintained significant continuities with Sanskrit theatre: They were "music-dance-oriented," employed locally popular musical styles, and "had grown up in the sophisticated feudal atmosphere and were patronized [primarily] by the kings, courtiers, and the upper class citizenry."[44] Panchal is writing only about a single part of South Asia, but these details likely apply more broadly, for the subsequent generation of Indian theatre forms (beginning in the sixteenth century) would continue to maintain many traits originally found in Sanskrit theatre. Most notable are the ritual preliminaries to performance as well as the presence of two distinct positions in the troupes of numerous theatre forms: the *sutradhara* (a director-manager who runs the troupe, performs the rituals, and appears as a meta-dramatic figure in the prologue) and the *vidusaka* (a jester or fool whose performance might be related only tangentially to the narrative of the show).[45] Such continuities would need to have been transmitted through the second-generation forms to the succeeding generation.

Kutiyattam is the only second-generation theatre form for which there is substantial information. It apparently emerged early in the tenth century on the Malabar coast (in what is now Kerala state). The local rulers, the Cheras, often contested with greater powers in southern India, but their small kingdom remained secure for hundreds of years, "being naturally rich and obtaining an adequate income from trade with west Asia."[46] The kingdom's native wealth was largely in the hands of the Hindu elite, and *kutiyattam*'s niche was in the temples they supported. Its performance was considered "a sacred event" that was traditionally arranged "at the request of temple authorities or a local ruler" and performed only for Brahmins and the royal family.[47]

As we have seen, Sanskrit theatre had certainly spread this far south in the preceding centuries, as evidenced by the trove of plays by Bhasa discovered in Trivandrum.[48] And whereas Sanskrit (along with the ancient Prakrit languages) was elsewhere in decline, Kerala "seems to have assimilated Sanskrit so totally that [the] literature of many disciplines was [still] written in that language."[49] This is likely why the ancient Sanskrit plays could find continued life in the Chera kingdom. They became the basis for *kutiyattam*, with comic stylings of the *vidusaka* spoken in the vernacular to introduce "the dominant note of keeping touch with contemporaneity."

Figure 6.2 *Kutiyattam*: Guru Ammanur Madhava Chakkyar performs the role of the demon Ravana in a contemporary production in Irinjalakuda. (Photo by Herve BRUHAT/Gamma-Rapho via Getty Images)

New plays for the form were also written, which (as Kapila Vatsyayan observes) "incorporated many elements of the Sanskrit theatre and yet imbued them with a local colour and a distinctive style which made them typically regional in character" (see Figure 6.2).[50]

Given the earlier-mentioned evidence from Gujarat, this sort of syncretism was apparently common for second-generation South Asian theatre. *Kutiyattam* drew "faithfully" from the older form, while having "unmistaken [sic] links with and elements from [local] traditions which have little or nothing to do with the Sanskrit theatre."[51] Whatever the texts involved in *kutiyattam*, however, Richmond reports that the actual "performance departs radically" from them.[52] A single performance can now take between five to twenty nights, with extensive preliminary activities performed each night and lengthy elaborations extemporized upon the text itself. As a result, a full performance generally presents only a single act of the play, for "to produce a whole play would probably require the better part of several months!"[53]

Richmond calls *kutiyattam* "the oldest surviving art form of the ancient world,"[54] and the form's continuance to the present day seems almost miraculous. One might well wonder how this survival has been possible, even as all the other forms of South Asia's second generation of theatre fell into desuetude. The Malabar coast's escape from Muslim conquest is the most obvious factor, but probably not the only one. Also relevant is the commercial strength of the coast, for as long as the temples' underlying source of wealth was undisturbed, the form itself could remain well supported. When third-generation theatre forms started to emerge in sixteenth-century Kerala, as we will see, they filled other niches and largely left *kutiyattam*'s temple-based niche undisturbed. But perhaps the most unexpected factor in the form's survival has been what Vatsyayan calls its "innovative flexibility," which has allowed "scope for renewal, re-interpretation and improvisation." Although difficult to trace in detail, the form's flexibility allowed it to continue functioning in its niche without its performances becoming "museum pieces."[55] Theatrical change is, paradoxically, a necessary component in theatrical continuity, for theatre forms cannot survive if they lose the support of their contemporary audiences and patrons.

North Africa

The last major stop on the southern sea route from China was Cairo, one of the leading cities of Islamdom. Even more than South Asia, perhaps, Islamic lands could claim to be "on the way to everywhere." The historian Richard Smith observes that Islamdom "was the consummate land–sea passageway, custom-made for middlemen. The Silk Roads system [i.e., the land route] provided a direct link from Persia to China, India was a monsoon's sail [away], Europe was just across the Mediterranean, the Black Sea provided access to the Russian river system, and West Africa was connected by camel caravan." Moreover, Islamdom "had an urban-based economy reaching back four millennia with active and savvy commercial classes, productive handicraft industries based on regional specialization, good ports, an experienced seagoing population, and a wide network of trade contacts already in place."⁵⁶ Arab merchants, meanwhile, were "pioneers in commercial institutions," creating the "legal instruments required for mercantile credit."⁵⁷ Europe in particular would come to rely heavily on Cairo (through the medium of coastal Alexandria) for access to goods from points east until the end of the fifteenth century, when Portuguese sailors would pioneer a sea route around Africa into the Indian Ocean.

Until then, Cairo was essential. By the eleventh century, as the capital of the Fatimid Dynasty, Cairo was already established as a "nexus of trade," serving as both an entrepôt and a center of production.⁵⁸ Egypt had long been a leading producer of grain; in the tenth century it also began producing sugar, cotton, rice, and citrus fruits, all introduced from India. Together, they "worked a small agricultural revolution" around the Eastern Mediterranean.⁵⁹ Cairo's role in international commerce climaxed in the early fourteenth century, under the Mamluk Dynasty. With the peace that followed the collapse of the last European Crusader States (in 1291) and the defeat of the invading Mongols (in 1303), a surge in population and the ever-expanding sea trade in South Asian and Southeast Asian spices brought prosperity to its peak.⁶⁰ It was in the Cairo of these centuries – the eleventh through the first half of the fourteenth – that a remarkable form of shadow theatre emerged: *khayāl al-zill* (literally, "shadows of fantasy/imagination").

This shadow theatre was likely not the first form of dramatic theatre in the Islamdom. Shmuel Moreh vigorously argues that even before the emergence of the shadow theatre, there was a form that was "performed by actors," sometimes dressed in character and using theatrical props.⁶¹ It was known originally as *hakāya*; the historical Averroës might well have encountered it in Islamic Spain. *Hakāya* seems to have been semi-literary, for one of its authors says of his own work, "This is the literature I have acquired from other writers, which I adorn myself," but the work itself was little more than sketch comedy.⁶²

It was the shadow theatre, however, that was apparently the leading form of theatre in Cairo.⁶³ Three plays written for *khayāl al-zill* are still extant – for the shadow theatre was, at least for a time, a literary form of theatre. The earliest mention of *khayāl al-zill* comes in the eleventh century,⁶⁴ but it seems the high point of the form arrived two centuries later, in the plays of the oculist and poet Muhammad Ibn Dāniyāl (1248–1311). Ibn Dāniyāl's poems were often satires of the daily life around him in Cairo; his plays were similarly satirical and incorporated numerous passages of his poetry.⁶⁵ Marvin Carlson writes that these plays "are the first elaborate, sophisticated, and literary dramatic works to be produced in the Islamic world and appear at a time when they are arguably the most ambitious theatrical works produced anywhere in the world."⁶⁶ In a prefatory note to one of his plays, Ibn Dāniyāl commented that he composed his works in response to a friend's complaint that "people have grown tired of [earlier] shadow plays and have been put off by their repetitive character."⁶⁷

Those earlier plays had enacted traditional topics that, according to M. M. Badawi,

> ranged from the heroic to the common and homely: armies fighting, land and sea battles, knights and infantry heavily armed with swords, spears and arrows, seamen on the decks of ships, soldiers routed and castles destroyed. The characters also include[d] supernatural beings of fearful appearance. At the other extreme we have fishermen catching fish with nets, fowlers spreading their [snares] for unsuspecting birds, benighted camels racing through the desert, [and] ships tossed by the waves or wrecked by sea monsters.⁶⁸

Given these subjects, it seems likely that the plays drew on popular tales such as can now be found in *The One Thousand and One Nights* (or, as sometimes called, *The Arabian Nights*), although it is unclear if the form could yet be called literary.

Ibn Dāniyāl's innovation was to introduce plays that were (as he claimed) "rather bawdy ... but in a high literary style nevertheless!"⁶⁹ The subject matter of his three plays was (as Carlson puts it) "the everyday life of Cairo, particularly its colorful, bohemian street life."⁷⁰ One play is essentially a farce, filled with strong sexual (often homosexual) content; another is largely a parade of street performers, each of whom offers a distinctive monologue.⁷¹ The third play is strikingly reminiscent, suggests Carlson, of the comedy of Aristophanes, being of similar structure and having an Aristophanic mix of obscenity and lyric poetry. Carlson argues that these similarities are not coincidental and that Ibn Dāniyāl might well have had access to the works of Aristophanes thanks to Cairo's frequent interactions with the Byzantine Empire.⁷²

Very limited information exists about the performance of Ibn Dāniyāl's plays, but it seems they were presented in taverns and private salons, presumably for audiences of well-to-do urbanites who could appreciate the playwright's self-proclaimed "high literary style."⁷³ Although each play was performed by a single puppet master, Li Guo suggests that it "would most likely [have been] an integral part of a variety show that combined music, poetry, dancing, and acting (live and puppetry), with fantastic lighting tricks."⁷⁴ The impression one receives is that the commercial centrality of Cairo had brought into being a class of wealthy merchants and shipowners – a new and moneyed niche for theatre. At first, the shadow theatre filled with this niche with plays on the previously mentioned "traditional topics," but as these grew tedious, Ibn Dāniyāl revitalized the form with his mix of bawdy yet poetic comedies.

A generation after Ibn Dāniyāl's death, Egypt was "hit by a catastrophic demographic event, the great plague epidemic in 1348," which was merely "the first in a series of crises that prevented the country and the city from making a lasting recovery."[75] Economic activity in the city did not completely cease, but one can easily imagine a drastic narrowing of the niche that shadow theatre occupied. And then, in 1451, the sultan "banned the shadow theatre and ordered the burning of all puppets," although Badawi reports that "we know from various references that shadow drama was performed in Egypt" in the succeeding centuries.[76] The theatre form survived, apparently, by seeking a new niche "as a popular form of entertainment, indulged in largely by the vulgar and poor"; the surviving plays from the seventeenth century and after "bear the unmistakable marks of folk art" that has been "transmitted orally from one generation of players to the next."[77]

CHAPTER 7

On the Margins of Eurasia

Europe

Across the Mediterranean from Egypt, the far-western peninsula of Eurasia would feel the economic influence of "the East" quite belatedly. Instead, the basis for its cultural crystallization (and for the theatre that would be part of that crystallization) was largely indigenous. But it was only after the peninsula became meaningfully engaged with the rest of Eurasia that its theatre would come fully into its own.

In the centuries following the disintegration of the Western Roman Empire, what we now think of as Europe was roiled by incessant raids, invasions, and migrations. Agricultural communities lived mostly at subsistence level while urban life was extremely limited; Rome itself was scarcely an echo of its former greatness. Degenerate offshoots of Latin emerged where the Western Roman Empire had once held sway; farther afield, a welter of Celtic, Germanic, and Slavic languages was spoken by peoples with limited knowledge of the long-fallen empire. According to the historian Charles F. Pazdernik, at no point before about 900 CE was "Europe, however it might be defined, a politically, culturally, or economically coherent entity."[1]

But by the tenth century CE, the social order had begun to change, bringing about a distinct European society – though few would have called it such for hundreds of years to come. The historian William H. McNeill specifies three important facets of change. First (and most fundamental) was agricultural expansion. McNeill emphasizes the increasing use of heavy moldboard plows that could work the waterlogged soil of western and northern Europe,[2] but at the same time European farmers were also planting previously undervalued grains (such as rye and oats) and experimenting with three-field crop rotation.[3] And it seems that a changing climate stimulated (or at least advanced the effectiveness of) the new European agriculture, for the Medieval Climate Anomaly, mentioned earlier, apparently began warming Europe in the ninth century.[4]

Thanks to its agricultural expansion, McNeill suggests, Europe became able "to sustain both a numerous military aristocracy and a vigorous town life."[5] The military aristocracy is McNeill's second facet of change. This "formidable class" would eventually become quite ostentatious, but because its tastes "were at first simple … even a thinly populated and commercially primitive Europe became able to support relatively large numbers of knights." With these warriors available for defense, "raiders and pirates soon lost their accustomed easy superiority [and] their depredations consequently slackened and soon ceased."[6] The historian Norman Davies suggests that the cost of maintaining this warrior class "provided the central rationale of feudal society." Hierarchies of power were soon established to support that cost, but feudalism was rife with "conflicting dependencies and loyalties, riddled with exceptions and exemptions" and unclear "lines of service."[7] The almost inevitable result was the emergence of multiple (and often warring) polities, each with its own ruler at the precarious top of the local hierarchy. The perpetually fractured politics of Europe would become one of its most abiding characteristics, with no polity ever managing to establish overall control.

McNeill's third facet of change is the growth of a "vigorous town life." The presence of the military aristocracy made it difficult for raiders and pirates to gain easy plunder in the now well-defended polities; instead, they settled down as agriculturalists themselves or turned to trade. Communities of merchants "establish[ed] themselves permanently at some convenient location" such as a bishop's seat, a wealthy abbey, or a feudal castle.[8] The increasing populations of these towns, suggests Norman Davies, created a labor force that could be "employed in new industrial enterprises such as mining and weaving," with "specialized textile towns" quickly becoming important.[9] Some towns also became centers of education, creating a new class of literate men who would populate the ranks of business, church, and state.[10]

Along with the facets of change identified by McNeill we must also recognize the ongoing Christianization of Europe. The domain of Latin Christendom roughly doubled in size between the tenth and fourteenth centuries, while also infilling those areas that had only nominally been Christian.[11] Two developments in Europe's Christianization are of special note. First are the structural changes within the Church itself, known collectively as the Gregorian Reforms (c. 1050–1080), that centralized Church power under the pope.[12] Second is the "investiture controversy" over whether the Church or secular rulers would appoint clergy. Its resolution gave the Church substantial freedom from secular authorities, enabling it to compete "for wealth and power with kings and emperors" and to grow into "a great superstate that was governed by the papal administration."¹³ The result was that for centuries to come, Europe would have an authoritative religious identity despite its many competing polities. With these two developments, writes the medievalist Robert Bartlett, "'Latin Christendom' can be used to designate not merely a [religious] rite or an obedience but a society."¹⁴ Europe's cultural crystallization had begun.

Religious institutions were among the earliest beneficiaries of Europe's increasing wealth, thanks in part to tithing from commoners and special bequests from aristocrats and royalty but also to the alacrity with which many of those institutions imposed serfdom on their own tenants.¹⁵ Wealthy institutions such as the Abbey of Gandersheim (where Hrotsvitha wrote Europe's first-known plays) and the monasteries of Saint Martial and Saint Gall (early adaptors of the *Quem queritis* trope) could allow their inhabitants to devote their time to the glory of God. Of the cities that developed in the shadow of one or another religious institution, the textile town of Arras (associated with the Abbey of Saint-Vaast) was among the wealthiest. By the late twelfth century, according to Carol Symes, Arras was "a creative maelstrom of conflicting politics, unprecedented economic opportunities, and unfamiliar types of social mobility." It was in this stimulating urban context that "five remarkable artifacts emerge: the earliest vernacular plays of medieval Europe."¹⁶

The newness of European theatre, whatever its language, needs to be emphasized. The ancient Mediterranean theatre region no longer existed; nor can it be said even that the emerging European theatre region was a continuation, after half a millennium, of the westernmost portion of the ancient region. Theatre in medieval Europe owed precious little to ancient theatre forms, either in its texts (no more classical heroes, scathing political satires, or carefully plotted comedies of urban life) or performance situations (no more state-supported festivals or games dedicated to Greek or Roman gods). And although ancient theatres littered the former areas of the Western Roman Empire, William Tydeman notes that "there is no evidence" that these theatres "ever housed medieval performances, being more usually employed as quarries, barracks, and forts, when not 'crumbling, overgrown or built-over'" – and this despite their original function being well understood.¹⁷ Europe would eventually gain a deep interest in the theatre of the ancient Mediterranean, but only after another half-millennium had passed. As V. A. Kolve bluntly states, "Medieval drama owes nothing to the tragedy and comedy of either Greece or Rome; it was a fresh beginning, unrooted in any formal tradition of theatre."¹⁸

The major exception to this lack of indebtedness is the work of Europe's first-known playwright. Hrotsvitha was a tenth-century poet who lived as a lay canoness in Gandersheim Abbey (in what is now Germany). This abbey, especially wealthy and well-connected to political power, "fostered an atmosphere of increasing cosmopolitanism and intellectualism" that included the study of ancient Latin texts.[19] In the preface to her six plays, Hrotsvitha acknowledges her debt to the Roman playwright Terence: "[I] have not hesitated to imitate in my writings a poet whose works are so widely read, my object being to glorify, within the limits of my poor talent, the laudable chastity of Christian virgins in that self-same form of composition which has been used to describe the shameless acts of licentious women."[20]

Hrotsvitha's claim of "imitating" Terence is somewhat perplexing: Her Latin is medieval, not classical, and her often gruesome narratives of female Christian martyrs are deeply alien to Terence's secular comedies. The safest way to understand Hrotsvitha's preface is to focus on her claim to write "in the self-same form of composition" as Terence. That is to say, she was "imitating" Terence by writing *dramatic literature* – but using that literary genre to create something the likes of which Terence could never have conceived. Two further points are worth noting about Hrotsvitha's claim. First, although she suggests that Terence was well known among the literate few, he was of interest to them not as a playwright but as a master of Latin rhetoric, renowned for "his neat [Latin] phrases, which were liked for their compactness and quotability."[21] Second, while there are hints of stage directions in Hrotsvitha's plays, many scholars doubt they were intended for performance.[22] And even if they had been performed in Gandersheim, they were apparently a creative dead end, for the canoness had no known successors to build on her work and establish a theatre form. Whatever debt she owed to ancient theatre came to an end with her.

More significant to the development of what would become European theatre was the sketch comedy that was part of the repertoire of itinerant performers, sometimes called jongleurs, whom I briefly mentioned earlier.[23] These performers were undoubtedly active well before Hrotsvitha put pen to parchment, for attempts to suppress them date from the years 679, 747, 789, 835, and 960. Tydeman observes that "many authorities now believe that the Roman actors of mimes … joined forces with the main body of nomadic performers" as the Western Roman Empire collapsed.[24] It is worth recalling, however, that we have encountered similar kinds of variety-like performance (including comic sketches) in many other societies. Grace Frank's conclusion is apt: The jongleurs "did not preserve the continuity of the formal theatre of ancient Rome or create the formal theatre of the Middle Ages; they merely gave evidence in some of their exhibitions of the perpetuity of the dramatic instinct."[25]

The most original theatre of tenth-century Europe was its liturgical theatre, first seen in the *Quem queritis* trope (also known as the Visitation Exchange). The earliest sure evidence dates from 965–975, although this probably follows some years after the trope was created in French religious institutions.[26] Perhaps the central point to emphasize here is that just as European theatre was not the continuation of late Roman theatre, Europe did not need to "reinvent" theatre in Church ritual.[27] Given the innate human capacity to engage in make-believe, as well as the existence of jongleurs long before the tenth century, it is more accurate to say that churchmen, although theatrical amateurs, took advantage of the already familiar medium of dramatic theatre to enrich the musical dialogue of their liturgy.

Tydeman notes that "the precise development of the liturgical drama is impossible to chart," but it seems that Visitation Exchanges were known in England, France, and German-speaking lands by 1000 CE and "remained more or less unaltered for roughly a century." The quick spread of liturgical theatre was undoubtedly enabled by the close connections maintained between religious institutions in Europe. Subsequent to the Easter-based liturgical theatre, "comparable plays" were created for the Christmas liturgy; these apparently then back-influenced the Easter plays, with some churches "creat[ing] new versions of the plays by drawing on further gospel material for their subject matter." Tydeman emphasizes, however, that "such developments are not simply expansions or cumulative versions of an original nucleus … nor did any of the elaborate plays necessarily evolve from simpler versions according to a regular pattern."[28] The liturgical theatre always remained seamlessly embedded in its religious context. Nils Holger Petersen observes that "the ritual is not just representational, it is a ritual that points to its own meaning and foundation in the Resurrection myth."[29] Liturgical theatre was created to serve the action of ritual and always remained in its service. The Church provided a pair of narrow but well-supported niches (Easter and Christmas services) for it, and there it would flourish, with great variations of complexity, for hundreds of years to come.[30]

As Europe's economy expanded, urban growth allowed it to become more fully integrated into Eurasian commerce. According to the medievalist Eric Cantor, "The period from 1050 to 1130 was the period of enormous commercial expansion, of the well-known rise of urban communities, [and] of the first expression of political influence by the new burgher class."³¹ Although Europe had not completely lacked commercial contact with the rest of Eurasia before the First Crusade (in 1095), that and subsequent crusades (through 1291) "were the mechanism," according to Janet L. Abu-Lughod, that fully "reintegrated northwestern Europe into a world system from which she had been detached after the 'fall of Rome.'" This reintegration stimulated new tastes in Europe: "Spices, silk cloth and brocades, damascene blades, porcelain, and a variety of luxury goods previously undreamed of made a rich prize for the Crusaders," and when Crusader conquests failed to fulfill these new tastes, "purchases were necessary." In the end, "the need for items to sell in eastern markets stimulated European production, particularly of fine woolen cloth."³² By the close of the thirteenth century, writes the historian Richard Smith, "Europe had re-emerged as an engine in Afro-Eurasian commerce, if not yet on the scale of other engines, at least with considerable potential as partner or competitor."³³

Europe's urban development opened new niches for theatre. I have already noted that the textile town of Arras was home to the earliest vernacular plays of medieval Europe. Carol Symes reports that "in the thirteenth century, Arras was at the center of an increasingly urbanized, cosmopolitan, and swiftly changing world"; it was also a world "where vernacular literacy was beginning to challenge the hegemony of Latin."³⁴ Of its five vernacular plays, the most accomplished is Jehan Bodel's *Play of Saint Nicholas* (c. 1200), which combines a well-known legend about the saint with realistic and comical "low life" scenes set in Arras itself. The most amusing is *The Boy and the Blind Man* (c. 1265), an anonymous satirical sketch that "contains the universal characteristics of farce." The most musical is Adam de la Halle's *Play of Robin and Marion* (c. 1285), which takes "the theme of hundreds of lyrico-narrative *pastourelles* [pastorals]" and embellishes it with ample song and dance.³⁵ It is difficult to generalize about the five plays, but two points can be made. First, they are works of literary theatre (however much the comic episodes might have allowed for improvisation), with three of the plays having named playwrights. Second, they draw their stories either from well-known narratives or universal sketch-comedy themes such as failed seductions, cuckoldry, clever cheats, and (as in *The Boy and the Blind Man*) abuse of people with disabilities.

More famously, urban growth stimulated the emergence of devotional forms of theatre that drew on popular religious narratives for their stories. The dominant form on the European mainland was the Passion play; England preferred cycles of short plays (usually offered on the Feast of Corpus Christi) that spanned from Creation through Christ's Passion to the Final Judgment;[36] in both places there were also stand-alone plays based on the lives of saints. These devotional forms appear to have emerged around the start of the fourteenth century, at the apogee of the Eurasian convergence. It seems, though, that they gained a special salience and renewed development only after the mid-century spread of the bubonic plague.[37] While these forms were clearly devotional, they were also typically civic celebrations. Tydeman suggests that although "churchmen still played a vital rôle in guiding the endeavours of the organisers, performers, and craftsmen" of the performing communities, "the main initiative now passed to the citizens and municipal authorities: Each community felt free to follow its own system of play presentation, and the staging of the great annual cycle performances or of the occasional drama of epic proportions became a matter of intense civic pride."[38]

Neither the Passion plays nor the cycle plays should be seen as outgrowths of a liturgical theatre that had burst beyond the confines of the Church. Stanley J. Kahrl argues that it has been amply demonstrated "that the Latin liturgical plays never 'developed' or 'budded out' into anything new because as particular enhancements of the liturgy they fulfilled the function for which they had been invented, and remained part of the liturgy as long as that liturgy was performed."[39] The new devotional forms were organized by, and performed in, the towns while being funded by civic trade guilds, as opposed to being organized, performed, and funded by religious institutions. Their texts were structured differently, treating a far broader range of material than liturgical theatre, while also being written and performed in the vernacular rather than Latin. And they had different performance practices than did the dignified liturgical theatre, with an emphasis on vivid characterization and spectacle that made substantial use of scenery, props, and special effects.[40] All of which is to say that the devotional forms were original accomplishments that filled new urban niches made possible by Europe's reintegration into Eurasian commerce.

Japan

Beyond the opposite coast of the Eurasian landmass, Japan's history offers both contrasts and similarities to that of Europe. Its proximity to China had long allowed for extensive cultural transfers from the mainland; well before the tenth century, Japan had domesticated China's system of writing, calendar, law codes, Confucian principles, and Buddhism (which itself had originated in India).[41] But as Björn Wittrock observes, its cultural crystallization followed a familiar pattern: "Japanese developments in the beginning of the second millennium CE exhibit many of the features characteristic of both Europe and China during this period. Thus in Japan there was also rapid growth in agricultural production, growth of urban life, [and] increasing commerce both domestically and externally."[42] To these we can add a general increase in literacy, such as we have already observed in Europe and China.[43]

Japanese society between the tenth and fourteenth centuries had three distinct power bases, which the historian Mikeal S. Adolphson refers to as the country's "ruling triumvirate." First was "the court nobility, consisting of the imperial family and the capital [city] aristocracy, [which] held the administrative and ceremonial aspects of the state." Second was the "religious establishment," whether Shintō or Buddhist, which "supplied the state and its members with spiritual protection" even as elite temples represented the state "through their many branch temples and extensive land possessions in the provinces." Third was "the warrior aristocracy," which was "responsible for keeping the peace and physically protecting the state."[44] This aristocracy was led by a *shōgun*, essentially a military dictator, who ruled through his *bakufu* (literally, his "tent government"; sometimes also called the *shōgunate*). The *shōgun* was supported by local lords (known as *daimyō*), each of whom controlled subordinate *samurai*. Up until the fourteenth century, the *bakufu* was on equal footing with the formal government of the emperor and his nobles, but thereafter the *shōguns* became "the de facto rulers, indicating that Japan had been ushered into a new age" of military dominance.[45]

Beneath this ruling triumvirate was a large class of agriculturalists who took advantage of Champa rice (introduced from China by the fourteenth century) to greatly expand the supply of food. There was also a smaller but growing class of trade-oriented town and city folk energized by a cash-based economy that relied on the massive importation of coinage from China.[46] Notably, the warrior aristocracy and the temples also greatly benefited from agricultural expansion and commercial growth, for the *daimyō* held large estates, while the temples were not only landholders themselves but also managed most international trade under the sponsorship of the *bakufu*.[47]

As a result of Japan's historical development, its theatre was directly influenced by China in the centuries *before* the Eurasian rising tide of theatre that began in the tenth century. But it was later indirectly influenced by the post-tenth-century contact that expanded its agriculture and commerce to the benefit of the ruling triumvirate. Japan's major contribution to Eurasian theatre's rising tide came when the growing power and riches of that triumvirate created the niche for *nō* (sometimes transliterated as *noh*; literally, "skills/artistry").

The history of Japanese theatre in the centuries before *nō* is deeply uncertain, owing to limited evidence and the "confusing usages" of various terms.[48] An early theatre form was known as *kagura*, a word whose original meaning is obscure but that has long been written to mean something like "god-music" or "entertainment for the gods."[49] Performances of *kagura*, which continue in many subforms to this day, begin with a ritual to gain the presence of divinity, but then might include virtually anything believed to entertain "the illustrious divine guest."[50] Beyond *kagura*, one can broadly divide Japan's early theatre forms into two groups: those that originated in China and were subsequently domesticated by Japan's imperial court and those that emerged in Japan itself.

Gigaku and *bugaku* were among the earliest known forms in the court, having apparently been brought from China (perhaps via Korea) in the seventh and eighth centuries, respectively.[51] Although *gigaku* was closely associated with Buddhism, its short, dance-based sketches, performed by masked characters, "contain[ed] satiric, erotic, or comic flavors seemingly contradictory to Buddhist morality."[52] *Bugaku* was somewhat more "dignified," and although it too had masked performers, it apparently contained little if any mimetic action.[53] As *gigaku* lost popularity in the court, around the twelfth century, some of its traits (in particular, certain dances and masks) were taken up by *bugaku* performers, but a particular Chinese-originated trait of *bugaku* itself is of special note: the *jo-ha-kyū* compositional structure that would eventually come to undergird *nō* theatre.[54]

Two indigenous Japanese forms are also of particular importance. *Sangaku* (roughly meaning "miscellaneous entertainments") was "the generic designation for all popular entertainments which did not belong to the canon of 'officially' recognized state entertainments." It was essentially variety performance, and included acrobatics, juggling, illusionist tricks, miracle cures, dance, music, and comic sketches.[55] When the form was eventually taken up by the imperial court (circa the eleventh century), it was renamed *sarugaku*;[56] concurrently it shifted its focus more toward mimetic performance.[57] It also seems to have adopted some of the ceremonial characteristics of the courtly *bugaku*,[58] which helped to further distinguish it from the ongoing popular *sangaku*. The other significant indigenous form was *dengaku* ("rice-field entertainment"), which began as a festival theatre "in connection with the rice-culture among the common people" but eventually became professionalized as well. Colorful costumes, dance, acrobatics, and stilt-walking were early staples of its performance, which helped *dengaku* troupes gain what Terauchi Noako calls "an overwhelming popularity" with all ranks of society.[59] Professional *dengaku* and *sarugaku* troupes interacted sufficiently for each to take on traits of the other, to the point that the forms could scarcely be distinguished from one another.[60]

The prehistory of *nō* (and of its comical companion form, *kyōgen*) lies in this set of theatre forms. The details of their interactions have not conclusively been sorted out,[61] but it is safe to suggest that by the mid fourteenth century, these forms held many theatrical traits in common, while other traits – even if unique to one or another of the forms – were available to artists talented and fortunate enough to take advantage of them.

The decisive moment came in 1374, when the *shōgun* Yoshimitsu visited the Imakumano Shrine in Kyoto to attend the performance of a particular *sarugaku* troupe; the troupe's leader was Kan'ami, and among its performers was his son Zeami.[62] H. Paul Varley writes, "Seldom in cultural history are single events of great significance, but one exception was the visit by Yoshimitsu to Imakumano Shrine." Yoshimitsu (who was seventeen at the time) was undoubtedly impressed by the performance – but he became infatuated with the twelve-year-old Zeami, "who seemed a dreamlike vision … a youth of infinite grace and elegance of manner."[63] Yoshimitsu brought the troupe under his patronage and Zeami into his bed (a cause of scandal not for its homosexuality but for its misalliance of *shōgun* and actor) in what was possibly the most serendipitous case of lust in the entire lusty history of theatre.[64]

The emergence of *nō* out of *sarugaku* and its related forms took place over the careers of Kan'ami and Zeami. What might have begun as the predilections of one *sarugaku* troupe became identifiable as something different and new, however substantial the continuities with earlier theatre forms might have been. Scholars do not agree on any *single* decisive innovation of Kan'ami. One notes that Kan'ami introduced the "inspired creation" of a synthesis between "the popular dramatic mimetic element and the elegant, sophisticated spectacle attuned to the aristocratic taste of the Shogun's court."[65] Another points to Kan'ami's authorship of highly literary plays that yielded "far more complexities of plot than the older dramatic forms permitted."[66]

Zeami proved a worthy successor to his father, taking over leadership of the troupe while revising Kan'ami's plays and writing some fifty of his own.[67] Again, scholars do not agree on any single decisive innovation. One suggests that whereas most *sarugaku* troupes favored "forceful performances of demon roles," Zeami "must have realized that demons lacked the lyricism to keep Yoshimitsu's attention" and so "worked to intensify the musical and choreographic interest"; in addition, he was less interested in "plot development," per se, than in allowing "a sequence of musical components" to set the play's structure.[68] Another observes that Zeami created an entire class of *nō* plays with warriors as their leading characters, "no doubt in part to appeal to and flatter Yoshimitsu."[69] A third scholar emphasizes "a reduction in the number of roles in a play and in the number of scenes, a restriction of the action to a single location, and a prominence of monologue over dialogue," all of which provided the plays with "a unity of time and characterization."[70] Presumably these many innovations (along with others unmentioned here) worked together to distinguish the troupe of Kan'ami and Zeami from their competitors.

In addition to his playwrighting and performing, Zeami authored a set of "secret treatises" that established what amounts to a philosophy of *nō* aesthetics and practice. Two concepts set forth in these treatises are especially noteworthy. First is *yūgen*, the aesthetic ideal that suffuses *nō*. Early on, Zeami seems to have used the word to mean something like "'grace' or 'elegance,'" while in his later writings it takes a "darker coloration," suggesting a "presence" that is "mysterious" and "indefinable."[71] Although Zeami sometimes associated the idea of *yūgen* with nobility, he insisted that it refers not necessarily to a particular class of characters but to something more ineffable.[72] Over the course of his career, he placed increasing importance on *yūgen*, perhaps at the expense of the principle of *monomane* – which literally means "imitation" but, given that word's English-language implication of realistic acting, is probably better translated as "role playing."[73] Zeami himself wrote that *yūgen* "can be regarded as the highest principle" of *nō*.[74]

The second aspect of Zeami's philosophy to note is the *jo-ha-kyū* compositional structure that, as previously mentioned, originated in the court-based *bugaku*. Zeami gave this structure a central position in *nō*, and for many hundreds of years it has been rigorously applied throughout the theatre form.[75] According to Thomas Rimer and Yamazaki Masakazu, *jo* "is sometimes translated as 'introduction or 'prelude,' suggesting the slow and stately tempo at the beginning of the play"; *ha* "is sometimes translated as 'development or exposition,' but a literal translation, 'breaking,' suggests the increased dramatic and musical energy level after the more composed and stately *jo*"; and *kyū* "is sometimes translated as 'climax,' or 'finale,' but a literal translation, 'rapid,' conveys the quick tempo appropriate for the end" of *nō*.[76] The "three-phase" rule of *jo-ha-kyū*, writes Ortolani, structures not only the composition of each *nō* play but "is also to be found within the subdivisions of each act and scene"; indeed, "it exercises the function of a universal organizational principle in each part of both text and performance of dance and music."[77] It was also used to structure entire theatrical events, which traditionally included five *nō* plays, along with interpolated *kyōgen* plays. According to Donald Keene, this progression of plays "was intended to provide the audience with a complete theatrical experience."[78]

Suffused with *yūgen* and structured according to the rule of *jo-ha-kyū*, *nō* was a fully literary theatre form – likely the first in Japan – that drew heavily upon the Japanese literature of the previous few centuries.[79] The most oft-used source for warrior plays was *The Tale of the Heike*, an epic work that offers "the richest legends and the most vivid impressions of the medieval mind at the time when ... the country was plunged into an age of warriors." The earliest (thirteenth century) version was likely rather brief, but as it was retold by "blind itinerant priests who traveled the countryside chanting their tales" it was "extensively revised and reshaped."[80] By Zeami's time, *The Tale of the Heike* was known to much of the Japanese population. But although Zeami "declared in his critical writings that texts based on this work must be faithful to the original," his own plays using this source "are free, not only in language but in emphasis."[81]

Another well-known narrative upon which *nō* drew was *The Tale of Genji*, a novel written in the early eleventh century. It too was subsequently disseminated by storytellers and came to exert a powerful influence on Japanese poetry as well as on *nō*.[82] Janet Goff notes that "following Zeami's advice, playwrights placed *Genji* poems at high points in a play and wove them into the imagistic and thematic structure." Playwrights also used elements of *Genji*'s narrative, but "whereas the *Genji* deals with *this* world, the noh plays nearly always treat the world of the *Genji* as a dream of long ago," as the story of a character's past retold in a moment of great distress.[83] In this way the narratives of *nō* were familiar and yet transformed into something new (see Figure 7.1).

While Kan'ami was alive, his troupe remained committed to performing for all classes of society, but under Zeami the troupe (and thus, the nascent theatre form) settled into the comfortable niche of performing for the ascendent warrior aristocracy. The warrior plays based on *The Tale of the Heike* were of obvious appeal to this audience, but the form as a whole flattered them by providing them "with the trappings of cultural legitimacy" and embodying "the aesthetic ideal of elegance and grace" to which they aspired.[84] Steven T. Brown tartly observes that "although Zeami described noh as 'a prayer for peace to reign over the entire country,' ... it might

Figure 7.1   *Nō*: a scene from *Matsukaze*, a play begun by Kan'ami and expanded by Zeami. Artwork by Kogyo Tsukioka (1898), from his series "Pictures of No Performances (Nogaku Zue)." (Photo by Heritage Art/Heritage Images via Getty Images)

also be viewed as a supplication to those elite members of the warrior class who held the reins of power."[85] And because under Yoshimitsu the military government moved its seat to near the imperial court in Kyoto, warriors and courtiers "intermingle[d] socially to a much greater degree than before and … share[d] patronage of the arts."[86] This expanded and further enriched *nō*'s niche. Zeami "accepted immersion in the elite social world of Kyoto" and, to suit his audience, "elevated noh to the supremely refined and courtly art we know today."[87]

Moreover, whereas earlier Japanese theatre forms were largely identified with either Buddhism or Shintō, *nō* fit comfortably in both religious contexts. Donald Keene observes that *nō* plays "often describe Shinto gods, but a strong Buddhist coloring runs through them."[88] Zeami's play *Yōrō* has a mountain god proclaim "Whether kami [that is, god] or Buddha, it is like water and waves [the essence is the same]. To save all living beings, Buddha appears in the guise of a god."[89] In sum, the niche for *nō* quickly came to include all three bases of Japan's "ruling triumvirate." This substantial niche was deeply conservative, much invested in the grace, beauty, and solemnity of *nō*. The preference for these characteristics apparently encouraged such stately performances that by the nineteenth century, each play lasted about twice as long as it had centuries earlier – the kind of change that kept the form well-fitted to its niche as a "ceremonial art."[90]

But a full *nō* program of plays was far from unrelentingly serious. At first, music and dance were used as filler between the plays of a program, but by the mid fifteenth century, short comedies known as *kyōgen* (literally, "wild words") had taken over that function. Developed from the comic sketches that were part of earlier forms, *kyōgen* presents "a different world from that of noh. Here there are no aristocrats, no legendary warriors, no beautiful poetesses"; instead, its plays are largely concerned with the world of "rural villages and estates."[91] As such, this companion form was little interested in the elegance of *yūgen* and instead leaned heavily into the role-playing of *monomane*.[92] Its plays incorporated "Buddhist and secular folktales and anecdotes, proverbs, and popular songs" into plots that "range from auspicious dance to comedy of manners, slapstick to dark comedy, absurd fantasy to noh parody."[93] And not only did the *kyōgen* actors perform their own short comedies between the *nō* plays, they also served as tertiary characters in the interludes of *nō* plays that happened to have two distinct acts. These characters were usually rustics whose colloquial language could help clarify to the audience "the story so cryptically related elsewhere in the play."[94] In this way, *kyōgen* lent further support to the *nō* program. Conjoined, these two new forms would satisfy their elite audiences until the Tokugawa Dynasty was overthrown by the Meiji Restoration in 1868.

In Part III of this book, we have traced the convergence of societies throughout Eurasia, seeing how increased commerce – founded on agricultural expansion, situated in growing cities, and abetted by technological innovations and transfers – brought on an overall growth in wealth that stimulated numerous cultural crystallizations. These generative disruptions enlarged some theatrical niches while also opening niches for new theatre forms. Coming into the tenth century, the ancient Mediterranean region was scarcely a memory; only South Asia had a clear theatrical identity. Elsewhere in Eurasia, theatre seems to have been a blurry assortment of local or semilocal sketch comedy, ritual, and folk traditions. But by the mid fourteenth century, numerous theatre regions had established themselves. The full geographic extent of each region at the time remains unclear, but certainly their core areas come into focus in East Asia, Southeast Asia,

Islamdom, Latin Europe, and Japan. In these areas, theatre artists drew upon their societal and theatrical contexts to create new forms suited to the various niches becoming available to them.

I want to focus here on the concept of *theatre regions*, which distinguishes between geographic areas specifically on the basis of their theatres rather than on their political, ethnic, religious, or linguistic affiliations.[95] The historian Marshall G. S. Hodgson suggests that each world region is an area in which there are "historical interrelations and interactions close-knit enough so that many questions can be dealt with in its terms without spreading out into a still wider region," such as Eurasia as a whole.[96] Along the same lines, the geographers Martin W. Lewis and Kären E. Wigen write that world regions are "more or less boundable areas united by broad social and cultural features"; they also note that while world regions "may not be *fundaments*" in the sense of being permanent and unchanging features of global geography, "they are nonetheless *fundamental* to understanding how the world is put together."[97]

To delineate the world's theatre regions, we need to identify areas over which single forms have spread and/or multiple forms have had meaningful "interrelations and interactions" (to repeat Hodgson's phrase) that result in theatrical homologies of one sort or another. It would be a misunderstanding to assume that these areas necessarily align with those of polities, ethnicities, religions, or languages. It is convenient sometimes to refer to Indian theatre, but the South Asian theatre region of the tenth century extended well beyond the bounds of the long-departed Gupta Empire, as well as beyond the borders of current-day India. And yet one can speak of a South Asian theatre region not only because of the widespread distribution of Sanskrit theatre through the post-Gupta centuries but also because of its apparent influence on later emerging forms in Gujarat (and likely elsewhere) as well as its obvious influence on *kutiyattam*. It is similarly convenient sometimes to refer to Chinese theatre, but political control of the East Asian theatre region was split for many years between the Mongol's Yuan Dynasty and the Southern Song Dynasty, and there seems to be no evidence that the theatre region of the time extended into what are now the westernmost portions of China. And yet one can speak of an East Asian region because despite the split of imperial control, *nanxi* and Yuan *zaju* had clear homologies, most notably their reliance on role categories that each derived from Song-era *zaju*.

As these examples from South Asia and East Asia should indicate, it would also be a misunderstanding to assume that any theatre region could be discussed in terms of a single "archetypical" theatre form. Instead, we need to recognize the diversity of theatre forms in all regions. In discussing Europe, we noted the sketch comedy of jongleurs, the liturgical theatre, the early vernacular plays of Arras, and the civic-based Passion plays and Corpus Christi cycle plays – and this is, to be sure, but a partial list of European theatre forms of the period. Similarly, in discussing Southeast Asia we observed not only the highly influential *wayang kulit purwa* but also the scores of forms descended at least in part from it, while also considering the large-puppet theatre forms in what are now Thailand and Cambodia, as well as *hat cheo* and water puppetry in what is now Vietnam. And again, this is but a partial list of Southeast Asian theatre forms that could have been noted. But binding together the diversity of forms in a given region are the various homologies that arise from interactions between them. If theatre form *A* has significant homologies with theatre form *B*, which itself has homologies with theatre form *C*, we can see them as being "close-knit enough" (to return to Hodgson's phrase) to belong to the same world region of theatre.

None of this should be taken to deny that within most theatre regions it is also possible to identify theatre *subregions* that more closely align with political, ethnic, religious, and/or linguistic affiliations. Indeed, a portion of the diversity to be found in each region is the direct result of one or another of these affiliations: It is easy enough, for example, to see that although *nanxi* and Yuan *zaju* are related theatre forms, southern and northern China have long been distinctive subregions of East Asian theatre. Conversely, it is also possible to identify what can be called theatre *megaregions*, in which "historical interrelationships and interactions" have spilled out, if only to a limited degree, beyond the individual regions themselves. By the mid fourteenth century, to take the primary example here, the various regions of Eurasia (including North Africa and the various islands that flank the Eurasian landmass) had been in sustained contact for hundreds of years. Although each region was undergoing its own cultural crystallization and developing its own complex of theatre forms, the material basis for many of those forms came from participation in a pan-Eurasian pattern of agricultural expansion, urban growth, and technological innovation and transfer. No one could possibly confuse, say, Corpus Christi cycle plays and *nō*, but both were made possible because England and Japan existed in the same megaregion.

The magnificent *nō* would be the last major creation in Eurasia's post-tenth-century rising tide of theatrical innovation. For even as *nō* emerged, the convergence of societies across Eurasia would be dealt a pair of crippling blows: the spread of bubonic plague and the collapse of commerce following the fall of the Mongol Empire. Performances of existing forms of theatre would certainly continue through the years that immediately followed these disasters, but the conditions that had stimulated the centuries-long efflorescence of new theatre forms were brought to an abrupt conclusion. A new stimulus would be required for the next efflorescence of theatre across Eurasia.

PART IV

The Eurasian Resurgence (starting c. 1500 CE)

During the sixteenth and early seventeenth centuries, Eurasia experienced an unprecedented wave of theatrical change. Even though established forms such as *kutiyattam* and *nō* carried on in their accustomed niches, new theatre forms emerged and gained dominance almost everywhere. The predicate for this wave of change was a pair of related events, briefly mentioned at the end of Chapter 7, that took place back in the fourteenth century: the demographic catastrophe brought on by the bubonic plague and the collapse of interregional commerce that followed the breakup of the Mongol Empire. Each was devastating in its own way. Together, and in association with the onset of the Little Ice Age as well as more localized crises, they had a crippling impact across Eurasia.

The most detailed information about the bubonic plague comes from Western Europe: Contemplating the three waves of plague that struck there between 1347 and 1375, the historian James Belich writes that "the nightmarish notion of demographic halving becomes really hard to avoid."[1] But the plague was not limited to Western Europe; as we have seen, it also devastated Cairo and, more broadly, Southwest Asia and North Africa. Beyond that, suggests the historian James L. A. Webb, Jr., "it is possible that the population of China decreased by as much as 50 per cent" from its pre-plague high, "although [deaths caused by] the Mongol invasions may have also been a major contributor to the decline." Webb adds that "a major lacuna in our knowledge is the extent of the population loss in other … densely populated areas such as Persia and India. Some historians have advanced estimates of the loss of population at 30 per cent or so, but the evidentiary basis of these estimates is not robust."[2]

Recent genetic research, as summarized by the historian Monica H. Green, suggests that during their thirteenth-century conquests, Mongol armies unwittingly spread the disease in animal populations in China, Mongolia, Siberia, and the Caucasus.[3] In the fourteenth century came the inevitable outbreaks as it passed into human populations. Even as the

Mongol Empire was being established, in other words, it carried within it the seeds of demographic disaster. The historian Richard Smith observes that the ensuing waves of plague "disrupted [Eurasia's] economic order. A smaller population meant a decrease in production, a plunge in demand, and an overall sharp decline in prosperity [as] long-distance trade experienced a drop in volume."[4] Two additional consequences, suggests the historian Janet L. Abu-Lughod, "were fairly universal": "One was a reemphasis on agricultural production, which absorbed a higher proportion of the smaller population than it had even decades before"; the other was "a drop in the rate of urbanization" as the plague hit hardest in crowded towns and cities.[5]

The second fourteenth-century development was the abrupt decline in interregional commerce brought about in part by the plague but also by the collapse of the Mongol Empire itself. By the late thirteenth century that empire had already fractured into four distinct but related entities; outbreaks of the plague soon helped undermine three of them, most importantly the Yuan Dynasty in China, which fell in the mid fourteenth century.[6] With the end of Mongol rule there, writes Richard Smith, "secure transcontinental [land] travel no longer existed."[7] This loss had a profound impact, for the land route had worked in concert with the two major sea routes in a well-developed system during the Mongol years: Competition kept shipping costs manageable, while temporary blockages of any one route could be overcome by switching to another. But with the fall of China's Yuan Dynasty, Abu-Lughod suggests, "the world lost the key link" that had connected the three routes; the ensuing "repercussions of this disjunction at the eastern end of the world system were felt throughout the trading world."[8] The historian Scott C. Levi remarks, "To those attuned to such things, the feverish trade and economic vitality of the Mongol era must have seemed an unstoppable force, even as the Mongol Empire itself fragmented …. But within a few years [in the aftermath of the bubonic plague] all seemed lost."[9]

And as if all that were not a sufficient dose of misery, nature itself "joined the conspiracy," as Richard Smith memorably puts it. The first stages of what is often called the Little Ice Age occasioned "sporadic crop failures in the fourteenth century" and brought about "a low in temperature in the fifteenth century."[10] The Little Ice Age, which would last through the eighteenth century, had a devastating impact on Eurasia's agriculture. The result of this mélange of disasters – not to speak yet of more localized political crises – was appalling. Only one century in human history seems to show an overall decline in global population: While the world total for

1300 is estimated at 431 million people, a century later it would be reduced to about 375 million.[11]

Eurasia would recover, but with that recovery would come a reconfiguration. Indeed, recovery and reconfiguration would be the main historical forces that stimulated Eurasia's soon-to-come wave of theatrical change. Populations rebounded, but new hierarchies, technologies, and ideologies would change the way those populations lived and thought. International commerce resumed, but it would be based on a newly important medium of exchange and take place on a hitherto unimaginable scale. Towns and cities were repopulated, but they would quickly be joined by countless *new* towns and cities that spread urban wealth far more widely than ever before. "Ironically," writes the historian Peter Frankopan, the disasters that befell Eurasia in the fourteenth century "often served as a catalyst to long-term growth."[12] Concurrently, powerful new governments invested in roads, caravansaries, canals, and ports, while providing sufficient social order to allow for the flourishing of commerce. The establishment of these governments, suggests the historian Jack A. Goldstone, "meant a growth in the ranks of officials, as well as the printers and booksellers, proprietors of shops and cafes, and artisans who served the burgeoning commercial and official classes." Eurasia, in brief, became "a much more populated, more urbanized, centrally ruled and administered place, with vastly expanded local, regional and international trade fueling the desire for goods and stimulating new ideas."[13] Among those new ideas would be new forms of theatre that could satisfy the audiences brought into existence by the Eurasian resurgence.

Even as all this was taking place, Western Europeans were reaching out to the broader world with their so-called voyages of discovery, stimulated in large part by a desire to gain direct access to the fabled riches of "the East" and cut out the northern Italian cities that had grown wealthy as the middlemen for that trade.[14] In 1488, Bartholomew Dias sailed around the southern cape of Africa into the Indian Ocean; his crew then refused to go any further, so it fell to Vasco da Gama, some ten years later, to be the first European to reach India by that route. He and his successors (at first fellow Portuguese, then also Dutch, English, and French) entered well-established Asian trading networks, but their sturdy galleons, armed with ranks of cannon, allowed for an unequaled projection of power. "The new European approach to trade-cum-plunder," writes Abu-Lughod, would eventually bring about "a basic transformation in the world system that had developed and persisted for some five centuries."[15]

At roughly the same time as Dias and da Gama, Christopher Columbus sailed west under the banner of Spain but with the same ambition of tapping directly into Asian riches. He failed because he grossly underestimated the circumference of the world – but his stumbling into the Americas was profoundly consequential. It initiated what the historian Alfred W. Crosby, Jr., calls the "Columbian Exchange": the transfer between the Old and New Worlds of plants, animals, diseases, and human populations.[16] The impact of the transfers *to* the Americas was almost immediate. A devastating plague in Mexico, for example, was as important to Hernando Cortez's conquest of the Aztec Empire as were his guns, courage, and duplicity. In the long term, the numerous Eurasian diseases brought to the Americas would lead to a horrific decline in the Amerindian population, easing the way for subsequent European settlers who would thrive on the Eurasian crops and livestock they brought with them.

The transfers *from* the Americas were less dramatic but no less important. The historian Ian Morris observes that New World crops such as maize (corn), white and sweet potatoes, and peanuts "grew where nothing else would, survived wretched weather [during the Little Ice Age], and fattened farmers and their animals wonderfully. Across the sixteenth century millions of acres of them were planted, from Ireland to the Yellow River."[17] Together, these crops (and later, tomatoes as well) allowed Eurasia not only to compensate for the ongoing "wretched weather" but also to support a far larger population than ever before. The environmental historian Robert B. Marks goes as far as to suggest that "much of early modern history turned" around the Columbian Exchange. He ranks it among the three most significant events in the long history of "the ways in which humans related to the natural world," after only the neolithic origins of agriculture and the nineteenth-century Industrial Revolution.[18]

European conquests in the Americas also made possible the expropriation of vast material wealth, most immediately of silver, which gave Europeans something highly desirable to trade in Asian markets; the historian Andre Gundar Frank suggests that Europeans used it to buy "a seat on the Asian [economic] train."[19] Within a few generations, however, European-owned sugar, tobacco, indigo, and cotton plantations in the Americas – worked almost entirely by millions of enslaved Africans – would further enrich Europe. An age of interregional, indeed truly global, activity had begun, and it changed the theatre in every society that it touched.

CHAPTER 8

Okuni's Crucifix

An Age of Conflict and Change

Details about the life of Izumo no Okuni are scarce. The dates of her birth and death are matters of speculation. Her father is said to have been a blacksmith, her mother possibly a temple priestess. What *is* known is that around the start of the seventeenth century, Okuni and her small troupe of actors gathered audiences in a dry riverbed in Kyoto and presented shows that conventionally mark the origin of *kabuki*.[1] This was toward the end of the wave of Eurasian theatrical change that had begun roughly a hundred years earlier, but the emergence of *kabuki* (and, along with it, the puppet theatre now known as *bunraku*) was in many ways paradigmatic of that wave. Societal change is inevitably idiosyncratic, but surging populations, technological improvements, fast-growing towns and cities, and expanding commerce – often abetted by powerful new regimes imposing sociopolitical stability – stimulated theatrical innovation across Eurasia. In Japan, all these elements were present when Okuni began performing.

The very word "*kabuki*" suggests the nature of Okuni's shows. Its earliest meaning was something like "to slant" or "to incline," but by Okuni's time, it meant "to speak or act in an ostentatious, antisocial, eccentric, or erotic manner" and was associated with the *kabukimono*: people engaged in deviant and outrageous behavior.[2] Before long, the word *kabuki* would be written with three kanji characters: *ka* ("song"), *bu* ("dance"), and *ki* ("prostitute"), the last of which would eventually be changed so that the meaning of *ki* became "skill."[3] The shifting meaning of the word *kabuki* offers, in effect, a synopsis of the form's first hundred years: It began as a radical affront to society, gained an almost immediate association with prostitution, and then eventually was recognized as a respectable theatre art.

Okuni's troupe was popular precisely because of the outrageousness of its performances. Its dances were perhaps derived from temple performance,[4] but the public was titillated by Okuni's sexualized interpretations of them. No less titillating were the troupe's dramatic sketches, which often centered on scenes of *samurai* procuring courtesans, with Okuni sometimes playing the male role, sometimes the female.[5] By 1610, after Okuni led her troupe on a tour that included Edo (now Tokyo), "kabuki fever was sweeping the country and numerous troupes sprang up to capitalize on the craze." As it happens, "nearly all of the imitators featured performances by prostitutes" who offered theatre by day and sex by night – no doubt an important factor in the popularity of the form.[6] Julie A. Iezzi observes, "The erotic dances, brothel scenes, noh parodies, references to contemporary events, and cross-gendered performances at the core of Okuni's kabuki remained central in prostitute's kabuki."[7] The outrages of *kabuki* did not, of course, please everyone. As one disgusted scholar wrote at the time, "The men wear women's clothing; the women wear men's clothing …. They sing base songs and dance vulgar dances; their lewd voices are clamorous." Despite such complaints, though, another contemporary noted that among the "many different things that are popular in Edo now, there is nothing to compare with the *kabuki* women."[8]

Okuni herself warrants a closer look (see Figure 8.1). It was not shocking for women in Japan to be public performers, for all-female troupes had long existed in *sarugaku* and a few other theatre forms.[9] What *was* shocking was Okuni's self-presentation: "Her androgynous hairstyle – cropped short, tied high on the head – [was] popular among the 'deviant' kabuki-mono [and] suited her portrayal of young sword-carrying samurai going to teahouses … to hire prostitutes." Moreover, Okuni accessorized herself with a large crucifix,[10] which certainly captures one's attention. How could Okuni have possessed such an item and why would she choose to wear it while performing? More broadly, what had been happening in Japan over the previous century-plus that would allow a sexualized performance that included the crucifix to be so profoundly appealing to audiences?

Japan was an anomaly in the broader Eurasian context because it suffered relatively little from the post-Mongolian decline of trade and even less from the bubonic plague. But it *had* suffered a commensurate set of miseries, brought on by nearly a hundred and fifty years of internal warfare, known as *Sengoku* ("The Age of Warring States"). The historian Marius B. Jansen relates that this unhappy age began in 1467, when "political order disintegrated almost totally after a shogunal succession dispute split the warrior leaders." Over the ensuing seventy-five years of near-continuous struggle, would-be *shōguns* "fought themselves to a standstill at the center" of power.[11]

An Age of Conflict and Change

Figure 8.1 *Kabuki*: an early performer, often claimed to be Okuni. Detail from a seventeenth-century painting (artist unknown). (History and Art Collection/ Alamy Stock Photo)

The standstill was broken in 1543, after a few Portuguese traders, passengers on a Chinese junk, landed in Japan. They carried with them gunpowder weapons (specifically, arquebuses) unknown in Japan. Japanese artisans got hold of the weapons and "speedily copied, improved, and produced" them in such numbers that they "transformed warfare and became the instrument of the unification of Japan."[12] Oda Nobunaga, one of the contestants for power, armed his men with thousands of these firearms and by the time of his death (in 1582) had gained mastery over about one-third of Japan.[13] His successor, Toyotomi Hideyoshi, "continued and completed the military unification of Japan" by 1590. Hideyoshi's rule "marked a culminating stage in the transformation of Japanese institutions" as he subordinated the far-flung *daimyō* to his direct authority while also transforming most *samurai* into a standing army, leaving the rest stranded without masters.[14] And yet Japan's time of trials was not yet ended, for upon Hideyoshi's death in 1598, a succession struggle ensued. The victor was Tokugawa Ieyasu, the third of the great "unifiers" of Japan.[15] In 1603 he became *shōgun*, establishing the dynasty that would bear his family name for the next two and a half centuries.

Through these long years of warfare, *nō* remained relatively secure in its niche among the warrior aristocracy. As urban life began to flourish in the late sixteenth century, a few *nō* troupes tentatively sought out a broader audience with a fresh repertoire of plays that emphasized "conflict and characterization,"[16] but the newer theatre forms that were soon to emerge – *kabuki* and *bunraku* – spoke far more directly to paying audiences composed primarily of townsfolk and *samurai*. *Nō* retreated to the safety of its existing niche, where it would endure until the end of the Tokugawa regime itself.

The turmoil of the Age of Warring States obscures the influence on Japan of the broad recovery already taking place elsewhere in Eurasia. The most immediate consequence of that influence had been the introduction of firearms by the Portuguese traders. But these traders were soon followed by others, coming from Portuguese bases in China and Malaysia. And then in 1549 came Jesuit priests.[17] Oda Nobunaga accepted their presence because they shared with him a hatred of Buddhist monks.[18] His successor, Toyotomi Hideyoshi, was at first also tolerant but later came to see them as the leading-edge of European power; he banished the Jesuits in 1587 and ordered a general persecution of Japanese Christians in 1597.[19] The crucifix that Okuni wore in her performances a few years later was symbolic of an alien and now-despised religion. As such, wearing it in public performances was a gratuitous insult to authority, much in keeping with the generally subversive ethos of early *kabuki*.

The resumption of Japanese trade with China was an even more important consequence of the Eurasian resurgence. In the late fifteenth and early sixteenth centuries, this trade had been conducted primarily on an extralegal basis, by so-called pirates. But China was "develop[ing] an 'insatiable appetite'" for the silver coming not only from the Americas but also from new Japanese mines, and so the piracy was tolerated. When China fully relegalized overseas trade in 1567, it resolved the piracy issue while also enriching the *shōgun*, who controlled the Japanese silver mines.[20] Thenceforth, Japan would cautiously limit European access to its markets, but "Japanese and other merchants could travel freely to Chinese and Southeast Asia ports," further enmeshing Japan in the expanding network of Eurasian commerce.[21]

With that enmeshment came urbanization. This process "began from a low base" because the Age of Warring States had weighed heavily on cities.[22] But Chinese-originated technologies brought about an agricultural "revolution" that doubled the extent of rice paddies and allowed for the growth of urban populations. Three cities served as the "major nodes in an urban system or network" that came to include many lesser Japanese cities and towns.²³ The imperial city of Kyoto was both a commercial center and a locus of Buddhist pilgrimage. Even as the city's artisans poured out an endless flow of luxury goods, "its streets were crowded with samurai, priests, acolytes, students and pilgrims."²⁴ The port city of Osaka, meanwhile, "became the center of the Japanese economy," with "lords from all parts of Japan" shipping their surplus rice to a "national commodities market" established there. Osaka's moats "were lined with warehouses" owned by merchants, run by managers, and manned by hordes of laborers.²⁵

Edo was the third and newest of Japan's leading cities. When Tokugawa Ieyasu chose it as headquarters for his *bakufu*, it was little more than a "sleepy, historic area," but within a hundred years it would be home to more than half a million people.²⁶ As the fast-growing city became the country's administrative center, it also became a center of consumption, driven in part by the new requirement that the *daimyō* (with their substantial retinues) live in Edo every alternate year,²⁷ in part by the numerous *samurai* who swarmed to the city, being either attached to the *bakufu* or newly without masters.²⁸ All these potential consumers needed goods to consume, and so "the food, clothing and building trades all flourished [as] artisans, shopkeepers and merchants naturally followed their potential customers to the city."²⁹

A "Floating World" of Entertainment

In brief, then, Japan's three major cities all developed substantial middling classes. The people of these classes of course wanted entertainment – and had the coins to pay for it. To satisfy their wants, the *bakufu* established "pleasure quarters" in each city: the Yoshiwara quarter in Edo, the Shimabara in Kyoto, and the Shinmachi in Osaka. The generic term for these quarters was *ukiyo* (literally, "floating world").³⁰ The middling classes that thronged to the *ukiyo* would be at the heart of Japanese theatre's efflorescence – and Izumo no Okuni would be among the earliest of theatre artists to capture their attention. Her *kabuki* was "an immediate success" not only with townsmen but perhaps even more with the *samurai* who "craved abandoned entertainment."³¹ As the form developed, its theatres would be built in the pleasure quarters, alongside numerous teahouses that provided food, drink, and prostitutes – practitioners of "the floating trade." Although the pleasure quarters were officially off-limits to *samurai*, a minimal disguise sufficed to avoid trouble; for all others, suggests Benito

Ortolani, the pleasure quarters served as "an island where social distinction did not count and only cash decided the issues."[32]

In 1629, the *bakufu* began issuing decrees to halt performances of women's *kabuki*. It was not motivated by a concern for public morality, for prostitution was legal in the pleasure quarters. Instead, it was responding to riots by audience members who hoped to secure the favors of the most appealing performers.[33] As a result of these decrees, troupes of young men became dominant; as with the women before them, they engaged in prostitution as well as in theatre. The young men's *kabuki* was itself first banned in 1652, again because of riots for the favors of the performers. Given all this rioting, one might wonder why the *bakufu* even tolerated *kabuki*. Apparently, it saw *kabuki* and prostitution – for they were deeply conjoined in these years – as a "necessary evil." Donald. H. Shively suggests, "These were the two wheels of the vehicle of pleasure, useful to assuage the people and divert them from more serious mischief." No doubt they "constituted social problems," but if suppressed, "more serious social, if not criminal, results would follow." The *bakufu* therefore accepted these activities while limiting them to the pleasure quarters "so that society as a whole would not be contaminated."[34] But public disorder, even in the pleasure quarters, was another matter entirely and demanded governmental response.

The bans on *kabuki* performed by women and young men left only mature men to perform. Even though the younger members of the men's troupes still engaged in prostitution, audiences became more attentive to the men's dramatic talents.[35] This led the troupes to look with envy to the *bunraku* puppet theatre that was developing at the same time (and to which I will return shortly). They learned from it "that sexy performers were not necessary to turn a profit – it was exciting drama that was attracting crowds to the puppet theatre."[36] Fuller dramatic development provided a way for the men's *kabuki* troupes to demonstrate their acting ability and compete for public favor in the newly developing niche for urban commercial theatre.

By the end of the seventeenth century, *kabuki* had established many traits that are still often maintained. Two styles of acting for the male leads predominated. First was *aragoto* ("rough style"), a hypermasculine performance that appealed not only to *samurai* but also to townsmen who fantasized about *samurai* power. *Aragoto* characters could fend off multiple enemies in a single fight, but according to a contemporaneous account, their routines also included "smashing gates, tearing tigers to shreds, ripping off enemies' heads, pulling huge trees up from the roots," and so on.[37] The second style for male leads was *wagoto* ("gentle style"), a far more romantic performance that appealed especially to the townswomen who attended *kabuki* no less avidly than the townsmen. *Wagoto* characters could be either *samurai* or townsmen and were often portrayed in scenes of visiting brothels – a reminder of the sort of performance that Okuni had given. More importantly, though, the *wagoto* men were willing to sacrifice themselves for the women they loved, even when those women were prostitutes.[38] The female characters in all *kabuki* plays were enacted by *onnagata*, the younger men of the troupe who cross-dressed for their roles. *Onnagata* actors did not burlesque femininity, but neither were they especially concerned with imitating real-world women. Stanca Scholz-Cionca and Nanako Nakajima write that "*onnagata* displayed an abstract femininity shaped by a male imagination that transcended borders of age and biological determination, marking the epitome of accomplishment in acting."[39] Only toward the end of the nineteenth century would women once again begin enacting female characters in *kabuki*.

The puppet theatre from which *kabuki* learned the importance of exciting drama is commonly known as *bunraku*, although that name is anachronistic.[40] The origins of puppetry in Japan are obscure, but puppet shows are clearly attested to as early as the eleventh century.[41] Their appeal waxed and waned through subsequent centuries, but during the tumultuous Age of Warring States, interest was again on the upswing,[42] perhaps because an entire show could be transported and performed by a single actor. Puppetry, though, is only one of the three basic components of *bunraku*. The second is the text recited by an onstage narrator who, in effect, carried on an established tradition of storytelling. A fifteenth-century romance called *The Tale in Twelve Episodes of Jōruri* was especially beloved; by the end of the sixteenth century, the term *jōruri* designated not only this tale but an entire storytelling tradition. An early name for *bunraku* was *ningyō-jōruri* ("human form" *jōruri*), which suggests the importance of these stories to the development of the form.[43] The third component of *bunraku* is the musical accompaniment played on the shamisen, a three-stringed instrument introduced (perhaps via Korea) from China in the 1560s. First praised for its novelty, its "expressive qualities" became essential to the form, with the instrument's "sharp, almost percussive [plucked] notes [being] ideally suited to guide the narrator in his delivery and the operators in maneuvering the puppets."[44]

No one can say precisely when the three components of *bunraku* were first brought together, but some now-unknown performers likely struck an alliance slightly before 1600.[45] The resulting shows were obviously satisfactory because other performers quickly followed suit. Although *bunraku* competed with *kabuki* for the same popular audience, its appeal was quite different, at least in its early years. The "live" form gloried in being licentious, while the puppet form emphasized the enactment of dramatic stories. These centered at first on heroes of history or legend, but other stories came to focus on townsfolk themselves, broadening the form's appeal by catering to different portions of its audience. Whatever the social status of the characters, a recurring theme in *bunraku* plays was the conflict between *giri* (social obligation or duty) and *ninjō* (personal human feelings).[46] In Chikamatsu Monzaemon's *The Battles of Coxinga* (1715), for example, a *samurai* has such a strong sense of duty that he kills his own son to save the emperor's child; in his *The Love Suicides at Amijima* (1721), a townsman and a prostitute are so desperately in love that they abandon their families to commit a double suicide.

Kabuki and *bunraku* would compete for public favor through much of the Tokugawa era. A 1681 map of Edo shows thirteen theatres crammed into a four-block area, with four *kabuki* theatres and six *bunraku* theatres, along with three variety theatres, all vying "for the same customers."[47] The competition between the two forms led them to shamelessly adapt whatever traits of the other might seem desirable. More than half of *kabuki*'s major plays were originally written for *bunraku*, thereby introducing into *kabuki* the narrator and shamisen music of the puppet theatre.[48] Conversely, early *bunraku* puppets were without functional arms or legs and were each operated by a single person. But by the eighteenth century, the puppets were becoming much more like *kabuki* actors, large enough to have fully functioning limbs and to require three men to operate each major puppet.[49]

A fascinating irony underlies the conjoined histories of these theatre forms. *Kabuki* reached its maturity only because a series of governmental decrees inadvertently led it to become more like the story-driven puppet theatre. *Bunraku*, meanwhile, would attain its status as one of the world's most admired forms of puppetry only because commercial competition encouraged it to use puppets that looked and moved like the men who performed *kabuki*. But by the late eighteenth century, the puppet theatre was clearly in decline.[50] Given the similarities that had developed in the two forms' narratives and artistic styles, one cannot help but think that the lively human presence of the *kabuki* actors made a critical difference. *Kabuki* had come a long way from Okuni's outrageousness, but the fundamental appeal of directly watching other people perform remained a constant throughout its history.

CHAPTER 9

Islamic Empires

The Legacy of Tamerlane

Timur the Lame, more commonly known as Tamerlane, was born either too late or too early; or perhaps he was just too impatient. He was "too late" because although he was a Mongol prince who claimed a distant relationship to Chinggis Khan, his birth in 1336 had him reaching maturity after the Mongol Empire had already fractured; he was "too early" because his death in 1405 did not allow his attempt to rebuild that empire to benefit from Eurasia's general recovery in the aftermath of the bubonic plague and the collapse of trade. And he was "too impatient" because he proved more interested in brutally conquering his empire than in effectively ruling it. The historian John Darwin remarks that "despite his ferocity, his military genius, and his shrewd adaptation of tribal politics to his imperial purpose, Tamerlane's system fell apart at his death."[1] His capital at Samarkand was glorified with brilliant architecture paid for by the spoils of incessant conquest; elsewhere, he left little more than a trail of terror and destruction.

In his wake, however, three Islamic dynasties carved out far more successful empires that would together span from Hungary and Algeria to beyond the delta of the Ganges River. The westernmost of these empires was the Ottoman, the easternmost was the Mughal; in the middle was the Safavid Empire in Iran. Much of the growth of these empires came between 1450 and 1650, as Eurasia recovered from the disastrous fourteenth century; they thrived as rebounding populations and the revival of commerce provided manpower and wealth. Ayşe Zarakol, a scholar of International Relations, explicitly identifies all three as "Post-Timurid empires" that (each in its own way) combined the Mongol tradition of sovereignty with a new Islamic identity;[2] they all relied on Mongol-derived military and logistical structures, while also being early adopters of gunpowder weaponry.[3] In contrast to Tamerlane's efforts, Marshall G. S. Hodgson writes, they were notable "not only for the extent and durability of their empires but also for the effectiveness of their absolutist rule."[4]

Despite the similarities between the three empires, however, the theatre forms that would emerge in them were quite different, for each empire had its own distinctive societal and theatrical contexts. They apparently shared a tradition of improvisational comedy. But beyond that, Ottoman theatre was dominated by the *karagöz* shadow theatre that emerged in the conquered Byzantine capital of Constantinople/Istanbul. Safavid Iran, newly converted to the Shiite branch of Islam, saw the lively development of religious storytelling and processional theatre, which would come together in the devotional form of *taʿziyeh*. Mughal India provided the richest harvest of new theatre forms, although South Asian theatrical innovation also took place in areas beyond Mughal control.

The Ottomans

The seed of the Ottoman Empire was a rural Turkic principality in northwestern Anatolia that gained its wealth by attacking the more urbanized lands nearby, especially in the aftermath of the two mid fourteenth-century crises. The historian Jerry H. Bentley writes that "famine, disease, and military casualties reduced the Christian population" in Anatolia, especially in the Byzantine trading cities on the coast; "many survivors fled before Turkish invaders; others fell captive and went into slavery."[5] By 1390, long-developing weaknesses in Byzantine control also opened the Balkans to the Ottomans.[6] The most notable setback to early Ottoman growth was defeat at the hands of Tamerlane in 1402, but the conqueror's failure to organize his conquests gave the Ottomans a critical reprieve; barely a decade later they had regained control of their nascent empire.[7] However much the Ottomans learned from Tamerlane, they were not to be ruled by him.

The most tempting target for the Ottomans was the Byzantine capital itself, which was ripe for the taking. Its decline had begun as early as 1204, when Western European participants in the Fourth Crusade made a deal with the Venetian merchants who provided them with ships: Before sailing to the Holy Land, they would *first* conquer Constantinople. After the Crusaders successfully assaulted the city – by far the wealthiest Christian city in the world – they never bothered to sail onward but returned home with their plunder. The Venetian merchants, for their part, established a Latin-ruled kingdom in the fallen city.[8] Even though Byzantine emperors eventually regained political control, the die had been cast. The Ottomans progressively stripped Constantinople of its imperial holdings even as the Italian merchants reduced the city to little more than a commercial entrepôt. Constantinople was then crippled by losses from the plague and the collapse of its overland trade with China. When the Ottomans finally attacked in 1453, only 7,000 able-bodied men remained in the city to fight.[9] The Ottoman army, 80,000 men strong, breached the city's walls thanks to clever tactics and the unprecedented use of gunpowder artillery,[10] then rampaged through Constantinople for three days. A contemporaneous (though perhaps sycophantic) account says that when the Ottoman sultan, Mehmed II, saw "the wholesale ruin of the city … tears fell from his eyes as he groaned deeply and compassionately, 'What a city we have given over to plunder and destruction!'"[11]

Mehmed II had long "seen himself as the heir to the classical Roman Empire and its Christian successor," writes the historian Lord Kinross. "Now his conquest of Constantinople confirmed him as such."[12] His "most imperative task was the rebirth" of the city, now renamed Istanbul. He immediately set about repopulating it with Christians and Muslims alike, bringing in "men of means, merchants, and artisans … to assist [in its] commercial and industrial development." Istanbul then continued to attract immigrants from all parts of the empire, so that within decades it "was once more a flourishing city of workshops and bazaars." By the end of the sixteenth century, it would be home to half a million inhabitants, more populous than any European city to its west.[13] And Ottoman conquests were not yet done. Within the next 100 years, they would double their empire's territory in Europe and gain control of North Africa, Arabia, and (for a while) Mesopotamia. The Byzantine Empire was, in effect, restored and even expanded, but also reconfigured as an Islamic empire.

Probably the most salient point in the societal context of the *karagöz* shadow theatre is that the Ottoman Empire was, indeed, an empire; Istanbul, as that empire's capital, had ample middling classes in regular contact with people from throughout the realm.[14] Nothing better illustrates this context than the cast of characters who regularly appeared in *karagöz* plays. The lead character is Karagöz ("black eye") himself, a "typical Turk" who "uses the language of the common people" but is "impulsive … in speech and behavior" and is little respected by others. Although always getting into trouble, he has an instinctive sense of morality that allows the audience to empathize with him despite his many flaws, the most striking of which is his uncontrollable phallus. Hacivat is Karagöz's neighbor and comic foil. He is "loquacious, credulous, and good-natured," but a font of superficial knowledge who apes "the moral principles of the upper class" to which he futilely aspires. As such, Karagöz never misses an opportunity to insult or assault him.[15] Around these two revolve a standard set of urban characters: an educated young man "whose love for a courtesan or a girl of good family" often motivates the dramatic action; an opium addict with the "bad habit of … falling asleep in the middle of a conversation"; a drunkard who brags of his strength but is fearful of fighting; a neighborhood "idiot" who "always arrives at the wrong time and is extremely difficult to get rid of"; and an array of women who are typically "flighty and given to intrigue."[16]

Many ethnically differentiated characters also regularly appear in *karagöz*, testimony to Istanbul's cosmopolitan nature. These characters, almost always the butts of humor, include a slow-witted Anatolian obsessed with his sweetheart back home; a boatman with "a strong Black Sea Coast accent" who talks too much to listen to others; an immigrant from the Balkans who is "proud of his wrestling abilities but actually loses his bouts"; a Kurd whose conversation is largely unintelligible; a Persian trader "in shawls, carpets and women's dresses" who exaggerates the limited profits of his trading; an Arab merchant or traveler "whose conversation consists merely of repetitive questions"; a foolish Albanian with an absurd accent; a European who is "a coward and unlikeable character"; a dour and ignorant Armenian; and a "malicious and vulgar" Jew who "is either a money lender, a second hand dealer, or a peddler."[17] These characters are all gross (and perhaps grotesque) stereotypes, but they suggest how the Turks of Istanbul viewed the many peoples of their multiethnic city.

The venues and performance occasions for *karagöz* were also deeply embedded in the form's societal context. While sometimes performed for the elite (indeed, even for the sultan) to celebrate auspicious events such as marriages and circumcisions,[18] *karagöz* was typically performed in coffeehouses, which by the sixteenth century had become popular in Istanbul and were seen as "a particular[ly] civilized feature of urban life."[19] A favorite occasion for these coffeehouse performances was the Islamic holy month of Ramadan,[20] which meant that any respectable puppet master needed at least twenty-eight different plays to keep the regular customers coming back each night.[21] *Karagöz* had no relationship to the religious rituals of the month, but the popularity of the coffeehouses at the end of each day's fast provided a ready-made audience for a theatre of social satire. Sabri Esat Siyavusgil suggests that the shadow screen presents "nothing other than one of the old *mahalles* (quarters) of Istanbul," with all its dramas transformed into comedy.[22]

The origins of *karagöz* are, one might say, rather shadowy. An oft-told story has it that when the Ottomans conquered Egypt in 1517, Sultan Selim

I ordered the Mameluke sultan to be hanged, but the rope broke twice. Afterward, Selim watched a shadow show that reenacted the hanging and made great comedy of the breaking rope. He was so pleased that he invited the puppeteer to perform in Istanbul for his son, thus beginning a traffic of Egyptian puppeteers to the imperial capital.[23] This story has limited bearing on *karagöz* as a theatre form, lacking any mention of its defining characters or typical narratives, but the idea of an Egyptian influence on *karagöz* is almost certainly correct. *Karagöz* puppets are controlled from behind, with the main control rod held perpendicular to the shadow screen, against which the puppets are pressed. This same kind of control existed in *khayāl al-zill*, the shadow theatre we have already encountered in Egypt. It is, however, fundamentally different than in shadow puppetry farther to the east, where the main rod is generally held upright from below the puppet. Metin And, the leading historian of Turkish theatre, plausibly concludes that "Turkish shadow theatre appears to be the product of a historical process whereby Mameluke-derived shadow play technique was taken over by Turks from a technical point of view" and then combined with native Turkish theatrical traditions of puppetry and live performance. By the start of the seventeenth century, And suggests, the various "elements" that would go into the form had "merged and fused," and *karagöz* "was fully identified."[24]

Karagöz eventually spread through much of the Ottoman Empire. The most well-studied location is Greece, where the form was first noted in 1799, though it likely had arrived somewhat earlier.[25] Originally a straight transference of *karagöz*, performed in Turkish for the Turkish ruling class, a Greek subform developed during the nineteenth century. By the end of that century, a thoroughly domesticated form called *karaghiózis* had emerged, performed in Greek for Greek audiences on Greek holidays.[26] *Karagöz* also spread to Turkish-ruled Egypt, Algeria, Tunisia, Morocco, Syria, Iran, and Bosnia-Herzegovina,[27] spawning an entire family of homologous theatre forms.

I mentioned earlier that all three of the Islamic empires had traditions of improvisatory comic theatre; in the Ottoman Empire, the relevant theatre form is *orta-oyunu*. The first scraps of evidence about its history come from the late seventeenth century, although Metin And suggests that it had developed from earlier kinds of live comic performance. He also observes that "anyone who has ever seen a [*karagöz*] shadow play notices immediately the similarity in characters, comic elements, and atmosphere" to *orta-oyunu*. Both forms were, at their core, social satires centered on a contrasting pair of comic characters.[28] The most obvious difference between the forms is that *orta-oyunu* was performed live rather than with puppets. Beyond that, the troupes of *orta-oyunu* were entirely male, with the men who played female roles using the gender incongruity for comic effect. Also, *orta-oyunu* was performed in the middle of its audience, with the form's name literally meaning "play-in-the-middle."[29] Interestingly, *karagöz* was the more respectable of the two forms, likely owing to the Islamic Sufi mysticism that saw shadow puppetry as a metaphor for Allah's control over human fates. As an Anatolian poet wrote: "Wise man seeking for the truth / Look up at the tent of the sky / Where the Great Showman of the World / Has long ago set up his Shadow Theatre. / Behind his screen he is giving a show / Played by the shadows of men and women of his creations."[30]

The Safavids

While the Ottomans had been able to reconstitute and expand their empire after a brief conquest by Tamerlane, Safavid Iran was built on what were essentially the ruins of Tamerlane's own short-lived empire. His successors' rule in Iran had collapsed in the mid fifteenth century, to be followed by a pair of even shorter-lived dynasties.[31] Lasting order was finally established by the founder of the Safavid Dynasty, Shah Ismail I (r. 1501–1524), who was inspired by a "messianic spirit" that "had its pendant in the religious mood of the people" – a mixture of Sunni and Shiite Muslims beset by "war, anarchy, bandits, catastrophes, plagues and famine" that gave rise to widely shared apocalyptic expectations.[32] Ismail rode a wave of "religious fanaticism" and established a Shiite theocratic state in 1502.[33] Upon gaining power, he began redeveloping trade routes through a network of caravanserais that (along with other measures) "invigorated trade and industry, so that the broad masses of the population also found that their standard of living was at first improved and ultimately reached a level never known up to that time."[34] The greatest glory of Safavid rule would come a century later, after Shah Abbas I (r. 1588–1629) moved the capital to Isfahan, where he encouraged the development of arts and literature. Notably, "the prosperity which the court blazoned over the face of [the capital] was not restricted to the court" or even to merchants and craftsmen: "Even the peasants seem to have lived, in some parts, substantially above the level of sheer subsistence."[35]

The combination of political order, religious enthusiasm, and renewed prosperity would prove potent: "The historical achievement of the Safavids," writes the historian H. R. Roemer, "was [to] establish a strong,

The Safavids

enduring state in Iran after centuries of foreign rule and a lengthy period of political fragmentation."³⁶ The official Shiism that Ismail established is of particular interest here because it would prove central to the theatre form most often associated with Iran: *taʿziyeh*.

As mentioned in Chapter 2, *taʿziyeh* is a form of devotional theatre.³⁷ Through cycles of up to fifty or more short plays, it relates the martyrdom of Husain (sometimes transliterated as Hussein or Husayn) during the Battle of Karbala (see Figure 9.1). Jamshid Malekpour writes that "a key element in understanding the philosophy of [both Shiism and *taʿziyeh*] is *shuhadat*, or 'martyrdom.' What drives the characters toward their tragic destiny in every play ... is *shuhadat*." Husain and his followers went to battle against the Sunni powers specifically "to be martyred in order to protect the basis of Islam." Husain's inevitable death when facing overwhelming odds "makes him a living symbol or role model for those who are in search of truth and justice in this world."³⁸

Taʿziyeh has a long prehistory in Iran. Although one need not agree with Malekpour that this prehistory can be traced back as far as the mourning rituals of ancient Persia and Egypt,³⁹ the tragic story of the pre-Islamic hero Siyavush (sometimes transliterated as Siyavash) certainly

Figure 9.1 *Taʿziyeh*: a contemporary performance at an arena theatre in Yazd, enacting the burning of the tents during the Battle of Karbala. (Photo by Bertrand Linet via Getty Images)

seems relevant. Stripped of its original Zoroastrian context, the story was recorded by Islamic historians and given a literary rendition in the poet Ferdowsi's great epic, *The Shāhnāmeh*.[40] Along with related stories, it became part of an "epic storytelling tradition" that was "very strong in pre-Islamic Iran [and] continued to be so after the Islamization of the country."[41] Certain details of Siyavush's story offer fascinating parallels to that of Husain. Most notably, the hero has foreknowledge of the inevitable suffering that awaits him and his family but does not hesitate to meet his destiny.[42] In both stories, the tragic fates of the heroes are emphasized explicitly to evoke the audience's empathetic connection to the hero. The story of Siyavush, one might say, predisposed Iranians to be responsive to that of Husain, even as the storytelling tradition associated with it was carried on in Shiite storytelling.[43]

Iran's tradition of storytelling, suggests Malekpour, provided the "first step toward the dramatization" of the story of Husain's martyrdom. Around the start of the Safavid Empire, with Shiism now the state religion, poets "unified all the elements of the Karbala [story] in an epic narrative structure that enabled each event to be presented independently while still maintaining a clear connection with the events of the Karbala cycle as a whole." At first, storytellers recited this work as an act of devotion, but public demand led to some performances becoming "commercial enterprises as well as religious events." Whether amateur or professional, the storytellers "not only narrated the stories, but acted them out. In their performances, they embodied the characters in a way that enabled the audience to see them and to empathize with them. This performance style of storytelling had a powerful influence on the Ta'ziyeh," especially "on the manner in which [it] was to be acted."[44]

Driving the storytellers was the desire to make the story of Husain's martyrdom emotionally compelling, and the best of them certainly succeeded. After their performances, audiences streamed into the streets, "singing and beating their chests" in mourning.[45] These informal processions themselves sometimes became semiprofessional, with mourners performing their sorrows while collecting alms from onlookers.[46] Perhaps this helped to stimulate the increasing elaboration of the processions, which came to include "symbolic theatrical properties such as the coffins of the martyrs, flags, banners, and animals such as lions and horses"; in time, the processions also included "actors impersonating the central characters of the Karbala story."[47] These performers usually enacted *tableaux vivants*, staged on processional floats, though in some cases they went so far as "playing episodes of the Karbala drama."[48]

None of this, writes Willem Floor, was "a conscious development, but a gradual evolution that coalesced around 1700 and thereafter grew into the passion play over the next decades."[49] Although the actors in *taʿziyeh* were sometimes professional (especially in the cities), they sought "to communicate to the public the [religious] emotion that filled them."[50] At crucial moments in the plays, the audience responded to the action "as if on cue," beating their breasts and producing "tears of sorrow" that evidenced their "oneness with the historical events being portrayed."[51] The Shiite religious authorities, interestingly, "strongly disapproved of this populist orgiastic outburst, which in their view made a spectacle of the Imams' lives." They were, however, largely powerless to stop it, for *taʿziyeh* was "idolized by the public."[52] It became the ultimate theatrical expression of Iranian Shiism.

Iran has also long hosted a form of improvisatory comic theatre, now usually called *ru-howzi*. Unfortunately, notes William O. Beeman, "it is only through the barest of clues that we can piece together a few guesses" at its history.[53] He suggests, however, that it reached "a point of rapid development during the Safavid era," when it was usually referred to as *taqlid* ("imitation") or *tamasha* ("comedy").[54] Its characteristics in its early years are largely unknown, but Beeman is willing to assert that "the *taqlid* form is in all essentials the same basic improvisatory comic theatrical form seen in Iran today."[55]

A few of *ru-howzi*'s basic traits stand out. First, it is an improvised social satire that "mocks and attacks the whole fabric of social and sexual structures which bind the spectators in their everyday lives."[56] Second, its troupes are entirely male, with female characters being enacted by men known as *zan-push*. Their performance of femininity is often carried out "in a burlesque fashion" that allows the audience to see their masculinity, though occasionally they offer a more "mimetic representation."[57] A third trait of *ru-howzi* is its performance in the middle of its audience, whether out in the open (in rural areas) or on a "platform over a [courtyard] pond" (which is the literal meaning of *ru-howzi*).[58] In all these respects it bears a distinct resemblance to the Turkish *orta-oyunu*. The only major difference is a fourth trait of the Iranian form: Its plays are centered on a single "clown,"[59] whereas *orta-oyuna* centers on a *pair* of comic characters. But Metin And suggests that in its "early days," *orta-oyuna* had also centered on a single "clown"; its shift to a central pair of characters was perhaps the result of its frequent interactions with the more respectable *karagöz* shadow theatre.[60]

An improvisatory comic theatre also exists in northwestern Afghanistan, which was at the border of the Safavid Empire in the early seventeenth century. Hafizullah Baghban reports that troupes of performers (who call themselves Magads) enact this Afghani form (as well as puppet shows and magic acts) at nomad encampments and peasant villages, with the performance being set in the middle of the audience.[61] As with *orta-oyunu* and *ru-howzi*, Magadi theatre is social satire that "deal[s] with the cultural surroundings of the performers and project[s] a realistic [though comically "exaggerated"] look at them."[62] The leader of each troupe serves as its central character, a "buffoon," while the young men in the all-male troupes perform the female roles.[63]

It is not unusual, of course, for a theatre form to have live actors offering social satire; nor to have its lead performer be a clown or buffoon; nor to have the men of the troupe perform female roles in a burlesque manner; nor, finally, for audiences to surround the performance space. But this specific combination of traits, as seen in the improvisatory comic theatre forms of Turkey, Iran, and Afghanistan, is unusual. It seems likely that these forms are homological rather than analogical – a likelihood given further credibility by the geographic contiguity of their homelands as well as by hints of similar forms in Central Asia.[64] Perhaps these forms share a common Central Asian ancestor or perhaps one might be ancestral to the others. Either way, their obvious similarities raise the prospect of an underexamined family of theatre forms.

The Mughals and Beyond

South Asia's theatrical efflorescence, like those occurring at roughly the same time in the Ottoman and Safavid Empires, was largely associated with the establishment of an Islamic empire.[65] As we have seen, Muslim warriors had been drawn to South Asia as early as the tenth century and had created numerous sultanates, the most notable being the Delhi Sultanate, established at the start of the thirteenth century.[66] This state's territory would wax and wane over the next three centuries, but its political and economic instability, along with frequent wars with its neighbors, was not especially conducive to the emergence of new theatre forms. The terminal breakup of the sultanate was instigated by Tamerlane. Having defeated (if only for a brief time) the nascent Ottoman Empire and taken control of Iran, Tamerlane invaded South Asia in 1398; his armies quickly overwhelmed the sultanate, sacking Delhi "in an orgy of rapine and killing." Then Tamerlane, ever impatient for new conquests, sought to invade China, only to suffer the inconvenience of dying from an unknown illness as he led his armies eastward. The defeated sultan of Delhi returned to his devastated capital, and two further dynasties would subsequently rule from there, but the sultanate's scope and power were permanently diminished.[67] A hundred or so years after Tamerlane's depredations came another conqueror, Zhair-al-din-Muhammad – better known as Babur (the "Tiger"). His father was descended from Tamerlane, his mother from Chinggis Khan: Babur saw himself as the heir to his glorious ancestors. After being stymied in his efforts to conquer Tamerlane's former capital in Samarkand, he turned his attention to South Asia, where he defeated the tottering Delhi Sultanate in 1526 and established the Mughal Empire.[68]

And then came Akbar (r. 1556–1605), the grandson of Babur. After his father had squandered much of the territory won by Babur, Akbar quickly reconquered it, then expanded his empire from Afghanistan to Bengal. In contrast especially to that of Tamerlane, this was not "a freebooter's empire that disintegrated as quickly as it had been assembled." Instead, writes John Darwin, Akbar "fashion[ed] a grander and more durable imperial system than previous Muslim rulers in India had been able to create."[69] The Mughal Empire "became legendary for its wealth and power …. Awash in New World and Japanese silver, and in close collaboration with the ubiquitous Hindu banking and financier castes, a new fiscal system and bureaucracy were developed, based on scientific surveys, which became effective instruments for the sustained and regularized collection of unprecedented amounts of revenue."[70] Notably, Victor Lieberman suggests that "Mughal towns and cities form[ed] an urban grid" that was almost as developed as China's, while being far in advance of Europe's; these towns and cities "served as centers of finance, crop marketing, and artisanry."[71] Prospering from domestic and/or international trade as well as from a newfound sense of political security, these towns and cities would offer numerous opportunities for emerging theatre forms.

No less important for South Asia's burst of theatrical innovation, however, was a Hindu religious movement known as *bhakti*. The word is usually translated as "devotion," but John Stratton Hawley, a scholar of Indian religion, emphasizes that *bhakti* is a "religion of participation, community, enthusiasm, song, and often personal challenge. … It implies a direct divine encounter, experienced in the lives of individual people."[72] The *bhakti* movement had been a religious force in southern India well before the tenth century CE. By the late fifteenth century – the period of the failing Delhi Sultanate – it had spread north, not only as a manner of worship but as an inspiration for religious literature.[73] This worship and literature (especially the poet Tulsidas's *Ramacharitmanas*) provided the basis for many of the devotional theatre forms that would emerge after the establishment of the Mughal Empire.

Given the importance of the *bhakti* movement for Indian theatre, it is important to observe, with the historian Marshall G. S. Hodgson, that "even in the first years of [Akbar's] reign his reforms took a direction that respected other faiths." Akbar abolished taxes that had long been imposed "on certain Hindu pilgrimages" and "not only disallowed [religious] persecution of any sort ... but contributed financially to the building of temples for various faiths."[74] Akbar's tolerance of Hinduism is evident in the third generation of South Asian theatre forms, many of which emerged during his long reign. Although his successors were often far less respectful of Hindu religiosity, *bhakti*-inspired devotional forms would prove irrepressible.

This presents an interesting issue, for, as Hodgson observes, "the culture of Muslim India can be seen with equal legitimacy" as belonging to Indian history and to Islamic history, "according to the sort of questions one is asking."[75] For questions of theatre history, the Indian perspective seems more relevant. Despite a clear Islamic influence on some theatre forms (as we will see), the theatrical efflorescence during the Mughal Empire was unmatched in the other Islamic empires. The emerging forms showed substantial continuities with earlier generations of Indian theatre, and the *bhakti* movement itself was the direct stimulus for some of the most important new forms. It seems that the essential precondition for this theatrical flowering was the fertile soil provided by the South Asian theatre region whose history already reached back well over a thousand years. Akbar's contribution was to provide security, prosperity, and an openness to Hinduism.

There are many ways to make sense of the multitudinous theatre forms of South Asia. Farley P. Richmond, Darius L. Swann, and Phillip B. Zarrilli categorize them on the basis of five "interlocking spheres of influence."[76] Putting aside the "classical" sphere (in which they include *kutiyattam* as well as Sanskrit theatre) and the "modern" sphere – both of which obviously fall outside the period under discussion here – the three remaining spheres are "ritual," "devotional," and "folk-popular."[77] I must also put aside the ritual sphere owing to the paucity of information about its forms' histories. This leaves the better-studied theatre forms of the devotional and folk-popular spheres, most of which had their origins in the sixteenth and seventeenth centuries. These two spheres are indeed "interlocking," since devotional forms could be immensely popular (and in some cases also possible to characterize as "folk"), while folk-popular forms usually included multiple rituals and sometimes enacted narratives drawn from the sacred epics.

Even so, one can broadly distinguish between these two spheres. Kathryn Hansen observes that devotional forms such as *raslila* and *ramlila* were brought into being by the *bhakti* movement: They "are meant to inspire reverence and love" for Krishna and Rama, respectively, "and they often produce audience emotion approaching rapture" (see Figure 9.2). Also, the devotional forms function "within a religious matrix presided over by priests, patrons, and high-status interpreters" and are presented in language that, while mostly vernacular, "is elevated and literary." Conversely, folk-popular forms such as *bhavai* and *swang* "evoke merriment, wonder, lust, even fear"; they "rely on their commercial appeal, offering diversion in exchange for a price"; and they are presented in everyday speech that is "accessible to all."[78]

Despite these differences, however, the devotional and folk-popular forms share many traits. They are often based in one or more of the numerous cities and towns of South Asia and performed in one or more vernacular languages. *Ramlila*, for example, might be the most widespread of the theatre forms, being presented across northern India, but in this vast region, the related vernaculars of Hindi and Urdu predominate.[79] Rather more localized is *bhavai*, a folk-popular form of Gujarat and neighboring states in northwestern India; it is offered in "a generous mix of Gujarati, Hindi-Urdu, and Marwadi, indicating the historical connections of many castes and communities" in this area.[80] Other traits shared by devotional and folk-popular forms, suggests Devendra Sharma, include "charming music, poetry, dramatic acting, extensive preparation and training," and "community patronage and participation."[81] In light of Sharma's comments, it seems justifiable to agree with Govardhan Panchal's general comment about South Asia's third generation of theatre forms: "These were truly the people's theatres, growing with the people, speaking their language, singing their songs, staging [performance] in their streets or near their temples."[82]

Dating the emergence of third-generation forms is difficult at best, for each form has competing theories as to its origin. But even before the Mughal conquests, the *bhakti* movement had found theatrical expression in *ankiya nat*, which emerged in Assam around the start of the sixteenth century.[83] It seems likely that at least some other *bhakti*-inspired forms would have emerged even absent the Mughal Empire. But it seems no less likely that the wealthy empire (along with Akbar's tolerance of Hinduism) combined with the performative impulse of *bhakti* to make available numerous niches for devotional theatre.

158 9 Islamic Empires

Figure 9.2 *Ramlila*: an actor portrays the monkey-god Hanuman (model of courageous devotion to Rama) in a contemporary performance in Ramnagar. (Photo by Frédéric Soltan via Getty Images)

Among folk-popular forms, meanwhile, *bhavai* might also have emerged especially early, for legend holds that it was created by a fourteenth-century Brahmin. Tellingly, Gujarat (where the form originated) was already under Islamic rule, and the form's dramatic sketches (*vesas*) often show "Hindus and Muslims living in harmony and peace."[84] Even if this early dating for the form is correct (and Vatsyayan, among some others, would date it to the sixteenth century),[85] it is easy to see how *bhavai*'s popularity would expand under the more consistently tolerant rule of Akbar. In Kashmir, *bhand jashna* (also known as *bhand pather*) first comes into historical focus in the mid fifteenth century, becoming better known after the Mughal conquest of Kashmir a century or so later.[86] This village-based form might well be homologous with the aforementioned comic-improvisational *orta-oyunu* (of the Ottoman Empire), *ru-howzi* (of Iran), and Magadi theatre (of Afghanistan). Like them, its lead characters are clowns (the word *bhand* means "jester, joker, or buffoon"), its female characters are played by cross-dressing men, and its performances take place in the center of its audience.[87] Also like them, it does not generally focus on "historical or mythological stories, romantic tales or folk heroes"; instead, "it mirrors social evils" such as "the cunning money-lender, the dowry system, the corrupt police, [and] the haughty officials ... giving [comic] relief to people who have led hard lives under monarchs and maharajas."[88] Javaid Iqbal Bhat refers to *bhand jashna* as a "syncretic theatre form," noting that while its performers and audiences are generally Islamic, some of its technical language and performance practices show Hindu influence.[89]

Tamasha, another folk-popular form, emerged in Maharashtra somewhat later, with sources dating it to either the late sixteenth century or the eighteenth century.[90] *Tamasha* is also clearly a syncretic theatre form. Tevia Abrams suggests that it "developed from decaying remnants of both the Sanskrit and Prakrit traditions, and from Moghul entertainments" brought "from the seat of imperial power in northern India."[91] Indeed, the name of the form itself derives from Iranian, and as we have seen, a contemporaneous theatre form in Safavid Iran bore the same name; it seems possible that *tamasha* is a more thoroughly Indianized homologue to the comic-improvisational family. Lieberman makes the general comment that the Mughal rulers were "heirs to three centuries of cumulative Indo-Islamic cultural accommodation,"[92] of which they took advantage as they consolidated their rule. Such "cultural accommodation" is certainly evident in the folk-popular theatre forms of northern India.

South Asian theatrical innovation, however, was by no means limited to Mughal lands. Far to the south, the Malabar coast had long been a critical node in interregional commerce. It was largely spared the misery of the fourteenth-century crises, but the explosion of international commerce in the sixteenth century brought new wealth and created new opportunities for theatre. We have seen how the Sanskrit-based *kutiyattam* long held onto its niche as a temple-based theatre form for the Hindu elite. The emerging third-generation theatre forms of the Malabar coast would similarly maintain at least some continuities with Sanskrit theatre (as well as with *kutiyattam*) but would serve new purposes for new audiences. Three of these forms are especially noteworthy.

Kathakali (literally, "story play") is the most widely known. It emerged "in the late sixteenth and early seventeenth centuries," writes Phillip B. Zarrilli, "under the patronage of regional rulers."[93] Zarrilli suggests that it "has always been both a popular and accessible form of theatre open to village communities, as well as a virtuosic genre appealing to connoisseurs and patrons of the art"; its performances were originally held outdoors, in family compounds or on temple grounds.[94] The popular appeal of *kathakali* is evident in its "spectacular scenes in which the use of torches, battle choreography, and realistic effects combine to produce striking results."[95] Its narratives are drawn in large part from the great epics, but although they include passages in Sanskrit, the performed texts are mostly in Malayalam, the local vernacular.[96] Notwithstanding these texts, however, the form is often referred to as a dance-drama, in which the dancing is notable for "its vigorous masculine style of physical movement, bold superhuman characterizations, and vivid emotionalism."[97]

While *kathakali* has been "a relatively popular dramatic form" traditionally offered in a "relaxed and festive" atmosphere,[98] the roughly contemporaneous *krishnattam* is very much a *bhakti*-inspired devotional theatre.[99] The form (and its standard cycle of eight plays) apparently emerged in the mid seventeenth century and was created as "a means of glorifying the name of Krishna, one of Lord Vishnu's most beloved incarnations"; the name of the form itself means "dramas/stories of Krishna."[100] *Krishnattam* shares many performance practices with *kathakali*, such as elaborate costumes and makeup;[101] its dance movements also "closely resemble those of *kathakali*" but "stress a lyrical, feminine quality of group movement" rather than "masculine vigour."[102] It also differs from *kathakali* in that its texts are performed in the sacred language of Sanskrit, with performances traditionally offered "only within the confines of the Guruvayur temple."[103] This temple was (and remains) a site of pilgrimage, which suggests relatively diverse audiences of Krishna's many devotees.

The third of the Malabar coast theatre forms I will mention is certainly the most anomalous. *Cavittu natakam* emerged in the mid sixteenth century for the express purpose of serving "the cravings of the Latin Christian communities for an entertainment centered around Christian subject matter." It was the creation of Jesuits, recently arrived in southern India, whose proselytizing was supported by Portuguese authorities. Curiously, performance is mostly given in Tamil, although the local language is Malayalam,[104] which suggests that the form might have originated at a Portuguese base on the southeastern coast (in what is now Tamil Nadu) and been brought west to the more vibrant port cities of the Malabar coast. But whatever difficulties its language might present are overcome thanks to the main comic character in the plays, who serves primarily "as commenter [and] translator."[105] This character is highly reminiscent of the *vidusaka* characters found in many South Asian folk-popular theatre forms and suggests the native influence on the form. In other respects, though, *cavittu natakam* is deeply alien to South Asia. Its plots center on "quasi-historical and mythological characters of Christian history," such as Charlemagne, Saint George, and Saint Sebastian.[106] No less notably, "the style of movement contrasts markedly with the Hindu theatre forms popular in the same region," with a heavy emphasis on foot stomping; indeed, the name of the form itself literally means "stamping/stomping drama."[107] *Cavittu natakam* is, to be sure, a relatively minor form of South Asian theatre. But its mere existence is evidence of a sixteenth-century world that was becoming ever more tightly integrated.

CHAPTER 10

Across the South China Sea

In the late sixteenth century, the South China Sea was arguably the most important body of water in the world. On its northern shore was the vast Chinese Empire, reunited under the Ming Dynasty and now fully returned to global commerce. To the south was maritime Southeast Asia, with its spice islands easily within reach, while to the east lay the Philippines, where fleets of Spanish galleons deposited American silver destined for the purchase of goods from China and the spice islands. To the west were the Malay Peninsula and the accessible Gulf of Thailand, which opened to mainland Southeast Asia. And just beyond the Malay Peninsula was the Strait of Malacca, the invaluable gateway from the South China Sea to the rest of Eurasia. As the disasters of the fourteenth century receded into memory, the resurgence and restructuring of Eurasia would stimulate the emergence of countless new theatre forms all around the South China Sea.

East Asia

By the mid fourteenth century, the Mongol's Yuan Dynasty in China had, in the words of the historian Harold M. Tanner, "plunged deep into a crisis that stretched the state's capabilities and resources to the breaking point." The crisis was brought on by "environmental catastrophe, epidemic disease, population decline, weak government, and massive rebellions" that seemed to be taking place "nearly *everywhere*."[1] In 1368, one of the rebellious warlords prevailed over the Mongols, as well as over the other contestants for power, and founded the Ming Dynasty.

The first Ming emperor established his dynasty's authority by "reasserting Han Chinese cultural identity ... ostentatiously presenting his government and its institutions as the restoration of ancient Chinese models."[2] Of particular note was "the restoration [after a lapse during the Mongol's Yuan Dynasty] of the examination system as the center of official life"; this provided a means to fill the civil service with neo-Confucian scholar-officials devoted to the imperial order.³ More broadly, however, China's recovery got off to an unsteady start, in part owing to ongoing struggles with the Mongol polities that still threatened from the west, in part to Ming mistakes. To take one instance: For nearly a hundred years, "the Ming state expropriated the large landholdings accumulated by entrepreneurial landowners, stifled commercial enterprise and overseas trade, and reverted to in-kind payments of goods and labor services in place of monetized taxes …. Only in the sixteenth century, with the original Ming fiscal institutions in ruin, did the Chinese economy regain its earlier dynamism."⁴

Four factors helped sixteenth-century China regain that dynamism. The first is the simplest: "All the evidence leads us to think that the population of China increased constantly between the end of the fourteenth century and the middle of the seventeenth," perhaps doubling in size.⁵ The second factor was an increase in Chinese productivity. Cotton and rice agriculture expanded into new regions while crops of maize, sweet potatoes and peanuts quickly spread after being introduced from the Americas. Also, the internal trade of manufactured goods was stimulated by a new monetary system as well as the rebuilding of the Grand Canal.⁶ The manufacturing itself could be quite intensive: By the end of the sixteenth century, for example, "there were 50,000 workers in thirty paper factories" in the province of Jiangxi alone.⁷

The third factor was a new pattern of urbanization that at once aided in and resulted from the increase in productivity. In earlier centuries, China had "vast numbers of people clustered in a few huge cities"; as we have seen, the massive Mongol and Southern Song capitals had created the niches for commercial theatre filled by Yuan *zaju* and *nanxi*. "But now provincial towns became better integrated into a national hierarchy [and] the urban population became more evenly distributed," bringing China to an unequaled level of urbanization.⁸ The fourth factor was that "in the mid-sixteenth century, Ming China [re]joined the global economy. It became the linchpin of a linked network of trade flows leading from Latin America through Europe to India, to Southeast and East Asia."⁹ Silver, mined in massive quantities in the Americas and Japan, became the leading international medium of exchange, and because China produced goods that were universally desired, the flow of silver into China powered "the birth of global trade in the sixteenth century."¹⁰

The historian Jaques Gernet comments that China's renewed economic dynamism engendered important societal changes, including "the formation of a proletariat and of [a widespread] urban middle class"; "the transformation of rural life, which was [now] permeated by the influence of the towns"; "and the rise of a class of important merchants and business men." These changes, he suggests, were "reflected in the upsurge and renewal of various literary genres, of thought, and of knowledge."[11] They also opened niches for an array of new theatre forms that could take advantage of the potential new audiences they engendered.

Following the fall of the Yuan Dynasty, *zaju* had survived reasonably well into the early Ming Dynasty; indeed, two Ming princes themselves wrote *zaju* plays.[12] Even more notably, scholars applied their skills to the form and by the mid sixteenth century were publishing compilations of Yuan *zaju* plays.[13] But even as the form was being memorialized, Ming-era *zaju* playwrights were toying with the structure and length of their plays, while also mixing in southern-style music and speech.[14] One gets the sense that they were searching for a formula that might retain the form's popular appeal in the face of competition with newer forms of theatre (shortly to be discussed). Their efforts, however, were in vain, perhaps because they adulterated the distinctive characteristics that had made *zaju* popular in the first place. A native of southern China went north in the 1630s hoping to hear the genuine music of *zaju*, but what he heard (he wrote in disappointment) had "lost its northern characteristics."[15] By the fall of the Ming Dynasty in 1644, *zaju* was no longer in performance.[16]

The career of *nanxi* was not nearly as successful as that of *zaju*, but ironically, it was the more seminal form. Its development had been interrupted when the Mongols conquered the Southern Song and brought *zaju* to the south, but after the breakup of the Yuan Dynasty, *nanxi* underwent a "gradual evolution" into what is usually considered a distinct form known as *chuanqi*.[17] The closest thing to a landmark in this evolution is Gao Ming's *The Story of the Lute* (sometimes called *Song of the Lute*, written in 1358), which retold the story of a *nanxi* play but "in elegant and polished poetry."[18] Before *Lute*, observes Grant Guangren Shen, *nanxi* plays were "routinely composed by theatre practitioners who had received little, if any, formal literary education. While a few of their scripts proved to be theatrically effective, the majority of them were marred by logic gaps, personality contradictions, structural defects and language flaws"; Gao Ming's play, however, was a "masterpiece" that gained widespread "literati admiration."[19]

There were many causes for *nanxi*'s evolution into *chuanqi*, one of which was certainly competition with *zaju* for the narrowing niche of popular theatre amid the troubled years of the Yuan Dynasty's decline. But the new form's literary quality, along with its frequent narratives of young scholars entangled in difficult romances, resonated deeply once the Ming

Dynasty (with its neo-Confucian ideals and reestablished exam system) took control in 1368. The form's popularity with the literati thereby gave it access to a new, well-resourced niche. *Chuanqi* would have a decisive influence on many subsequent forms of Chinese theatre, passing on the role category system it had inherited from *nanxi*, as well as its "presentation of time and space through conventional, stylized methodologies."[20] But *chuanqi* itself had a significant flaw: "Many critics faulted its songs and song sets, the sequence in which one song followed another, as disharmonious."[21] As with *nanxi* and Yuan *zaju* playwrights, *chuanqi* playwrights typically set their lyrics to popular melodies, but the results were often slipshod.[22] These flaws encouraged the development of more appealing musical systems.

I must pause here to reemphasize the central importance of music in Chinese theatre: "Until relatively recently, a Chinese audience would not have considered a piece to be theatre without music and singing of some kind."[23] The basic narrative of an established play could be (and often was) transformed into something new by setting it to a different musical system and adjusting its verse accordingly. Musical systems are by no means the sole defining trait of Chinese theatre forms, but they are a critical part of any such definitions. And by the late Ming years (roughly 1550 to 1644), music had become an ever more important factor in differentiating the theatre forms.[24] Indeed, the development of Chinese theatre starting in the sixteenth century is largely the story of a handful of widely disseminated musical systems. The most famous is the music of Kunshan, a city in the province of Jiangsu. But no less important are the musical systems known as *yiyang* (from Jiangxi province) and *bangzi* (from Shaanxi and Shanxi provinces); a few other systems (in particular *haiyan* music and *yuyao* music) were also widely influential.[25] The spread of these musical systems was made possible, above all, by "the heightened mobility" of Ming society, as China "experienced the deepening impact of commercialization" abetted by "the influx of silver [that] fueled an increasingly monetized economy" and escalated "the volume of long-distance travel" within China. Such travelers included countless merchants as well as the many scholar-officials who served in the imperial bureaucracy.[26]

In the sixteenth and seventeenth centuries, literally hundreds of theatre forms came into existence using one or another of these musical systems, or some combination thereof, usually in conjunction with local musical styles.[27] As in South Asia during the same period, an important reason for these theatrical riches was China's multiplicity of regional spoken languages. The sinologist Victor H. Mair observes that "it is commonplace to talk of Chinese 'dialects' as though there were only a single language in China with a dozen or so mutually intelligible varieties," but in fact "there are scores of [mutually *un*intelligible] Sinitic languages, which may be divided into hundreds of dialects and thousands of subdialects."[28] China's many spoken languages, in conjunction with its unparalleled riches and urban development, afforded ample opportunities for the emergence of new theatre forms, even as commercial and bureaucratic travel encouraged the spread of musical systems from one linguistic region to the next.

The music of Kunshan was the most sophisticated of China's newly developing musical systems. In the mid sixteenth century, Wei Liangfu spent ten years refining the music of his native city into a style "so smooth and delicate that it acquired the appellation 'water polished music.'"[29] The refinements included "filtering out all the elements considered coarse from Kunshan music," "absorbing the structural strengths of northern music," and "revamping the southern instrumental ensemble" from one that was predominantly percussion-based to one that included various string and wind instruments.[30]

His efforts were quickly taken up by his friend Liang Chenyu, who in 1579 applied the new musical system to the *chuanqi* play *The Girl Washing Silk* (with the last word of the title sometimes translated as *Gauze*). The play proved "immensely popular" both for its literary merits and for its employment of Wei's polished musical system.[31] Seeing its success, other theatre artists similarly reset *chuanqi* plays to Kunshan music, even as new plays were written specifically for that music. The result was the emergence of *kunqu* (literally, "music of Kunshan"), a theatre form especially suited "to the intimacy, enclosure, and refinement of the private stages" that elite patrons could provide.[32] Indeed, "almost all known private troupe owners belonged to three privileged social strata": the literati themselves, salt merchants enriched by their state-sanctioned monopoly, and "head eunuchs" empowered by the Ming bureaucracy. "By and large," writes Shen, "the Ming private theatre was a theatre of the elite, by the elite and for the elite," with "virtually all the best actors belong[ing] to literati troupe owners, and all the recognized playwrights, directors and critics [coming] from the social stratum of literati."[33] But although *kunqu* was (as Li Ruru puts it) "an art for a coterie,"[34] that coterie was far from insignificant. Approximately 900 *kunqu* plays were mounted in the late years of the Ming Dynasty, and one of the form's most enduring plays, *The Peach Blossom Fan*, was written by Kong Shangren in 1699, well after the start of the Qing Dynasty (see Figure 10.1) The form's popularity among the elite would decline only as the Qing Dynasty itself struggled for survival in the late nineteenth century.[35]

Figure 10.1 *Kunqu*: a scene from a contemporary performance of Kong Shangren's *The Peach Blossom Fan*, in Beijing. (Photo by China Photos via Getty Images)

In contrast to the elegant *kunqu*, the *yiyang* and *bangzi* musical systems held far greater appeal beneath the elite level, and each became the musical basis for numerous theatre forms. According to Wing Chung Ng, these musical systems were "more versatile and dynamic" than the music of Kunshan and "were particularly susceptible to a process of artistic amalgamation, picking up [local] folk tunes, expressions, and dialects" specific to various locales, "even as the imprints of their musical structure and plot designs remained apparent on the local stage."[36] The singing in theatre forms using these musical systems was far more rhythmic and direct than the melismatic stylings of *kunqu*. Among the characteristics of *yiyang*-based forms were "the use of drums and cymbals for the rhythm … and a brisk and loud [vocal] delivery" that led some to hear it as little more than "bellowing."[37] Forms using the *bangzi* system (generically known as clapper operas) were musically notable, above all, for the datewood blocks (i.e., clappers) that beat out the rhythm in accompaniment to the songs.[38] These two musical systems (as well as the others mentioned earlier) "travelled around with itinerant theatre troupes, adapting to new customs" wherever they went, "merging, borrowing, and appropriating from each other."[39]

Colin Mackerras suggests *yiyang* originated just before the start of the sixteenth century while *bangzi* originated in the mid to late sixteenth century.⁴⁰ By the end of the sixteenth century, the many demotic forms using these and other musical systems were already sufficiently popular for their artists to organize into trade guilds: "The number of actors, musicians, and others who relied on theater for livelihood was evidently growing steadily, and the need for coordination, mediation, mutual aid, and perhaps self-defense had reached a critical point for such effort to be warranted and for those concerned to back it up with financial resources."⁴¹ In sum, one might say (with a nod to Mao Zedong) that a hundred theatrical flowers bloomed in sixteenth-century China. Its many forms of theatre worked together, according to Cyril Birch, to make this "a time when the entire nation was mad about theatre. The news that a play was being put on could attract an audience anywhere in China, at any level of society, in any convenient location from village temple to city tea shop to emperor's private apartments."⁴²

The fall of the Ming Dynasty in 1644 did little to quell the Chinese enthusiasm for theatre. In the broad historical sense, the incoming Qing Dynasty (imposed from a base in Manchuria) chose not to reject Ming institutions but only to modify them; the civil bureaucracy of scholar-officials remained largely unaltered, as did the examination system with its emphasis on neo-Confucian orthodoxy. This was all "part of the bargain the Manchus made with local elites … to assure that their status would remain unthreatened by the new rulers."⁴³ Colin Mackerras observes that the dynastic change in 1644 "is no turning point in the history of Chinese theatre," however much theatre historians like to rely on dynasties to mark their historical periods.⁴⁴ The next "turning point" would come only around the start of the nineteenth century, when *jingju* (also known as Beijing opera) emerged amid what the historian Peter Purdue characterizes as "a catastrophic series of rebellions induced by environmental pressure, official corruption, and cultural conflict" with encroaching European imperialism.⁴⁵ But that was still far in the future.

Southeast Asia and the Philippines

Southeast Asia had a somewhat different experience than most of Eurasia in the aftermath of the two crises of the mid fourteenth century. As elsewhere, the fourteenth century saw "a relatively high discontinuity in the long-term pattern of Southeast Asian history," writes the historian Anthony Reid. Mainland Southeast Asia apparently "joined the common disease pool of Eurasia [around the time of the bubonic plague], suffering initial heavy losses in the pockets of dense population," while climate change beginning in the fourteenth century exacerbated the mainland's losses. Less information is available about maritime Southeast Asia, but the islands almost certainly had their own difficulties: "Tectonic mega-events including tsunamis, and volcanic eruptions that darken the skies and induce major crop failures, are likely to [have been] more important factors" in the islands' discontinuity than the introduction of a new disease.[46]

But owing to maritime Southeast Asia's position at the most vital node of Eurasian commerce, as well as to its much-desired spices, it was less affected than other regions by the mid fourteenth-century collapse of commerce – and it would recover even more quickly. Reid writes that during the "long sixteenth century" (from the mid fifteenth to mid seventeenth centuries), "Southeast Asia played its most central role in world history as a crucible for the birth of modernity and the unification of world markets."[47]

This "age of commerce," as Reid calls it, brought wealth and foreigners to Southeast Asia's port cities, the most notable of which was Melaka, strategically situated on the Strait of Malacca.[48] In 1468, the local ruler wrote, "We have learned that to master the blue oceans people must engage in commerce and trade. All the lands within the seas are united in one body. Life has never been so affluent in preceding generations as it is today." At roughly that time, the city's population of more than 100,000 included some 15,000 foreign merchants from virtually every portion of Eurasia. Upon arriving in Melaka in the early sixteenth century, the Portuguese diplomat Tomé Pires wrote that the city "was made for merchandise, fitter than any other in the world. Commerce between different nations for a thousand leagues on every hand must come to Melaka." And recognizing that control of the city would advance the Portuguese goal of cutting Italian middlemen out of the trade with Asia, he added that "whoever is lord of Melaka has his hands on the throat of Venice."[49]

Owing in large part to its critical role in interregional commerce, Southeast Asia was especially open to the influence of foreign religions. Even before the disasters of the mid fourteenth century, most of the mainland was proving receptive to Theravada Buddhism (in contrast to the Mahayana Buddhism that had earlier been part of the Hindu-Buddhist influence there). But it was during the commercial boom of the long sixteenth century that Theravada Buddhism was "consolidated as orthodoxy."[50] Many rulers on the mainland used it to control and expand their domains, which resulted in the rise of "powerful new states" in the areas of what are now Myanmar, Thailand, Cambodia, and Laos. The Theravada

Buddhism shared by these new states, however, "did not eliminate political and ethnic conflict among rival peoples."⁵¹ Indeed, the interactions associated with those conflicts would prove an important vector for the transmission of theatre forms between the states.

Theravada Buddhism's influence on theatre in mainland Southeast Asia is subtle but clear, especially in the stories that various theatre forms would enact. The Thai version of *The Ramayana*, known as *The Ramakien*, was apparently first written in the fifteenth century. In this version, the Hindu epic was "given a Buddhist character," with the god Rama himself being regarded "as a potential buddha (bodhisattva)."⁵² No less important were the concurrently imported *Jataka* tales which concerned "one or another of the previous births of the Buddha." These tales ranged from "beast fables" (along the lines of Aesop's fables) to stories of "common life" to "long romances." Above all, they were popular stories, whose "ethical teaching," suggests Ghulam-Sarwar Yousof, "is mostly that of the virtues of secular life and moral retribution as emphasized by the doctrines of karma and rebirth."⁵³

As I mentioned in Chapter 6, most parts of the mainland already hosted a pair of shadow-puppet theatre forms. One of these forms comes into clearer focus during the long sixteenth century. The first undoubted reference to *nang yai*, the Thai form in which dancers wielded large multicharacter puppets, is from 1458. The name of the form literally means "large puppet," and performance was reserved for the royal court.⁵⁴ By 1515, a new theatre form known as *khon* was also being performed for the court, with some of its traits being derived from *nang yai*. Most strikingly, its heavily made-up (or masked) live dancers "move[d] in a special sideways fashion, keeping in profile as much as possible" in imitation of the figures on the multicharacter *nang yai* puppets; they also used "visual friezes" as they assumed poses that correlated with *nang yai* puppetry.⁵⁵ As with *nang yai*, the stories enacted in *khon* generally involved characters from *The Ramayana*, but they came via the Thai *Ramakien* and were often used "to illustrate a Buddhist moral lesson."⁵⁶

Another theatre form reserved for the Thai court was *lakon nai*, a name shortened from either *lakon fai nai* ("inner court play") or *lakon nan nai* ("drama of women of the palace").⁵⁷ Because performances were by members of the royal harem, attendance was limited to the king, his invited guests, and royal attendants.⁵⁸ The form is generally said to have come to the court in 1431: When the Thai captured the Khmer capital, they kidnapped the Khmer royal dance troupe and musicians and brought them home as spoils of war.⁵⁹ In the process of making the dance their own,

Thai dancers simplified the steps and adjusted their meanings, creating "an 'alphabet' of dance that, in a modified form, is used in Thailand, Laos, and Cambodia today."[60]

In contrast to these court-based forms of theatre was *lakon nok*, meaning either "drama of the southern provinces" or "play outside [the palace]."[61] As is typical of many popular theatre forms, there is little evidence of when the form might have emerged, although there might be a reference to it as early as 1376.[62] *Lakon nok* is said to have its origins in ritual. James Brandon writes that as "performances ceased to be a religious act, the number of actors was increased, new stories were dramatized, and the orchestra was enlarged to include more melody-carrying instruments. Perhaps most important, dance was subordinated to the requirements of action. Popular audiences demanded fast action, colloquial language, lots of rough joking, and not too much boring dance."[63] Most of the stories it enacted were drawn from the *Jataka* tales.[64] But although *lakon nok* would eventually influence *lakon nai*, it "was excluded from the aesthetic standards of court theatre, because it was considered the theatre form of commoners."[65]

Maritime Southeast Asia was largely untouched by the Theravada Buddhism that had swept the mainland. Its most significant new religion was Islam, which had begun spreading in the region even before the long sixteenth century. Wherever trade was a way of life, Islam was supported by local officials who sought to attract Muslim merchants.[66] This embrace was especially strong in Java, Sumatra, and the Malay Peninsula. The societal impact of Islam could be transformative, suggests the historian Craig A. Lockard: "The mostly Islamic people of Melaka began calling themselves 'Malay' (Malayu) in the fifteenth century. Henceforth, the term applied to those who practiced Islam, spoke a version of the Malay language, and identified themselves as group members"; in this way "an ethnic category" was created.[67] And with the spread of Islam "came a network of scholars and manuscripts, as well as storytellers and their tales, translating the idioms of Arabic and Persian into Malay and Javanese."[68] This led to the emergence of Islamic forms of theatre along with changes in established forms to make them more acceptable to Muslims.

On the island of Java, for instance, *wayang kulit purwa* adjusted to the new religion. According to Brandon, "the present-day highly stylized shape" of the shadow puppets "dates from the sixteenth century" and follows from a Muslim ruler's order "to have a non-realistic puppet set made in order to circumvent the Islamic proscription against the portrayal of the human form in art."[69] Perhaps more notable was the introduction, in

Figure 10.2 *Wayang kulit purwa*: a pair of shadow puppets. The puppet on the left (with movable arms) apparently represents Judistira; the other puppet might represent Kresna (with multiple but nonmovable arms). (Photo by Pictures from History/Universal Images Group via Getty Images)

1630, of movable arms for the shadow puppets (see Figure 10.2). Brandon comments that "in the wake of this startling innovation must have come a virtual revolution in the art of puppet manipulation, particularly in the many fighting movements."[70] It is possible that this change reflects knowledge of shadow-puppet forms of the Eastern Mediterranean, where movable arms were commonplace, although *wayang* shadow puppets remained operated from below.

More broadly, suggests Ghulam-Sarwar, the Islamic influence helped *wayang kulit purwa* not only to survive but also to experience "one of the most exciting artistic transformations in the annals of theatre," thanks to "a fusion of aesthetic principles deriving from all cultures – animist, Hindu-Buddhist and Islamic – experienced by the Javanese before western colonization."[71] But it was less the changes in *wayang kulit purwa* that illustrate the Islamic presence than it was the explicitly Islamic forms of *wayang* puppetry that emerged. Of those, the most notable is *wayang kulit Menak*, which enacts heroic legends and fantasies about Amir Hamza, the Prophet Muhammad's maternal uncle and an early convert to Islam. Eventually another form, known as *wayang golek Menak*, would also enact tales of Amir Hamza, but using full-bodied puppets that reflected Islamic aesthetics.[72]

Whatever impact Islam might have had on maritime Southeast Asia, perhaps the region's theatre was most notable for its "eclecticism," brought about by the frequent movement of people from one locale to another. Anthony Reid notes that the port cities "became great centers of cultural exchange." A contemporaneous Malay text reports that even in relatively remote Sumbawa, "all kinds of entertainments" could be seen, including "Indian dances, Siamese theatre, Chinese opera, [and] Javanese puppet theatre."[73] This eclecticism led to complex (and largely uncharted) patterns of syncretism between Southeast Asian theatre forms.

Carriers of a third religion, Christianity, arrived in Southeast Asia in the sixteenth century. The Portuguese, who (as we have seen) were already aware of the value of the Melaka, sent a fleet that conquered the city in 1511. But ironically, "Melaka languished under Portuguese control, as fewer merchants chose to endure the higher taxes and the Portuguese intolerance of non-Christians"; to make matters worse, Portugal failed to provide enough settlers to offset the loss of non-Christian locals and merchants.[74] In the long run, Melaka proved of little value to the Portuguese. The Dutch East India Company (known by its Dutch initials as the VOC) had more success when it gained control of the northwestern Javanese town of Jakarta in 1619; this town, which the Dutch renamed Batavia, sat on the Sunda Straits and served as a meeting point for European and Chinese ships. The colony itself had few Europeans. Enslaved people (largely from other parts of Southeast Asia) made up at least a third of the total population, while Chinese settlers (primarily businessmen) accounted for almost half of the free adult male population.[75] At this early point, therefore, European theatre made little impression in either Melaka or Java.

The story was quite different in the Philippines, where the Spanish arrived in the 1560s, almost 200 years after Islam had reached the southern islands of the archipelago. The timing was propitious: Islam was not yet "entrenched" in the northern Philippine islands, while Spain could "draw on over seven decades of evangelizing [and colonizing] experience in Latin America."[76] They took quick advantage of the magnificent port of Manilla and the easy access it afforded to China, for they had something of immense value to the Chinese: silver. By 1575, fifteen ships crammed full of American bullion were arriving each year, firmly establishing the colony's economic viability.[77] Although the number of Spanish colonists was never large, Filipinos embraced Christianity far more readily than did the people of Melaka or Java. This was the result, in part, of the Spanish learning from their experience in Mexico. They gave their "missionaries special authority over the people and their land" but also allowed aspects of indigenous religions to shape Philippine Catholicism.[78] And they took immediate advantage of theatre as an ideological tool.

Numerous forms of Spanish theatre were brought to the Philippines over the years, but one of the earliest and most successful transplants was the Spanish folk form *Moros y Cristianos*, which takes as its historical referent the Christian "reconquest" of Moorish Spain. At the form's heart is a set of mock battles between masses of performers representing Moors and Christians; performances typically also include parades of the two sides, episodes of combative dialogue, and the ultimate conversion of the Moors.[79] Nicanor G. Tiongson observes that in the Spanish colonies of Mexico and the Philippines (in the latter of which it is called *komedya* or *moro-moro*), the form was intended "to convince the natives that the European and/or the Christian will always have moral and military superiority … because God himself will work miracles through the saints and angels in order to ensure" victory.[80] The form might not have been transferred to the Philippines directly from Spain but from the earlier-established Spanish colony in Mexico, carried by Mexican friars who became parish priests in the Philippines.[81] In Mexico, a land without Moors, Islamic characters were inherently exotic. That exoticism can also be found in *komedya*, for even though there were Muslims in the Philippines, there is little direct reference to them in the plays. Instead, the Moors are depicted as coming from Islamic Spain, Turkey, Persia, or Arabia. Isaac J. Donoso therefore argues that this Moorish presence shows the Spanish world as filtered through Mexican sensibilities, although the argument cannot yet be considered conclusive.[82]

Regardless of whether *Moros y Cristianos* was introduced into the Philippines directly or indirectly, its "efficacy as an ideological tool of the establishment should not lead to the impression … that the natives simply accepted the colonial messages of the plays."[83] Filipinos domesticated the form to suit their own traditions and tastes, to the point that the resulting *komedya* stands as a theatre form in its own right. Of particular note, writes Tiongson, was the introduction of a recurring jester/clown figure called the *pusong*: "Through his scripted and spontaneous comments and ad lib gestures and movements," the *pusong* "punctured the pretensions" of the plays' "world of royal make-believe"; he also "satirized social and political practices that mimicked the culture of the overlords."[84] The "Filipinization" of the form, argues Donoso, was further abetted by incorporating the local style of martial arts (known as *arnis*) as well as local musical styles, while also having the characters speak in local languages.[85] Tiongson notes, finally, that the plays were often "performed on occasions originally devoted to the celebration of indigenous rituals held sacred by the natives, or in honor of Christian saints who were clearly meant to replace their native counterparts."[86] The Spanish might have seen *komedya* as a way of asserting their supremacy and converting the locals, but the Filipinos used it to take ownership of the new religion, just as they took ownership of the theatre form.

Indeed, the same basic point can be made of almost all the theatre forms that emerged in the long sixteenth century – not only in the Philippines but also in mainland and maritime Southeast Asia. Brandon comments that although many of these forms are "deeply indebted to outside literary sources" brought by new religions and/or rulers, "time and time again foreign dramatic materials are 'localized.'" "Foreign stories" such as *The Ramayana* are typically "presented to an audience as if they were local stories …. In Thailand, Rama is a Thai prince [who] wears Thai dress, follows Thai court etiquette, listens to … Thai music, and watches Thai dancing"; and "since Thailand is a Buddhist country, Rama is Buddha in a previous life." In Java, meanwhile, "Rama is a Javanese prince …. Java was Hindu-Brahminic and now is Moslem, so Rama is a reincarnation of Vishnu, a descendant of Adam, and a child of Allah."[87] As theatre forms (and the literature on which they are based) were transferred to lands with differing theatrical and societal contexts, theatre artists found syncretic ways to make the forms and the literature their own.

CHAPTER 11

Erasmus's Prophecy

A Renewed Europe

In 1517, the famed Dutch humanist Desiderius Erasmus suffered an unexpected bout of optimism.[1] Writing to a friend, he insisted that although "it was no part of my nature … to be excessively fond of life … at the present moment I could almost wish to be young again, for no other reason but this, that I anticipate the near approach of a golden age." Erasmus was thinking primarily about politics and religion, and in these matters he would be sorely disappointed. But his optimism extended more broadly to the success of the humanist project, for he noted that "polite letters, which were almost extinct, are now cultivated and embraced" through much of Europe. This led him "to a confident hope, that not only morality and Christian piety, but also a genuine and purer literature may come to renewed life or greater splendor."[2] In some ways, and despite the ongoing political and religious strife, the "renewed life" had already begun. Even as Europe was recovering from the disasters of the fourteenth century, humanists were looking to the ancient past to inspire new European arts. Within a hundred years of Erasmus's prophecy, the art of theatre would most certainly find itself in the midst of the "golden age" for which Erasmus yearned.

Four socioeconomic factors helped prepare the ground for Europe's theatrical efflorescence. The most obvious was its repopulation in the wake of the bubonic plague: By the late sixteenth century, Europe's population had regained its pre-plague level and would keep increasing from there.[3] This restored population, however, was differently situated than before, owing to the second socioeconomic factor: urbanization. By the end of the fifteenth century, roughly a quarter of all European villages had been abandoned, owing not only to losses during the bubonic plague but also to migration to towns and cities.[4] European cities (aside from Constantinople/Istanbul) had never been large by standards elsewhere in Eurasia. Madrid was a small town in 1561 when King Philip II moved his court there, but by 1700 it contained over 100,000 people. Seville, meanwhile, became a commercial "boom town in the sixteenth century" as the main Spanish port for silver bullion imported from the Americas.[5] In England, the population of London swelled from about 50,000 in the 1520s to upwards of 500,000 by 1650, fed by London's preeminence as a center of both politics *and* commerce.[6] Indeed, the city grew so rapidly that "the Crown became alarmed," and King James I complained that soon "England will onely [sic] be London."[7]

The third socioeconomic factor was technological advancement, particularly in the ships that would help Europe reach the Americas and trade in Asian markets. Many of the technologies used in these ships had come from abroad: Gunpowder weapons, compasses, and the stern-rudder post had all originated in China, while the lateen sail was first developed by Arab sailors. But Europeans "refined, accumulated, and combined" these technologies "to the point that they at least matched and most often exceeded the technological development of other peoples."[8] Another technological advance came in mid fifteenth century, when Johannes Gutenberg reinvented the moveable-type printing press (first invented in eleventh-century China); moreover, although Gutenberg had originally printed onto parchment, Europeans soon began using paper (also invented in China) to inexpensively spread knowledge.[9] The fourth socioeconomic factor was the Columbian Exchange: Conquests in the New World gave Europe access to American foodstuffs as well as to the American silver necessary for trade with Asian lands.

Italy led the way in Europe's recovery. To be clear, there was no Italian nation-state, only a miscellany of squabbling republics, duchies, kingdoms, and Papal states. But Italian cities – in particular, Venice, Genoa, Milan, and Florence – were the wealthiest and most commercially sophisticated in Europe thanks to their long-standing control of trade with Asia.[10] The fourteenth-century disasters had dealt these cities a powerful blow, but in the fifteenth century, suggests the historian Richard Smith, "starting in Italy and spreading north and west, [Europe's] population grew, urbanization revived, production increased, commodity prices stabilized, and trade and commerce flourished."[11] The voyages of Vasco da Gama and Columbus near the end of the fifteenth century foretold a coming crisis, when the center of European commerce would shift from the Mediterranean to Atlantic ports, but that was still somewhat in the future. In the fifteenth century, writes the historian Fernand Braudel, "the glory born of material wealth was the long-effective secret of the power" held by the major Italian cities.[12]

Europe's recovery gave new life to existing forms of theatre. Alan E. Knight comments that "in the late Middle Ages, the theatre in France, as elsewhere in Europe, experienced an unprecedented flourishing."[13] In German-speaking cities such as Lucerne and Innsbruck, marketplace performances of Passion plays attained a new level of extravagance.[14] England's Corpus Christi cycle plays also thrived with the renewal of urban life, drawing support from the growing wealth of artisan guilds. Pedagogically minded morality plays had their heyday as well. These offered "moral instruction" through allegorical dramatic action, with the protagonist generally being "a figure of all men" (e.g., Everyman or Mankind) and other characters being "polarized as figures of good and evil" (e.g., Mercy, Lechery).[15] The earliest of these plays dated from before the mid fourteenth century, but it was only as Europe recovered that the form became especially "abundant," sometimes as "large-scale" plays mounted by communities, sometimes as "small-scale" plays (often called "interludes") mounted by traveling professional troupes for private dinners and banquets.[16]

The endurance of these and other theatre forms leads Alexandra F. Johnston to observe that "the distinction between 'medieval drama' and 'Renaissance drama' can no longer be clearly drawn" on a chronological basis; in the mid sixteenth century, "medieval morality forms co-existed with [humanist-inspired] school plays with no apparent sense of incongruity," while biblical cycles were "being performed in all their 'medieval' glory after the opening of the professional theatre in London."[17] There was, in other words, a considerable overlap between the old and the new, just as there were continuities between them: Molière's comedies, for example, happily drew from earlier French farces, while Christopher Marlowe's *Doctor Faustus* "puts the morality formula in the service of a devastating cultural critique," even borrowing the well-worn device of parading the Seven Deadly Sins across the stage.[18] But although no clear chronological demarcation can be drawn, the theatre forms that had originated before the sixteenth century would slowly be overwhelmed by newly emerging forms that took advantage of Europe's socioeconomic resurgence and drew on a potent new ideology.

That ideology was the humanism espoused by luminaries such as Erasmus. According to Fernand Braudel, to refer to humanism as "an ideology is to identify it as a loose system of ideas, beliefs, declarations, [and] prejudices, connected by a sometimes less than perfect logic, but connected all the same." A central aspect of this ideology was the recuperation of ancient Greek and Roman learning that had previously been undiscovered, overlooked, or misunderstood. But humanism was not merely antiquarianism; it paradoxically "return[ed] to the past" to chart a course of future "progress."[19] The historian John Hale observes, "Whatever was brought to the surface from the deep strata of antiquity was interpreted by individuals in their own terms" – and "whatever was made in Italy in the fifteenth and sixteenth centuries was subject elsewhere to local adaptation" in the face of "personal genius" and "national temperament."[20]

It was not by chance that Italy was at the forefront of humanism. The Italian heritage extended back to ancient Rome, so the recovery of Latin texts was a point of obvious interest. And although the texts of ancient Greece were forbiddingly alien, Italy's commercial relations with (and proximity to) Constantinople would make them accessible as well. Through the decades of Ottoman pressure that culminated in that city's conquest in 1453, numerous Greek scholars fled to Italy, bringing editions of ancient texts. When they arrived, writes Deno John Geanakoplos, "they were amazed and horrified by the corruption of the ... manuscripts of Greek works utilized by the [medieval] Scholastics and even by the humanists"; they were able, however, to provide better texts, along with others that "were either unknown in the West or [had been] left untranslated."[21] This is not to suggest that humanism originated with the arrival of Greek scholars – but they provided a critical stimulus, especially regarding Greek materials. Thanks to their contributions, humanists were enabled to see the ancient texts as models they could use "for their own increasingly complicated urban society and culture."[22]

A Theatrical "Golden Age" Begins

Richard Andrews writes that "it was Italian Humanists [circa 1500] who set in motion a series of major transformations" in how European theatre "was conceived and managed."[23] Whether independently or in association with one or another academic institution, humanists studied the surviving plays of ancient Rome and Greece. In Italy, some humanists quickly turned to using the ancient plays as models for new ones, which they wrote in the vernacular. The result is known as *commedia erudita* ("comedy of the learned"), primarily a literary movement that offered occasional amateur and semiprofessional performances under the sponsorship of local courts or patricians.[24] The humanist network, however, was not limited to Italy. It amounted to "a transnational community of intellectuals" who engaged in the frequent "exchange of ideas."[25] Gutenberg's press (and the use of paper rather than parchment) was critical in this exchange, for it made "the labours of classical scholars more and more conspicuous in booksellers' shops" across most of Europe.[26]

Theatrical development played out under humanist influence in numerous academic institutions, with students studying and/or performing ancient plays as part of their education, first in their original languages (with Latin comedies predominating), then in translation.[27] Before long, professors began using the ancient texts as models for their own plays, also intended for study and production. One feature of the humanist-influenced plays is especially notable: Their monologues and dialogues were generally spoken, with singing either being recognized within the narrative *as* song or used outside the narrative for prologues, interludes, or finales. The relative absence of song (and of dance as well) will seem bizarre from a non-European perspective but likely followed from the humanists basing their work on ancient texts that provided words alone. To them, this is what *serious* comedy looked like.

Commedia erudita might not have been a fully fledged theatre form, but it soon helped to inspire one: *commedia dell'arte* ("comedy of the profession").[28] The first solid evidence for this professional *commedia* is a contract signed in 1545 between members of a theatrical troupe.[29] Within fifteen years, *commedia* troupes had begun to include women, a development that "helped to balance the comedy by giving more realism to the romantic plot lines" favored by the troupes – while also being "a calculated bid for greater commercial appeal."[30] Even at that early point, *commedia* troupes were far more than the illiterate street performers they are sometimes made out to be.[31] The surviving *commedia* scenarios and plot outlines, notes Ollie Crick, "show a clear understanding of multi-character plot development, and the structural and compositional device of both a three-act and five-act play." The *commedia dell'arte* troupes had learned from *commedia erudita* to develop plays that could "keep the audience's interest over several hours, by the unfolding of a dramatic story."[32] And although their various masked characters (such as Arlecchino/Harlequin, Pulcinella/Punch, and Pantalone) are justifiably renowned, *commedia* troupes had also learned to build their madcap comedies around the tribulations of sympathetic young lovers – a plot device borrowed from *commedia erudita* that effectively "exploit[ed] sexual reference and the erotic appeal of actresses."[33]

Thanks in part to their theatrical sophistication, *commedia* troupes could suit their shows to the many different audiences for which they played. The well-known formula of stock characters, masks, *lazzi* (comic business), and structured improvisation (on the basis of a prepared scenario) was but one

A Theatrical "Golden Age" Begins   181

of their many modes of performance, which could also include "written comedies, tragi-comedies, tragedies, tragedies set to music, and pastoral plays," depending on the troupe.[34] In Italy, the troupes' willingness to tour gave them access to numerous towns and cities, where they could perform on the street, in public halls, or for private audiences. Their adaptability made their work eminently suitable for export, a path already well-worn by countless other bearers of Italian Renaissance culture (see Figure 11.1). By the 1570s, *commedia* troupes were widely touring, with audiences ranging from the "plebeian" and "semi-bourgeois" to "princes, aristocrats [and] great lords."[35] The troupes' foreign language does not seem to have presented much of a barrier because they could vary the emphasis on dialogue as the occasion demanded. Indeed, the formula of stock characters, masks, *lazzi*, and structured improvisation "may have been largely developed for, or during, foreign touring and residence."[36]

Commedia dell'arte was clearly a somewhat amorphous theatre form. But as its name suggests, perhaps its most important characteristic was the fact that its actors "were committed to the theatre as a way of earning a living."[37] Ferdinando Tavioni remarks that *commedia* "stood out because it

Figure 11.1 *Commedia dell'arte*: the Gelosi troupe in performance. The female lead is possibly Isabella Andreini, coleader of the troupe; opposite her is the character Pantalone. The painting is by either Hieronymus or Frans (the elder) Francken, circa 1590, just after the troupe's first visit to Paris. (Photo by Photo12/Universal Images Group via Getty Images)

consisted of theatrical enterprises which sold performances by persuading spectators to buy tickets."[38] When its troupes first traveled abroad, none of the lands they visited had a body of performers nearly as artistically competent or professionally committed. But that would shortly change, thanks to the influence of *commedia dell'arte* itself, in conjunction with school-based humanist efforts. The result would be the emergence of three early subforms (Spanish, English, and French) of European spoken theatre.

These subforms shared numerous traits still common to the form, three of which are especially noteworthy. The first (and most obvious) is that they followed the model of *commedia erudita* and humanist-influenced school plays by having their characters speak their lines. But beyond the occasional inclusion of diegetic song and dance, spoken theatre troupes found additional ways to include these crowd-pleasing elements in their theatrical programs. In late sixteenth-century Spain, for instance, a performance of what was originally called *comedia nueva* ("new comedy"; note the single "m" in the first word) was accompanied by a variety of other entertainments, including opening songs and/or dances as well as a concluding *baile* (a dance that was mixed with a monologue or dialogue).[39]

A second trait shared by the three subforms is that they filled niches for urban commercial theatre that were opening as the economic center of Europe shifted from the Mediterranean to the Atlantic coast. As had occurred elsewhere in the world, suggests the historian Peter Burke, "the growth of cities [in Western Europe] led to the commercialization of leisure – the rise of the theatres for instance," for "as cities grew, it was possible for actors to remain in the same place and still perform for a different audience every night."[40] And because a portion of the urban wealth was now accruing to the middling classes, the audiences were at once substantial and variegated. In Spain, *comedia nueva* came into its own by the 1580s as "a genre which produced that comparatively rare thing, a truly popular great art." Audiences in the *corrales* ("theatres") of Madrid and Seville "represented a good cross section of urban society – nobles, prelates and the wealthy in the boxes, traders, shopkeepers and artisans on the benches and raked seating, manual workers, soldiers, servants, young bucks and those who lived by their wits in the patio."[41]

At roughly the same time, professional spoken theatre also emerged in London. According to the historian Peter Hall, this city was undergoing "nothing less than an economic revolution," carried on in good part by "a class of 'New Men': clothiers, financiers, merchants, entrepreneurs who owed their power not to owning land but to business ability" and who were abetted by numerous clerks, apprentices, and wage laborers – all of

A Theatrical "Golden Age" Begins 183

whom found themselves with a few pence to spare for entertainment. Also abounding were a growing number of lawyers and governmental functionaries, as well as aristocrats in search of fresh distractions. The implications for theatre were immediate. As Hall suggests, "In one sense, the question – why did London theatre happen – hardly needs answering: London's theatre arose because the audience was waiting."[42]

The emergence of spoken theatre in Paris was somewhat delayed compared to Spain and England. As late as the 1620s, theatre in "the city was on the level of any provincial [French] town, the inhabitants of which were only provided with theatrical performances when a strolling company stopped there for a few days in the course of its wanderings."[43] There is no generally agreed upon reason for the relative tardiness of Parisian commercial theatre: Perhaps it was the fault of plebian audiences and the playwrights who wrote down to them; or perhaps it was the lack of "refinement" among the Parisian elite.[44] But one should not underestimate the impact of the French Wars of Religion that had raged through the second half of the sixteenth century. In the 1590s, the population of Paris collapsed from a high of some 400,000 (swelled by impoverished refugees from elsewhere in France) to a low of about 200,000, following a "massive exodus" of Parisians fleeing siege and a new outbreak of plague.[45] Paris's population implosion seems to have hobbled the prospects for urban commercial theatre if only because the potential audiences were so limited. But by the 1630s, Paris had regained and surpassed its earlier population; its commercial theatre entered into its glory years, with audiences that were "for the most part bourgeois, with at least a sprinkling of noblemen" as well as some people from "the lower orders."[46]

A third trait (or rather set of traits) shared by the subforms of spoken theatre concerns the texts they enacted. These followed the precedent of *commedia erudita* and humanist plays in offering complex (usually secular-oriented) plots whose reliance on dialogue and monologue allowed for characters to be portrayed in great psychological depth. But the three subforms also followed the example of *commedia dell'arte* in being composed for commercial success. With troupes outsourcing the task of playwrighting to one or more authors, they could appeal to audiences with an almost endless flow of new material. In early sixteenth century Spain, "approximately a hundred theatrical managers were active, each of whom staged from twenty to forty plays yearly."[47] In London, a single troupe (in the 1594–1595 season) "offered their audience a total of thirty-eight plays, of which twenty-one were new to the repertory, added at more or less fortnightly intervals."[48] Even in Paris, the rag-tag touring troupes of the early sixteenth century were able to offer numerous plays; Alexandre Hardy, the leading French playwright of the era, claimed to have written 600 of them over a career of some forty years.[49]

Yet again, though, localized differences marked the three subforms. The plots of the Spanish *comedia* "tend[ed] to be complicated, usually action-packed"; their emotions were "correspondingly intense, even exaggerated"; and "love and honor [were] the two overriding matters of immediate concern."[50] Of little concern to this subform were the neoclassical "rules" of theatre derived from misreadings of Aristotle's *Poetics*.[51] English playwrights were even less bothered by those rules. Their plays sprawled across time and space while "deploy[ing] a range of genres responding to the changing pulses and tastes" of their audience. Especially popular early on were history plays treating "the societal situation, the dynamics of dynastic conflicts ..., and the question of the legitimacy of royal domination" – all matters of pressing concern in a country facing dynastic uncertainty under the childless Queen Elizabeth I. Among other popular genres were Italian-based romantic comedies as well as satirical comedies frequently set in London itself.[52] In France, however, the neoclassical rules served, in effect, as the theatrical expression of an absolutist state obsessed with maintaining order. They included what were called "the three unities" (time, space, and action), but no less important were *vraisemblance* ("verisimilitude"), which required that nothing in a play should strain the audience's credulity, and *les bienséances* ("the proprieties"), which insisted that "each character speak according to his condition, his age, and his status."[53] Seventeenth century French theatre trended toward an ever increasing obedience to these rules, suggests John Lough, although most playwrights did not forget the "higher rule" of "giving pleasure" to the audience.[54] Insofar as French audiences (as well as playwrights, actors, and critics) were themselves increasingly indoctrinated to accept the rules, this did not necessarily lead to any contradiction.

One final point about the three early subforms of spoken theatre deserves mention. Although female actors were not unprecedented in European theatre history, they were nonetheless a rarity.[55] But the women of the touring *commedia dell'arte* troupes provided a tempting model and (in Spain and France especially) a competitive challenge. Women were accepted onstage in Spain by 1587, when an Italian troupe was licensed to include them; in short order, Spanish troupes were also being granted such licenses.[56] Their acceptance was, however, somewhat grudging, for female actors "remained a target for moralists and detractors throughout the seventeenth century."[57] France was next to succumb, and again it seems that the influence of the Italian *commedia* was significant, given its popularity there. Although French "actresses may have been rare at the beginning of the [seventeenth] century," there were certainly at least a few by the 1620s. And while their morals were often impugned, "for aesthetic and other reasons actresses were quickly to constitute one of the main attractions of theatre as it gradually became a fashionable form of entertainment."[58]

England's belatedness in allowing women onto the public stage was, as Stephen Orgel comments, "anomalous" when "viewed in a European context."[59] Perhaps this anomaly was related to the relative infrequency of visits by Italian troupes and the resulting absence of a competitive model that needed to be emulated.[60] But English playwrights were certainly aware of *commedia*, while English visitors to the European mainland were fascinated (if sometimes appalled) by women on stages there. Orgel suggests that behind England's "outrage of public modesty" was "a real fear of women's sexuality, and more specifically, of its power to evoke men's sexuality": Given the choice between cross-dressing boys and real women, the latter presented the greater societal danger.[61] Laurence Senelick, however, argues that this was "a period when a boy was a culturally acceptable equivalent of a woman" as the locus of male desire; indeed, "the boy player's personal charms ... were not concealed but enhanced by his female accoutrements."[62] Neither of these suggestions, however, can account for why England alone held out against female actors: Were Englishmen more fearful of women or attracted to boys than were the men of France and Spain?

A better explanation for the anomaly of cross-dressing boys might be that the playwrights who created English spoken theatre – the so-called University Wits – were well-accustomed to working with boys from their days at Cambridge and Oxford; some of these playwrights also worked with the Boy Companies that flourished for a brief spell in London.[63] Despite limited information about the boys who enacted women's roles on the professional stage, at least a few are known to have performed in academic institutions or in the Boy Companies.[64] There was presumably a stream of stage-worthy boys available to the professional troupes – and at minimal cost, for the boys were hired as apprentices to troupe members and so were not paid.[65] Once the practice of using cross-dressing boys was established, subsequent audiences would have accepted it as the right and proper norm, especially absent the direct competition of *commedia*. Indeed, playwrights could even take advantage of the practice for gender-bending plays (such as Shakespeare's *Twelfth Night*) that used boys to enact female characters who disguised themselves as men.[66] When English theatres were shut down with the onset of the English Civil War in 1642, the tradition of cross-dressing boys came to a swift end. Upon King Charles II's return from exile in France in 1660, audiences in the reopened theatres were happy to follow the lead of the Frenchified court and enjoy female characters enacted by women.

Even as the three subforms of spoken theatre emerged in the decades around 1600, a radically different theatre form was beginning its career in Italy. This form, now known as opera, was also inspired by humanist study, but here the focus was on Greek tragedy. Ottavio Rinuccini, librettist for one of the earliest attempts at opera, stated the challenge: "The ancient Greeks ... in representing their tragedies on stage, sang them throughout. But until now the noble manner of recitation has been neither revived nor (to my knowledge) even attempted by anyone."[67] Although Rinuccini was mistaken in thinking that tragedy was sung "throughout," his misunderstanding would prove immensely productive. David Kimball suggests that "there was scarcely one of the first generation of opera composers who did not rationalize the new genre by explaining that it was an attempt to revive the tragic art of the Ancient Greeks."[68] Notably, however, it would prove to be "the mythological handbooks rather than the Greek plays themselves that provided the subjects for the new musical dramas until the late eighteenth century."[69] The strictly antiquarian interest, in other words, was quickly subordinated to the question of how to employ ancient ideas for contemporary purposes, albeit with a "classical" gloss.

According to Ruth Katz, the "puzzle" for a shifting circle of Florentine humanists known as the Camerata de' Bardi "was to discover the ideal combination of words and music such that ... each in its own way and in juxtaposition to the other, could be maximally effective in communicating not just sensory pleasure [but also] the specific meanings and emotions appropriate to the text."[70] It was difficult, however, to imagine how the polyphonic and contrapuntal music of the time could be made to support singing in which the words might be comprehensible. The Camerata's first successes – *Dafne* (1597–1598) and *Euridice* (1600) – were created for "specific political or social occasions, and were performed before an invited patrician audience," with virtually unlimited budgets.[71] Their major conceptual breakthrough was to replace polyphonic singing with a "monodic style": a fixed melody line for the singer, supported by limited, noncontrapuntal orchestration. But as the novelty of this new style wore off, suggest Donald Jay Grout and Hermine Weigel Williams, its defects became inescapable: weak characterization, a limited range of emotion, careless musical organization, and above all the monotony of solo singing.[72]

The puzzle of combining words and music remained to be solved by Claudio Monteverdi. In 1607 he presented his landmark opera, *Orfeo*, which pushed the monodic style in a pair of contrasting directions: toward the open structure of recitative, which allowed "for a dynamic integration of the dialogue into the flow of action," and toward the song-like structure of the melodic aria, which "halts the action, allowing externalisation of affect or a contemplative moment of introspection."[73] And because Monteverdi saw music not merely as the servant to the text but as its equal, he increased the role of orchestration, enabling the music to participate fully in the creation of dramatic meaning. Through these and other innovations, Monteverdi "achieved the unity of drama and music of which the Florentines only dreamed."[74]

Although Monteverdi's first operas were limited to the same sort of elite audiences that had attended the earlier efforts, this changed when he moved to Venice in the late 1630s. According to Ellen Rosand, "The audience for [Venetian] opera, drawn from the carnival crowds that annually swelled the population of the city, was unusually large; it was also unusually diverse …. When foreign tourists took their places in the theaters, they were surrounded by the full spectrum of Venetians, from the patricians in the boxes to the volgo in the stalls." Between 1637 and 1678, nine different theatres presented a total of more than 150 operas; for those theatres, "commercial success was of primary concern, and that could be achieved only by creating works with broad audience appeal."[75] The transition from private to public performances was the first change of niche in opera's illustrious career – but would not be its last.

Ballet also had its prehistory in the festivities of sixteenth-century Italian patricians, whose entertainments often included "elegant social dances" known as *balli* and *balletti*.[76] As Fernand Braudel comments, ballet began as "an Italian initiative that underwent unexpected and expansive developments in France" when a Florentine noblewoman, Catherine de Medici, married into the French royal court and began importing Italian dance masters.[77] The most significant early step in the form's development was the *ballet de cour* ("court ballet"), established with the *Ballet Comique de la Reine* (1581). This carefully choreographed work included a pseudoclassical narrative that sought above all to glorify the French court. As the dance master himself wrote to the king, "And now, after so many unsettling events … the ballet will stand as a mark of the strength and solidity of your Kingdom."[78]

In England, meanwhile, the royal court sought to celebrate its own glory. Under Queen Elizabeth I, royal progresses had already grown quite elaborate, making ample use of mask and costume and incorporating what Martin Butler calls "semi-dramatic" elements. At the tail end of Elizabeth's reign, and even more under her Jacobean successors, these self-celebrations lost their peripatetic aspect and turned into court masques. In this theatre form, "scenery, song, and speech were brought together within a single integral fable that accommodated flattery of the monarch with an opportunity for social dancing between masquers and audience."[79] The form attained its full elaboration in the early 1600s. The design of its productions drew on the full panoply of Italianate staging, while its texts gave the form a literary quality far beyond that of the more dance-oriented *ballet de cour*. What these two forms had in common, above all, was their willingness (indeed, their explicit desire) to expend prodigious resources to glorify their monarchs.[80] What most differentiated them were their fates. The court masque would not survive the English Civil War (1642–1660), aside from a few minor exceptions.[81] Ballet, on the other hand, would continue to develop within the French court until the French Revolution, after which it would switch niches and become (for a while) a popular commercial form of theatre.

The prophecy of Erasmus, in sum, had come true, at least as it pertained to theatre. The sixteenth and early seventeenth centuries were very much a theatrical "golden age" in Europe. And although this account has focused primarily on Italy, Spain, France, and England, humanist playwrights could be found in most of Europe; Italian *commedia* troupes toured in Germanic- and Slavic-speaking lands; and the spoken theatre that had emerged in rough synchronicity in three countries quickly spread outward. William N. West notes that "in the 1670s the repertoire of a company in Bavaria included works by Kyd, Marlowe, Shakespeare, Lope de Vega, Calderón, Andreas Gryphius, and the Dutch playwright Joost van den Vondel, as well as Italian operas."[82] Those operas would prove especially influential in France, Austria, and Russia, each of which would go on to develop its own important operatic tradition. But whatever the national traditions of spoken theatre and opera might have been, the forms themselves were well on their way to becoming virtually pan-European.

I have argued in Part IV of this book that the predicates for Eurasia's theatrical resurgence in the sixteenth and early seventeenth centuries were the disasters of the bubonic plague and the post-Mongol collapse of trade, along with the onset of the Little Ice Age and more localized political crises, such as beset Japan. In their wake came generative disruptions that created new possibilities for theatrical innovation: populations rebounded; new technologies and ideologies were created or adapted; and new social hierarchies took shape, usually dominated by powerful regimes but often featuring fast-growing, urban-based middling classes. All of which is to say that as Eurasia recovered it was also reconfigured. That reconfiguration was further stimulated by the resumption of intersocietal contact across Eurasia – and now also with the Americas, resulting in the Columbian Exchange. The upshot of Eurasia's recovery and reconfiguration was a theatrical resurgence, with scores of new forms being created to satisfy the interests and desires of new audiences. As should be clear, it was not Europe alone that experienced a golden age of theatrical innovation; instead, the golden age extended across the breadth of Eurasia.

Much of this can easily appear to exist beyond the human scale and therefore raises the question of human agency. Fernand Braudel, a leading exponent of histories written on massive geographic and temporal scales, certainly wrestles with that question. He asks: "By stating the narrowness of the limits of [human] action, is one denying the role of the individual in history?" He answers, "I think not" – but he then adds, "When I think of an individual, I am always inclined to see him imprisoned within a destiny in which he himself has little hand, fixed in a landscape in which the infinite perspectives of the long term stretch into the distance both behind him and before."[83] Michael Adas is one of many historians who, while being sympathetic to Braudel's approach, have insisted on the significance of human agency. Adas writes: "In and of themselves, institutions, systems, and processes cannot account for historical change or causality. Rather, they comprise the contexts (essential to historical analysis) in which human agents, both as individuals and as members of social collectives, make history"; he adds that "of course, the contexts themselves have been constructed by other human agents over a great span of time."[84] Even such matters as epidemic disease and climate change should be understood as "contexts" (however favorable or unfavorable) in which people "make history."

Throughout Eurasia in the sixteenth and early seventeenth centuries, recovery and reconfiguration opened countless new niches that theatrical innovators could fill, but there was no necessity that they be filled in the ways that they were. Theatre artists, whether as individuals or working collectively, took what they could find in their societal and theatrical contexts and shaped it to suit their own talents and purposes. Sometimes this resulted in theatre forms that ended up competing for the same new niche, as with the competition between the *kabuki* originated by Okuni and the *bunraku* created by anonymous storytellers, puppeteers, and musicians; at other times the result was a single theatre form that could serve in multiple geographically distinct niches, as with the three early subforms of European spoken theatre. Sometimes an ideological development would lead to the emergence of a narrow but perfectly suited theatre form, such as *taʿziyeh*, which was the theatrical embodiment of Iranian Shiism; at other times a no-less singular ideology, such as South Asia's *bhakti* movement, could spawn multiple theatre forms, such as *raslila*, *ramlila*, and *krishnattam*. Sometimes a theatre form would, in effect, be outright appropriated, as with the Thai capture of the Khmer royal dance troupe; at other times the appropriation would be more covert, as with the Filipino domestication of the *Moros y Cristianos* introduced by Spanish conquerors; and sometimes the appropriation would be based on a fortuitous misunderstanding, as with European opera's attempted appropriation of Greek tragedy. My point is that none of this *had* to happen in the way that it did: Among the countless variables involved in all of this, one must include the agency of the theatre artists themselves.

By the middle of the seventeenth century, however, the pace of theatrical innovation seems to have flagged. Some historians speak of a general Eurasian "crisis" having occurred between roughly 1620 and 1690, although even those who accept this idea cannot quite agree on its geographic extent, temporal duration, or basic cause.[85] If indeed there was such a crisis, one can imagine it imposing constraints on theatre in at least some regions. But however that might be, it is certainly the case that the new social orders brought into being during Eurasia's recovery and reconfiguration were becoming more rigid over time – and that social stability, for all its virtues, tends to limit the sort of generative disruptions that open new theatrical niches. For theatre artists of the late seventeenth century, the best opportunities could usually be found by working *within* theatre forms that were well established but still relatively fresh. The Eurasian theatrical resurgence, unprecedented in its suddenness, breadth, magnitude, and variety, was by then an accomplished fact of which they could readily take advantage.

PART V

The Global Transformation (starting c. 1800 CE)

A person touring Eurasia in the mid eighteenth century would have encountered a few theatre forms that had emerged during the rising tide that started in the tenth century (e.g., *kutiyattam, nō, wayang kulit purwa*) and many more that had emerged during the wave of change that began in the sixteenth century.[1] If this person were adventurous enough to travel beyond Eurasia, most of the theatre to be seen would be indigenous forms with uncertain histories, along with a salting of European forms in scattered colonial settlements. But a century and a half later, a tour of the world's theatre would reveal a transformed landscape. Although many of the established forms would still be in performance, scores of important new forms would have emerged during a new wave of theatrical change that was truly global in scale.

This transformed theatrical landscape came into being because the world itself had radically changed. The historian Jürgen Osterhammel writes that in the eighteenth century, "all societies on the planet were still stuck in a universal premodernity" that was notable above all for its vast distances. But "by the eve of the First World War, a new and unprecedented stage of [global] modernity, however fragmentary and imperfect, had been reached."[2] European-originated revolutions in transportation and communication had breached the barrier of distance, enabling the global expansion of European empires and European-centered capitalism.[3] Europe had never previously been notably wealthy or powerful among the regions of the world. But as modernity took hold, its global reach would disrupt societies almost everywhere.

This is, to be clear, a delicate subject. The historian R. Bin Wong observes that "the writing of global history in the early twenty-first century has become sensitive, even allergic to the faintest hint of Eurocentrism." But although he "shares the aspiration to avoid privileging European actors and processes," he "recognizes that the nineteenth century is the period of greatest European impact globally – if ever Europe came to dominate the world politically and economically, it did so in the nineteenth century."[4] Just as the Mongols had dominated the world within their reach at the start of the fourteenth century, so Europe dominated the world within its reach in the nineteenth century; the difference is that this reach now included much of the world.

According to Osterhammel, "The basic connections of the nineteenth-century system of trade were in place by the middle of the eighteenth century," for Europe was already colonizing the Americas while engaging directly in Asian commerce.[5] But between roughly 1750 and 1850, Great Britain's industrial revolution transformed imperialism through technological improvements in transportation (e.g., steam-powered ships and trains), communications (e.g., the telegraph), and production (e.g., of textiles, iron, and steel).[6] Industrialization spread quickly from Britain: "Steamships, railways and the electric telegraph had been widely adopted in Europe and North America from the 1830s and '40s," writes the historian John Darwin. "By the 1870s they were colonizing vast new areas of the world, carving corridors of access into regions where travel had been difficult (and costly) and information scarce"; indeed, "by the end of the century, no part of the world could be considered immune from the transforming effects" of the new technologies.[7] The global impact of industrial imperialism was profound, not only politically and economically but also culturally. Darwin suggests that "the cultural theory of this imperial world was perhaps its most pervasive departure [from earlier imperialisms]. Europeans convinced themselves, and persuaded others, that while non-European civilizations and cultures were exotic, fascinating, romantic, or beautiful, they were at best a series of culs-de-sac."[8]

How shall we understand the global changes wrought by all this? The historian Sebastian Conrad identifies three overarching conceptual frameworks. The first suggests that "the birth of cultural modernity was … a thoroughly European affair"; only after Europe's "cultural achievements" had "reached maturity" were they "released into the wider world, and over time their light also reached traditional societies in Africa and Asia." A contrary framework condemns rather than celebrates "the spread of the modern worldview," emphasizing the malign impact that Europeans had upon the world at large. But as Conrad notes, "even in this postcolonial reading, cultural modernity remains a European development that gradually spreads its influence throughout the world." A third framework "follows a different logic" by "tracing parallels in cultural development and looking for autochthonous processes of rationalization that occurred independently of Europe, but with similar outcomes." As Conrad observes, however, even this framework ultimately "posits the same goal as standard histories – a modern, capitalist society."[9]

Conrad suggests that "it is less instructive to search for the origins of cultural development" than "to focus on the global conditions and interactions through which the modern world emerged."[10] Globalizing forces, after all, did not come *only* from Europe. Massive population movements in the nineteenth century included diasporas of Africans, Chinese, and Indians, as well as of Europeans themselves;[11] the various regions of Asia gained new or deeper understandings of each other not only through these population movements but also because of a growing realization that such knowledge might be useful in countering European and American power.[12] And of course any aspect of "modernity" that might have been introduced into a given locale was modified in one way or another by the people *of* that locale. The historian Kaoru Sugihara writes: "Western technology and institutions became a global influence, not because they were universally applicable, but because local and regional efforts neutralized their cultural and environmental specificity. In other words, the diffusion of industrialization was the result of multipolar agency."[13]

Taking all this in sum, one can agree with the historians Charles Bright and Michael Geyer: "In the vortex of the global transformation" that began in the nineteenth century, "all societies ... were thrown into nerve-wracking processes of radical self-transformation that remade them, from the inside out, by recombining themselves and their ways with adaptations and imports from all sides."[14] That vortex undoubtedly began in Europe, but each society contributed to it in the course of its own self-transformation. For theatre, all this disruption created numerous new opportunities in theatre regions around the world (see Figure PV.1).

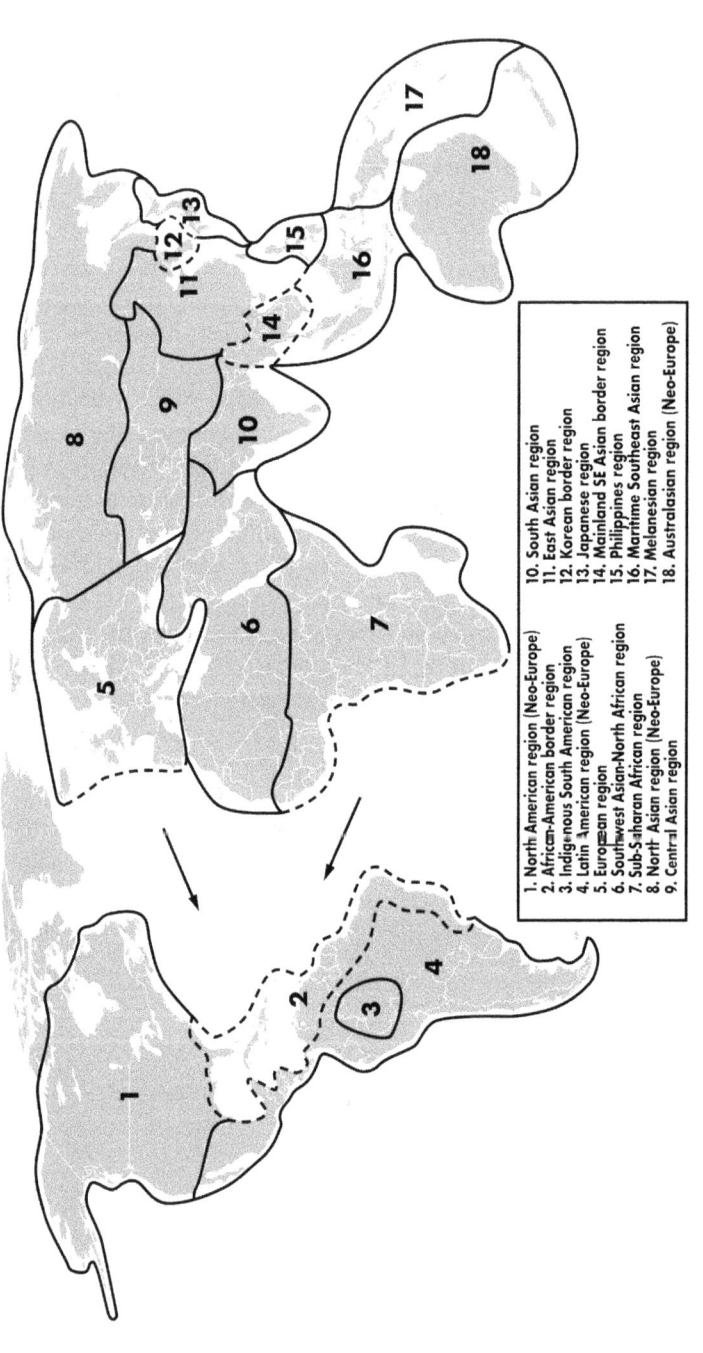

Figure PV.1 Theatre regions of the world, circa nineteenth and twentieth centuries. This map shows the approximate extent of eighteen world theatre regions over the past two centuries or so. The solid lines should be understood as border zones (of uncertain dimensions) in which the theatres of adjacent regions might overlap to some degree; the dotted lines indicate the boundaries of border regions, which are regions that have been strongly influenced by multiple other regions but have distinctive theatre forms of their own. Three of the regions are delineated on the basis of limited evidence: Indigenous South America, Central Asia, and Melanesia; the borders given to the first two of these are especially uncertain.

modernity, realism was, in effect, the very means by which modernizing Europe tried to make sense of itself. According to Osterhammel: "The novelty in nineteenth-century Europe was that … branches of knowledge arose with the aim of *describing* the contemporary world and grasping the patterns and regularities beneath the surface of phenomena." Throughout the century, "new genres of social reportage and empirical inquiry came into being."[10] It is no coincidence that the fields of sociology (applied primarily to Europe), anthropology (applied primarily to non-Europeans), and psychology – along with archive-based national histories – were nineteenth-century developments.

The inescapable problem in discussing *theatrical* realism is that there are many aspects of a theatrical performance that can be treated "realistically," including a play's subject matter; the identities of its characters; the psychological depth given to them; and the look, sound, and movement of the actors playing them. "Realism" might also refer to the social setting of a play or to the scenic depiction of that setting, or (according to Bertolt Brecht) it might apply to the deeper social reality that lay hidden beneath all those surfaces.[11] Confusion about what counts as "realism" is compounded because realist aspects of a performance are often combined with aspects that are deeply stylized. To further complicate matters, the term "naturalism" is often used synonymously with "realism," although scholars try (in various and often contradictory ways) to distinguish between the terms. It is perhaps best to think of naturalism as an extreme kind of realism that presents a play's plot, characters, *and* setting in a virtually clinical manner, rather like a scientific experiment intended for careful observation.[12]

Theatre in Europe took many paths forward through the nineteenth century, with those paths often combining romanticism and realism. Coming into the century, ballet and opera were well-established theatre forms that would be profoundly impacted by romanticism but also touched by realism. Paris was the center of ballet, where it could be seen both as a divertissement in opera and as a theatre form in its own right. In the eighteenth century its dominant subform had been the *ballet-d'action*, which was notable for its emphasis on narrative, its highly standardized choreography, and its "belief in hierarchy and in the truth of social distinction."[13] After decades of difficult transition following the French Revolution, it shifted niches in the 1830s by embracing romanticism. The development of dancing *en pointe* by ballerinas, along with the new invention of gas lighting, favored dances that responded to modernity by escaping into a fantastical world of imagination. The ballet

198   12 The Dynamo of Transformation

La Sylphide (1832) established the template: The ethereal female, dancing as if on air in the mysterious moonlight, became the form's archetypical subject, helping to establish romanticist ballet as a commercial theatre for the moneyed bourgeoisie (see Figure 12.1).[14]

Figure 12.1   Ballet: Marie Taglioni in *La Sylphide*, as performed in Vienna in 1833. (Historisches Museum Der Stadt Wien; Photo by DeAgostini via Getty Images)

Come the start of the twentieth century, though, a renegade troupe called the Ballet Russes would explode upon Paris with a radically new choreography. It would be too much to speak of a pervasive realism in their productions, but reality intruded to a shocking degree, including the dancer Vaslav Nijinsky miming masturbation in a dance that was "not sexy but sexual – a clinical and detached depiction of desire." Jennifer Homans writes, "Nijinsky modernized ballet by making it ugly and opaque: 'I am accused,' he boasted, 'of a crime against grace.'" In his choreography, the awkward realities of human movement – including "hunched figures [who] shuffled, stomped, and turned their feet into awkward pigeon-toed poses with arms curled and heads askew" – found a place on the ballet stage.[15]

Opera, meanwhile, was even more widely established at the start of the nineteenth century but was no less nimble in seeking out new theatrical niches. According to Vlado Kotnik, "The secret of opera's success and popularity" over the centuries is that it "has been the privileged place for enacting the fantasy of a mythical or 'imagined community.'" In the seventeenth century it had supported fantasies of absolute monarchy, most notably in France; in the eighteenth it had offered the "illusion of the enlightened society"; in the nineteenth it came to serve "as the foundational myth of the nation-state, [as] the previous court opera evolved into the 'state opera.'"[16] Only in Italy was opera "a real specialty for *il Popolo*," but even there it responded to modernity by flavoring its romanticism with nationalism.[17] This combination was even more evident in German-speaking lands, where the composer-librettist Richard Wagner created operas that celebrated German artistry and glorified Germanic legend.[18]

Wagner's centrality was not limited to his romanticist nationalism. As Christopher Innes observes, "The mythic material and heroic treatment of his librettos, the musical 'leitmotifs' that lent a dramatic complexity to his music dramas, and the sheer scale upon which the dramas were conceived required a unified presentation that could only be provided by [a] director"; in his maturity Wagner himself served that function.[19] This consummate artist-as-heroic-genius was an important figure in the development of the stage director, which would have profound implications for spoken theatre as well as opera. With the director, writes Nicola Savarese, each theatrical production became understood "as an autonomous work of art," being "the personal synthesis of an artist who interpreted the dramatic text and, through the creation of the performance, expressed his/her own idea of the world and the feelings that pervade it."[20]

As had happened in ballet, realism found a way into opera toward the end of the nineteenth century, especially with Italian opera's *verismo* (literally, "realism") movement. The characters of these operas were typically commoners living in (and struggling through) modern times, as in Giacomo Puccini's *La bohème* (1896). Alan Mallach suggests that "the *verismo* composers strove for what might be called a melodramatic reality, attempting to create the illusion of unmediated reality in service of melodramatic artifice."[21] The fit between realism and opera seemed inherently awkward to at least some people: A contemporaneous composer complained that the whole concept was "untenable," for "people performing actions while singing" makes sense only in the realm of "the incredible, the untrue, the improbable."[22] But this was more an expression of formal expectations than of logical necessity, for numerous theatre forms around the world have successfully enacted aspects of "real" life through song.

Less imposing than opera was operetta ("little opera"), which developed in the mid nineteenth century. Romanticism and realism mixed to varying degrees in operetta's French, British, and Austro-Hungarian subforms, but as Zoltán Imre suggests, the form as a whole "defined and shaped the illusions, desires and expectations of millions and millions of [middle class] spectators."[23] Similarly influential was a related Spanish form known as *genero chico* ("little genre") which had emerged by the 1880s. Deriving from the opera-like romanticist *zarzuela* (which had itself succumbed to competition from Italian opera) *genero chico* replaced *zarzuela*'s "exquisite verse" with "realistic everyday language," making it especially accessible. The form was called *chico* ("little") because each of its plays lasted only about an hour, being performed as part of a program of two or three such pieces. Its subject matter was at once "sentimental and cynical [and] romantic and realistic," writes Christopher Webber, with the form's "prime characteristic" being its roots in "the life of the people, presented for the people."[24]

The most immediately effective combination of romanticism and realism, however, was in melodrama, the first major theatre form to emerge in the tumult of Europe's modernization, right at the start of the nineteenth century. The French playwright Émile Zola dismissed melodrama as "that middle class offspring of the romantic drama."[25] Its romanticism is evident in the way it appeals to the audience's passions through Manichean conflicts between overtly "good" and "evil" characters, as well as by its elaborate stagecraft and insistent musical underscoring. Melodrama's response to modernity was to sympathize with those who felt abused by what seemed a newly unfair world and to present them with "a fantasy of *agency*, the possibility of being able single-handedly to challenge authority and change it."[26] But if romanticism was one of melodrama's parents, realism was its often-unacknowledged *other* parent. Jim Davis suggests, "The fact is that melodrama, however heightened through spectacle, conventional plotting, and character stereotyping, works because it is rooted in the real."[27] It often presented characters who might have stepped onto the stage from everyday life; indeed, "while melodrama may have provided escapist entertainment for some [of the audience], it also provided opportunities to come to terms with, and to negotiate the fact of, modernity."[28]

Melodrama was popular not merely with the middle class, as Zola had suggested, but also with the working class: The form's first great playwright, Guilbert de Pixérécourt, openly stated, "I am writing for those who cannot read."[29] It had many modes in its early decades, but by the 1820s, domestic melodrama had become especially important. In this mode, writes Matthew Buckley, "society was presented in precisely contemporary terms; its figures, crises, and fears were local and ordinary, if exaggerated in tone." Melodrama thus became "a drama not only of tragic nightmare, of historical myth, and national military, political, and social struggle, but of contemporary day-to-day existence, the waking experience of emotional relations, and the psychological negotiation of familial and personal life."[30] In melodrama's portrayal of that existence, Martha Vicinus suggests, "the good hero or heroine confronts a variety of evil forces threatening to destroy the family, but never loses faith that justice will ultimately triumph," for "the fault lies not in him, but in society, which must change."[31] Perhaps Eric Bentley comes closest to capturing the dual nature of melodrama when he refers to it as "the Naturalism of the dream life."[32]

Although I have been treating melodrama as a distinct theatre form, it was obviously closely related to Europe's spoken theatre. Indeed, the public appetite for melodrama sometimes shaped the repertoire of spoken theatre itself. The nineteenth-century critic Horace Foote noted that William Shakespeare's "*Richard III*, *Othello* and *Macbeth* were the most popular 'legitimate' dramas for the simple reason that they were 'the most melodramatic.'"[33] Notwithstanding the preference for its melodramatic plays, however, the cultural importance of spoken theatre remained unchallenged, with its leading playwrights being prized for their contributions to national *literature* even more than for the stage-worthiness of their plays. This emphasis on plays-as-literature helps to account for the relatively limited impact that romanticism had on spoken theatre. In the late eighteenth century, members of the German-language *Sturm und Drang* ("storm and stress") movement were among the earliest romanticist playwrights. They "paid attention first and foremost to elements of poetry," suggests Simon Williams; "dramatic features of importance to the practical theatre, such as clarity of structure, consistent characterisation, and an economical and well-paced action were of secondary concern."[34] In Britain, romanticist poets such as Samuel Taylor Coleridge, Percy Bysshe Shelley, and Lord Byron also tried their hands at playwrighting, but to little avail. Erika Fischer-Lichte rather glumly observes, "A rift seems to have arisen between the public institution of theatre and aesthetically-advanced dramas," which became "dramas to be read" rather than seen. Romanticist spoken theatre stood its best chance in France, thanks to the towering figure of Victor Hugo and his controversial play *Hernani* (1830). And yet within a couple decades, the romanticist flame in spoken theatre had guttered there as well.[35]

One can broadly suggest that in an age dominated by working- and middle-class audiences, the romanticist approach to spoken theatre was overwhelmed by competition not only from the forms already mentioned but also from a subform of spoken theatre that explicitly favored stage-worthiness over aesthetic ambition. Middle-class audiences found what they wanted in the "well-made play" (in the original French, *pièce bien faite*), pioneered by the French playwright Eugène Scribe (1791–1861). Some well-made plays had contemporary settings and characters, others were historical; their tone might be dramatic, comic, farcical, or any combination thereof. But it scarcely mattered, for their main attraction was the formulaic but propulsive construction of their plots. Scribe understood "that all drama, in performance, is an experience in time, and that therefore the first essential is to keep one's audience attentive from one moment to the next"; John Russell Taylor comments that while this ambition is not "the most one might hope for from a playwright," it is "a very proper and by no means despicable minimum."[36] Filled with well-prepared surprises and logical conclusions, the well-made plays sought above all to offer (in Scribe's own words) "relaxation and amusement."[37]

Eric Bentley, though willing to defend the often-scorned melodrama, refers to the well-made play as "this least intellectual form of drama," emphasizing that its plays were "put together according to a mechanical scheme, not, like any really good work of art, according to an organic scheme."[38] But many middle-class theatregoers had little evident concern for "really good work[s] of art." They flocked to see well-made plays, presented in respectable theatres, that offered clever entertainment "coupled with a sane, though certainly not weighty, moral content."[39] The realist possibilities of the well-made play were developed by Alexandre Dumas *fils* in works such as *La Dame aux Camélias* (often simply called *Camille*, 1852), which centered on the tribulations of a Parisian prostitute. But despite its superficial realism, the play did not attempt a serious examination of its characters' psychology or social world; instead, it settled to "contrive" for its audience the comforting illusion of redemption "through love and suffering."[40]

Breaking the "Three Great Taboos"

Psychological and sociological examination were, however, to be the hallmarks of the more stringently realist spoken theatre that was subsequently developed in the works of playwrights such as Henrik Ibsen, August Strindberg, and Anton Chekhov. Ibsen shocked Europe with plays such as *A Doll's House* (1879) and *Ghosts* (1881), which used the plot formula of the well-made play to create psychologically complex characters and examine contentious social issues such as feminism and venereal disease (see Figure 12.2); a British editorial called *Ghosts* "an open drain, a loathsome sore unbandaged, a dirty act done in public."[41] Strindberg was no less shocking with plays such as *The Father* (1887) and *Miss Julie* (1889), which laid bare the raw brutality of intimate human relations. A Danish reviewer wrote of *The Father*, "Despite the talent revealed in the technical construction of the play, it nevertheless remains a bitter, unpoetic fruit on the arid tree of realism."[42] Chekhov was gentler in realist plays such as *The Seagull* (1896) and *Uncle Vanya* (1899), which presented sympathetic but penetrating character studies of the Russian gentry confronting a changing world. Maurice Valency comments, "His great talent lay in the sensitive depiction of the life around him, the physical and psychical landscape in which he lived."[43]

"The new paradigm of realism," writes Peter W. Marx, carefully examined its characters' psychology even as it "explore[d] issues of social change" and the "phenomena that were considered the symptoms and causes of social distress." It brought socially repressed topics to the fore and turned theatre into a forum "for political debate."[44] But the public was often censorious, while the plays themselves were sometimes subjected to governmental censorship. Theatre troupes wanting to mount realist plays frequently resorted to small, noncommercial venues. Eric Bentley points out these venues existed primarily to present plays that broke "the three great taboos in middle class culture – sex, religion, and economics."[45] In so doing, realist playwrights preferred the satisfaction of confronting reality (as they saw it) over that of appealing to large audiences.

Realist spoken theatre itself was soon outflanked in its taboo-breaking, beginning with Alfred Jarry's *Ubu Roi* (1896). Innes observes that the

Figure 12.2 Spoken theatre: Hedvig Winterhjelm and August Lindberg in a scene from the first German production (1883) of Henrik Ibsen's *Ghosts*. (Teaterhistorisk samling, Oslo Museum; CC BY-SA /4.0)

realist desire "to attack society for its hypocrisy" aroused vehement indignation – but was still "intellectually acceptable." With *Ubu Roi*, Jarry attacked "the fundamental concepts of western civilization, accompanied by the satiric denigration of everything bourgeois."[46] Also under attack was the dogged plainness of spoken theatre's stringent realism, in response to which numerous theatre artists and critics called for a "re-theatricalization of theatre."[47]

In the first half of the twentieth century, according to Stefan Hulfeld, the two main lines of this "re-theatricalization" were "a modernist return to pre-modern traditions and a modernist search for a 'theatre of the future.'"[48] These lines can be epitomized by the works of Antonin Artaud and Bertolt Brecht, respectively. Notably, non-European theatre was influential in both lines – for the modernization of European theatre was brought about not only by changes within European society itself but also by Europe's increasing interactions with the rest of the world. These interactions, argues Min Tian, opened a "neo-Orientalist discourse," in which "the Western avant-garde … perceive[d] Asian theatres as their ally in their struggles against European realism and in their searches for a universal language of theatre"; within this discourse, "Asian theatres [were] praised, displaced, reconstructed, and appropriated as materials in the service of the desires, investments, and projections of their competing and ever-renewing experiments and theories."[49]

In 1931, Artaud attended a set of Balinese dances at the Colonial Exhibition in Paris; in them he saw "the concretization" of a theatrical idea he had long cherished. Artaud "had no particular predilection for the theatres of the East," notes Nicola Savarese. "Rather, his passion for 'otherness' was fueled by his total rejection of Western civilization." Upon viewing the Balinese dances, Artaud saw in them "the theatre he had sought for and dreamed of, and, at the same time, *possible theatre*."[50] Rustom Bharucha acerbically comments that "in his eclectic, almost frantic need to absorb non-western cultures," Artaud created his own "imaginary Orient, from which he derived sources of rejuvenation" while being "totally oblivious of their historicity and indigenous meaning."[51] What most appealed to Artaud was what he mistook to be the ritualistic primitivism of the Balinese dances. He wrote that the Balinese performance "restores the theater, by means of ceremonies of indubitable age and well-tried efficacy, to its original destiny," with its various elements "fused together in a perspective of hallucination and fear."[52] This fascination with primitivism and ritualism, Innes comments, "is what distinguishes avant garde aims most clearly" from the alternative line of retheatricalization that emphasized "socially or politically committed drama."[53]

That alternative line was influenced by non-European theatre in 1935, when Brecht saw the work of *jingju* artists touring from China. It helped confirm to him two key ideas he had been developing. The first was that actors should not be "completely transformed" by their roles; instead, the Brechtian actor "underlines the technical aspect and retains the attitude of someone just making suggestions" about the role.[54] This distance between actor and role was intended to support Brecht's second key idea, the *verfremdungseffekt* (translated as either the "alienation" or "estrangement" effect), whose purpose is to disrupt the audience's empathetic response to the characters and to provoke instead a critical analysis of the underlying social reality presented by the play.[55] But as Min Tian observes, Brecht entirely misunderstood what the *jingju* artists were doing, for in Chinese theatre "it is through the performer's identification [with his character] that the spectator is drawn into the dramatic situation emotionally, spiritually, and aesthetically and identifies himself/herself in varied degrees with the character."[56]

Artaud and Brecht, in sum, "started from the same point, the rejection of naturalism,"[57] but they took very different approaches to retheatricalizing European theatre. Whereas Artaud desired a return to primitive ritual as a way of *erasing* bourgeois society, Brecht wanted to advance society *beyond* bourgeois dominance. Christopher Balme comments that the influence of Asian theatre forms on Artaud and Brecht (along with others such as William Butler Yeats, Peter Brook, and Ariane Mnouchkine) amounted to "a kind of 'blood transfusion' … for a moribund theatrical aesthetic."[58] The effectiveness of this transfusion is certainly a matter for debate. But it is undeniable that Europe's increasing presence throughout the world not only had an impact on non-European theatre, as we will see, but also changed European theatre itself. In the maelstrom of the nineteenth and early twentieth centuries, such change was inescapable, for modernity was never a one-way street.

CHAPTER 13

The Neo-Europes

Europe's New Worlds

Europe's imperial adventures did not, of course, begin in the nineteenth century but with the colonies it had established in the Americas three centuries earlier. The original colonizers thought of themselves as belonging to one or another "home" European country. But generations later, those who lived in those once-colonial lands staked a claim to more localized identities, even while retaining a sense of connection to Europe. How then are we to make sense of the theatres that developed in these now-former colonies?

The historian Alfred W. Crosby has introduced the useful concept of "Neo-Europes" for the lands beyond Europe that were subjected to extensive European settlement. These lands have climates similar enough to Europe's to allow for the transfer of the plants and animals on which Europeans have historically depended. Further, the colonizing Europeans established familiar institutions that helped them to subordinate the indigenous populations – and eventually to outpopulate them as well, thanks to warfare, disease, further waves of immigration, and (in some cases) intermarriage with native peoples. The lands Crosby identifies as Neo-Europes include Australia and New Zealand (taken together, Australasia), North America, and much of Latin America; he refers to Siberia as a "Neo-Europe manqué," mostly because it does not produce the "colossal surpluses of food" typical of other Neo-Europes.[1] For theatre history, it is clearly a Neo-Europe, but because information about its theatre is so limited, I will pass over it here.

Crosby makes little mention of the lands in or around the Caribbean Sea, which are unique because the colonizing Europeans and the indigenous Amerindian peoples were not the only players in their colonial histories. Between the sixteenth and nineteenth centuries, some ten to twelve million enslaved Africans were transported to the Americas, most often to the Caribbean islands and Brazil but also to elsewhere in Latin America as well as the United States.² The geographers Martin W. Lewis and Kären E. Wigen designate these areas as a global region unto itself, which they call "African America."³ It is, in effect, a Neo-European *border* region long controlled by Europeans, populated largely by Africans, but geographically and culturally associated with the Neo-Europes of Latin and North America.

The four European nations that took the lead in creating the Neo-Europes of the New World were Spain, Portugal, France, and England; Holland also had a few colonies, but these were either small or short-lived, so I will overlook them here. The different motives and means of the Spanish and Portuguese colonialists on the one hand and the French and English on the other explain much about the different directions taken by the various colonies and their theatres.

As Columbus's successors soon realized, he had failed to pioneer the desired shortcut to Asia – but the Americas offered their own possibilities. The Treaty of Tordesillas (signed in 1494) granted Spain colonization rights to most of the Americas but (owing to a faulty sense of global geography) gave Portugal rights to what is now Brazil. With those rights in hand, the two Iberian countries quickly turned to extracting American resources and Christianizing Amerindian populations. Given these tasks, the Iberian colonizers were almost entirely male, being soldiers, administrators, or missionaries. Many of them soon took up with Amerindian women, inevitably resulting in substantial mestizo classes. These classes, along with the general success of the evangelical mission, partly bridged the cultural distance between the colonizers and the colonized. During the nineteenth century, immigration drastically increased, with some eight million people "from the Iberian and Italian peninsulas mov[ing] to South America's frontier societies, Brazil and Argentina in particular."⁴ What had begun as rapacious commercial enterprises and hotbeds of missionary activity took on the appearance of settler colonies, albeit with a substantial Amerindian intermixture.⁵

The French and British, for their part, blithely ignored the Treaty of Tordesillas and in the early seventeenth century established their own colonies in North America. These differed from the Iberian colonies because virtually from the start they were settler colonies. Although they made an effort to extract resources (primarily animal furs) and convert the occasional native, the French and British colonies were largely peopled by families rather than soldiers and missionaries. Their primary desires were to keep Amerindians as distant as possible, while extending their own land claims as far as they could. No mestizo classes bridged the cultural gap between the settler and native populations, nor was there widespread conversion of Amerindians to Christianity. Subsequent immigration only increased the Neo-European appetite for land, and by the end of the nineteenth century the much-diminished Amerindian population in North America was largely hemmed in on "reserves" or "reservations."

The African American border region presents a third model of colonization. It was predicated on plantations that used enslaved Africans to produce massive quantities of rice, tobacco, cotton, indigo, and (most importantly) sugar. On the seventeenth-century Brazilian sugar plantations, writes the historian Wolfgang Reinhard, "it was claimed that a slave would earn his master his purchase price back in just sixteen months," providing "no incentive to treat the slave workforce humanely. As a Jesuit missionary observed in 1627, 'A sugar mill is Hell on Earth. Their owners are all damned.'"[6] Perhaps that would eventually be the case, but while they lived the plantation owners were also often fabulously wealthy, whether they resided in their home countries or in a cocooned colonial world far removed from the hell of their enslaved workforce. Although masters often imposed sexual relations on enslaved women, the offspring of these alliances were (by definition) slaves themselves, and so did little to bridge the racial bifurcation that was the central characteristic of plantation colonialism in the African American border region.

Latin America

Theatre in what would become the Latin American Neo-Europe long predated the voyages of Columbus, although little of it remains. Philippa Brown Yin writes that "history, religion, great deeds, acts of heroes and devils, nature's marvels, and comic relief were acted, sung, danced, or all of these, with musical accompaniment, in the major population centers" of the great Amerindian empires.[7] The Inca Empire had "numerous performance traditions related to historical and military affairs whose primary function was to inculcate ethical values and to ensure political cohesion by celebrating the deeds of Inca warriors." But a seventeenth-century account also notes that there were "comedies" as well, whose plots "were about farmers, agriculture, and household affairs."[8] Even more striking is a sixteenth-century dramatic text from the Maya Empire (in what is now Guatemala), known as *Rabinal Achí* (*Rabinal Warrior* or *Man of Rabinal*).[9] No such play texts survive from the Aztec Empire, but some "poems include passages in dialogue as well as choral sections interspersed with descriptions of pantomimic dance," suggesting the presence of dramatic theatre. There is also Spanish testimony "of what sounds like pure entertainment in Aztec culture," in which players "provoked gales of laughter by their portrayals of comically afflicted persons seeking cures from the gods."[10]

The Iberian conquistadors and missionaries were quick to take advantage of the Amerindians' theatrical inclinations by enlisting their participation in European-derived theatre forms, most notably *autos sacramentales* (the Iberian version of miracle plays), *pastores* ("Shepherds' Plays"), and *Moros y Cristianos*.[11] In 1538, for example, an *auto* entitled *The Fall of Adam and Eve* was "presented by the Indians 'in their native language'" in Spanish Mexico. Susan Castillo comments that the play's "depiction of the expulsion of the unhappy pair from a Paradise of abundance and beauty to a desert of forced labour and privation would have resonated greatly with the Nahua spectators who had experienced the violence of the Conquistadores at first hand only a generation earlier."[12]

More spectacular were the 1539 productions of *The Conquest of Rhodes* (in Mexico City) and *The Conquest of Jerusalem* (in Tlaxcala), both of which were indigenized versions of the Spanish *Moros y Cristianos*.[13] Once again, though, what the Amerindians took away from the performances was likely not quite the intended glorification of Christian conquerors. Peculiarities in the plotting and performance of these conquest plays lead Castillo to suggest that "the indigenous performers [were] in effect, staging a counter-Conquest, appropriating the ideology that had apparently given supremacy to the Iberian invaders and inverting the discourse that would view the natives of the New World as less civilized or human." The "real barbarians," from the Amerindian perspective, were "perhaps not the indigenous groups of the Americas, but rather the Europeans."[14] This suggestion comports with Max Harris's argument that these plays contained "a hidden transcript" understood only by the Amerindians, one "strand" of which "dreamed of future liberation" from European domination.[15]

Be that as it may, Judith A. Weiss et al. observe that the high culture of the developing Latin American colonies "was predominately an extension of the ideological apparatus of imperial Spain and Portugal."[16] For theatre, that especially meant the spoken theatre that had emerged in late sixteenth-century Spain. As it happens, a Mexican woman, the illegitimate child of a Basque landowner and a Creole mother, was arguably the last of the great playwrights of that Spanish "Golden Age." Sor Juana Ines de la Cruz (1648–1695) was widely recognized for her brilliance, though compelled to retreat to a convent to carry on her studies and writing.[17] Her theatrical work consists of eighteen *loas* (either freestanding or affixed to full-length plays), three *autos*, two *sainetes* (one-act farces), and two *comedias*.[18] The *loa* affixed to one of the *comedias* (*The Divine Narcissus*) is of special interest, suggests Castillo: It "stages an extraordinarily rich and allusive Creole performance of the collision between two local narratives, that of Spanish missionary Catholicism at the service of Empire and that of enduring indigenous belief systems." The *loa* is, in effect, a continuation of the syncretism "in which indigenous performance forms are amalgamated with certain features of European theatrical tradition."[19]

Perhaps even more syncretic is a folk play called *El Güegüence, o El Macho Ratón* (*The Old Man, or The Billygoat-Mouse*), for which a single seventeenth-century text exists in what is now Nicaragua.[20] Written in a "hybrid Nahuatl-Spanish language," this musical dance-drama has elements "that defy the standard Spanish drama" of the time (including a lack of female speaking roles and an excess of verbal repetitions), even as its setting is a colonial city and many of its characters are European or mestizo. Weiss et al. see it as "fundamentally a satire of the corruption and the abuse of power by whites" and suggest that since it is neither "a purely Native American play" nor a European one, it should be understood as a "mestizo play."[21]

By the late eighteenth century, the tastes of the Iberian-born or Iberian-descended elite had shifted away from the earlier Spanish *comedias*. Philippa Brown Yin suggests that the preference was now for plays that could be justified "on the grounds that [they] would provide forums for the honest portrayal of good behavior, language, and general civility" – a moralism common in Enlightenment European theatre but that held limited popular appeal.[22] Such theatre soon met its match amid the rumblings of revolution that echoed through Latin America as its peoples sought independence from Europe.

Although differing political situations in the various Latin American colonies/countries affected each one's theatrical development, a broad similarity between them extends through the nineteenth and early twentieth centuries. Most notable was the ongoing influence of European theatre, even as it was modified by local tastes and considerations. Fernando Peixoto observes of Brazil: "We inherited from [European] romanticism and realism an interest in modern themes, including social concerns …. The unresolved conflict of the time was between the Portuguese style of representation and the Brazilian national style. And even if the official colonial links were broken during the 19th century, the country remained subordinate to Europe."[23] Mexico was similarly "ripe for the Romantic movement which swept through Europe." Mexican romanticism "indulged the emotions, making a virtue of extremes of passion, and drew upon the folk life, local color, national history and literature that constituted [the] cultural patrimony." And "although Mexican theatre continued to rely heavily upon both plays and performing artists from Spain ... Mexican nationalism found various means of expression both on the stage and in the audience."[24] During Mexico's War of Independence (1810–1821), Mexico City's leading theatre "was filled with *costumbrismo*, plays depicting local customs, atmosphere, and modes of speech, all of which reinforced a sense of Mexican identity distinct from that of the mother country." That identity was fundamental to a population "with great numbers of mestizos" who maintained "certain aspects of the indigenous culture" that "permeated all levels of the colonial social hierarchy, excepting perhaps those ... born in Spain."[25]

Referring to Latin America as a whole, Philippa Brown Yin comments:

> What is perhaps most interesting is that while Europe looked to past glories ... and far-off lands for exotic images to strengthen their national images, the Latin American countries discovered themselves. They found the exotic on their doorsteps and their national images in their own making.... The interplay of the sentiments of the romantic and the more historically accurate realism provided ample ground for most dramatists.[26]

And yet French operetta also came into vogue after mid-century, appealing especially to the newer immigrants from Europe. Referring to one of Jacques Offenbach's greatest works, a contemporaneous account from Rio de Janeiro reports that "the larger part of the populace which does not consist of blue-blooded noblemen and has no access to an easy and light genre of entertainment similar to [that] in European capitals" welcomed "the lively and cheerful" *Orpheus in the Underworld* "with great enthusiasm."[27]

After operettas, *zarzuelas* (Spanish-style musical theatre) became popular in the expanding cities of the late nineteenth century, with many being created by local artists and given local settings and characters.[28] The one-act Spanish comedy form known as the *sainete* gained the favor of the urban masses, especially in Chile, Uruguay, Peru, and Argentina,[29] in the last of which a subform called the *sainete criollo* ("Creole *sainete*") was immensely popular (see Figure 13.1). The nature of these short plays can be seen in a list of their typical settings: "poor rural or suburban homes, *conventillo* patios, the open streets of popular neighborhoods, carnivals, bars and late-night cafes, factories, shantytowns, and even garbage dumps." The form's "spaces and characters," in other words, came "from everyday life," and its plays addressed "pertinent themes from a perspective the popular sectors could relate to."[30] The playwright Alberto Vacarezza outlined a typical

Figure 13.1 *Sainete criollo*: a scene from Alberto Vacarezza's 1929 play *El conventillo de la Paloma* (*The LaPaloma Tenement*), as remounted in 2013 by The Teatro Nacional Cervantes in Buenos Aires. (Photo by Gustavo Gorrini, Teatro Nacional Cervantes, Argentina)

plotline: "A *conventillo* [tenement] patio / an Italian *encargao* [manager] / a leathery Spaniard / a broad, a smooth-talker / two thugs with knives / flirtatious words, a love affair / obstacles, jealousies, arguments / a duel, a knifing / uproar, shooting / help, cops … curtain."[31]

In the twentieth century, immigration and economic growth produced both "a middle class [and] a working class with increased spending power and cultural aspirations." Even though these classes were socially dominated by the old-guard elite, the theatrical repertoire they favored "often reflected their social and political aspirations."[32] This allowed for the emergence of a deeper psychological and social realism along the lines established by Ibsen, which was almost inevitably followed by a theatrical avant-garde that even more resolutely rejected commercialism and instead "point[ed] to a spirit of renovation in the theater."[33] In Mexico, "the nationalist ideals" of important playwrights "prompted them to turn to the European avant-garde as a source of inspiration for renewing Mexican drama." They and others were influenced by modern theatre that ranged from realism to "abstract and symbolic dramas" to expressionism, intermixing well-known European plays with original Mexican ones.[34]

Two themes should be clear from this quick overview of Latin American theatre. First, from the arrival of the Iberians, the region was dominated by a series of theatre forms and theatrical movements that had originated in

Europe. But second, the non-elite Latin Americans themselves (whether Amerindian or mestizo or immigrant) often domesticated these forms and movements to suit their own interests. The near-total destruction of Amerindian theatre at the hands of Iberian conquistadors and missionaries had virtually assured that Latin American theatre would be European in orientation – but the theatre that resulted was anything but a pale imitation of Europe's.[35]

African America

The development of theatre in the African American border region was not at all like that of Latin America, especially in the Caribbean islands, which are the core of the region and on which I will focus here. One fundamental difference was the virtual annihilation of the Amerindian populations in the Caribbean during the earliest European invasions, which resulted in the islands becoming a kind of "tabula rasa" on which were created "new kinds of society consisting wholly of nonindigenous outsiders": Europeans who understood the islands' potential for cash crops and Africans who were brought across the Atlantic to slave on the plantations that produced those crops. The result was a deeply bifurcated society in which Europeans (about 10–30 percent of the overall population, depending on the locale) held absolute sway.[36] This bifurcation was a second fundamental difference between African America and Latin America: There would be precious little interaction (in life or in theatre) between the two populations until late in the nineteenth century, well after the institution of slavery had been abolished.

The European populations of the Caribbean up to the nineteenth century consisted of plantation owners, overseers, and specialists (along with the families some brought along), as well as soldiers and sailors garrisoned to protect the colonies from competing European empires. What the "white plantocracy" sought in their theatre, suggests Kole Omotoso, "was not just imitations of what went on in the mother-country. Rather, as much as it was possible, it was the fare of the mother-country itself."[37] Aside from occasional amateur performances, this fare was provided by professional touring troupes with a repertoire that ran (depending on the colony) from Shakespeare and Molière to farces and melodramas to *zarzuelas* and operas.[38] But the transplanted European theatre had shallow roots and bore little Caribbean fruit. The main theatre in Havana hosted eighty-six performances in 1791, but only a single Cuban play was performed.[39]

More interesting is what was happening among the enslaved Africans. They "came from many if not all of the African [slave] exporting regions," resulting in a "cultural diversity" that encouraged syncretism.⁴⁰ "The slaves may have crossed the Atlantic empty-handed," writes Osita Okagbue, "but definitely not empty-minded. Each carried within them their own portion of Africa" that helped them "retain their humanity." Individual African languages could scarcely survive in these multicultural communities, but traditions of music and dance were easily shared and combined; the syncretic styles that emerged would become "key structural elements" in "Afro-Caribbean" performance.⁴¹ John Thornton notes also that the styles' creators "stood to benefit if they could also include elements drawn from the music of their ... masters, as winning their patronage promised even greater rewards. Thus, African American musicians adopted instruments and musical elements from European cultures as well."⁴²

One striking theatrical manifestation of pan-African syncretism was called *jonkonnu* (or *johnkannaus*, or John Kannú, or John Canoe).⁴³ The form apparently emerged in eighteenth-century Jamaica and was named for a West African chieftain who had fought against Dutch slavers.⁴⁴ This chieftain, though, was not so much a character in *jonkannu* as he was a locus of celebration in the face of oppression. The form itself was structured along the lines of West African masquerade traditions; it was offered on festive occasions and filled with elaborately masked and costumed singers and dancers. Owing to the prominence of these features, writes Peter Reed, early accounts of *jonkonnu* "tended to discuss it as a transplanted feature of African culture" that was "primitive and extravagantly exotic." But despite its African characteristics, it was an original Afro-Caribbean creation that enacted "a constant tension" between the culture of the enslaved Africans and that of their masters, with performances that "actively engaged the processes of expropriating, transporting, and exploiting countless Africans."⁴⁵

Errol Hill argues that after the development of *jonkonnu* and similar theatre forms, "the next logical phase in the emergence of an indigenous Caribbean theatre should have occurred when gifted individuals began to perform" for "edification and entertainment" – but this did not happen. Instead, "the formal theatre adopted in the Caribbean" continued to come "neither from Africa nor from Afro-Caribbean experience, but from Europe," as "a ready-made package, wrapped in the glory of its acknowledged achievement."⁴⁶ In Cuba, the Hispanic urban population had grown sufficiently by the early nineteenth century to allow for "Romantic drama with its characteristic idealization of individuality and nationalism" to find receptive audiences, to be followed by "realistic social problem plays from France and Spain." By the late nineteenth century, however, a "distinctly Cuban" form of musical theatre finally emerged; known as *bufos habaneros*, it "used situations from working class Cuban life to mock the showier Spanish *zarzuelas*" that also remained popular.[47]

In Jamaica, meanwhile, the usual diet of European theatre continued to be served even after the abolition of slavery in the mid nineteenth century. Only at the end of the century did the separation between African and European-based performance break down when Christmas Morning Concerts (a European variety format) began including Black performers. Half a century later, British-style pantomime introduced the African-originated trickster character Anancy (also known as Anansi). Henceforth, pantomime "became identifiably Jamaican in its use of indigenous material including dance, music, song, drama, improvisation, and pithy commentary on the contemporary social and political scene."[48] Hill seems rueful that Caribbean theatre was "fashioned" on the European form,[49] but the refashioning of alien theatre forms has, as we have seen, long been a common practice and need not be understood as a moral or artistic shortcoming.

One last aspect of theatre in African America deserves mention. After slavery was banned, plantation owners on some islands turned to South Asia for their labor force, introducing yet another nonindigenous element into their populations. Some "forty percent of the one million or so people living in the Republic of Trinidad and Tobago," for example, "have distinctly South Asian ancestry" and "hold tightly to an Indian identity" even as they also see themselves as Trinbagonian. David Mason reports that in the autumn, "roughly coincid[ing] with the Dussehra holiday as observed in India – between twenty and fifty Ramlilas are performed."[50] At least one of these *ramlilas* (known locally as *ramdilla*) explicitly connects the ancient story of Rama with the current lives of Hindu Trinbagonians.[51] Muslim Trinbagonians from South Asia similarly hold annual performances of the Shiite *taʿziyeh*, here called *hosay* (after the name of *taʿziyeh*'s central figure, Husain); these are, however, primarily processional, with little of the dramatic performance of Iran's *taʿziyeh*.[52] This is likely because Shiites had settled in South Asia well before the emergence of Iran's fully dramatic *taʿziyeh* and had never developed "staged dramas of Husayn's martyrdom."[53] In its Caribbean context, *hosay* is primarily a raucous street festival, attended by Muslims and non-Muslims alike. Kole Omotoso observes that "there is no doubt that [it] has become far more secularized than it could ever be in the Shiite communities" of South Asia.[54] The Caribbean *ramdilla* and *hosay* should remind us that the movement of populations was a key feature in the upheavals of the nineteenth century.

North America

Relatively little is known about Amerindian theatre in North America before the nineteenth century. Jeffrey Huntsman suggests this is because French and English settlers had limited interest in understanding their neighbors; by the time their descendants became curious, many of the Amerindians' hundreds of societies had been driven from their homelands or outright destroyed. And when nineteenth-century ethnologists finally began studying the surviving societies, "they were too interested in finding support for preconceived notions about 'primitive' theatre or the 'origin' of drama and often too unwilling to attribute the art they sometimes recognized as anything more than 'primitive intuition.'"[55]

The earliest manifestations of European theatre in North America came from Spain and France. In 1598, a conquistador heralded the Spanish crown's triumphant arrival at what is now the Rio Grande by putting on a performance of some unidentified sort;[56] this introduced a Hispanic element into North American theatre that would extend well into California by the start of the nineteenth century.[57] A few years later and thousands of miles to the northeast, the French garrison at Port Royal greeted its returning founders with a *reception* they called *Le Théâtre de Neptune* (1606). David Emmett Gardner comments that this "parade of short poetic monologues" offered "a strong sense of individuality in the twelve speaking roles, and a healthy adaptation of the neoclassic forms and imagery of Europe to the immediacy of a particular North American situation."[58] Thus began a tradition of French-language performance that would endure in Canada to the present day, although until the twentieth century it would rely heavily on plays imported from France.

Despite these Spanish and French head starts, British theatre would become dominant in North America. In English-speaking Canada, British plays (along with a few translated French ones) ruled the stage: "Not until the mid-nineteenth century do we see any significant number" of Canadian-authored plays, which were themselves characteristically based on European models.[59] The same domination prevailed in the colonies that would become the United States. When George Washington wanted to rally his revolutionary troops during the brutal winter at Valley Forge, he turned to British theatre, ordering that Joseph Addison's heroic tragedy, *The Dying Cato*, be staged "to encourage his troops to accept their hardships with the same Stoic resignation as that portrayed by the play's titular hero as he faces his own death." John O'Brien dryly notes that the troops' "reaction is unrecorded."[60] Even after the war, the American repertoire remained largely British, while touring British stars were often relied upon to attract audiences.[61]

Through the nineteenth century, the most important theatre form in the United States would be European-derived melodrama. It was a natural fit, suggests Daniel C. Gerould: "Crude, violent, dynamic in action, psychologically and morally simple, reliant on machinery and technological know-how for its powerful effects, melodrama became the direct expression of American society and national character."[62] The spoken theatre of the time – primarily well-made plays and lightweight farces – found a less substantial but somewhat more respectable audience, whether offering British plays or "crude and inexpert" imitations thereof. But as William Coyle and Harvey G. Damaser comment, most nineteenth-century British theatre was itself "imitative and second-rate" – so one could scarcely expect the North American versions to exceed it.[63]

One might wonder at the regularity with which early North American settlers aped European theatre. Gardner suggests: "The superiority of the mother country is an accepted fact of colonial life and imitation is its sincerest form of flattery .... When deviations from the original (and, expected) norm appear, they are construed as ... the gaucheries of a distant and provincial child."[64] But even after thirteen colonies banded together to declare independence from Britain in 1776, the imitations continued. Perhaps the best explanation is that European theatre was, in effect, the native theatrical language in Canada and the United States. In Latin America, as we have seen, there was at least a modicum of syncretization with Amerindian theatre, especially after the rise of mestizo classes. North America lacked this syncretism because of the French and English style of colonial settlement. But a different kind of syncretization eventually *did* occur, more in the United States than in Canada. It would not break the North American connection to European theatre, but it made possible three theatre forms that were distinctly American: minstrel shows, Tom shows, and musicals.

The demographics of the United States can help explain the emergence of these forms. North American slavery dates from 1619, when "twenty Negars" were imported to the Jamestown colony.[65] But in North America, slavery was not nearly as deadly as on Caribbean and Brazilian plantations; moreover, the enslaved population was decidedly more balanced between men and women. For these reasons, by the start of the nineteenth century, most of that population in the United States was native-born.[66]

While these men and women retained a strong cultural memory of Africa, they developed their own dialects of English, accepted Christianity, and took up "the egalitarian ideal of liberty that informed the revolutionary age" and inspired calls for Abolition.[67] Slaves in the United States lived in the northern reaches of the African American border region and partook of the theatre traditions of that region. Peter Reed observes that "in her 1861 autobiography *Incidents in the Life of a Slave Girl*, Harriet Jacobs writes of popular holiday slave performances she calls 'Johnkannaus'" – the Jamaican *jonkonnu* discussed earlier.[68] In New Orleans, meanwhile, "slaves gathered to sing and dance in a variety of musical styles, including ones based on African or Afro-Caribbean forms." Joseph R. Roach notes that Euro-American witnesses displayed a deep "ambivalence" toward these performances: Even though they were "scandalized" by what they saw, "they pushed and shoved to obtain a better view."[69]

This same fascination was at the root of the theatre form known as minstrelsy. Minstrel shows presented Black music and dance, along with dramatic sketches ostensibly based on the lives of the enslaved – but all safely sanitized because it was performed by White men wearing blackface. Minstrelsy is usually dated to 1828, when Thomas Dartmouth Rice (an actor who had performed occasional blackface roles in spoken theatre) darkened his face with burnt cork to perform his "Jim Crow" dance.[70] The formal structure of minstrelsy quickly settled into a three-part performance. Shows opened with comic repartee between two endmen (called "Tambo" and "Bones," after the instruments they played) and an interlocutor; they continued with specialty acts (especially song and dance); and they concluded with a dramatic sketch, typically a "plantation scene with dancing 'darkies,'" a burlesque of Shakespearean drama, or a short melodrama.[71] "Burlesque" was indeed central to minstrelsy, but it extended far beyond absurd renditions of Shakespeare. Robert B. Winans argues that the "essence" of the form was burlesque: "The very presence of those comic, pseudoblack performers onstage was a burlesque of all serious theatrical and concert performances. Beyond this general principle, all sorts of specific burlesques were staged," including "burlesque lectures," burlesque dance, burlesque opera, and burlesques of all manner of music.[72]

The sanitized and burlesqued version of Blackness served up by minstrel shows was immensely popular among working-class audiences in northern cities but was also intrinsically political. Eric Lott argues that in the decades before the American Civil War (1861–1865), the form "acknowledged and absorbed black culture even while defending white America against it."[73] Alexander Saxton contends that prewar "minstrelsy not only conveyed explicitly pro-slavery and anti-Abolitionist propaganda; it was, in and of itself, a defense of slavery because its main content stemmed from the myth of the benign plantation."[74] These interpretations are given additional credibility by the career of minstrelsy outside of the United States. Minstrel tours to Ontario were frequent enough that, in 1840, Black Canadians petitioned to have the shows banned on the grounds that they "turn into ridicule and hold up to contempt the coloured population, caus[ing] them much heart-burning and lead[ing] occasionally to violence.'" Minstrel troupes also traveled to Britain and to "British imperial sites across Africa, South Asia, the Antipodes, and the Caribbean," offering "the predominantly antiblack, proslavery, white Anglophone public a figure affirming their social power and feelings of racial superiority through performances of black abjection."[75]

That said, however, "the greatest [popular] success in the history of American theatre" was found in the dramatic adaptations of Harriet Beecher Stowe's novel *Uncle Tom's Cabin* (see Figure 13.2). Numerous such adaptations began in the 1850s and long held the stage, for even as the century turned there were some 500 "Tom" companies touring the country.[76] Judith Williams notes that "'Tom shows' incorporated the blackface, music, and spectacle of the minstrel show with the pathos and abolitionist sentiment of Stowe's novel."[77] This combination of minstrelsy and "abolitionist sentiment" is highly incongruous, but once slavery was abolished after the Civil War, audiences were able to enjoy the plays both for their "melodramatic pleasures – excitation at flight and pursuit, and moral outrage at the victimization of innocence" – and for the pleasures of their "minstrel interludes, animal acts, cakewalk contests, and song and dance routines." The "Tom show," had become, in effect, a syncretic theatre form in its own right, but what had begun as an overwrought but sincere indictment of slavery ended up as little more than melodramatic excess and racist voyeurism. By the mid twentieth century, writes Daniel C. Gerould, "*Uncle Tom's Cabin* seemed a grotesque reminder of a shameful past, something almost obscene, that was best buried and forgotten [sic]."[78]

Blacks themselves had begun working in minstrel shows even before the Civil War and carried on in far greater numbers afterward. They often performed for Black audiences, who "did not conflate blackface with the performers' race ... but understood [it] as a specialty act that facilitated the display of particular sorts of acrobatic, comedic, dramatic, and musical flair."[79] For the performers themselves, minstrelsy provided, above all, an opportunity. Douglas Jones suggests that "despite its racist degradations and grotesqueries," it appealed to Black performers and entrepreneurs

Figure 13.2 Tom show: a color lithograph poster by W. J. Morgan & Co. for an 1881 stage production of *Uncle Tom's Cabin*. In this scene, slave catchers have unleashed their hounds as the runaway slave Eliza escapes with her child across the icebound Ohio River. (Library of Congress, Reproduction Number: LC-USZC4-1298)

because it offered satisfying work and "outlets for their creativity." These minstrel troupes would prove highly influential in subsequent American culture, playing a formative role "in the development of the Broadway musical, vaudeville, ragtime, the blues, and jazz."[80]

The White minstrel troupes that did not turn to "Tom shows," meanwhile, moved on from racial matters to more contemporary topics in the aftermath of the Civil War. To understand this shift, we need to look again to the demographics of the United States. Between 1820 and 1920, roughly thirty-three million European migrants arrived, mostly from Germany, Ireland, Italy, and Eastern Europe.[81] Chinese laborers, meanwhile, crossed the Pacific to work in California's gold rush and to help build America's railroads. Though many would return to China, enough remained to justify setting up Chinese-language theatres in San Francisco. Euro-American audiences curious enough to visit those theatres could make nothing of the plays and often found the music "discordant" and "deafening" – but they were dazzled by the spectacle.[82]

Robert Toll observes that when "faced with basic changes in American society as well as with increased entertainment competition that included large numbers of black minstrels," White troupes turned their attention to the "immigration, urbanization, and modernization" that were transforming the United States. But minstrelsy could not keep up with the changes because the form "had its roots in caricature, not characterization" and so "could not easily capture human complexity."[83] It had been simple enough to caricature distant Black slaves and the occasional big-city Black dandy and then to similarly caricature the new immigrant ethnicities. But as immigrants became a familiar presence, this became anachronistic. The times were changing faster than minstrelsy could, and newer theatre forms could outcompete the minstrel shows for audiences that were increasingly composed of immigrants themselves.

The theatre form that eventually supplanted minstrelsy was the Broadway musical. Its prehistory is usually said to have begun with *The Black Crook* (1866), an implausible melodrama interlarded with occasional songs and beautified by ballerinas who (as a scandalized contemporary wrote) "seem to wear little else than satin slippers, with a few rose-buds in their hair." Despite (or because of) its literary and moral failings, the play was a spectacular success, running for an unprecedented 475 consecutive performances.[84] Although *The Black Crook* demonstrated the appeal of musical theatre, it was a one-off freak. The Broadway musical itself would be woven from the syncretism of four distinct strands of theatre.

One of those strands was ethnic musical comedy as pioneered by Edward Harrigan and Tony Hart, whose plays "gave comic voice to the experience of immigrants and working-class New Yorkers" of the late nineteenth century. Although Harrigan and Hart came out of White minstrelsy and the vaudeville variety theatre that was minstrelsy's immediate successor, they wrote full-length musical plays that "found humor largely in the conflicts that arose" among New York's immigrant groups, even while imbuing the characters "with degree of humanity."[85] The second strand was Black musical theatre, which came out of Black minstrelsy and also passed through vaudeville.[86] Bert Williams and George Walker were its leading exponents, with their play *In Dahomey* (1903) being "the first full-length all-black musical to play a legitimate Broadway theatre in season."[87] Critics were impressed by the play's comedy, but its music and dance proved especially influential; among other things, it introduced the practice of having its choruses simultaneously sing *and* dance.[88] The third strand was British musical comedy, the biggest hits of which were exported throughout the English-speaking world.[89] Especially important to these lightweight confections were simple but catchy songs and female leads and choruses that gave the plays a sexiness that audiences (especially the men, one assumes) found irresistible.⁹⁰ The final strand came from European operetta, first popularized in importations from France, Britain, and Vienna.⁹¹

The Broadway musical emerged in the first decades of the twentieth century. George M. Cohan (the grandson of Irish immigrants) and Irving Berlin (a Jewish immigrant from Russia) each combined the traits of ethnic and English musical comedies, while Sigmund Romberg (a Hungarian immigrant) and Rudolf Friml (a Czech immigrant) emphasized operetta. Joseph P. Swain suggests that "the first maturity" of the Broadway musical was attained in 1927 with *Show Boat*, composed by Jerome Kern with a libretto by Oscar Hammerstein II.⁹² Interweaving the various strands that could go into a musical, *Show Boat* offered a sprawling story filled with spectacle and driven by an "all-American" score that evoked "a panorama of vernacular music from nineteenth-century minstrel shows to 1920s jazz."⁹³ Gerald Bordman writes that "it presented possibly the most important breakthrough in the history of our musical stage," being "the first real 'musical play': a lyric piece with a relatively serious romantic story about essentially everyday people."⁹⁴ Although *Show Boat* would have no equal until the opening of *Oklahoma!* in 1943, it pointed the way to a musical theatre that could be romanticist and realist, comic and dramatic, artistically accomplished and highly popular – and all at the same time.

Australasia

Finally, a few words about the Neo-Europes of Australasia – a sociogeographic concept that makes sense only in the aftermath of British colonization. The colonization of Australia began in 1788 with the establishment of a penal colony in Sydney; eventually some 162,000 convicts would be transported. Within a few decades, free colonization to Australia had also begun and by the mid nineteenth century free settlers far outnumbered convicts.⁹⁵ New Zealand, meanwhile, was a settler colony from its start in the 1840s. As with British settler colonialism in North America, Australasian relations with the indigenous peoples were predicated on the principle of keeping them distant while appropriating their land. The result was that, through the nineteenth century at least, the theatre of the British settlers would remain thoroughly British.

The theatrical pattern was set almost immediately when, in 1789, a group of convicts in Australia performed *The Recruiting Officer*, a British play from earlier in the century. Jim Davis notes that "the social function of the theatre in nineteenth-century Australia, at least officially, was to uphold British values." Touring troupes from Great Britain arrived regularly, serving "very much [as] cultural ambassadors, upholding the values of the mother country." In practice, this meant an emphasis on the plays of Shakespeare, whom a British actor of the time extolled as a civilizing force around the globe, 'making his way through distant climes and foreign regions, vanquishing race after race, as our conquerors did of old.'" There was, however, an "ambivalence in Australian reactions" to the touring troupes, "suggestive of a nationalistic desire not to be imposed upon by European culture." Australians sometimes claimed ownership over British theatre traditions, "transforming them into something specifically Australian along the way."[96] But as late as the 1890s, "Australia was still a provincial outpost of British theatre" that "remained largely dominated by performers and managers who had come from abroad."[97] Theatre in New Zealand was no less dependent on British theatrical models (sometimes filtered through Australian touring troupes), despite the development of locally situated melodrama in the late nineteenth century.[98] More than in the other Neo-Europes, theatre in the Australasian colonies remained largely a mirror, however imperfect, of theatre from the colonizing homeland.

None of this should be taken to suggest that the indigenous peoples of what are now Australia and New Zealand themselves lacked theatre, even if its historical details are at this point untraceable. Maryrose Casey notes that Aboriginal Australian performance "can be divided into three major types; ceremony, public performances based in Dreaming stories and performances based on topical issues for entertainment."[99] The enactment of narrative is an obvious element in performance of stories about Dreamtime (a term that "generally refers to the period when the land was created and shaped" and each Aboriginal group was given its own specific land, language, and protocols); enacted narratives were also central to "topical" entertainments (whose "stories often offer a keyhole view into social events, run away lovers, broken hearts, celebration of country, celebration of hunting prowess," and so on). But even in ceremony, "Aboriginal people through dance, music, song, mime, story and body art connect with their spiritual beliefs."[100] Nor should it be imagined that these performances were the same across Australia, for "Indigenous Australian as a collective label represents more than 250 separate nations or groupings speaking different languages, living in radically different physical environments, with different histories, modes of subsistence, cultural practices and technologies."[101] One must assume there existed (and to some degree still exist) many distinct local or semilocal theatrical traditions, each with its own history.

But well into the twentieth century, the British settlers and their descendants had scant regard for any of this. They scarcely "recognised or valorised [Aboriginal performance] as theatre," writes Casey, because it had not made "the same journey through text-based 'drama' to contemporary 'physical' theatre" that was familiar from European theatre.[102] Instead, the vague label of *corroboree* has been used to encompass "all Aboriginal ceremonies and rituals and entertainments involving singing and dancing."[103] These *corroborees* were of interest to the settlers primarily as anthropological or touristic curiosities, but because *corroborees* did not fit the dominant European conception of theatre, they were largely excluded from Australian theatre historiography until recently.[104]

CHAPTER 14

Colonial Experiences

Conceptualizing Colonial-Era Theatre

There is no *single* colonial experience, even if one limits discussion to European colonialism in the last few hundred years. The historian John Darwin comments, "The drama and violence of Europe's takeover of Africa has ... encouraged the idea that it was the 'classic' case of European imperialism. In fact tropical Africa was no more typical of European expansion than was the commercial imperialism practised in Latin America and China, the settler imperialisms of North America and Australasia, or the imperialism of rule fashioned by the British in the Indian subcontinent."[1] Especially after the mid nineteenth century, the industrial might of Europe's leading countries allowed them to project military and economic force to coastlands – and thence, to hinterlands – wherever they saw fit. But there was no uniformity to their actions once they arrived, for each colonized region presented its own challenges and opportunities. Along with European military and economic force inevitably came a cultural force, which derived at least in part from the attractiveness of certain aspects of European culture. But this force also had a highly variable impact in the colonized regions, and even among different groups of people within each region. For theatre, we can say that because each region already had its own unique complex of theatre forms coming into the nineteenth century, the impact of European military, economic, and cultural forces compelled each to create its *own* version of theatrical modernity.

Many theatre historians rely on a fundamental dichotomy between "traditional" theatre and "modern" theatre when discussing non-European theatre. Traditional theatre, in this formulation, is that which existed before European intervention; modern theatre (or, as it is sometimes called, "literary theatre") is the European spoken theatre transferred in toto in the aftermath of that intervention. But David Kerr, writing about African theatre, observes that "an almost teleological perspective is applied to the impact of colonialism, so that it seems part of an inevitable evolution toward major post-colonial forms of literary theatre."[2] The same can be said of theatre beyond Africa, for the dichotomy between traditional (i.e., precolonial) theatre and modern (i.e., European-style spoken) theatre is regularly suggested for many of the world's theatre regions. Traditional theatre might be treasured for its "authenticity" or scorned for its "backwardness," but in either case, modern theatre is understood to be a more advanced kind of theatre. The traditional–modern dichotomy is, in effect, a restatement of the Standard Western Approach to theatre history.

Another flaw with the traditional–modern dichotomy is that it overlooks scores of theatre forms, emerging especially between 1850 and 1950, that were at once indigenous *and* influenced by the changes brought on by colonialism. To account for them, some scholars posit that between the "traditional" and "modern" categories exists a category of "transitional" theatre forms. In Asian theatre studies, Kathryn Hansen notes, this category is "often associated with the period of British colonialism and 'Western' practices such as commercial companies, the proscenium stage, and the prevalence of melodrama."[3] Although this intermediate category works for at least some of the forms left out of the traditional–modern dichotomy, it preserves (and makes even more explicit) the teleology of that dichotomy, for "transitional" theatre forms are understood to be little more than waystations on the road to a more European-like modernity.

Another term sometimes used for this intermediate category is "hybrid-popular." Andrew B. Killick writes that "what distinguishes hybrid-popular theatre" from earlier theatre forms in most of Asia "is that elements of … local narrative and dramatic traditions are brought together with conventions deriving from Western theatre: performances are given in an enclosed space open to all those, and only those, who will pay the price of admission; the subject matter is more human; and the presentation is more realistic."[4] This neatly sidesteps the teleological implications of "transitional" theatre but excludes from consideration any recently emerging theatre forms that have largely eschewed Western conventions. It also fails to account for long-established theatre forms that have been somewhat influenced by European theatre but that are still understood to be "traditional." And it can scarcely work in Japanese and Chinese theatrical contexts, where performances have for centuries been presented in "enclosed spaces open to all" for the "price of admission."

A different conceptual framework is necessary to make sense of the many paths that theatre has taken over the past two centuries. This framework can begin with forms such as European spoken theatre that were transferred in toto from one region to another, often to be domesticated through a syncretic process to better fit the local societal and theatrical contexts. The transference of theatre forms was by no means unprecedented, as we have seen with the transfer of *wayang* shadow puppetry to mainland Southeast Asia, *karagöz* to Ottoman-controlled lands in Europe and North Africa, and *Moros y Cristianos* to Spanish-controlled Mexico and the Philippines – but never before had it been such a wide-ranging phenomenon.

Transference in toto, however, was by no means the *only* path forward. Two pairs of variables are especially relevant for recognizing the range of other possible paths. First, a given theatre form might have been established before the transformations of modernity, or it might emerge during those transformations. Second, the traits of a given form might strongly be indigenous in their origins, or the form might make significant syncretic use of nonindigenous theatrical traits. A simple diagram shows the four possible combinations of these variables. When we include in that diagram the transference of complete theatre forms from one region to another, we can get a fuller sense of world theatre's range of possible paths during the global transformation that began in the nineteenth century (see Figure 14.1).

Forms in the *established indigenous* quadrant of this diagram are typically referred to as "traditional." They existed locally before roughly 1800 and have remained relatively stable since then, although likely not without some changes introduced either through theatrical syncretism or the

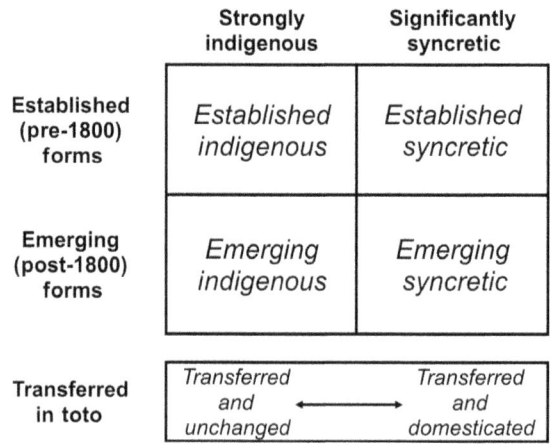

Figure 14.1 Conceptualizing multiple theatrical paths.

adoption of modern construction, lighting, and/or sound technologies. Forms in the *established syncretic* quadrant are those that existed before roughly 1800 but that have since been significantly altered by the introduction of theatrical traits from beyond the home region of the form, to the extent that the forms are sometimes even given new names. Forms in the *emerging indigenous* quadrant developed after 1800 or so but are deeply rooted in the theatrical histories of their indigenous cultures and exhibit few if any intercultural syncretic traits. Forms in the *emerging syncretic* quadrant have also developed in the past two centuries but exhibit inter-regional syncretism, usually from their very origins; these are the forms sometimes referred to as "transitional" or "hybrid-popular."

Finally, there are theatre forms that are *transferred in toto* from one region to another. In the past 200 years or so, European spoken theatre is the most obvious instance. But it is not the only one, for numerous theatre forms have been transferred by diasporic communities, such as the Chinese forms brought to San Francisco and the *ramdilla* and *hosay* brought to the Caribbean. Any transferred form might remain relatively unchanged in its new environment (especially if performed exclusively within the diasporic community) or it might be domesticated in various ways to give it a better fit in its new environment. All these possibilities exist because the tumult of modernity allowed – indeed, compelled – theatre artists to think anew about their artistic choices. We have already seen how this played out in Europe and the Neo-Europes; now we will turn to those parts of sub-Saharan Africa and Asia that Europeans directly colonized.

Sub-Saharan Africa

Europeans had been involved in transatlantic slave-trading since the sixteenth century, but by the time their empires engaged in what historians call the "scramble for Africa" in the 1880s, that slave trade had largely been extinguished.[5] It was imperial competition between European states that brought on the scramble and led to the partition of Africa. The historian Frederick Cooper refers to this competition as "pre-emptive colonization," for "as soon as one European power made a move, its rivals had to follow." This "helps to explain why the scramble for Africa was so intense and why, once colonized, the European powers did relatively little [at first] with the territory that they had taken over. Conquest was easier than administration."[6]

But having made their conquests, the imperial powers wanted them to pay off. One such payoff was material, for parts of Africa were rich with resources such as gold, diamonds, rubber, and oil. Another payoff was ideological, powered by a Christian missionary zeal and/or a deeply racist sense of what was called a "civilizing mission."[7] And so the European conquerors established bureaucratic, commercial, and religious structures to wrestle their new colonies under control. However dubious in motive and baleful in execution, this spasm of European imperialism led sub-Saharan Africa to create its own "modernity." The result was the emergence of numerous theatre forms that would join with previously established ones.

The very existence of those established forms has long been a subject of debate. Osita Okagbue refers to some doubting scholars as "evolutionists," who see in precolonial African performance a "primitivity" that had not yet evolved from ritual into dramatic theatre in the manner presumed to have occurred in ancient Greece. He identifies other scholars as "relativists," who in their determination to oppose the evolutionists broaden their definition of "drama" to such an extent that virtually "every performance, every theatre event, has to be drama."[8] Okagbue's comments echo an analysis by Biodun Jeyifo, who suggests a third approach that neither denies the existence of precolonial African dramatic theatre nor proclaims *all* African performance to be dramatic theatre. Jeyifo's approach instead addresses issues such as "*which* African or European sources and influences do we find operative and combined in any given African theatrical expression" and "what motivates the interaction and combination of the 'foreign' and the 'indigenous.'"[9]

The framework I have proposed aligns with Jeyifo's approach. Without being so "relativist" as to explode any meaningful definition of dramatic theatre, one can certainly contest the claims of the "evolutionists" and affirm the existence of established indigenous forms of dramatic theatre. Those forms (including the *kote-tlon* of the Bamana people, as described in Chapter 2) are undoubtedly different than European spoken theatre – but the same can be said of most of the world's theatre throughout history, including that of Europe itself. Many of the established indigenous forms of sub-Saharan Africa are performed in the context of more comprehensive theatrical events known as masquerades. These events include masked and costumed performers who embody the entrance of supernatural spirits into the human world, which can "arouse awe and fear in the spectator." But there are also "human and animal masquerades [that] often contain a high degree of entertainment, comedy and informality and are valued for their play qualities." Masquerade audiences often take a critical view of the individual performances, which are "judged and appreciated" both for "the appropriateness of the movements to a character" and for "the degree of skill" in the performance.¹⁰ There is nothing alien to the idea of dramatic theatre in this, especially if one does not insist that dramatic theatre be secular (see Figure 14.2).

Figure 14.2 *Gelede* masquerade: a performer in Cove, Benin, wearing a female mask and costume. *Gelede* celebrates female elders, ancestors, and deities. It is also performed by the Yoruba in Nigeria. (DEA/M. BORCHI/Contributor via Getty Images)

Okagbue notes significant similarities among the many African masquerade traditions "in terms of their stories of origin, organizational structure and support, actual performance processes, and social and aesthetic functions."[11] But countering a common assumption, the anthropologists Walter E. A. van Beek and Harrie M. Leyten point out that "most African cultures do not have masks at all, just as most African countries do not house masquerade traditions"; instead, their domain is limited to three specific "zones."[12] Along with the similarities between these traditions, their peculiar geographic distribution suggests that they belong to a homologous family. Figure 14.3 shows the three masquerade zones,

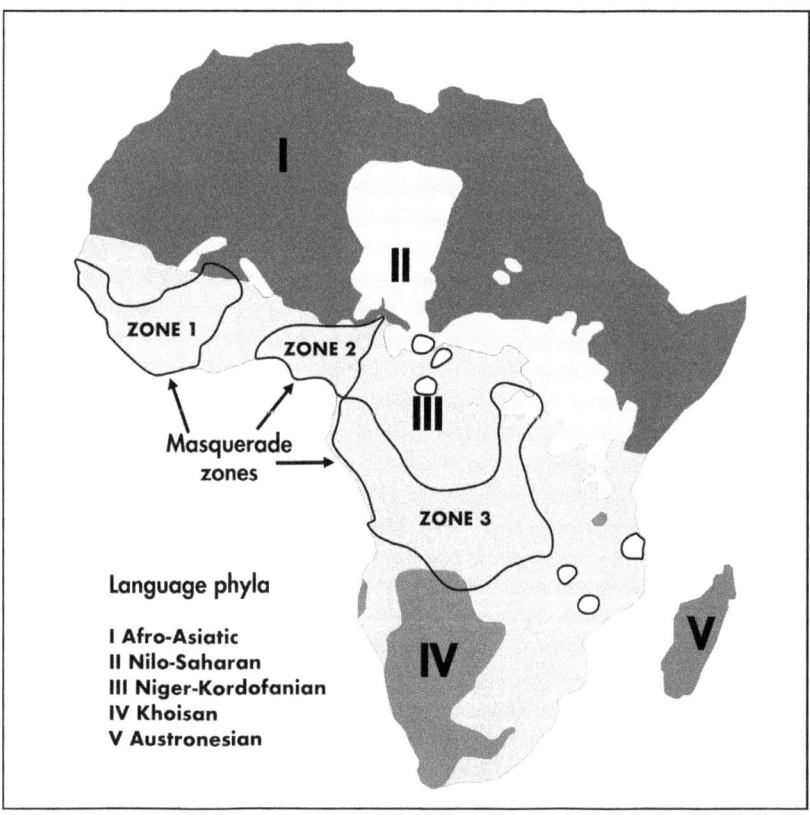

Figure 14.3 Masquerade traditions and language phyla of Africa. Boundaries of masquerade zones based on Walter E. A. van Beek and Harrie M. Leyten, *Masquerades in African Society: Gender, Power, and Identity* (Boydell & Brester, 2023), 9 (Map 1).

as identified by van Beek and Leyten, in which seventy-seven "ethnic groups" host such traditions.[13] Plotting these zones on a base map of the major language phyla of Africa shows that all the masquerade traditions are hosted by speakers of the Niger-Kordofanian languages – or, more specifically, this phylum's Niger-Congo branch of languages. This seems relevant to the distribution, for one of the signal events in African history was the expansion (starting about 4,000 years ago) of peoples whose descendants now speak one or another of these languages. These peoples were sub-Saharan Africa's first agriculturalists, and many of their societies share the similarities of being based in self-sufficient agricultural villages in which women are the primary producers of food and there is little heritable wealth (and therefore "an orientation toward symbolic capital and visual aesthetics").[14]

Note, though, that masquerade traditions are not found *throughout* the Niger-Congo language area, so other factors also clearly weigh on the distribution. The most important of these is apparently ecological. Van Beek and Leyten observe that although the ecologies of the three masquerade zones are somewhat different, they have in common a wet and forested environment that hosts the tsetse fly, a disease vector to which the dominant African species of cattle (the zebu) has no resistance.[15] The specific boundaries of the masquerade zones are in large part determined, they suggest, by the absence of cattle herding and the heritable wealth that such herding makes possible.[16]

The historical relations between the various masquerade traditions are unclear, but it seems relevant that the greatest variety of traditions can be found in west-central Africa (around the border between present-day Nigeria and Cameroon), which is also where one finds the greatest linguistic and genetic diversity of Niger-Congo speaking peoples.[17] Raphael Chijioke Njoku argues that this area "is the birthplace of the masquerade culture" because it is there that "the most intricate masquerade rituals with out-of-this-world costuming were developed …. Moving out from this culture area, the masquerade traditions found in other parts of West and Central Africa exhibit a clear regressive involvement with religious ideologies, the exercise of political authority, and the weight of privileges assigned to masquerade cults."[18] Historical evidence concerning masquerade traditions before the nineteenth century, however, is scarce, and it might be that the *idea* of the masquerade (as well as of some specific masquerade practices) was spread between neighboring peoples who shared similar societal structures. Whatever the relations between masquerade traditions, those traditions clearly include performances that count as indigenous theatre forms established long before contact with Europeans.

This is not to suggest, however, that the forms exist in some ahistorical state of purity. The art historian Susan Elizabeth Gagliardi rightly insists that "no masquerade performers are timeless reproducers of some fixed norm, and observers' experiences of the art in all its heterogeneity have often contradicted their own communally bound interpretive frameworks" of traditionality.[19] As Okagbue notes, "The indigenous forms are constantly reviewing and revising themselves in response to their ever-changing historical and cultural contexts," adapting to "new or foreign material, such as technology ... and to changing life patterns of their communities."[20] But notwithstanding such changes, he suggests, these and many other precolonial forms have "remained true to their original forms and processes"; they continue to be performed to this day, having "kept their developmental paths firmly rooted in their native cultures."[21] The typical niches for masquerade traditions are specific festivals celebrated in their agricultural villages. Such niches are narrow, but the forms are especially well-fitted to them. As long as the festivals are maintained, in the face of urbanization, modernization, and the expansion of Islam and Christianity, the masquerades will likely continue, with whatever changes might keep them relevant.

Another form of African theatre from before colonialism is *alarinjo* (also known as *apidán*). The British explorer Hugh Clapperton saw a performance in the 1820s and was not amused by its inclusion of a comically hapless White man for whom he was likely the model.[22] According to oral histories, the form emerged around the start of the seventeenth century, following the Yoruba court's return to Oyo-ile (Old Oyo) after years of exile.[23] *Alarinjo* took up certain elements of its performance from Yoruba *egungun* masquerades, but through much of its career it had professional troupes that worked primarily at the court while also giving occasional public performances.[24] The number and quality of troupes decreased after the demise of the Yoruba Kingdom in the mid nineteenth century, but *alarinjo* still continues to be performed.[25] These performances remain largely unaltered by colonialism or its aftermath, although they have come to include not only outsiders like Clapperton's White man but also a variety of more contemporary figures.[26]

Even as established indigenous forms have carried on with only modest change, new indigenous forms have also emerged. Perhaps because these are mostly rural in origin, they are relatively unknown. One such form is *kwagh-hir*, which emerged among the Tiv people (in Nigeria) in the 1960s;

despite its recent origin, *kwagh-hir* is said to be "a purely rural traditional art."²⁷ The explanation for this apparent paradox is that while the elements of the form (puppetry, masquerade-like costumes, satirical sketches, storytelling, music, and dance) have long existed among the Tiv, this particular combination is quite novel. Performances are usually competitions between troupes from different villages, resulting in a series of variety-like shows.²⁸ The judges presiding over the competition render a judgment that "seeks to relate the depiction of modern Tivland to established traditional aesthetics."²⁹ Modern realities, in brief, can be addressed in new but strongly indigenous forms, especially where the impact of colonialism has been relatively muted.³⁰

But in the fast-growing colonial cities, it was emerging syncretic forms that filled newly opening niches for commercial theatre. One of these forms, known as Concert Party theatre, emerged in the coastal cities of Ghana. In the 1920s, "Teacher" Yalley (an educator at a Methodist-run school) organized vaudeville-style shows presented "in English, in posh venues, for élite [African] audiences" and the occasional European, in which he performed in a comical outfit that included blackface. The form gained a broader popularity in the 1930s, when some of Yalley's students (most notably, Bob Johnson) mixed in local languages and performed in inexpensive theatres, drawing audiences from the Ghanaian middling classes. By the 1950s, the form's transition to an urban commercial theatre was completed, with plays presented entirely in local languages.³¹ In the course of its development, Concert Party artists "appropriated material from American movies, Latin gramophone records, African American spirituals, Ghanian *asafo* [warrior-dance music of the Fante people], and 'highlife' songs," along with a trickster character similar to Anansi (a well-known figure in West African folklore). Catherine M. Cole comments that the Concert Party is representative of how African theatre artists "have creatively responded to the tumultuous changes wrought by colonialism, industrialization, postmodernity, and the current neocolonial age."³²

Amid all this syncretism, what stands out to many outside observers is the form's use of blackface, which harkens back to American minstrel shows. But as Cole notes, Concert Party artists themselves are usually "unaware of the history and ideological significance of blackface as practiced outside of Ghana." They wear blackface, as one performer explained, because "it is attractive" and "when you wear the trant [i.e., blackface] it creates laughter." No doubt that the appropriation of blackface involves a misunderstanding of its meaning in minstrel shows, but then, Antonin Artaud and Bertolt Brecht also misunderstood the meanings of the Balinese and Chinese performances that influenced *them*. Cole notes that while "scholars are caught in a gridlocked debate about the concert party's hybridity or authenticity, concert party practitioners themselves are much less concerned about the origins of their art form."[33] The scholarly debate is misguided, both for the Concert Party and for other syncretic forms of theatre: There is no necessary opposition between "hybridity" and "authenticity," for once theatre artists make a theatrical trait their own, it becomes "authentically" theirs, even if it is not part of some long-standing local "tradition."

At roughly the same time as the Concert Party was finding its niche in Ghana, Yoruba Travelling Theatre (also known as Yoruba Popular Theatre) was emerging in Nigeria. From the start of the twentieth century, British colonialism had "accelerated the formation of new classes," including a "small, highly educated African bureaucratic élite" and an "amorphous" middling class "made up of wage laborers, artisans, traders, providers of services of all kinds, low-paid civil servants, [and] employees of big trading companies." Especially during the Second World War and the postwar economic boom, "the sector of paid employees" greatly expanded, "putting money into [peoples'] pockets."[34] It was by and for this class that Yoruba Travelling Theatre was created.

The new Nigerian theatre form was no less syncretic than the Ghanian Concert Party but drew from decidedly different sources. The British had introduced Christian missions into Nigeria; by the early twentieth century, a popular form of performance in some mission churches was the cantata, which offered "dramatized versions of well-known Bible stories, rendered entirely or almost entirely in song."[35] In the mid 1940s, a choirmaster named Hubert Ogunde began creating his own rather conventional cantatas, but then radically reshaped the cantata form. He introduced secular plots and themes (including folkloric and anticolonial material); made extensive use of drumming and chanting (both taken from *alarinjo*); added improvised dialogue between the set-piece songs; and professionalized his troupe, which he took on tours through the urban and semi-urban areas of Yorubaland, performing in movie houses, nightclubs, town halls, and community centers.[36] The church cantata format was at the base of the Yoruba Travelling Theatre, but the form's unique theatrical syncretism, along with its immense popularity, gives the lie to any claim that it lacked "authenticity."

It was, however, the spoken theatre transferred in toto from Europe that eclipsed other African theatre forms "in terms of sheer social and cultural power." In writing those words, John Conteh-Morgan refers specifically to former French and Belgian colonies, but the point holds true elsewhere in sub-Saharan Africa. Despite the popular appeal of the emerging syncretic forms, spoken theatre (or, as Conteh-Morgan calls it, "literary drama") "has become the hegemonic form." In the French and Belgian colonies, it began its career as an entertainment primarily for Europeans in colonial cities such as Dakar and Leopoldville. But "it was through the medium of the school … that French drama was to take root in Africa," with students studying French plays and writing original works in French.[37] For the French-educated elite, European-style spoken theatre "became a symbol of their modernity, new status and aspirations." They would eventually inherit political control when their lands gained independence, and "their cultural production" would come "to define the identity of their nations in a way that those nations' indigenous cultures, with all their acknowledged vitality, have not."[38]

Mineke Schipper observes that "the so-called modern African theatre" is usually written and performed in a European language; emphasizes the verbal element rather than music, song, and dance; separates the audience from the stage by using a proscenium and curtain; presents plays that are much shorter than the full evenings typical of indigenous theatre; focuses on contemporary themes; and is mostly attended by "a small upper class of the population."[39] African spoken theatre, in short, fills a very different niche than either the established indigenous forms based in communal festivities or the syncretic forms that emerged to serve the urbanized middling classes; it is for the African elite who can understand a European language and accept the conventions of spoken theatre.

Understandably, the choice to write and perform in a European language can be controversial. Christopher Balme points to the "lively discussion on the question of using colonial languages as an adequate and legitimate means of literary or theatrical expression." He notes the playwright Ola Rotimi's view that "the use of the colonial language has certain advantages in terms of mutual understanding in a linguistically heterogeneous" country but observes that it is inherently exclusionary, since relatively few people speak a European language.[40] Moreover, it can be seen as implicitly legitimizing European colonialism. Playwrights such as Ngugi Wa Thiong'o have insisted on writing their plays in their mother tongue (even if they might then translate them into a European language), seeing their choice as "part and parcel of the anti-imperialist struggles" of sub-Saharan Africa.[41]

But writing in a local language is only one way that African playwrights have tried to domesticate spoken theatre. Perhaps more frequent has been their focus on pertinent issues of African history, politics, and society, along with the infusion of indigenous traits of actor movement, improvisation, collective creation, and audience participation.[42] Especially important has been the effort to break down the spoken-ness of spoken theatre by incorporating indigenous music and dance traditions into new plays, as can be seen in Wole Soyinka's *Death and the King's Horseman* (1975). Okagbue writes that the "integrated" use of music and dance in "the hybridised literary theatre of western educated African playwrights" is "part of their postcolonial quest for an African identity that is neither enslaved by nor ashamed of its colonial experience."[43] Whatever language a play might be written in, the spoken theatre originally transferred in toto from Europe has largely been domesticated into a new and *African* version of that form.

South Asia

In the centuries following Vasco da Gama's visit to South Asia in 1498, business interests from Portugal, Holland, France, and England set themselves up in more than a dozen cities along the eastern and western seaboards. The Mughal Empire could offer little opposition as it crumbled under the weight of "religious wars, court incompetence, greedy factionalism, and traditional invasions from the northwest."[44] Neither the Portuguese (beyond Goa) nor the Dutch would have a significant South Asian presence by the start of the eighteenth century, during which century British interests would prevail over those of France.[45] I refer to "interests" because the colonial competition in South Asia was carried on between governmentally supported private trading companies expected to be profitable enough to defend themselves. After pushing out the French, the British East India Company (often referred to as the EIC) continued its expansion, bringing to heel the multitude of post-Mughal successor states. By the start of the nineteenth century the EIC had gained effective control over most of South Asia.[46]

After some fifty years of relative peace, suggests Jürgen Osterhammel, the British came "to believe not only that their Indian subjects accepted them as rulers but also that they were acting as benefactors by bringing them a superior civilization. The reality, and the British appreciation of it, changed within a few weeks" in 1857, when "British rule collapsed in large parts of northern India."[47] The British refer to this collapse as "the Indian Mutiny"; Indians call it "the National Uprising" or "the First War for Independence."[48] In the wake of this mutually disastrous conflict, the British Parliament dissolved the EIC and established direct colonial rule that would last until 1947.⁴⁹ The new British Raj built out railroad and telegraph networks to allow for "closer co-ordination of imperial policies and more supervision from London," while also establishing schools that emphasized English-language education.⁵⁰ The goal was not merely to create a class of Indians to help run India but to form an elite that was, in the words of Thomas Babington Macaulay, "Indian in blood and color, but English in taste, in opinions, in morals, and in intellect."⁵¹

At what point in all of this can one say that South Asia's "modernity" began? Osterhammel recognizes that there are rarely neat temporal boundaries in history but argues that "the beginning of European colonization … presented an epochal break in nearly all parts of Asia and everywhere in Africa."⁵² In South Asia, the British presence became tangible first in the cities under EIC control, then extended outward under the imperial Raj. For theatre, Aparna Dharwadker suggests that modernity's "period of inception" lasted from around 1790 until 1870. These years were "marked by a strong critical interest among the urban intelligentsia, especially in the Calcutta and Bombay regions, in the potential value of Western-style theatre for Indian audiences in Indian languages." This period of inception, though, did not yet see the creation of "stable forms of artistic, institutional and material organization" for such theatre.⁵³

The development of modern theatre, however, was not limited to the urban intelligentsia. Even as they were considering the possibilities of "Western-style theatre," South Asia's innumerable established forms continued in performance. Many remained relatively secure in their niches, although they were not untouched by change. For generations, the city of Ramnagar ("Rama's city") had been an important site for the performance of *ramlila*. Near the start of the nineteenth century, a local prince brought *ramlila* performance in Ramnagar under his patronage and developed it "on a scale that would attract national attention." Princely support was something new, for elsewhere the form was typically supported by neighborhood committees; the national interest in one locale's *ramlila* was also new.⁵⁴ These conditions apparently led to the Ramnagar performances becoming what Pamela Lothspeich calls "preservationist," with a deep interest in adhering "to nineteenth-century conventions of tableau-style devotional theatre."⁵⁵ The attempt to freeze the form as a model for India seems to have been a response to the societal changes already taking place under the pressure of British colonization, and so itself can be considered a reactive aspect of modernity.

The Ramnagar performance style, however, is "not representative of the way in which the vast majority of Ramlilas are performed and therefore experienced"; for in fact the character of the form beyond Ramnagar "has changed immensely since the early nineteenth century." Through most of that century, *ramlilas* remained "stylistically in conversation" with the Ramnagar *ramlila* but not "derivative of it." Subsequently, a "'Ramlila renaissance' saw an explosion of new, 'realistic' Ramlilas inclined toward mimetic theatre and performed on outdoor proscenium stages."[56] What we see with *ramlila* is an established indigenous form that in one locale has remained relatively unchanged for the past 200 years but that in others has taken on syncretic traits without losing its distinctive historical identity.

The more secular theatre form of *tamasha* – which like *ramlila* had emerged in the sixteenth century – underwent rather different changes. These were less the result of theatrical syncretism than of the broader societal transformations taking place in modernizing India. After the British had extended their rule into Maharashtra (in central India), "many of the folk artists" of *tamasha* "turned to themes of a social and political nature." By the start of the twentieth century, reports Tevia Abrams, themes such as "the prevailing caste system, illiteracy, outmoded superstition, and the oppression of women" rose to the fore. The movement toward national liberation then led *tamasha* to become "a viable medium for anti-British propaganda," especially because it was free of the censorship that hobbled the politicized spoken theatre concurrently developing in major cities.[57]

New indigenous theatre forms have also emerged during the past two centuries. One of the most interesting is *nautanki*, which apparently developed out of *swang* (also known as *svāng*) and/or *bhagat*, though the precise relationship between these various forms is uncertain.[58] What seems clear is that in the 1850s, a particular troupe began performing a play about a certain Princess Nautanki. When this proved successful with audiences, the play (along with the style in which it was presented) was taken up by other troupes as well, and the name *nautanki* came to signify the entire emerging form, even as it added other narratives.[59]

According to Hansen, *nautanki* "is rooted in the peasant society of premodern India," but its audiences are not only villagers but also working-class migrants from the countryside to the towns and cities. The form clearly fills a commercial niche there, but rather than identify it as "either a city or village form," Hansen prefers to see it as a "conduit in the cultural flow that connects the urban centers and the hinterlands."[60] Five distinct "schools" of *nautanki* developed rather quickly, with two of the most important being in Hathras ("a small town with virtually no industry") and Kanpur ("a large industrial city" that served as a military station for the British).[61] A notable difference in the *nautanki* of these locales is the greater syncretism found in the city with a strong British influence. In Hathras, for example, *nautanki* is performed on a slightly raised stage fully surrounded by the audience, but in Kanpur, it is done on a European-derived "picture-frame stage" with a drop curtain. For these and similar reasons, Balwant Gargi complains that Kanpur's *nautanki* has "absorbed all the vices of the decadent professional theatres."[62] But as Hansen notes, *nautanki* relies neither "on the patronage of a Westernized middle class" nor on that class's "imported substratum of ideas and texts."[63] It is an indigenous form touched by theatrical syncretism only where the European influence was at its strongest (see Figure 14.4).

More thoroughly syncretic from their very emergence were the Parsi, Marathi, and Bengali theatres that developed in colonial cities "apart from the traditional hierarchies and distinctions in Indian performances."[64] The community that created the Parsi theatre, on which I will focus here, was descended from Iranian Zoroastrians who had migrated to India nearly a thousand years earlier. Now serving as the "brokers of European mercantile houses" in Bombay, Parsi businessmen "interacted with colonial elites and were exposed to English education." Young Parsi men took an interest in theatre while students at a British-run college; by the late 1860s, their amateur theatrical performances proved so popular that they turned professional.[65] Hansen observes that European melodrama, brought by touring British troupes, was a formative influence on Parsi theatre.[66] The Parsi troupes learned from them the appeal of spectacular scenic effects as well as of a semblance of realism. Many of their plays "dwelt on the

Figure 14.4 *Nautanki*: Devendra Sharma and Palak Joshi in a contemporary production of *Sultana Daku*. (Photo by Swagato Basumallick, CC BY-SA 3.0, via Wikimedia Commons)

web of relationships within the family [and] on the profound sociality of everyday existence. They engaged with distinctions of ethnicity and class, looking to servants, retainers, or outsiders as examples of difference."[67] But in "important respects," writes Hansen, Parsi theatre also "revealed its distinctive Indian character," for it dealt with Indian subject matter and included music and dance derived from "the Indian dramatic tradition."[68]

Parsi theatre troupes "operated under Parsi management well into the twentieth century," but "its actors were drawn from the ranks of Parsis, Muslims, Hindus, Anglo-Indians, and Jews," while its audiences were no less diverse.[69] As the form gained popularity, its troupes benefited from colonial India's new railroads, which allowed them to tour extensively and exert a widespread influence: In the cities to which they traveled, Hansen reports, "offshoots of the original Bombay companies sprang up. The lure of Parsi-style musical productions, rich in spectacular scenery and effects, was contagious."[70] Indeed, the touring of the Parsi troupes was not limited to India. Taking advantage of European-run steamship lines, they brought their shows to foreign ports such as Colombo, Rangoon (now Yangon), Penang, Singapore, Surabaya, and Batavia (now Jakarta). "Due to its sophistication and charm," Hansen suggests, "Parsi theatre was welcomed everywhere it went" – and almost everywhere it went it was "copied and adapted into local languages and genres."[71]

Of no less enduring impact, of course, was the spoken theatre transferred in toto by the British. It was introduced into South Asia in the mid eighteenth century as entertainment for the growing number of British soldiers, administrators, clergy, and merchants; by the early nineteenth century, British touring troupes were presenting shows in theatres that were virtual copies of those back home.[72] As we have seen, spoken theatre soon caught the attention of the native intelligentsia being educated in British schools. By the close of the nineteenth century, Indian troupes were presenting original plays written in native languages and – much to the consternation of British authorities – were using them "as a forum for social and political ideals designed to influence opinion and raise social consciousness."[73]

This is a recurring theme with spoken theatre in the European colonies of the nineteenth and early twentieth centuries: As the form was taken up by the local intelligentsia – themselves often the products of a European-style education – it was turned against the colonizers. The main consolation for the colonizers was that the niche for spoken theatre was relatively narrow, especially at first. In India, established forms such as *ramlila* and *tamasha* had niches beyond the European base cities, so generally escaped colonial control; *nautanki*'s niche spanned between the countryside and the cities, but as we have seen, it remained strongly rooted in the peasant society. The Parsi theatre was more urban in orientation but was a commercial theatre form that desired only to entertain India's burgeoning middling classes. Spoken theatre, however, was addressed primarily to educated urbanites and potentially challenged British rule among those whom the British were most concerned with controlling.

Spoken theatre's appeal was enhanced by an almost immediate effort to domesticate it into something identifiably Indian. "Despite the apparent dominance of western influences," writes Dharwadker, "the overwhelming creative impulse in modern Indian theatre of the later nineteenth century was to indigenize and assimilate the 'foreign' models to performative structures that would be intelligible in the linguistic and cultural registers of their immediate audiences." She goes on: "While modes such as realism, naturalism and symbolism informed the text of drama [after about 1870], indigenous traditions of music, dance and spectacle came to dominate the styles of presentation. More ambitiously, the creative and theoretical constituents of modernity were carefully accommodated to classically derived concepts." Further advancing the process of domestication was the use of "major Indian languages such as Bengali, Marathi, Hindi, Urdu, Gujarati and Kannada ... as the primary media of original theatrical composition."[74] This contrasts with the development of spoken theatre in sub-Saharan Africa, where European languages remained dominant. Perhaps the difference can best be explained by two factors. First, South Asia had a tradition of literary theatre that extended back almost 2,000 years; sub-Saharan Africa did not. Second, whereas sub-Saharan Africa is linguistically fragmented and has relatively small numbers of people speaking each indigenous language, the major languages of India each have tens or even hundreds of millions of speakers, thereby allowing spoken theatre in those languages to have a chance at developing (and being sustained by) substantial audiences.

The trend toward domesticating spoken theatre continued even more vigorously in the twentieth century, especially after India gained independence in 1947. What has been called the "theatre of roots" (TOR) has an explicit sociopolitical agenda. The term itself was coined by Suresh Awasthi in 1985 to describe "the new unconventional theatre, which has been evolving as a result of its encounter with tradition"; Awasthi saw TOR as "part of the whole process of decolonization of our lifestyle, values, social institutions, creative forms, and cultural modes."[75] In practice, this has meant incorporating a wide range of indigenous theatrical traits, such as the "dramaturgical structure of *kutiyattam*," the "actor training methods of *kathakali*," and the "structures, aesthetics and techniques [of] *yakshagana*."[76] The central goal of TOR is said by some to be the creation "of a 'decolonized' modern Indian theatre," by others to be something "that is *neither* 'Western' *nor* 'Indian,'" but "*both* 'Western' *and* 'Indian.'"[77] Despite the differences in these two formulations, they express the shared desire to continue domesticating spoken theatre.

It is worth noting, however, that some Indian scholars object to TOR. Rustom Bharucha, for example, is disturbed by post-independence Indian artists and scholars "who have 'invented' a 'tradition' based on principles of 'authenticity' and the search for 'roots.'" His immediate concern is that they have stripped localized theatrical practices from their specific societal contexts; his broader concern is that "'Indian culture' is being reduced to a commodity by our own government and a new breed of [theatre-oriented] bureaucrats, who have shaped, marketed and transported this 'culture' to different parts of the world."[78] These concerns have merit, but as we have seen, the decontextualization of theatrical practices (whether from one's own society or from foreign societies) is a recurring feature of theatre history, and never more so than in the nineteenth and twentieth centuries. The modern practice of commodifying a national culture, meanwhile, is scarcely limited to India alone, for governments of numerous countries now support theatre either for export or to promote international tourism. One might applaud or deplore the governmental commodification of culture, but it seems an almost inevitable feature of a globalizing world. For their part, exponents of TOR, along with theatre artists in many other places, have been grappling with the paradox of maintaining a distinctive societal identity even as their society engages in the difficult task of self-modernization.

Southeast Asia

Coming into the mid eighteenth century, the Dutch retained their maritime base in Java and controlled the valuable spice islands of the Maluku archipelago, while the Spanish remained masters in the Philippines; the rest of Southeast Asia was still under native control. But the whirring motor of European-based commerce had already begun to drive change throughout the region. The historian Anthony Reid writes that "there is no doubt that the Southeast Asian economies underwent a marked expansion in the late eighteenth and early nineteenth centuries." In part this was owing "to the expansion of tobacco, coffee, and sugar cultivation" in Java and the Philippines, but it was happening even "faster in that great majority of the region that lay outside effective European control" as the increasingly globalized economy stimulated mining and cash-cropping.[79] Aside from Java and the Philippines, the stirrings of Southeast Asian modernity were felt even before the onset of direct European colonization.

Such colonization began in the 1850s, with the period of European dominance lasting until 1940.[80] The Dutch expanded outward from Java and the Maluku archipelago; the British colonized the Malay Peninsula and Burma (now Myanmar); and the French controlled the lands they called Indochina (now Vietnam, Laos, and Cambodia). Only Siam (now Thailand) escaped colonial rule, serving as a neutral buffer between French and British territories. But from the mid nineteenth century, Siamese kings sent embassies to study in Europe while also hiring European technical advisors, so even independent Siam felt a European influence.[81] Colonization spurred the pace of urbanization, especially along the coasts: "Of the eleven Southeast Asian cities with more than 100,000 population in 1910, seven were colonially created port-centers." These cities would become hotbeds of theatrical syncretization: "A bewildering variety of shows passed through the urban spaces of Southeast Asia around the turn of the [twentieth] century, offering precious opportunities for its plural populations to wonder and laugh at each other."[82] Rural areas, though, underwent a "peasantization," with their populations turned to "small-scale production" under "a hierarchical and static social order."[83] For theatre, this meant that indigenous forms beyond the port cities would have a reasonable chance for survival through and beyond the nineteenth century, although they would need to adjust to societal changes.

Wayang kulit purwa, as we have seen, had emerged in Java about a thousand years ago and is arguably as "traditional" as an established theatre form can be. Generations of Dutch scholars in particular have been fascinated by it. Sadiah Boonstra argues that they have valued it as "a never changing tradition," while paying "inordinate attention" to its "mystical, philosophical and religious elements."[84] There is a clear scent of exoticism in their fascination, tinctured perhaps with colonial guilt. But as with many other established forms, *wayang kulit purwa* has continued to develop without abandoning the virtues that made it appealing in the first place. We have already noted some of its changes over the centuries; more recently, *dalangs* – the form's puppeteers/narrators – have incorporated international characters into their plays "to appeal to local audiences and to familiarise Indonesia's youngsters with *wayang*. They [also] use international languages and develop their work in response to international networks and audiences."[85] Jennifer Goodlander observes: "Traditional performance has survived in many cases because it has remained relevant to the societies producing it – negotiating modernity and technology will continue to be an important part of that relevance moving into the future."[86] *Wayang kulit purwa*, one might say, has survived as an established indigenous form precisely because it has *not* become a museum piece from the premodern world.

Zat pwe is not nearly as long-lived as *wayang kulit purwa*, having emerged in eighteenth-century Burma "as a vehicle for the portrayal of historical or religious themes in a stylized manner."[87] The form originated in the royal court, but after Burma's subsumption into the British Raj in 1886, it needed a new niche. Over the next few decades, writes Hansen, it "transformed from a courtly artefact with a limited audience to a mass entertainment with unquestioned commercial appeal. Companies grew increasingly prosperous and well organised. Cities, towns, and countryside were linked in a vibrant entertainment network with a star system, spectacular performance styles, and new music and dance items." Interestingly, it was at this time that the aforementioned Parsi theatre was internationally touring, and for a brief period competed with *zat pwe*, especially in the heavily Indian port city of Rangoon. But as Hansen suggests, "The Parsi theatre in Burma flared, flickered, and then died out. The resilience of the Burmese performing arts was surely a major factor in minimising its impact." Even as *zat pwe* "adapted to conditions under the British, its structures provided strong frames. New inputs did not overwrite them but were assimilated with little fundamental change." In the face of colonial conquest, *zat pwe* was "far from static," to the point that some locals "decried [it] as decadent,"[88] but it survived thanks to its newfound niche as a popular form of theatre.

Other established theatre forms in the Southeast Asian regions were far more affected by European colonization and the new theatrical ideas that came in tow. We have already encountered *lakon nai*, which had previously been restricted to the Thai royal court. Under the modernizing King Chulalongkorn (r. 1868–1910), it was freed to "spread out into Bangkok and the provinces." This was, in a sense, a shift of niche similar to that of *zat pwe*, but the result was a more thoroughly syncretic transformation. Mattani Mojdara Rutnin suggests that with the form now being offered in public theatres, "producers had to find new ways to attract customers." As it took on traits from other Thai forms and from European theatre, new and more popular forms were created out of *lakon nai*.[89] In some of these descendent forms, the stories "are mostly concerned with everyday domestic problems in a contemporary setting, or are adaptations of foreign tales"; the dialogue is "modern and colloquial" in tone; the music and lyrics express "great emotion" and are sung with such "deep feeling" that audience can be moved to tears; and the costumes and European-style sets "are as contemporary as the situations of the plays." One obvious point here is a "trend toward realistic presentation" along with "an attempt to balance [that] realism with romanticism: that is, to present the romantic, mythical, and heroic stories of Thai classical dance-drama in a more realistic way for the purpose of communicating better with modern audiences."[90] Realism, by this account, is less a teleological necessity (as the Standard Western Approach would have it) than an adjustment that can be made to fit a theatre form to a new niche.

Notwithstanding the impact of colonization, some emerging theatre forms remain distinctly Southeast Asian in inspiration and style. One of these, *likay* (sometimes transliterated as *liké*), is also from Thailand, where it emerged toward the end of the nineteenth century. *Likay* was syncretic from its start, but it was an *intra*cultural syncretism of existing Thai forms. The name *likay* probably derives from "ceremonial Muslim chanting and incantation," but the form is anything but spiritual.[91] It borrows elements from the Thai court theatres of *lakon nai* and *khon*, as well as from the village form of *lakon nok*, to create an appealing confection of "romanticism, exaggeration, and superfluous beauty, together with a belief in karma."[92] Gary Bryden Carkin notes that for its rural and working-class audiences, *likay*'s "traditional elements give a sense of belonging to a national culture" and offer "a feeling of heritage and pride."[93] But although the stories it tells are generally old (including traditional tales of court life as well as a mix of fairy tales and local legends), *likay* also incorporates contemporary issues such as "the price of gasoline, the presence of 'chicos' or street toughs, [and] the use of toilet paper as a sign of civilization." Carkin notes in all this that the form "works on two levels: establishing the past with the present, and sustaining time-honored traditions in demonstrating solutions to present concerns."[94]

Other emerging theatre forms were created through *inter*cultural syncretism.[95] *Bangsawan*, for example, emerged in late nineteenth-century Malaysia.[96] Although the Malaysian government identifies the form as "traditional," recent scholarship has no doubt that it was a new and commercial theatre form that incorporated "Malay, Western, and other foreign influences" as it aimed "to suit the tastes of [its] audience."[97] Tan Sooi Beng observes that the form emerged in a colonial society undergoing "rapid socio-economic, political, cultural, and demographic changes."[98]

The onset of Malaysian modernity opened a niche for urban commercial theatre that would serve "audiences with spare cash and leisure time …. *Bangsawan* was developed to entertain" those audiences.[99] Because it drew on earlier forms of Malay theatre, it provided enough continuity to be seen as "traditional." But the form's more wide-ranging syncretism is reflected in many of its foundational traits. Its narratives are drawn not only from local history but from Arabia, China, Europe, Indonesia, and Thailand.[100] Other traits include European-style "painted backdrops and wings presented on a proscenium-style stage, which represented all that was new and modern to local viewers" (see Figure 14.5).[101]

Even after it had become established, *bangsawan* "was constantly adapting to audience preferences." With "the rise of Malay nationalism," for example, more contemporary "Malay stories with Malay costumes and sets were introduced. With the greater exposure" to "western" films and books, "audiences began to prefer realism to fantasy, and *bangsawan* responded accordingly."[102] The form also eventually had to compete with

Figure 14.5 *Bangsawan*: a scene from an unidentified play mounted in Penang, circa 1895. (Royal Netherlands Institute of Southeast Asian and Caribbean Studies and Leiden University Library, via Wikimedia Commons)

newer forms for its commercial niche. Despite *bangsawan*'s moves toward nationalism and realism, a form called *sandiwara* proved more suited to the post–Second World War "mood and spirit of anti-colonialism." While many of *bangsawan*'s traits were taken over by *sandiwara*, the new form's advantage was largely the result of fully scripted plays that dealt directly with current politics and were presented with a realism of settings, costumes, and characters that *bangsawan* could not match. Confronted by *sandiwara*'s competitive success, *bangsawan* eventually shifted to a new niche: Since the 1970s, it has been supported by the government as a means of "promoting national unity."[103] This probably accounts for the government's claim that *bangsawan* is a "traditional" form of theatre. But in fact it was merely one of the many emerging theatre forms in Southeast Asia that pieced together traits from earlier indigenous forms with theatrical traits newly arrived from Europe and, to a lesser degree, India and China.

Europe's colonization of Southeast Asia brought with it the usual cultural accoutrement of European-style education. At first, the Europeans "extended their home education to the colonies primarily to educate their own sons," but soon these schools were "expanded to cope with ever-greater proportions of Asian students." As in Africa and South Asia, "a fundamentally new elite class was produced in the western schools," having "a privileged relation to colonial modernity through their education. Typically detached from traditional cultures, they eagerly devoured debates on how to create new national ones."[104] One of the means they almost inevitably latched onto was the spoken theatre they had studied in European-run schools.

This spoken theatre goes by various names in Southeast Asia: *pya zat* ("new plays") in Burma/Myanmar; *kich nôi* ("spoken play/drama") in Vietnam; *lakhon vao* ("spoken drama") in Laos; and *drama moden* ("modern drama") in Malaysia.[105] In Thailand it was originally called *lakon phut* ("spoken theatre") – but as Rutnin comments, it "has not seemed to catch on with Thai audiences, except among the intellectual and Westernized elite …. Serious social and political plays, though attracting intellectuals, have very little chance even in contemporary theatre, whereas melodramatic, historical, domestic, and straight-forward patriotic plays with songs and dances gain favorable responses."[106] The same can be said of spoken theatre (under whatever local name) throughout Southeast Asia. And even with elite audiences, spoken theatre truly gained purchase only when theatre artists ceased directly imitating their European models and turned to anticolonial advocacy, critiques of the societies and regimes that followed independence, and examinations of social issues such as urbanization and modernization.[107] As in sub-Saharan Africa and South Asia, Southeast Asian theatre artists have also made efforts to create a "fusion of western, or western-inspired, dramatic texts with elements of local culture and performance traditions," writes Michael Bodden. These artists seek both to "participate in and perform a global culture" and to "create novel ways of performing modern theatre that highlighted the cultural identity of these newly independent nations as something distinctive and 'local.'"[108]

I need briefly mention that non-European theatre forms were also transferred to Southeast Asia. James R. Brandon notes that immigrants from three different parts of China brought their own local forms to the Malay peninsula (especially to the British-developed port city of Singapore). These remained almost exclusively in niches provided by the Chinese communities,[109] rather in the same way that Chinese theatre functioned in nineteenth-century San Francisco. Similarly, Chinese immigrants brought a form of hand-puppet theatre to Java at the start of the twentieth century. In this form, curiously, "Chinese stories are performed by Chinese-costumed puppets, but the language the puppets speak is Indonesian" – even though performance is confined to Chinese Buddhist temples and never offered to the larger public.[110] With the change of language, we see at least a hint of domestication. These various Chinese theatre forms, however, are evidence that Southeast Asia's swirl of theatrical modernity was not *just* a function of European colonialism. Rather, theatre artists in the various countries of Southeast Asia have sought to forge their own versions of modernity.

CHAPTER 15

Pacific Lands

The Wages of Success

In the year that barbarians from the far west called 1790, a pair of proud empires sat astride the Sea of Japan, each seemingly invulnerable to external threat. The Qianlong Emperor in China celebrated his eightieth birthday, having already sat on the throne of Qing Dynasty China for more than fifty years. "Internal peace, as well as expansion along China's frontiers," writes the historian Morris Rossabi, "gave birth to an optimism that pervaded" the Qianlong Emperor's reign.[1] The *shōgun* in Japan was Tokugawa Ienari, eleventh in the line of Tokugawa *shōguns* to rule in the name of Japan's figurehead emperors. He was in only his third year of power, but the military government he led had not faced a serious challenge, foreign or domestic, for generations. On the southwestern reaches of the Sea of Japan, meanwhile, lay Korea, where King Chŏngjo was the twenty-second ruler of the Chosŏn (also known as Yi) Dynasty. Although Korea had earlier experienced invasions from China and Japan, it had now been at peace with both for nearly 200 years and relations with China were friendly enough that King Chŏngjo sent a personal embassy to the birthday festivities of the Qianlong Emperor, where it was received with honor.[2] Each of these three societies, in brief, could justifiably see itself as a success, and as with successful societies everywhere, each was strongly inclined to maintain its well-established socioeconomic order.

The good times were soon to end. Within the next 100-odd years, China's Qing Dynasty would collapse, the Japanese emperor would wrest power from the Tokugawa *shōguns*, and Korea would fall under Japanese domination. Behind these radical changes were encounters with European and American powers that threw China, Japan, and Korea headlong into their own crises of modernity. It was not European colonialism, per se, that drove the resulting changes on the shores of the Sea of Japan; only China was compelled to offer colonial concessions, which were limited to a handful of cities. Instead, it was the realization (slowly dawning in China, more abrupt in Japan, and imposed upon Korea) that radical change was necessary for survival in the face of modern European technology.

Historians have passionately debated how Europe gained its nineteenth-century technological advantage.[3] Some have credited a singularly European "path of social development" (as with Max Weber's idea of a Protestant work ethic or Karl Marx's argument about the rise of capitalism) dating as early as the sixteenth century.[4] But many world historians are now inclined to see the advantage being gained only toward the end of the eighteenth century, for until then China and Japan were surprisingly similar to Europe in "combining sophisticated agriculture, commerce, and nonmechanized industry."[5] The historian R. Bin Wong argues that eighteenth-century China and Japan did not lack the ability to industrialize; they lacked the *need*, thanks to their surpluses of inexpensive labor.[6] Many additional factors might also be mentioned (such as Europe's easy access to the wealth produced by mines and plantations in the Americas), but the irreducible fact is that Europe *had* gained a technological advantage. Around the start of the nineteenth century, the Pacific lands were unavoidably confronted by that fact.

Japan

When Commodore Matthew Perry of the United States Navy steamed into Edo Bay in 1853 to demand that Japan open itself to American trade, his four "black ships" were mounted with sixty-one cannons – an unimpressive display of arms in a European context, but "more firepower than all the guns in Japan combined" after hundreds of years of peace.[7] It was immediately apparent that the Tokugawa era's tight regulations on direct trade could no longer be maintained; Japan soon granted the United States access to a pair of ports, with various European nations demanding and receiving similar rights shortly after.[8] Given its evident weakness, the Tokugawa regime itself came under domestic challenge. On January 3, 1868, the court in Kyoto proclaimed "the Restoration of Imperial Rule of Old."[9] Jürgen Osterhammel observes that the Meiji Restoration was "an act of pure usurpation," but it set the stage for the world's "most thoroughgoing revolution of the middle decades of the nineteenth century." The Japanese "needed relatively little force to achieve far-reaching changes," without ever having suffered "significant foreign military intervention" or "colonial subjugation."[10]

Although Japan was never colonized, its modernizers were attracted to European and American military and industrial models, as well as to their cultural models. The historian Irokawa Daikichi writes: "The influence of European and American civilization on Japan during the 1860s and 1870s was traumatic and disruptive," but "for a time any thought of defending traditional culture was scorned as an idle diversion from the critical need to respond to the urgency that faced the country. What had to be done was to penetrate the enemies' camp, grasp their weapons of civilization for use against them, and then turn to use them in the national interest."[11] In the event, suggests the economist Kaoru Sugihara, Japanese industry learned from Europe and the United States but did not imitate them: "Recognizing that both land and capital were scarce while labor was abundant and of relatively good quality, the new [Japanese] strategy was to encourage ... the conscious adaptation of Western technology to [Japan's] different conditions."[12] But there remained "widespread confusion and ambivalence," writes John K. Gillespie: "If Japan became a modern nation, could it retain Japanese qualities? Did becoming modern mean becoming less Japanese or, worse, western? What did it mean to be Japanese in the modern world?"[13]

These questions had a special urgency when it came to theatre. Although *bunraku* was already in steep decline by the start of the nineteenth century, *nō* and *kabuki* were still going strong. But the Meiji Restoration "totally upended the theatrical establishment," suggests Jonah Salz. "Instantly, crucial aspects of [the] entire repertoire [of the two forms] were made obsolete. Confucian ideology and Buddhist philosophy were officially disdained," while "feudal hierarchies were abandoned for the all-important imperial mission of building a modern state."[14] The prospects for *nō* were especially grim, for its centuries-long base of support – the Tokugawa military aristocracy – no longer existed. As a result, "a great number of performers had to abandon their art, many *nō* stages were destroyed ... or converted to other uses, and invaluable *nō* masks and costumes were sold."[15] In the words of Donald Keene, the form "was in disgrace," along with the regime it had served.[16]

And yet *nō* serendipitously survived to become enshrined in a new niche. Early in the 1870s, a court official named Iwakura Tomomi led an embassy to Europe, where he was "stunned to see western leaders entertaining [foreign] dignitaries with plays, which would have been inconceivable in Japan."[17] After returning to Japan, Iwakura arranged in 1876 for a performance of *nō* for the imperial family, arousing interest in what remained of the form. Three years later, Ulysses S. Grant, former president of the United States, became the first head (or former head) of a foreign state to visit Japan, and the imperial court was unsure of how to entertain him. Recalling his experience in Europe, Iwakura arranged for Grant to see a *nō* performance, hosted by the emperor.

One might not expect Grant – formerly a hard-drinking soldier – to have been especially interested in the ancient theatre form, and it is no surprise to learn that he slept through much of the show. But afterward he reportedly proclaimed, "So noble and beautiful an art is easily cheapened and destroyed by the changing tastes of the times. You must make efforts to preserve it." His words were "taken to heart" by the imperial court, which empowered Iwakura to establish a society for the preservation of *nō*. Subsequently, the form would become a bulwark of Japanese identity in a time of radical societal change, the embodiment of "'pure' Japanese culture uncontaminated by foreign influences."[18]

Japan's modernity had a more complicated impact on *kabuki*. By the mid nineteenth century the form had its own deeply entrenched traditions, despite a "continuous history of reform and change" that had allowed it to retain its popular appeal. Still, as Thomas Leims comments, "novelties" in *kabuki* had always been introduced "with a certain responsibility towards the conservation of what may be termed the essence of their art, i.e., the actors' performance."[19] Some *kabuki* plays in the repertory had been written in the seventeenth century, while others were from the Genroku period (1688–1704) or the early nineteenth century, when a new genre of playwrighting emphasized "the sentimental, the grizzly, and the grotesque."[20] But even these newer plays largely maintained traditions of costuming and makeup, as well as the long-established *aragoto* (powerful male), *wagoto* (romantic male), and *onnagata* (men cross-dressing for female roles) styles of performance.

With the abrupt modernization that followed the Meiji Restoration, *kabuki* took multiple paths. One of these involved a "process of crystallization" rather like *nō*'s, leading the form away from its accustomed "immediacy and responsiveness" to public tastes.[21] Other paths aimed to maintain the form's commercial appeal by embracing modernity, but did so in differing ways. One modernizing path emphasized nationalistic themes, especially in the decades between the Sino-Japanese War (1894–1895) and the end of the Second World War. Most notable during this latter war was the introduction of "overnight pickle" plays (*ichitazuki*), which "directly dramatized current military actions."[22] Similarly nationalistic were "new-history" plays (*shin-jidaigeki*) that retold familiar tales from Japanese history, but now with reference "to the contemporary ideal of loyalty to the emperor … anachronistically attributed to warriors, generals, and shoguns from the feudal past."[23]

Another modernizing path for *kabuki* was to move cautiously toward syncretism with European cultural and theatrical traits. In 1872, the actor Ichikawa Danjūrō IX proclaimed the need to "clean away the decay" of *kabuki* and emphasize realism. At about the same time, "crop-hair plays" emerged, featuring "surface elements of Western culture and modernity," with actors favoring "western suits, bowler hats and pocket watches," even as the plays themselves largely maintained "traditional kabuki dramatic structures and performance conventions."[24] Slightly more syncretic was *shin* ["new"] *kabuki*, which made greater use of "contemporary themes and psychological realism." Although it too was generally performed with the look and feel of *kabuki*, it "avoided certain standard techniques, such as *mie* (climactic poses), attempting greater verisimilitude. Even the accompanying music was different," especially in being "less pervasive" than was traditionally the case. But despite (or perhaps because of) the European influence, *shin kabuki* had limited success, being "never as popular as the old, unreformed favourites."[25]

Around the start of the twentieth century, even before *shin kabuki* had reached its full development, a somewhat more thoroughly syncretic theatre had emerged: *shinpa* (sometimes transliterated as *shimpa*; meaning "new wave" or "new school"). Benito Ortolani writes that *shinpa* was "the first" Japanese theatre form "to develop outside the *kabuki* world after the Meiji Restoration as an attempt to modernize and westernize Japan's drama."[26] The emerging form became popular for a while by choosing "timely themes" such as "war plays and plays adapted from successful novels and newspaper serials," even as it incorporated ample amounts of spectacle and emotion. But it never attained much stability; its contemporaries saw it, above all, "as a kind of curiosity."[27] Gillespie notes that *shinpa* has variously "been characterized as an offshoot of *kabuki*, an early modern form, and a bridge between the traditional and the modern."[28] I would call it an emerging syncretic theatre form and note that despite its limited durability in Japan, it would exert a strong influence on theatre in both Korea and China (as we will see), giving it greater historical importance than its intrinsic merits might suggest.

Far more consequential for Japan would be the emergence of *shingeki* ("new drama"), which at its start was simply European spoken theatre transferred in toto to Japan. It is an open question among Japanese scholars whether *shingeki* grew out of *shinpa* or was an independent development.[29] *Shinpa* had certainly been influenced by European theatre but was seen by advocates of *shingeki* as being insufficiently "modern."[30] Those advocates desired to transfer spoken theatre without making any compromises to Japanese theatrical traditions, so while they were likely influenced by *shinpa*, they intentionally chose a different, more radical path. Spoken theatre was brought to Japan not by Europeans (as had been the case in sub-Saharan Africa, South Asia, and Southeast Asia) but by Japanese academics themselves. *Shingeki* "was born," writes Ortolani, "around two major Tokyo universities" and was based on "the serious study, translation, and performance of western dramatic literature," with the hope of developing "a Japanese dramatic literature comparable to that of the West."[31]

Carol Fisher Sorgenfrei emphasizes how thoroughly *shingeki* "turned its back on Japanese tradition. *Shingeki* was (and remains) primarily interested in making theatre reminiscent" of spoken theatre's text-based "psychological realism"; she notes also that this interest dovetailed with the contemporaneous cultural and political "desire to reject tradition and to learn from and surpass the West."[32] But she perhaps overstates the case, for as the theatre critic Senda Akihiko comments, "From Ancient times the Japanese have introduced and assimilated with ardent curiosity entirely different cultures of alien lands such as China, America and various European countries. Whatever could be converted to the native style took root in Japanese soil, enriching in a somewhat chaotic manner the culture there, which has come to be characterised by a hybrid nature."[33] Even if *shingeki* was originally intended as a direct transfer of spoken theatre, in other words, it was soon "converted to the native style," much as the technological models transferred from Europe and the United States were reconceived to suit Japanese conditions.

In the years before the Second World War, *shingeki* was performed mostly in small theatres that catered to educated audiences interested in the form's psychological realism and/or political commentary – a relatively narrow but influential niche.[34] Virtually from the start, its plays were presented in Japanese.[35] A diversity of approaches quickly developed within *shingeki*, which could be safely indulged because the form's artists "shunned commercialism, and worked mostly outside Japan's professional entertainment world."[36] Gillespie suggests that "once the obeisance paid to translated western plays subsided, once activists surged past orthodox *shingeki* to realize a truly indigenous Japanese drama, the new voice gained timbre, though only amid the din of competing voices."[37] *Shingeki* proved to be the leading theatrical voice of modern Japan, but the nineteenth- and twentieth-century developments in *nō* and *kabuki* demonstrate that theatrical modernity did not require the sacrifice of a distinctly Japanese past.

Korea

Korea's theatrical modernity came about in a unique way. Nineteenth-century Europe and the United States were not disinterested in what they sometimes called the Hermit Kingdom, but Korea was little more than an afterthought. Koreans themselves "seem to have remained on the whole strangely unmoved and unchanging despite … foreign pressures."[38] Rather than Europe or the United States, it was Japan that instigated Korea's modernization. Quickly industrializing after the Meiji Restoration, Japan is sometimes said to have wanted "to leave Asia" and become part of "the West," but in truth what the Japanese wanted toward the end of the nineteenth century was "to expand their power over their East Asian neighbors."[39] One of their most immediate targets was Korea. After decades of unequal trade relations, Japan reduced Korea to a protectorate in 1905, then subjected it to outright annexation in 1910.

Up until then, Korea's established theatre forms had remained largely undisturbed for generations. In the Introduction I mentioned the *pyŏlsin-gut* of Hahoe Village, which is but one of Korea's many folk forms of mask or puppet theatre;[40] the court of the Chosŏn Dynasty (1392–1910) had its own long-lived forms of mask theatre, along with a satirical form of unmasked theatre.[41] But by far the most popular Korean theatre form was *p'ansori* (a word of uncertain origin). In this form, "a single vocalist … delivers an entire story, or more commonly an episode from one, taking on the roles of the various characters in turn and also acting as a third-person narrator." The performance involves "three distinct techniques: singing (*ch'ang*) with a distinctive husky and emotionally intense vocal timbre; stylized speech (*aniri*); and mimetic or expressive movement (*pallim* or *norumsae*)."[42] There were surprisingly few stories performed in *p'ansori*: Oh-kon Cho notes that "only five pieces [currently] exist, although there once were up to twelve"; but substantial improvisation added variety to these well-known stories.[43]

Despite the Japanese annexation in 1910, many of the established folk forms would carry on, largely unchanged, to the present day. *P'ansori* would survive as well, but from it would also spring a syncretic form known as *ch'anggŭk*. Before turning to this form, however, we need to confront a curiosity: "At the dawn of the twentieth century," writes Andrew P. Killick, Korea "lacked a theatrical tradition to compare with those of China or Japan" – by which Killick means a tradition with purpose-built theatres and scripted plays comparable to *jingju* or *kabuki*. He suggests that this lack was probably because "Korea had never developed the kind of substantial moneyed merchant class that supported professional indoor theatre."⁴⁴ This seems plausible, but it is also worth noting that while the capital city of Seoul had a population of some 200,000 people as early as the seventeenth century, that number remained relatively steady until the start of the twentieth century.⁴⁵ We have seen in many instances that upsurges in urban population can bring about the development of potential new audiences, which are critical for the emergence of commercial theatre forms. Seoul's stability through the latter centuries of the Chosŏn Dynasty suggests the absence of an audience that would demand something *other* than the familiar *p'ansori*.

With the coming of Japanese investment and annexation, however, Seoul's population suddenly grew, creating new opportunities for theatre. One form that took advantage of these opportunities was *ch'anggŭk* (literally, "sung drama"), which was originally based in a small theatre (mostly used for silent movies) operated by the American-owned Seoul Electric Company. The form itself was apparently created by a Korean who had studied in Japan and seen *shinpa* there; upon coming home he "brought a group of *p'ansori* singers together to perform a drama that we would now recognize as *ch'anggŭk*."⁴⁶ Meewon Lee explains that the form is essentially "a role-divided P'ansori, where each actor plays a role [along] with a main narrator." According to contemporaneous critics, *ch'anggŭk* performances were considered "obscene, lewd, and filthy."⁴⁷ But as is often the case, this objectionable entertainment was what the new urban audiences wanted. *Ch'anggŭk* played into its popular appeal, writes Killick, by "absorb[ing] imported concepts of acting, costumes, and stage scenery. Eventually – with the addition of an accompanying orchestra, chorus of extras, other kinds of music besides *p'ansori*, various styles of dance, and the technical capabilities of the modern theatre – the genre would approach the proportions of grand opera" (see Figure 15.1).⁴⁸

Although *ch'anggŭk* was certainly a creation of modernizing Korea, Lee suggests, it was intellectually conservative, taking no interest in "expressing ideas of modernization."⁴⁹ But modernizing ideas would shortly also arrive from Japan, in the forms of *shinpa* and *shingeki*. Hong Seunyong notes that *shinpa* in Korea was originally offered for Japanese audiences by Japanese touring troupes. But "a new phase" of Korean theatre dawned by the 1920s as Koreans who had studied in Japan returned to create their own Korean-language versions of *shinpa* and *shingeki*, known in Korea as *shinp'a* (or *shinp'agŭk*) and *shingŭk*, respectively.⁵⁰ This of course created a pattern already familiar from European colonization: The Koreans took the colonizing Japanese theatre as a model, even as they resented the Japanese colonization.⁵¹

Figure 15.1 *Ch'anggŭk*: a scene from a contemporary production in Seoul of the traditional *p'ansori* story-song *Sugungga*. (Photo by Seung-il Ryu/NurPhoto SRL/Alamy Stock Photo)

The plays of *shinp'a* were "set in the present time and dealt with contemporary events in Korean life," being mostly "military plays, detective plays, and domestic plays" that were especially popular because they showed the Japanese occupation as "the cause of individual and national suffering."⁵² The plays had "many characteristics of western melodrama" as filtered through *shinpa*, including an appeal to the emotions and an emphasis "on the promotion of virtue and the reproof of vice."⁵³ Korea's *shingŭk* was rather different, following the Japanese *shingeki* in being a transfer in toto of European spoken theatre, though at the start this was an indirect transfer, consisting of "Korean translations of Japanese translations of Western dramas."⁵⁴ Korean students, however, soon began writing their own spoken theatre plays "focused on social problems such as sexual taboos, early marriages, and patriarchal tyrannies. They used everyday language and detailed descriptions of environments following the footsteps of western realism."⁵⁵

One might well wonder if *shinp'a* and *shingŭk* are to be understood as the result of European cultural imperialism, even if that imperialism came indirectly, via Japan's own imperialism. Jinhee Kim insists that "Korean audiences are capable of responding, within the framework of the traditional values of their culture, to plays based on Western models performed in Western-style productions." Or, to put the matter more broadly, the domestication of a foreign theatre form "does not deprive indigenous populations of their cultural roots," since "non-Western audiences," and, for that matter, theatre artists, "are not, and cannot be, mere passive receivers of hegemonic Western texts and their accompanying ideologies."[56] In Korea as elsewhere, those artists were the creators of their own modernity, employing whatever useful tools might have been at hand.

East Asia

The celebrations for the eightieth birthday of China's Qianlong Emperor in 1790 were by all accounts a splendid affair, notable especially for their theatrical presentations. The emperor was "famous for his fondness for spectacular shows," and during his long reign he had increased the number of court-based performers from a hundred to a thousand. He also had an unusual interest in the diversity of China's theatre forms. During six visits to southern China, for example, "he enjoyed a variety of popular theatres" not typically seen in Beijing.[57] In return, for the occasion of his birthday celebrations, officials and merchants in the southerly province of Anhui sent theatre troupes to Beijing. These troupes were remarkably versatile, performing both *kunqu* (the elegant theatre form especially appreciated by the elite) and *huidiao* (a popular theatre form that used the *erhuang* musical system, itself a spinoff of the *yiyang* system); they were also noted for their acrobatic skills.[58] Their performances at the emperor's birthday celebrations are conventionally regarded as the birth of *jingju* (also known as *jingxi* and Peking/Beijing opera). By all appearances, *jingju* is a "traditional" form of Chinese theatre, despite its relatively recent emergence (see Figure 15.2). Its development, however, would be shaped by China's confrontation with European imperialism and so it serves as a sort of hinge in Chinese theatre history. In one sense it is the product of centuries of indigenous theatrical experience, but in another sense, it is China's first "modern" theatre form, with its development being intimately connected to nineteenth-century British incursions into China's soon-tottering empire.

Coming into the nineteenth century, Great Britain did not have diplomatic relations with China, but the British East India Company (EIC) had already established a commercial base in Canton (now Guangzhou). The EIC had a problem, though. The British had a growing appetite for Chinese goods: porcelain and silk, as always, but now especially for Chinese tea, to be sweetened with sugar from plantations in the Caribbean. But

Figure 15.2 *Jingju*: a scene from a contemporary production of *Hegemon King Says Farewell to His Queen*. (Photo by K-King Photography Media Co. Ltd. via Getty Images)

what commodity could the British use to offset the cost of these imports? Although it does them little honor to say it bluntly, the British turned to drug-dealing.

Opium grown in British-controlled India could easily be shipped to China, so the EIC invested in opium fields; in the early decades of the nineteenth century, they managed a fivefold increase in shipments of the drug. When the EIC's China monopoly officially ended in 1833, numerous British merchants joined in the lucrative trade. In 1839, the Chinese government banned the drug's importation, jailed some British merchants, and confiscated vast amounts of opium. The British responded by declaring war in the name of free trade. Its navy blockaded or bombarded coastal Chinese cities and penetrated up the Yangtze River.[59] The Treaty of Nanjing ended the war and rewarded Britain with control over Hong Kong, access to four additional ports (most importantly, Shanghai), and compensation for war costs as well as for the confiscated opium. But in 1856 a Second Opium War broke out, with the British this time being aided by the French; it ended with China completely legalizing the opium trade and providing additional enclaves for European merchants.⁶⁰ And these wars were accompanied by a series of internal rebellions, the deadliest being the Taiping Revolution (1850–1864), led by a Chinese man poorly educated in Christianity who claimed to be the younger brother of Jesus. The Taiping effort to establish a millennialist state led to large portions of southern China being devastated by warfare, famine, and disease. By the time military forces aligned with the government put down the rebellion, tens of millions were dead and countless more were driven from their homes.⁶¹

And yet it was in the context of the Opium Wars and the Taiping Revolution that *jingju* came into its own. This will seem paradoxical because devastating warfare is typically not conducive to the emergence of theatre forms. But Beijing itself was well north of the various war zones. Many refugees fled to the relative safety of the capital, where (among other necessities) they sought entertainment. Li Ruru observes that this suddenly enlarged Beijing audience was "no longer content with the old repertoire of romantic sentiments and elegant music," as was the regular fare in *kunqu* especially, "but needed a theatre that could express their anxiety and indignation, conveying the spirit of militancy and austerity demanded by the time."⁶² *Jingju* would exemplify that spirit, Fu Jin observes, by quickly filling its repertoire with plays about "political and military conflicts inside the court or between two nations" that could easily arouse "the audiences' sensations."⁶³

Actors and theatre troupes from the troubled areas of China also took refuge in Beijing, where they found the waiting audiences. Of special note were troupes that came from Hubei province. As with the troupes from Anhui that had earlier come for the emperor's birthday celebrations, these Hubei troupes used *erhuang* music, but they also employed *xipi* music, derived from the *bangzi* (clapper music) musical system. The troupes from the two provinces soon began working together, as well as with troupes from elsewhere that had also come to Beijing. Together, they developed a modified musical system known as *pihuang* (a combination of *xipi* and *erhuang*) that "became the basic structure for future *jingju* music."⁶⁴ Over the next generation, yet additional troupes from beyond Beijing would arrive to add further complexity to the emerging theatre form, which became "a vibrant fusion of strands drawn from other genres [that] evolved an exceptional ability to assimilate different styles of dialect, song, music and acting conventions."⁶⁵ That fusion held great appeal to Beijing audiences: Wherever in China they might have come from, they could find something familiar in it. And when they eventually returned to their homes, they took with them a taste for *jingju*, which would help make it China's first truly national theatre form. The form appealed to the imperial court as well, whose insistence on a "high standard" of performance "enhanced [its] overall artistic quality."[66]

Even after its extended period of emergence, *jingju* continued to change, undergoing perhaps its most significant "reform" after it was introduced to Shanghai. The European presence there was far more inescapable than in Beijing and helped to bring about a split in *jingju* between *haipai* ("Shanghai-style") and *jingpai* ("Beijing-style") subforms. Fu Jin comments that "the locals" in Shanghai "wouldn't mechanically copy" the Beijing style, for they "had their bright alternative."[67] *Haipai* proved to be the "more flexible" of the subforms, "readily adopting modern mechanisms, techniques, and acting styles from other genres, including Western theatre and cinema."[68] Among other changes, it "overthrew the essential concept of conventionalization by using contemporary costumes and make-up." This might seem a relatively minor matter, but as Li Ruru writes, it "actually changed *jingju*'s aesthetic approach from abstract, symbolic and expressive to concrete, real and representing reality."[69] For the first time, a Chinese theatre form that had been created through *intra*cultural syncretism was stimulated by *inter*cultural syncretism.

Such syncretism would play an even larger role as the Qing Dynasty collapsed under external pressure from European empires and Japan (which had taken control of Taiwan even before it annexed Korea), along with internal pressure from a secret society known as the Boxers (the Chinese name means "Righteous and Harmonious Fists"), who violently opposed the foreign presence in China and blamed the Qing Dynasty for accepting that presence. Chinese theatre artists (and the intellectuals who spurred them on) looked for ways to modernize their work even more thoroughly than the Shanghai-style *jingju*. Shanghai was the crucible of change because it contained an International Settlement (populated mostly by British, Japanese, and Chinese), a specifically French Concession, and a Chinese-controlled area. Siyuan Liu suggests that "the lack of a hegemonic cultural force and the presence of a large immigrant population, both Chinese and international, made Shanghai an ideal site for the emergence of a hybrid theatre."[70] There was also the influence of nearby Japan, which was already decades into its own self-modernization.

In 1907, Chinese students studying in Tokyo became interested in Japan's *shinpa* and were inspired to mount plays of their own. Their first effort was a single act of *Camille*, the "well-made" French play by Alexandre Dumas *fils*. They followed with a full-length adaptation of the

American antislavery novel *Uncle Tom's Cabin*, which they entitled *The Black Slave's Cry to Heaven*. This might seem a curious choice of texts, but the Chinese-language adaptation focused attention on "the rebellious and triumphant George Harris." In doing so, it emphasized his "unjust suffering" and linked "American slavery directly to the fate of Chinese laborers in the United States" and to "the national fear of succumbing to colonialism"; the clear implication was the ability of China to overcome the foreign powers that oppressed it.[71]

The play was successful enough that when some of its creators returned to Shanghai, they mounted another version there. The performance itself was deeply syncretic, with a "reliance on speech, [a] five-act structure, a complete script, ensemble acting, as well as (semi)realistic costume, set, and makeup," while also including ample amounts of Chinese-style "singing and dancing" as well as cross-dressed men playing the female characters.[72] Chinese audiences were apparently unsure what to make of *Black Slave's Cry* and the ensuing plays that took up its syncretic formula. They referred to the emerging theatre form as *wenmingxi*, meaning "civilized drama," owing to the theatrical traits it had taken from Europe.[73] But as one *wenmingxi* director wrote about a subsequent show: "The bones of this production were Western, its flesh and joints were Japanese [based in *shinpa*], and its skin was Chinese."[74] The form gained a modest popularity but "was plagued with low-quality productions and actors, which in turn affected its survival" in the face of competition from other theatre forms, most notably the Shanghai-style *jingju*.[75]

As with many emerging syncretic forms of theatre, *wenmingxi* has been given little respect by theatre scholars, being neither "traditional" Chinese theatre nor the "modern" spoken theatre that would shortly be transferred there in toto. Liu observes that "wenmingxi remains in a theoretical limbo in search of a paradigm that defines its place" in Chinese theatre history. While *Black Slave's Cry* "has been credited as the beginning of modern Chinese theatre, the ideologically and theatrically hybrid decade that followed the production has ... [been] seen as a failed experiment in modern theatre that is separate to huaju, a name that denotes the spoken theatre since the 1920s and is exclusively synonymous with modern Chinese theatre."[76] As I noted earlier, emerging syncretic forms such as *wenmingxi* are sometimes referred to as "transitional," as if their only function were to prepare non-Europeans for the superior European-style spoken theatre that would follow. But this demeans *wenmingxi* no less than it does other such forms, each of which deserves respect as an original attempt to treat the issues of modernity.

Huaju itself was far more radical than *wenmingxi*, both theatrically and politically; indeed, these radicalisms were intimately connected. The form emerged shortly after the Qing Dynasty was overthrown in 1911, as China attempted to sort out what it meant to be a republic. "The advocates of *huaju*," notes William Dolby, "tended very much to be young intellectuals," often "strongly influenced by Western education"; they were also "self-consciously concerned with promoting bold ideas for social change." The European playwrights they studied and translated included Henrik Ibsen, August Strindberg, Anton Chekhov, and George Bernard Shaw – a veritable who's who of politically engaged realist theatre.[77] As a contemporaneous Chinese critic wrote, the "purpose" of *huaju* "was to comment on the miseries of the current situation and to warn our fellow citizens," as well as to "mobilize the hitherto hidden wave of nationalism," adding that "from now on, drama has to be real and it has to record reality." This purpose entailed an almost complete rejection of existing Chinese theatrical practices and narratives; instead, the emphasis would be on contemporary topics presented as naturalistically as possible.[78]

Huaju, in short, began as a direct transference of spoken theatre. Its greatest successes came in the 1930s, when (as Dolby suggests) "the persistent inspiration provided by European and American playwrights manifested itself most strikingly in Cao Yu … generally acclaimed as the greatest of all Chinese *huaju* playwrights."[79] But even as Chinese theatre artists were inspired by spoken theatre they had begun to domesticate it: One especially successful *huaju* play included an "extensive infusion of jingju performance" techniques to add "to the play's appeal."[80] The success of the Communist Revolution in 1949 brought obvious complications for *huaju* playwrights, as their "choice of theme and its form of expression were sure to be bounded by the confines allowed by the ideology of the new regime."[81] Through it all, though, *huaju* never filled more than a relatively narrow niche in the complex of Chinese theatre forms. Liu reports that even after the Second World War, the audience for *huaju* was limited "to the urban elite and occupied a tiny fraction of the theatre market when compared to indigenous theatre."[82] As almost everywhere else in Asia and sub-Saharan Africa, spoken theatre (however thoroughly domesticated) was artistically and politically important but scarcely popular.

With all the attention that can rightfully be paid to *jingju*, *wenmingxi*, and *huaju*, it is easy to overlook the numerous Chinese theatre forms that existed before 1800 and continued in performance well into the twentieth century without significant syncretism. One of the more obscure of these is *yangge*, a folk theatre that has apparently existed in northwestern

China for many centuries.[83] Its distance from the coast, as well as its base in villages, kept it at a remove from intercultural syncretic influence. As with many folk forms, *yangge* showed substantial variation from place to place, but its dramatic theatre was generally embedded in nondramatic performances such as parades, dances, and martial arts displays, typically offered during Lunar New Year celebrations.[84] The form's repertoire was surprisingly large: One troupe (made up mostly of illiterate farmers) had memorized forty-eight plays, which in print total some 700 pages.[85] And the form was remarkably popular: In 1944, almost a thousand troupes were counted in the Shaan-Gan-Ning border region.[86] At around that time, the Chinese Communist Party created its own subform of *yangge*, intended explicitly for propaganda – and yet the folkloric version of *yangge* was still being performed decades after the Communist Revolution.[87]

It is also too easy to overlook Chinese theatre forms that emerged after 1800 but that are strongly indigenous in their content and style. One such form is *huju* (also known as Shanghai opera). It emerged in the same way as had *jingju* – through *intra*cultural syncretism – but did so in the early 1900s. *Huju*'s roots are in a pair of ballad-singing traditions. One of these was based in the nearby countryside and was notable especially for its "wholly salacious songs and dialogue," presented by a pair of performers, originally male and female. When some of these performers moved to Shanghai, they encountered urban ballad-singers with whom "they shared a number of traditional plots."[88] The rural and urban performers began working together – and as they encountered yet other performers "they gradually adopted new stylistic traits." Being in multicultural Shanghai, the emerging form also picked up traits from European theatre: European "instruments, harmonization, and metrical structures" were incorporated, even as "traditional melodies remain paramount." By the 1920s, *huju* troupes were performing "fully staged and costumed opera."[89] Romantic love stories dominated the repertoire, to the point that female performers not only returned to the form (after having been governmentally prohibited for some decades) but came to dominate it, with at least a few troupes being all-female.[90]

As China struggled to modernize, in brief, Chinese theatre was anything but an inevitable progress from the indigenous "traditional" to the European-derived "modern." It was and remains a mix of established forms and newer ones, with some of its forms remaining strongly indigenous and others borrowing from European theatre to a greater or lesser extent; of course there is also the domesticated version of spoken theatre transferred in toto from Europe. If China's mixture of theatre forms seems especially complex, it is likely because its self-modernization was especially tortuous, with its magnificent culture having been buffeted for well over a century by one disaster after another.

As we reach the end of Part V, one question deserves further consideration: How can we account for the transference of European spoken theatre to so many parts of the world, to the point that it is often considered the quintessential "modern" theatre?

The form's transference to the American and Australasian Neo-Europes is simple enough to understand, for it was in effect the native theatrical language of Neo-European settlers and immigrants. Insofar as their descendants retain cultural links to their ancestral homelands, European spoken theatre remains an important model. As for sub-Saharan Africa and the various regions of Asia, a first pass at the question yields an easy (and not inaccurate) answer: In the nineteenth and early twentieth centuries, Europe was always the colonizer and never the colonized. But matters are not quite that simple, for as we have seen, Japan was never colonized, and colonization in China was limited to a handful of locales. Although European imperialism is a necessary part of any explanation for the transference of spoken theatre, it is not sufficient in itself.

As Kevin Wetmore, Jr., Siyuan Liu, and Erin B. Mee point out, the form's transference was brought about, above all, by "people attached to particular universities or even secondary schools. Indeed, much modern drama [in Asia] evolves out of both foreign language programmes at Asian secondary schools and institutions of higher learning";[91] the same, as we have seen, is true of sub-Saharan Africa. But it is worth noting that although one or another European language (and the spoken theatre composed in it) might have been imposed upon the students at those schools, few societies were compelled to forswear their native theatre forms, however much those forms might have been disparaged. It is also worth noting that in Japan and China, the educational institutions were not generally run by Europeans. For students and teachers in those institutions, it was quite plainly the model of European culture (and of spoken theatre) that beckoned.

It is evident, then, that some people actively *chose* to transfer spoken theatre to their homelands. Why would they make this choice? Erika Fischer-Lichte argues that "the adaptation of the foreign is sparked off by a problem which has arisen in the traditional theatre (and in extreme cases, the culture) … that cannot be solved within the scope of existing theatrical forms."[92] The "problem" at hand was that established indigenous theatre forms could not adequately address the psychological, social, and political issues that most concerned the students, activists, and intellectuals in sub-Saharan Africa and the regions of Asia. Some indigenous forms (e.g., *nō*) had what were, in effect, closed canons of texts; others had content that was thematically circumscribed in one way or another (e.g., *raslila* and *wayang kulit purwa*); commercial theatre forms might have been somewhat more open but could scarcely risk offending the audiences on which they depended (e.g., *jingju* and *kabuki*). Some newly emerging syncretic forms (e.g., Parsi theatre and *bangsawan*) similarly depended on popular audiences, although a few could go further, as with the Yoruba Travelling Theatre's willingness to broach anticolonial themes and *wenmingxi*'s *Black Slave's Cry to Heaven*.

But spoken theatre as written by realist playwrights such as Ibsen, Strindberg, and Chekhov was specifically created to engage with psychological, social, and political issues. Moreover, it was readily adaptable by non-Europeans to their own concerns, the most immediate of which were nationalist reactions to European imperialism. As a result, spoken theatre in sub-Saharan Africa and the regions of Asia quickly "developed into an anti-colonial dramaturgy."[93] But anticolonialism was not the only theme taken up by the transferred form: Confrontations between traditional family structures and the modernizing world were also frequently addressed, as were issues with postcolonial governments. Spoken theatre, in brief, offered people beyond Europe a useful tool for the creation of works that could address difficult issues in their modernizing societies.

It also helped that spoken theatre *seemed* relatively easy to mount. In contrast to many theatre forms (including European opera and ballet), it required no extensive training in vocalization or movement; no costly costumes or complex makeup or masks; and no musical accompaniment. But the ease of spoken theatre was only apparent, for it presented its own set of challenges. For Africans and Asians, these challenges were exacerbated by their familiarity with indigenous performance practices. As an early *wenmingxi* director commented: "When we perform in new drama, we wear regular clothes, walk in a natural gait, and use ordinary gestures …. In short, there is no convention that constricts us. Since there is no convention, is it easy? The answer is no. In fact, it is hundreds and thousands of times more difficult than old theatre."[94]

Notwithstanding the successes achieved by theatre artists in sub-Saharan Africa and the regions of Asia, spoken theatre has generally been confined to a limited niche in each locale's complex of theatre forms. Wetmore, Liu, and Mee note that the domesticated versions of spoken theatre in regions of Asia are "by and for (and ultimately about) the educated middle class who could afford tickets, were interested in modern drama, and were educated to understand Ibsen, Chekhov, Strindberg, and others";[95] the audience for spoken theatre in sub-Saharan Africa, meanwhile, is even more restricted because (as we have seen) its plays are usually presented in European languages not understood by most people. The narrowness of spoken theatre's niche is not difficult to explain. Although the details vary from place to place, one can broadly say that the form intentionally eschews many of the traits that have made other theatre forms so popular, such as familiar narratives, exciting music and dance, elaborate stage effects, sentimentality, and overt appeals to emotion. One can plausibly argue that it is to spoken theatre's credit that it is more interested in challenging its audience than in satisfying them with easy comforts – but many audiences remain unmoved by or resistant to the challenges it offers.

The limited appeal of spoken theatre beyond Europe and the Neo-Europes, even after a hundred or more years of performance, undermines any claim that it is *the* "modern" theatre. There is no teleological necessity to its widespread transference, nor is it the necessary end state to which all theatre aspires. Its transference was everywhere a choice made by a minority of theatre artists who saw it as a useful tool for engaging with issues that mattered to them. But that choice is neither irrevocable nor conclusive; other choices can and will be made as the history of world theatre continues to unfurl.

Conclusion

Three aspects of world theatre history call for final comment, not only because of what they suggest about theatre's past but also for what they might hint about its future. First is the immense impact that broad historical forces have had on theatre history, especially at its major inflection points; second is the frequency with which theatre forms have been shaped by syncretism, whether *intra*cultural or *inter*cultural; and third is the depth of attraction that dramatic theatre has exerted upon people through the centuries and around the world.

The very structure of this book emphasizes *the impact of broad historical forces*. A global perspective makes it possible to see that it was not some ineffable "genius" of Greek society (or for that matter, of Indian society) that made possible the breakthroughs to literary theatre. Examining the Greek and Indian breakthroughs in tandem allows for the identification of a specific set of societal conditions that no other society would happen to share for centuries to come: a literate class, a well supported niche that encouraged the development of new plays, and a storehouse of popular narratives that playwrights could shape to their own ends. It is no coincidence that when that same set of societal conditions came to exist elsewhere, new forms of literary theatre (such as *nanxi*, Yuan *zaju*, *khayāl al-zill*, *nō*, and the early vernacular forms of Europe) soon followed.

For the past 1,000 years, the nontheatrical forces that influenced the three major inflection points in world theatre history were not specific to one or two societies but were pan-Eurasian or even pan-global. First, the convergence of Eurasian societies beginning in the tenth century was stimulated above all by agricultural advances, the growth of towns and cities, and the development of interregional commerce driven by Chinese productivity. The resulting increases in (and redistributions of) wealth encouraged cultural crystallizations throughout Eurasia that allowed societies to develop their own distinctive identities, including in their forms of theatre. Second, sixteenth-century Eurasia experienced a grand resurgence in the aftermath of the bubonic plague and the post-Mongol collapse of trade. Populations rebounded; urbanization resumed; and interregional commerce was restored and elevated to new levels, especially as the wealth of the Americas began to filter through Eurasia. Its recovery, and the socioeconomic reconfigurations that ensued, made possible an unprecedented efflorescence of new theatre forms. Third, the nineteenth-century industrialization that began in Europe allowed for the conquest of distance; it brought about a global transformation in which societies everywhere were compelled to create their own modernities. These were expressed in an even grander efflorescence of new theatre forms, many of which were interculturally syncretic or were domesticated versions of forms that had been transferred in toto.

Common to these three inflection points are a few interrelated factors: technological advancements (including agricultural, industrial, and communication technologies), escalating intersocietal contact (including commercial, religious, and militaristic contact), and accelerating urbanization, all of which were spurred on by increases in population.[1] These factors are long-standing (though variable) historical trends, but they are especially notable at theatre history's major inflection points, when relatively sudden upsurges in one or more of them disrupted the status quo of multiple societies in rough synchronicity, opening numerous new niches for theatre. To be clear, these upsurges were not the *only* nontheatrical forces involved in the opening of new niches. New secular and/or religious ideologies (such as the *bhakti* movement in India, humanism in Europe, neo-Confucianism in China, Shiism in Iran, and anticolonial movements in Africa and the various regions of Asia) helped shape numerous theatre forms, while the establishment of stable governance after a period of societal disarray (as in Tokugawa Japan, Ming China, and Mughal South Asia) provided the security that allowed the new forms to flourish.

The fact that these various nontheatrical forces have had a profound impact on theatre history does not imply that theatre's history has been *determined* by them; it means only that theatre does not exist outside of human time and space. The same forces might impact multiple global regions (or multiple societies in a given region, or multiple social groupings in a given society) at roughly the same time, but the responses of theatre artists in those regions, societies, or social groupings depended on artistic choices made in specific theatrical and societal contexts. During the Eurasian resurgence that began in the sixteenth century, the development of urban middling classes in Europe and Japan allowed for the convergent analogy of purpose-built, price-segregated theatres. But even if we were to focus just on the spoken theatre and *kabuki* that held the stages of those theatres, it would be obvious that these were radically different theatre forms. And even as spoken theatre was being presented in the European theatres, that region also saw the emergence of opera, ballet, and court masques, which served very different audiences than spoken theatre and resulted from very different artistic choices. Japan, meanwhile, saw the continuance of *nō*, more secure than ever in service to the Togukawa warrior aristocracy, as well as the emergence of *bunraku*, which was no less popular than *kabuki* but emphasized narrative rather than licentiousness. The various nontheatrical forces, in brief, created opportunities for theatre artists but did not determine how they took advantage of what was newly possible.

The nature of theatre itself explains why nontheatrical forces weigh so heavily on its history, for theatre is inherently a *social* art. A person can engage in poetry and painting on a solitary basis, perhaps with the hope of finding some future audience, but perhaps merely for personal pleasure. Theatre artists, however, cannot stash their performances in a desk drawer or dusty attic. By most definitions (including the one I have used), theatre requires the copresence of actors and their audience. One can dance in one's bedroom, sing in one's shower, or recite speeches to one's mirror, but theatre requires a direct relationship between actors and their audiences.

This is why theatre is especially open to broad historical forces. It is typically performed in a language shared by the actors and their audiences, even though a form might become sufficiently long-lived or well-traveled to bring it to times or places where that vernacular is either archaic (as with the Japanese of *nō*) or foreign (as with the Italian, French, or German of operas performed beyond those language areas). No less notable, however, is the source material upon which theatre draws, which is also shared by actors and their audiences. We have seen that Athenian tragedy and Sanskrit theatre drew most of their narratives from the great epics of Greece and India, respectively; Yuan *zaju* drew from China's *chuanqi* literature; *nō* drew from *The Tale of the Heike* and *The Tale of Genji*; European Passion plays and Corpus Christi cycle plays drew from the Bible, and so on. Day-to-day social life also offers copious source material for theatre. Forms as wildly divergent as European spoken theatre, the *karagöz* shadow theatre of the Ottoman Empire, the *kote-tlon* of the Bamana people, India's folk-popular *bhavai*, and the Argentine *sainete criollo* have all offered incisive portrayals of the world in which their audiences live. When a society rather abruptly changes – whether owing to upsurges in technology, intersocietal contact, and/or urbanization, or to the introduction of new ideologies or the reestablishment of social order – theatre artists are presented with opportunities to expand their existing audiences or to develop new ones. And so it happens that the three major inflection points in theatre history's past 1,000 years are aligned with major moments of pan-Eurasian or pan-global historical change.

The second aspect of world theatre history I mentioned earlier is *the frequency with which theatre forms have been shaped by syncretism.*² A popular saying holds that "nothing comes from nothing," and it is surely the case that new theatre forms are not created *ex nihilo*. We have seen, for example, how *likay* was created out of a melding of traits from existing Thai theatre forms; likewise, *jingju* drew on existing musical systems to create its own *pihuang* system even as it continued the long-standing Chinese tradition of employing role categories to people its plays. Numerous theatre forms, meanwhile, have also taken advantage of traits drawn from nondramatic kinds of performance. Again, to offer but a few examples: Iran's *ta'ziyeh*, Japan's *bunraku*, and Korea's *ch'anggŭk* all built on established traditions of storytelling; the Philippines' *komedya* incorporated the martial arts tradition known as *arnis*; and medieval Europe's liturgical theatre elaborated on the ritual liturgy in which it was embedded.

The examples in the preceding paragraphs are of theatre forms being shaped by *intra*cultural syncretism, but *inter*cultural syncretism has also played a major role in shaping many forms of theatre. Such syncretism is, in effect, a sort of cultural compromise in which theatre forms, or certain traits thereof, are fitted into the framework of a society other than the one in which they had originated. The Yoruba Travelling Theatre, for example, had its basis in Christian church cantata, but it also employed the drumming and chanting of *alarinjo*, while its plots often derived from traditional folklore or contemporary anticolonialism. Intercultural syncretism is also evident when theatre forms transferred in toto become domesticated in their new homelands. Such was the case when the Ottoman *karagöz* was transferred to Greece and, through a century of domestication, became the new, fully Greek form of *karaghiózis*; a similar process of domestication led to the emergence of Mexico's *Moros y Cristianos* and the Philippines's *komedya* out of the transfer of Spain's *Moros y Cristianos*. And, of course, the transference in toto of European spoken theatre led to the emergence of homologous theatre forms such as China's *huaju*, Vietnam's *kich nôi*, and Japan's *shingeki* – which itself, when transferred to Korea, would lead to the emergence of *shingŭk*.

In all of this intercultural syncretism we see a process of what can be called *productive reception*. Although theatre artists might take an interest in foreign theatre forms or in certain traits of those forms precisely because they are foreign, they take advantage of the foreign for their own purposes. The initial intent of the artists might sometimes be to replicate the foreign form or traits, but their transference into different theatrical and societal contexts generally leads to a process of domestication. It is sometimes the case, however, that artists misunderstand (in part or whole) the forms or traits of which they seek to take advantage. We have seen this sort of productive misunderstanding in the European humanists' desire to recreate Greek tragedy, which led to the emergence of opera; we have also seen it in the transference of blackface performance from American minstrel shows to the Concert Parties of Ghana, where it is devoid of the racist burlesque it had originally signified.

Whether *intra*cultural or *inter*cultural, theatrical syncretism raises an issue much debated for the past few decades. All of the instances of intercultural syncretism just mentioned involve cultural appropriations of one sort or another, and additional instances (both intra- and intercultural) can easily be cited: American minstrel shows appropriated not only the *look* of enslaved Blacks but also the music and dances they created; India's Parsi theatre appropriated European melodrama's spectacular scenic effects and semblance of realism; and the Thai *lakon nai* was brought into being after the literal kidnapping of the royal dance troupe of the Khmer Empire.

In brief, cultural appropriation is endemic in theatre history, just as it is in general history. This is because, as the historian William H. McNeill observes, "Ideas ... are the most contagious aspects of human culture, even though, when translated into a new language and required to fit into a different social context, they have a chameleon-like capacity to change meaning, sometimes only slightly, sometimes radically."[3] Whatever the vector of their transmission might be – perhaps commercial relations, military conquests, demographic movements, religious interactions or conversions, or simply the voluntary emulation of an appealing model – the contagion of theatrical ideas (whether entire theatre forms or specific traits thereof) is a fact of theatre history, as is the subsequent domestication of those ideas in the places to which they have spread.

Moral objections can be raised against at least some instances of cultural appropriation. The philosopher Erich Hatala Matthes writes: "There is general agreement that if cultural appropriation is morally objectionable, it is only objectionable when a member of a dominant cultural group appropriates from a member of a marginalized group: no reasonable person thinks that, for instance, an indigenous person does something wrong by employing some Western artistic style."[4] But although dominance might sometimes be easy to ascertain in the context of individual societies, it can be far less clear when referring to the relations *between* societies. Dominance might refer to political influence, military power, economic strength, or cultural suasion – which do not always go hand in hand. And dominance can be even more difficult to determine when the relations between groups *within* a society might contrast with the relations *between* societies: Okuni's crucifix was certainly a cultural appropriation from a marginalized social group within Japan, but the power relationship between Portugal and Japan, circa 1600, was at the very least ambiguous.

Moral objections to appropriation often rely on the argument that certain ideas *belong to* one or another society or social group. Susan Scafidi, a law professor, defines cultural appropriation as "taking intellectual property, traditional knowledge, cultural expressions, or artifacts from someone else's culture without permission."[5] But defining theatrical ideas in this way presents a problem, for those ideas themselves are often an amalgam of ideas drawn from yet other cultures. Echoing (and extending) the point made by McNeill, the philosopher Kwame Anthony Appiah writes: "All cultural practices are mobile; they like to spread, and almost all are themselves creations of intermixture."[6] To take but one example: *Wayang kulit purwa* originated in Java but drew heavily from Indian texts for its narratives and was likely eventually influenced by Islamic traditions in the design of its puppets. Can one claim that the form is *entirely* the intellectual property of Java? It then spawned (or at least influenced) the emergence of scores of other theatre forms through most of Southeast Asia. Are those descendent forms to be understood as morally objectionable appropriations of Javanese culture? The need for *permission* also presents a problem, for it is often quite unclear who (if anyone) might be in a position to grant it. Again, to take but one example: Peter Brook's controversial play *The Mahabharata* (first presented in 1985) drew its plot from the Indian epic of the same name.[7] Whatever the merits of the show, one wonders just whose permission Brook might have sought to use the epic material. The notion of needing permission (in this or any other instance) also raises the prospect of censorship, for if some sort of authorization is required to use a theatrical idea, then presumably that authority could also limit or control the ways in which that idea is used.

According to Appiah, "The real problem isn't that it's difficult to decide who owns culture; it's that the very idea of ownership is the wrong model"; he contends instead that "usually, when there's a [moral] problem worth noticing, it involves forms of disrespect compounded by power inequities."[8] This seems a reasonable position, especially when set against the futility of assigning exclusive ownership of theatrical ideas to particular societies or social groups. Ideas cannot be contained, but disrespect (especially when compounded by obvious power inequities) can certainly be deplored. It is worth noting, however, that comedic performances around the world have often relied on disrespect, frequently finding expression in stereotypical or grotesque caricatures, as we have seen in theatre forms such as the *karagöz* shadow theatre, American minstrelsy, and *alarinjo*'s hapless European explorer. However much one might want to deplore such mockery, it would be naïve to think that people will ever stop creating comedy at the expense of others.

The third aspect of world theatre history I mentioned earlier is *the depth of attraction that dramatic theatre has exerted upon people*. I argued in Part I that this attraction derives from the universal human characteristic of childhood pretend play, which is associated with the characteristics of language and theory of mind in being an expression of the evolutionary development of advanced symbolic thinking. The counterfactual "realities" of pretend play become a fully social activity when audiences imaginatively play along with the enactment of a "make-believe" narrative that is made vivid through the presence of the actors, the artistry of their performances, and the empathy that their fictional characters can draw from the audience.

Even if one is unwilling to accept this Darwinian argument, dramatic theatre's depth of attraction should still be self-evident. People regularly engage in theatrical behavior without the slightest thought, whether by imitating others or by physically and vocally enacting the stories they tell. Organized dramatic theatre is obviously less common owing to constraints of time, effort, and cost – as well as to occasional societal disapproval – but a dizzying array of theatre forms has nevertheless flourished around the world. The many theatre forms discussed in this book are a mere fraction of the world's forms, but in themselves should be sufficient to demonstrate the universal appeal of theatre.

It also seems the case, however, that there has been a relative decline in emerging theatre forms since the mid twentieth century. Although it is not surprising that the onrush of technological change, intersocietal contact, and urbanization has narrowed or closed niches long occupied by local and/or rural theatre forms, these societal upheavals have not been as productive of new forms of theatre as one might expect. Instead, we have seen the emergence and global spread of drama performed via radio, film, and video, rather than live. Each of these media has its own specific characteristics, but they share the critical trait of relying on the availability of electricity and so can be grouped together as electronic media. Although most live theatre with access to electricity will take advantage of it, it obviously does not *require* electricity in the same way as the electronic media do. But with most of the world now having at least semi-regular access to electricity, drama presented via electronic media has become, in effect, the near-universal competition to live dramatic theatre.

This competition is decidedly unbalanced because performance via electronic media is frequently more physically accessible to audiences while also often being less expensive on a cost-per-viewing basis. Moreover, electronic media can offer remarkable production values thanks to their economies of scale: A single film or television show might cost a fortune to create, but it can attract a mass (even global) audience vastly exceeding that of any live production. None of this is to suggest that live dramatic theatre and drama performed via electronic media are quite the same thing, but they certainly share what Tobin Nellhaus calls a "family resemblance":[9] In both cases, actors seek to attract and hold the attention of their audience through the artistry of their performances and the empathy that their characters draw forth. What electronic media *cannot* offer is the sense of presence that results from actors and their audiences being in the same physical space – but electronic media have compensatory advantages, such as the variety of recording and editing techniques that live theatre can scarcely emulate.

None of this means that drama via electronic media can or will replace dramatic theatre. The value of the actors' presence remains a vital part of live theatre's appeal and can still be exploited to great effect, not only in ways already established but no doubt also in ways as yet undeveloped. But it does mean that electronic media have become an important part of world theatre history. From thousands of years ago until the end of the nineteenth century, all dramatic performance was of necessity *live*; even puppetry required one or more live actors to create the performance. That is no longer the case, and however much lovers of live dramatic performance might prefer it to electronically mediated dramatic performance, it would behoove them to recognize the important continuities between the two, the most essential of which is the unceasing attraction of dramatic performance itself. An alternative name for the human species might as well be *Homo dramaticus*.

Notes

Abbreviations for Frequently Cited Collective Sources

AEW	*An Emerging World: 1750–1870*, eds. Sebastian Conrad and Jürgen Osterhammel (Harvard University Press, 2018).
CCGT	*The Cambridge Companion to Greek Tragedy*, ed. P. E. Easterling (Cambridge University Press, 1997).
CCTH	*The Cambridge Companion to Theatre History*, eds. David Wiles and Christine Dymkowski (Cambridge University Press, 2013).
CGACT	*The Cambridge Guide to African and Caribbean Theatre*, ed. Martin Banham, Errol Hill, and George Woodyard (Cambridge University Press, 1994).
CGAT	*The Cambridge Guide to Asian Theatre*, ed. James R. Brandon (Cambridge University Press, 1993).
CGT	*The Cambridge Guide to Theatre*, ed. Martin Banham (Cambridge University Press, 1995).
CHCL	*The Columbia History of Chinese Literature*, ed. Victor H. Mair (Columbia University Press, 2001).
CHTAEmp	*A Cultural History of Theatre in the Age of Empire*, ed. Peter W. Marx (Bloomsbury Academic, 2017).
CHTAEnl	*A Cultural History of Theatre in the Age of Enlightenment*, ed. Mechele Leon (Bloomsbury Academic, 2017).
CHTEMA	*A Cultural History of Theatre in the Early Modern Age*, ed. Robert Henke (Bloomsbury Academic, 2017).
CT:OPD	*Chinese Theater: From Its Origins to the Present Day*, ed. Colin Mackerras (University of Hawaii Press, 1983).

CTTP	*Chinese Theories of Theater and Performance: From Confucius to the Present*, ed. and trans. Faye Chunfang Fei (University of Michigan Press, 1999).
CtWH	*A Companion to World History*, ed. Douglas Northrop (Wiley Blackwell, 2012).
CWH1	*The Cambridge World History, Vol. 1: Introducing World History, to 10,000 BCE*, ed. David Christian (Cambridge University Press, 2015).
CWH4	*The Cambridge World History, Vol. 4: A World with States, Empires and Networks, 1200 BCE–900 CE*, ed. Craig Benjamin (Cambridge University Press, 2018).
CWH5	*The Cambridge World History, Vol. 5: Expanding Webs of Exchange and Conflict, 500 CE–1500 CE*, eds. Benjamin Z. Kedar and Merry E. Wiesner-Hanks (Cambridge University Press, 2015).
CWH6.1	*The Cambridge World History, Vol. 6: The Construction of a Global World, 1400–1800 CE; Part 1, Foundations*, eds. Jerry H. Bentley, Sanjay Subrahmanyam, and Merry E. Wiesner-Hanks (Cambridge University Press, 2015).
CWH6.2	*The Cambridge World History, Vol. 6: The Construction of a Global World, 1400–1800 CE; Part 2, Patterns of Change*, eds. Jerry H. Bentley, Sanjay Subrahmanyam, and Merry E. Wiesner-Hanks (Cambridge University Press, 2015).
CWH7.1	*The Cambridge World History, Vol. 7: Production, Destruction, and Connection, 1750–Present; Part 1, Structures, Spaces, and Boundary Making*, eds. J. R. McNeill and Kenneth Pomeranz (Cambridge University Press, 2015).
CWH7.2	*The Cambridge World History, Vol. 7: Production, Destruction and Connection, 1750–Present; Part 2, Shared Transformations?*, eds. J. R. McNeill and Kenneth Pomeranz (Cambridge University Press, 2015).
E&E	*Empires and Encounters: 1350–1750*, ed. Wolfgang Reinhard (Harvard University Press, 2015).
EAT	*Encyclopedia of Asian Theatre*, 2 vols., ed. Samuel Leiter (Greenwood Press, 2007).
ELAT	*Encyclopedia of Latin American Theater*, eds. Eladio Cortés and Mirta Barrea-Marlys (Greenwood Press, 2003).

HGT	*A History of German Theatre*, eds. Simon Williams and Maik Hamburger (Cambridge University Press, 2008).
HIT	*A History of Italian Theatre*, eds. Joseph Farrell and Paolo Puppa (Cambridge University Press, 2006).
HJT	*A History of Japanese Theatre*, ed. Jonah Salz (Cambridge University Press, 2016).
HRGD	*A Handbook to the Reception of Greek Drama*, ed. Betine van Zyl Smit (Wiley Blackwell, 2016).
IMM	*Inside the Minstrel Mask: Readings in Nineteenth-Century Blackface Minstrelsy*, eds. Annemarie Bean, James V. Hatch, and Brooks McNamara (Wesleyan University Press, 1996).
IT:TP	*Indian Theatre: Traditions of Performance*, eds. Farley P. Richmond, Darius L. Swann, and Phillip B. Zarrilli (University of Hawaii Press, 1990).
MAT:PT	*Modernization of Asian Theatres: Process and Tradition*, eds. Yasushi Nagata and Ravi Chaturvedi (Springer, 2019).
NWH:TC	*The New World History: A Teacher's Companion*, ed. Ross E. Dunn (Bedford/St. Martin, 2000).
OHWH	*The Oxford Handbook of World History*, ed. Jerry H. Bentley (Oxford University Press, 2011).
OTAGB	*The Origins of Theatre in Ancient Greece and Beyond: From Ritual to Drama*, eds. Eric Csapo and Margaret C. Miller (Cambridge University Press, 2007).
PGH	*The Prospect of Global History*, eds. James Belich, John Darwin, Margret Frenz, and Chris Wickham (Oxford University Press, 2016).
RCP-RCN-EL	*The Routledge Companion to Performance-Related Concepts in Non-European Languages*, eds. Erika Fischer-Lichte, Torsten Jost, and Astrid Schenka (Routledge, 2024).
RHAT	*Routledge Handbook of Asian Theatre*, ed. Siyuan Liu (Routledge, 2016).
RtP	*Representing the Past: Essays in Performance Historiography*, eds. Thomas Postlewait and Charlotte M. Canning (University of Iowa Press, 2010).
TME	*The Theatre of Medieval Europe: New Research into Early Drama*, ed. Eckehard Simon (Cambridge University Press, 1991).

Introduction

1. Jean-François Lyotard, *The Postmodern Condition: A Report on Knowledge*, trans. Geoff Bennington and Brian Massumi (University of Minnesota Press, 1984), xxiv; Michel Foucault quotation is in Lawrence W. Besserman, "The Challenge of Periodization: Old Paradigms and New Perspectives," in *The Challenge of Periodization: Old Paradigms and New Perspectives*, ed. Lawrence W. Besserman (Routledge, 1996), 16.
2. This account of the Standard Western Approach draws from Steve Tillis, *The Challenge of World Theatre History* (Palgrave Macmillan, 2020), 61–92, 132–37, and 251–56.
3. Marshall G. S. Hodgson, *Rethinking World History: Essays on Europe, Islam, and World History*, ed. Edmund Burke III (Cambridge University Press, 1993), 7–8.
4. Edward W. Said, *The World, the Text, and the Critic* (Harvard University Press, 1983), 21.
5. Edwin Wilson and Alvin Goldfarb, *Living Theatre: A History of Theatre*, 7th ed. (McGraw-Hill, 2018).
6. Marshall G. S. Hodgson, "Hemispheric Interregional History," in *NWH:TC*, 119.
7. James R. Brandon, "Introduction," in *CGAT*, 9.
8. Leonard C. Pronko, *Theatre East and West: Perspectives toward a Total Theatre* (University of California Press, 1967), 4.
9. Brander Matthews, *A Study of the Drama* (Houghton Mifflin, 1910), 96. https://archive.org/details/astudydrama02mattgoog/
10. Wang Guowei, "Wang Guowei on Theatre," in *CTTP*, 107.
11. Farley P. Richmond, "Characteristics of Sanskrit Drama and Theatre," in *IT:TP*, 72.
12. The first English translation of *Orphan of Zhau* was by William Hachett in 1741; the first English *Sakuntala* was by William Jones in 1789. J. I. Crump, *Chinese Theater in the Days of Kublai Khan* (University of Arizona Press, 1980), 350; Romila Thapar, Śakuntalā: *Texts, Readings, Histories* (Anthem Press, 1999), 199–200.
13. Peter Burke, "Western Historical Thinking in a Global Perspective: 10 Theses," in *Western Historical Thinking: An Intercultural Debate*, ed. Jörn Rüsen (Berghahn Books, 2002), 18.
14. William H. McNeill, *Mythistory and Other Essays* (University of Chicago Press, 1986), 122.
15. Lawrence W. Levine, "Looking Eastward: The Career of Western Civ," in *NWH:TC*, 21.
16. Shannon Jackson, *Professing Performance: Theatre in the Academy from Philology to Performativity* (Cambridge University Press, 2004), 87, 86.
17. Jackson, *Professing Performance*, 88.
18. Sheldon Cheney, *The Theatre: Three Thousand Years of Drama, Acting and Stagecraft*, rev. ed. (Longmans, Green, 1952), 4.

282   *Notes to pages 6–11*

19. Glynne Wickham, *A History of the Theatre*, 2nd ed. (Cambridge University Press, 1992), 33–34.
20. Alan Woods, "Emphasizing the Avant-Garde: An Exploration in Theatre Historiography," in *Interpreting the Theatrical Past: Essays in the Historiography of Performance*, eds. Thomas Postlewait and Bruce A. McConachie (University of Iowa Press, 1989), 166.
21. Cheney, *Theatre*, 4 (italics in the original), 6.
22. Wickham, *History of the Theatre*, 14.
23. Pamela Kyle Crossley, *What Is Global History?* (Polity, 2008), 6.
24. Wolfgang Reinhard, "Introduction," in *E&E*, 12.
25. "Around 1990 only one fifth of the world's states claimed that one ethnonational group amounted to more than 90 per cent of the population; in one third official statistics placed its share at 75–89 per cent, and in the rest it amounted to less than half." Dirk Hoerder, "Migrations," in *CWH7.2*, 24.
26. David Reich, *Who We Are and How We Got Here: Ancient DNA and the New Science of the Human Past* (Vintage Books, 2018), 268.
27. Maik Hamburger and Simon Williams, "Introduction," in *HGT*, 6.
28. For the difficulties associated with national theatre histories, see *Writing and Rewriting National Theatre Histories*, ed. S. E. Wilmer (University of Iowa Press, 2004).
29. Thomas Postlewait, *The Cambridge Introduction to Theatre Historiography* (Cambridge University Press, 2009), 189.
30. Marshall G. S. Hodgson, *The Venture of Islam: Conscience and History in a World Civilization, Vol. 1: The Classical Age of Islam* (University of Chicago Press, 1974), 48.
31. This account of "world history" and "world theatre history" draws from Tillis, *Challenge of World Theatre History*, 11–15 and 55–56.
32. Jerry H. Bentley, "The Task of World History," in *OHWH*, 1.
33. Dominic Sachsenmaier, "The Evolution of World Histories," in *CWH1*, 75.
34. Jürgen Osterhammel, "Global History and Historical Sociology," in *PGH*, 31.
35. This understanding of "world theatre" differs from the ways that "world literature" is understood in literary studies, which David Damrosch notes has sometimes been defined in terms of "classics," "masterpieces," or "windows on the world." He defines it as "a subset of the plenum literature" that "encompass[es] all literary works that circulate beyond their culture of origin, either in translation or in their original languages." *What Is World Literature?* (Princeton University Press, 2003), 15, 4. "World theatre," as I use the term, makes no presumptions about what might be a classic, masterpiece, or window, nor is it limited to the subset of interculturally circulating plays or theatre forms. It is simply theatre in all its global variety.
36. James Belich, John Darwin, and Chris Wickham, "Introduction: The Prospect of Global History," in *PGH*, 10.
37. Catherine M. Cole, *Ghana's Concert Party Theatre* (Indiana University Press, 2001), 21–29.
38. Quoted by John-Paul A. Ghobrial, "Introduction: Seeing the World Like a Microhistorian," *Past and Present* 242, Supplement 14 (2019): 1–22, 14.

39. Christian G. De Vito, "History without Scale: The Micro-Spatial Perspective," *Past and Present* 242, Supplement 14 (2019): 348–72, 352.
40. John Darwin, "Afterward: History on a Global Scale," in *PGH*, 183.
41. Douglas Northrop, "Introduction: The Challenge of World History," in *CtWH*, 7.
42. McNeill, *Mythistory*, 100.
43. Janet L. Abu-Lughod, "The World-System Perspective in the Construction of Economic History," in *World History: Ideologies, Structures, and Identities*, eds. Philip Pomper, Richard H. Elphick, and Richard T. Vann (Blackwell Publishers, 1998), 73.
44. Northrop, "Introduction," 7.
45. This account of the meaning of "theatre" draws from Tillis, *Challenge of World Theatre History*, 14–21.
46. Richard Bauman, "Performance," in *Folklore, Cultural Performances, and Popular Entertainments*, ed. Richard Bauman (Oxford University Press, 1992), 41.
47. Erving Goffman, *Frame Analysis: An Essay on the Organization of Experience* (Doubleday, 1974), 124.
48. P. E. Easterling, "Form and Performance," in *CCGT*, 166.
49. Eli Rozik, *The Roots of Theatre: Rethinking Ritual and Other Theories of Origin* (University of Iowa Press, 2002), 153.
50. Quoted in Jeffrey Huntsman, "Native American Theatre," in *American Indian Theatre in Performance: A Reader*, eds. Hanay Geiogamah and Jaye T. Darby (UCLA American Indian Studies Center, 2000), 88.
51. Quoted in Glenn Odom, *World Theories of Theatre* (Routledge, 2017), 39.
52. Zeami, *On the Art of the Nō Drama: The Major Treatises of Zeami*, trans. J. Thomas Rimer and Yamazaki Masakazu (Princeton University Press, 1984), 10.
53. Tang Xianzu, "Tang Xianzu on Theatre," in *CTTP*, 55.
54. Dennis Tedlock, ed. and trans. *Rabinal Achi: A Mayan Drama of War and Sacrifice* (Oxford University Press, 2003), 2.
55. Claire Sponsler, *Ritual Imports: Performing Medieval Drama in America* (Cornell University Press, 2004), 24.
56. Quoted in Alice Henson Ernst, *The Wolf Ritual of the Northwest Coast* (University of Oregon Press, 1952), 30.
57. Maryrose Casey, *Telling Stories: Aboriginal Australian and Torres Strait Islander Performance* (Australian Scholarly, 2012), 19.
58. Osita Okagbue, *African Theatre and Performances* (Routledge, 2007), 4.
59. Roger D. Abrahams, "Introduction," in *African Folktales*, ed. Roger D. Abrahams (Pantheon Books, 1983), 8.
60. Khalid Amine, "Introduction" [to Arabic concepts], in *RCP-RCN-EL*, 225.
61. Quoted in Kendall L. Walton, *Mimesis as Make-Believe: On the Foundations of the Representational Arts* (Harvard University Press, 1990), 89.
62. This account of theatre history's inflection points draws from Tillis, *Challenge of World Theatre History*, 249–51, 256–67, and 269–70.
63. John Russell Brown, "Introduction," in *The Oxford Illustrated History of Theatre*, ed. John Russell Brown (Oxford University Press, 1995), 7.

64. Quoted in Postlewait, *Cambridge Introduction to Theatre Historiography*, 165.
65. Ross E. Dunn, introduction to Part Seven, "Periodizing World History," in *NWH:TC*, 360.
66. Adam McKeown, "What Are the Units of World History?," in *CtWH*, 82.
67. Steven Pinker, *How the Mind Works* (W. W. Norton, 1997), 310, 312.
68. Some authors prefer the term "genres" to that of "forms," but the former carries literary connotations (e.g., the genres of comedy and tragedy) that might be misleading. This account of "theatre forms" draws from Tillis, *Challenge of World Theatre History*, 105–18.
69. M. Cody Poulton, "World History and Modern Japanese Drama: The Case of Hirata Oriza's Plays," in *Historical Consciousness, Historiography, and Modern Japanese Values*, ed. James C. Baxter (International Research Center for Japanese Studies, 2006), 265.
70. David Hackett Fischer, *Historians' Fallacies: Toward a Logic of Historical Thought* (Harper and Row, 1970), 160.
71. Joseph Fletcher, "Integrative History: Parallels and Interconnections in the Early Modern Period, 1500–1800," *Journal of Turkish Studies* 9 (1985): 37–57, 39.
72. This roster revises and expands the one published in Tillis, *Challenge of World Theatre History*, 305–10.
73. William A. Green, "Periodizing World History," in *NWH:TC*, 386.
74. Dunn, introduction to Part Seven, 359–63.
75. Victor Lieberman, *Strange Parallels: Southeast Asia in Global Context, c. 800–1830, Vol. 2: Mainland Mirrors: Europe, Japan, China, South Asia, and the Islands* (Cambridge University Press, 2009), 895.
76. Fischer, *Historians' Fallacies*, 181.
77. A. M. Nagler, *The Medieval Religious Stage* (Yale University Press, 1976), xi.
78. Among the most impressive works on theatre by a team of experts is *A Cultural History of Theatre*, eds. Christopher B. Balme and Tracy C. Davis (Bloomsbury Methuen Drama, 2017). This six-volume work, focused primarily on the ancient Mediterranean and Europe, runs over 1,600 pages.

Part I The Deep History of Theatre (starting c. 50,000 BCE)

1. Jorge Luis Borges, "Averroës' Search," in *Collected Fictions*, trans. Andrew Hurley (Penguin Books, 1998), 236, 239, 241.
2. Shmuel Moreh, *Live Theatre and Dramatic Literature in the Medieval Arab World* (New York University Press, 1992) 111, 117. Generations of European scholars have similarly referred to nontheatrical works (such as novels and films) as tragedies and comedies, knowing full well that Aristotle used these words in the context of theatre.
3. Pronouncements of universality are tricky because ethnographic reporting is incomplete and of variable quality; because "human behavior is so complex and malleable that any trait or complex can only approach near universality"; and because in some individuals an otherwise universal behavior

can be impaired. For these reasons, "anthropologists draw attention to the distinction between universals and 'near universals' generally to argue that the distinction is not important." Donald E. Brown, *Human Universals* (McGraw-Hill, 1991), 43–44.
4. Richard Schechner, "Victor Turner's Last Adventure," in Victor Turner, *The Anthropology of Performance* (PAJ Publications, 1986), 10.
5. Brander Matthews, *The Development of Drama* (Charles Scribner's Sons, 1906), 41. www.google.com/books/edition/The_Development_of_the_Drama/2S6bKAhM5EsC?hl=en&gbpv.
6. Victor Turner, *From Ritual to Theatre: The Human Seriousness of Play* (PAJ Publications, 1982), 79.
7. Francis MacDonald Cornford, *The Origin of Greek Comedy* (Edward Arnold, 1914).
8. Gilbert Murray, "Excursus on the Ritual Forms Preserved in Greek Tragedy," in Jane Ellen Harrison, *Themis: A Study of the Social Origins of Greek Religion* (Cambridge University Press, 1912).
9. Jane Ellen Harrison, *Themis: A Study of the Social Origins of Greek Religion* (Cambridge University Press, 1912).
10. William Ridgeway, *The Drama and Dramatic Dances of Non-European Races* (Cambridge University Press, 1915).
11. Eric Csapo and Margeret C. Miller, "General Introduction," in *OTAGB*, 3.
12. Kimberley C. Patton, "Discussion," in *OTAGB*, 374.
13. E. T. Kirby, *Ur-Drama: The Origins of Theatre* (New York University Press, 1975), 19, 5.
14. Eli Rozik, *The Roots of Theatre: Rethinking Ritual and Other Theories of Origin* (University of Iowa Press, 2002), 72.
15. Steve Mithen, *The Singing Neanderthals: The Origins of Music, Language, Mind, and Body* (Harvard University Press, 2007).
16. Brian Boyd, *On the Origin of Stories: Evolution, Cognition, and Fiction* (Harvard University Press, 2009), 114–15.
17. Bruce McConachie, *Evolution, Cognition, and Performance* (Cambridge University Press, 2015), 70.

1 The Wellspring of Theatre

1. Jorge Luis Borges, "Averroës' Search," in *Collected Fictions*, trans. Andrew Hurley (Penguin Books, 1998), 236.
2. Sabine Doebel and Angeline S. Lillard, "How Does Play Foster Development? A New Executive Function Perspective," *Developmental Review* 67 (2023), 101064, 1–9, 4. https://doi.org/10.1016/j.dr.2022.101064.
3. Patrice Pavis, *Dictionary of the Theatre: Terms, Concepts, and Analysis*, trans. Christine Shantz (University of Toronto Press, 1998), 268.
4. Kedar A. Kulkarni, "Introduction" [to Indian Languages concepts], *RCP-RCN-EL*, 502–503.
5. Heike Oberlin, "Āṭṭam vis-a-vis Kūttu and Līlā," in *RCP-RCN-EL*, 524.

6. Philip Adédọ̀tun Ògúndèjì, "Eré," in *RCP-RCN-EL*, 60; Siyuan Liu, "Xiju and Xiqu," in *RCP-RCN-EL*, 127.
7. Bruce McConachie offers a related argument for the pretend-play roots of theatre. *Evolution, Cognition, and Performance* (Cambridge University Press, 2015), 29–64.
8. David M. Buss et al., "Adaptations, Exaptations, and Spandrels," *American Psychologist* 53, no. 5 (May 1998): 533–48, 535.
9. Buss et al., "Adaptations, Exaptations, and Spandrels," 537. An additional way to explain a characteristic is as "noise," which "is distinguished from incidental by-products in that it is not linked to [any] adaptive aspects of design" (538).
10. Darwin's term "preadaptations" is now rarely used because it might seem to imply that the characteristics evolved in anticipation of the function they would eventually serve.
11. Buss et al., "Adaptations, Exaptations, and Spandrels," 539.
12. Daniel C. Dennett argues that "if you go back far enough, you will find that every adaptation has developed out of predecessor structures each of which either had some other use or no use at all" (quoted in Buss et al., "Adaptations, Exaptations, and Spandrels," 542). Buss et al. counter that "understanding the degree to which a new function is superimposed on a predecessor structure that already existed as an adaptation or as a by-product may … shed light on its nature" (542).
13. John Tooby and Leda Cosmides, "Does Beauty Build Adapted Minds? Toward an Evolutionary Theory of Aesthetics, Fiction and the Arts," *SubStance* 94/95 (2001): 6–27, 7; italics suppressed.
14. Tooby and Cosmides, "Does Beauty Build Adapted Minds?," 12.
15. Caren Walker and Alison Gopnik, "Pretense and Possibility: A Theoretical Proposal about the Effects of Pretend Play on Development: Comment on Lillard et al. (2013)," *Psychological Bulletin* 139, no. 1 (2013): 40–44, 40.
16. Angeline S. Lillard et al., "The Impact of Pretend Play on Children's Development: A Review of the Evidence," *Psychological Bulletin* 139, no. 1 (2013): 1–34, 2.
17. Brittany N. Thompson and Thalia R. Goldstein, "Disentangling Pretend Play Measurement: Defining the Essential Elements and Developmental Progression of Pretense," *Developmental Review* 52 (2019): 24–41, 27.
18. Borges, "Averroës' Search," 236.
19. Thompson and Goldstein, "Disentangling Pretend Play Measurement," 24.
20. Angeline S. Lillard, "Why Do the Children (Pretend) Play?," *Trends in Cognitive Sciences* 21, no. 11 (November 2017): 826–34, 826.
21. Lillard et al., "Impact of Pretend Play," 25, 19.
22. Lillard, "Why Do the Children (Pretend) Play?," 831.
23. See, for example, Peter Langland-Hassan, "Pretense, Imagination, and Belief: The Single Attitude Theory," *Philosophical Studies* 159 (2012): 155–79, and Heather V. Adair and Peter Carruthers, "Pretend Play: More Imitative than Imaginative," *Mind & Language* 38 (2023): 1–16. https://doi.org/10.1111/mila.12417.

24. Ori Friedman and Alan M. Leslie, "The Conceptual Underpinnings of Pretense: Pretending Is Not 'Behaving-as-if'," *Cognition* 105 (2007): 103–24, 120.
25. Friedman and Leslie, "Conceptual Underpinnings of Pretense," 121.
26. Angeline Lillard, Ashley M. Pinkham, and Eric Smith, "Pretend Play and Cognitive Development," in *The Wiley-Blackwell Handbook of Childhood Cognitive Development*, 2nd ed., ed. Usha Goswami (Wiley-Blackwell, 2011), 294–95.
27. Lillard, "Why Do the Children (Pretend) Play?," 826.
28. Henry M. Wellman and Karen Lind, *Reading Minds: How Childhood Teaches Us to Understand People* (Oxford University Press, 2020), 41.
29. Paul Hernadi, "Literature and Evolution," *SubStance* 94/95 (2001): 55–71, 56.
30. Kendall L. Walton, *Mimesis as Make-Believe: On the Foundations of the Representational Arts* (Harvard University Press, 1990), 4; italics in the original.
31. Walton, *Mimesis as Make-Believe*, 190; italics in the original.
32. Walton, *Mimesis as Make-Believe*, 272–73; italics in the original.
33. Walton, *Mimesis as Make-Believe*, 273–74.
34. Previous theories of theatre as a kind of "game" (such as offered by Johan Huizinga and Roger Callois) "tend to reduce theatre to the experience of role-playing. None pay much attention to the communication that takes place between the stage and the audience." Jean Alter, *A Sociosemiotic Theory of Theatre* (University of Pennsylvania Press, 1990), 41.
35. Walton, *Mimesis as Make-Believe*, 39; italics in the original.
36. Walton, *Mimesis as Make-Believe*, 209.
37. Stanca Scholz-Cionca and Nanako Nakajima, "Introduction" [to Japanese concepts], in *RCP-RCN-EL*, 415.
38. Walker and Gopnik, "Pretense and Possibility," 42.
39. To suggest that theatre is inherently pleasurable does not imply that every theatrical experience will *be* pleasurable.
40. Steven Pinker, *How the Mind Works* (W. W. Norton, 1997), 524.
41. Pinker, *How the Mind Works*, 543.
42. Michelle Scalise Sugiyama, "Reverse-Engineering Narrative: Evidence of Special Design," in *The Literary Animal: Evolution and the Nature of Narrative*, eds. Jonathan Gottschall and David Sloan Wilson (Northwestern University Press, 2005), 186, 188.
43. Joseph Carroll, *Literary Darwinism: Evolution, Human Nature, and Literature* (Routledge, 2004), xxii.
44. Carroll, *Literary Darwinism*, 108, 198.
45. Carroll, *Literary Darwinism*, 198.
46. Jacqueline Martin and Willmar Sauter, *Understanding Theatre: Performance Analysis in Theory and Practice* (Almqvist & Wiskell International, 1995), 85, 90–91.
47. Samuel L. Leiter, *New Kabuki Encyclopedia: A Revised Adaptation of* Kabuki Jiten (Greenwood Press, 1997), 260.
48. Martin and Sauter, *Understanding Theatre*, 80–81.

49. Quoted in Leonard C. Pronko, *Theatre East & West: Perspectives toward a Total Theatre* (University of California Press, 1967), 170.
50. Martin and Souter, *Understanding Theatre*, 82.
51. Walton, *Mimesis as Make-Believe*, 273.
52. Kendall L. Walton, *In Other Shoes: Music, Metaphor, Empathy, Existence* (Oxford University Press, 2015), 9.
53. Clive Gamble, "Humanity from the Ice: The Emergence and Spread of an Adaptive Species," in *The Oxford Illustrated History of the World*, ed. Felipe Fernández-Armesto (Oxford University Press, 2019), 37.
54. Gamble, "Humanity from the Ice," 15.
55. Gamble, "Humanity from the Ice," 19.
56. Julia Galway-Witham, James Cole, and Chris Stringer, "Aspects of Human Physical and Behavioural Evolution during the Last 1 Million Years," *Journal of Quaternary Science* 34, no. 6 (2019): 355–78, 363. For arguments that advocate for revolutionary change, see Steve Mithen, *The Prehistory of the Mind* (Thames and Hudson, 1996), and Ian Tattersall, "A Timeline for the Acquisition of Symbolic Cognition in the Human Lineage," in *The Oxford Handbook of Human Symbolic Evolution*, eds. Nathalie Gontier, Andy Lock, and Chris Sinha (Oxford University Press, 2024), 71–96.
57. Gamble, "Humanity from the Ice," 18.

2 The Social Uses of Theatre

1. See, for example, Ross E. Dunn, introduction to Part Seven, "Periodizing World History," in *NWH:TC*, 362–63.
2. Andrew Shyrock and Daniel Lord Smail, *Deep History: The Architecture of Past and Present* (University of California Press, 2011), 7.
3. Edward Burnett Tylor, *Primitive Culture: Researches into the Development of Mythology, Philosophy, Religion, Art, and Custom*, 2 vols. (John Murray, 1871), vol. 1, 28.
4. Lewis Morgan, *Ancient Society, or Researches in the Lines of Human Progress, from Savagery through Barbarism to Civilization* (Charles H. Kerr and Co., 1909), vii.
5. Robert Ackerman, *J. G. Frazer: His Life and Work* (Cambridge University Press, 1987), 79.
6. Glynne Wickham, *A History of the Theatre*, 2nd ed. (Cambridge University Press, 1992), 18.
7. The following paragraph draws from Steve Tillis, *Rethinking Folk Drama* (Greenwood Press, 1999), 41–45.
8. Richard M. Dorson, *The British Folklorists: A History* (University of Chicago Press, 1968), 166–86; 271–76; 301–15; Stith Thompson, *The Folktale* (Holt Rinehart, and Winston, 1946), 385–90.
9. William Bascom, "Folklore and Anthropology," in *The Study of Folklore*, ed. Allan Dundes (Prentice-Hall, 1965), 31.

10. Dipesh Chakrabarty, "The Climate of History: Four Theses," *Critical Inquiry* 35 (Winter 2009): 197–222, 214.
11. Quoted in Chakrabarty, "Climate of History," 214.
12. Eli Rozik, *The Roots of Theatre: Rethinking Ritual and Other Theories of Origin* (University of Iowa Press, 2002), xi.
13. Stephen Bates and Anthony J. Ferri, "What's Entertainment? Notes toward a Definition," *Studies in Popular Culture* 33, no. 1 (Fall 2010): 1–20, 2.
14. Bates and Ferri, "What's Entertainment?," 11–13.
15. Bates and Ferri, "What's Entertainment?," 14.
16. Phillip B. Zarrilli, "Introduction to the Ritual Traditions," in *IT:TP*, 123; italics suppressed.
17. Balwant Gargi, *Folk Theatre in India* (Rupa and Company, 1991), 53–56, 77–78.
18. Grace Frank, *The Medieval French Drama* (Oxford University Press, 1954), 20, 21–22.
19. Choe Sang-Su, *A Study of the Mask Play of Ha-Hoe* (Korea Books Publishing, 1959), 1; Oh-Kon Cho, *Traditional Korean Theatre* (Asian Humanities Press, 1988), 115.
20. Cho, *Traditional Korean Theatre*, 115.
21. Choe, *Study of the Mask Play*, 4.
22. Cho, *Traditional Korean Theatre*, 118.
23. For an overview, see Kamran Scot Aghaie, "The Origins of the Sunnite-Shi'ite Divide and the Emergence of the Ta'ziyeh Tradition," *TDR: The Drama Review* 49, no. 4 (Winter 2005): 42–47.
24. Peter J. Chelkowski, "Ta'ziyeh: Indigenous Avant-Garde Theatre of Iran," in *Ta'ziyeh: Ritual and Drama in Iran*, ed. Peter J. Chelkowski (New York University Press and Soroush Press, 1979), 2.
25. Milla C. Riggio, "Ta'ziyeh in Exile: Transformations of a Persian Tradition," *Comparative Drama* 28, no. 1 (Spring 1994): 115–40, 127, 121.
26. Donald Keene, "Introduction," in *Chūshingura (The Treasury of Loyal Retainers)*, trans. Donald Keene (Columbia University Press, 1971), 1–7.
27. Osita Okagbue, *African Theatre and Performances* (Routledge, 2007), 136.
28. James T. Brink, "Time Consciousness and Growing Up in Bamana Folk Drama," *Journal of American Folklore* 95, no. 378 (October–December 1982): 415–34, 420–23.
29. Okagbue, *African Theatre and Performances*, 173.
30. Brink, "Time Consciousness and Growing Up," 422.
31. Okagbue, *African Theatre and Performances*, 166.
32. Bertolt Brecht, *Brecht on Theatre*, ed. and trans. John Willett (Hill & Wang, 1964), 30, 71.
33. David Barnett, "Naturalism, Expressionism, and Brecht: Drama in Dialogue with Modernity," in *HGT*, 219. *Thingspiele* were mounted only for a few years, in part because Hitler himself was more interested in using Wagnerian opera "to celebrate significant moments in the Nazi calendar." Stephen Wilmer, "Nationalism and Its Effect on the German Theatre," in *HGT*, 237.

34. Colin Mackerras, "Theatre and the Masses," in *CT:OPD*, 172.
35. Quoted in Frances Harwood, "Myth, Memory, and the Oral Tradition: Cicero in the Trobriands," *American Anthropologist* 78, no. 4 (1976): 783–96, 784.
36. Ronald M. Berndt and Catherine H. Berndt, *The World of the First Australians: Aboriginal Traditional Life: Past and Present*, 5th ed. (Aboriginal Studies Press, 1999), 443, 282–85.
37. Nicanor G. Tiongson and Ramon M. Obusan, *Dulaan: An Essay on Philippine Ethnic Theatre* (Sentrong Pangkultura ng Pilipinas [Cultural Centre of the Philippines], 1992), 33.
38. "William Tell Open-Air Theatre in Interlaken," www.interlaken.ch/en/planning/events/top-events/william-tell-open-air-theatre-interlaken; "Wilhelm Tell Festival, New Glarus, WI," https://wilhelmtellfestival.org.
39. Max Harris, *Aztecs, Moors, and Christians: Festivals of Reconquest in Mexico and Spain* (University of Texas Press, 2000), 31–63.
40. Peter Thomson, "Sadler's Wells Theatre," in *CGT*, 957.
41. Tracy C. Davis and Peter W. Marx, "Introduction: On Critical Media History," in *The Routledge Companion to Theatre and Performance Historiography*, eds. Tracy C. Davis, and Peter W. Marx (Routledge, 2020), 3.
42. Richard Schechner, *Introduction to Performance Studies*, 4th ed. (Routledge, 2020), 7–9.
43. Davis and Marx, "Introduction," 7.
44. See, for example, Anita Gonzalez, "Seeking Critical Frameworks for Global Majority Theatre," *Theatre Journal* 75, no. 4 (December 2023): 511–17.

3 Inventing Literary Theatre

1. Gerald F. Else, *The Origin and Early Form of Greek Tragedy* (Harvard University Press, 1967), 49.
2. Paul Cartledge, "'Deep Plays': Theatre as a Process in Greek Civic Life," in *CCGT*, 22–23.
3. Cartledge, "'Deep Plays,'" 23.
4. Eric Csapo and William J. Slater, *The Context of Ancient Drama* (University of Michigan Press, 1995), 107–08.
5. Ananda Lal, ed., *The Oxford Companion to Indian Theatre* (Oxford University Press, 2004), 182.
6. Aparna Dharwadker, "Representing India's Pasts: Time, Culture, and the Problems of Performance Historiography," in *RtP*, 173.
7. See, for example, Vasudev Vishnu Mirashi and Narayan Raghunath Navlekar, *Kālidāsa: Date, Life and Works* (Popular Prakashan, 1969), 29; and Ram Gopal, *Kālidāsa: His Art and Culture* (Concept Publishing, 1984), 14.
8. Ashvini Agrawal, *Rise and Fall of the Imperial Guptas* (Motilal Banarsidass, 1989), 174–75.
9. Stanley Wolpert, *A New History of India*, 4th ed. (Oxford University Press, 1993), 89.

10. Lal, *Oxford Companion to Indian Theatre*, 55, 53.
11. Farley P. Richmond favors dating Bhasa to around 400 CE, and Kalidasa to shortly after; he suggests that Asvaghosa is the earliest known Sanskrit playwright and that he lived a few hundred years earlier ("Characteristics of Sanskrit Drama and Theatre," in *IT:TP*, 54, 63, 53). This still places the emergence of Sanskrit theatre around the second century CE.
12. John Keay, *India: A History* (Grove Press, 2000), 90.
13. Richmond, "Characteristics of Sanskrit Drama and Theatre," 54.
14. Eric Csapo and Margaret C. Miller, "General Introduction," in *OTAGB*, 8; Peter Levi, *A History of Greek Literature* (Viking, 1985), 133–34.
15. David Depew, "From Hymn to Tragedy: Aristotle's Genealogy of Poetic Kinds," in *OTAGB*, 129.
16. Else, *Origin and Early Form*, 47; italics in the original.
17. Manohar Laxman Varadpande, *History of Indian Theatre*, vol. 1 (Shakti Malik, Abhinav Publications, 1987), 21–46.
18. Gargi Bhattacharya, "A Discourse on *Nāṭya* (Indian Drama): Origin, Development and Technicalities," *postScriptum: An Interdisciplinary Journal of Literary Studies* 3, no. 2 (July 2018): 178–89, 181.
19. V. Raghavan, "Sanskrit Drama and Performance," *Sangeet Natak* 38, no. 2 (2004): 15–36, 15.
20. Kedar A. Kulkarni, "Introduction" [to Indian Languages concepts], in *RCP-RCN-EL*, 496.
21. Farley P. Richmond, "Origins of Sanskrit Theatre," in *IT:TP*, 31. The other two ways are "through pictures which illustrate the story" and "through words alone."
22. V. Raghavan, "Sanskrit Drama in Performance," in *Sanskrit Drama in Performance*, eds. Rachel Van M. Baumer and James R. Brandon (University of Hawaii Press, 1981), 13.
23. Raghavan, "Sanskrit Drama in Performance," 11.
24. Varadpande, *History of Indian Theatre*, 207–67.
25. For the Greek influence on South Asian coinage, architecture, and art, see Chandima S. M. Wickramasinghe, "The Indian Invasion of Alexander and the Emergence of Hybrid Cultures," *Indian Historical Review* 48, no. 1 (2021): 69–91.
26. Bhattacharya, "Discourse on *Nāṭya*," 180–81.
27. Indū Shekhar, *Sanskrit Drama: Its Origin and Decline*, 2nd ed. (Munshiram Manoharlal Publishers, 1977), 57.
28. Raghavan, "Sanskrit Drama and Performance," 18.
29. Bhattacharya, "Discourse on *Nāṭya*," 181.
30. Bhattacharya, "Discourse on *Nāṭya*," 183.
31. Rosalind Thomas, *Literacy and Orality in Ancient Greece* (Cambridge University Press, 1992), 8; italics in the original.
32. Thomas, *Literacy and Orality in Ancient Greece*, 11.
33. Thomas, *Literacy and Orality in Ancient Greece*, 92.
34. Csapo and Slater, *Context of Ancient Drama*, 1.

35. Klaus Karttunen, "Orality vs. Written Text: Mediaeval Developments in Vedic Ritual Literature," *Folklore (Estonia)* 8 (December 1998): 114–26, 123. https://doi.org/10.7592/FEJF1998.08.veda.
36. J. A. B. Van Buitenen, "Introduction," in *Two Plays of Ancient India*, trans. J. A. B. Van Buitenen (Columbia University Press, 1968), 9.
37. Van Buitenen, "Introduction," 11.
38. Bhattacharya, "Discourse on *Nāṭya*," 186. There are exceptions to this language distribution. For example, kings suffering poverty might speak in a Prakrit language, while anyone can use Sanskrit to quote divine speech (186).
39. David Wiles, *Greek Theatre Performance: An Introduction* (Cambridge University Press, 2000), 167.
40. This paragraph draws from Steve Tillis, *The Challenge of World Theatre History* (Palgrave Macmillan, 2020), 208–11, 230–31.
41. Jean Pierre Vernant and Pierre Vidal-Naquet, *Myth and Tragedy in Ancient Greece* (Zone Books, 1990), 23, 25.
42. Csapo and Slater, *Context of Ancient Drama*, 3–4.
43. Simon Goldhill, "The Audience of Athenian Tragedy," in *CCGT*, 54; italics in the original.
44. Goldhill, "Audience of Athenian Tragedy," 67.
45. Vernant and Vidal-Naquet, *Myth and Tragedy*, 257, 33.
46. Goldhill, "Audience of Athenian Tragedy," 66.
47. Edith Hall, "The Sociology of Athenian Tragedy," in *CCGT*, 109.
48. Helen P. Foley, *Female Acts in Greek Tragedy* (Princeton University Press, 2001), 335.
49. Chester G. Starr, *A History of the Ancient World* (Oxford University Press, 1991), 298, 307, 313.
50. Wiles, *Greek Theatre Performance*, 34–35.
51. Wiles, *Greek Theatre Performance*, 34–35, 53.
52. See Zachary P. Biles, "Aeschylus' Afterlife Reperformance by Decree in 5th C. Athens?" *Illinois Classical Studies* 31/32 (2006–2007): 206–42.
53. The complexity of the "New Music," with its greater rhythmic and melodic complexity, "was a major factor in the diminution of the chorus' role," being better suited for trained, professional soloists than for choral performance. Csapo and Slater, *Context of Ancient Drama*, 333–34.
54. Harry Falk, "The Tidal Waves of History: Between the Empires," in *Between the Empires: Society in India 300 BCE to 400 CE*, ed. Patrick Olivelle (Oxford University Press, 2006), 45.
55. Michael Witzell, "Brahmanical Reactions to Foreign Influences and to Social and Religious Change," in *Between the Empires: Society in India 300 BCE to 400 CE*, ed. Patrick Olivelle (Oxford University Press, 2006), 467.
56. Romila Thapar, *The Penguin History of Early India: From the Origins to AD 1300* (Penguin Books, 2015), 224–25.
57. Keay, *India*, 131.
58. Shonaleeka Kaul, "South Asia," in *CWH4*, 498.
59. Falk, "Tidal Waves of History," 146.
60. Raghavan, "Sanskrit Drama in Performance," 42.

61. Shekhar, *Sanskrit Drama*, 128.
62. Shekhar, *Sanskrit Drama*, 137, 144–45.
63. Shekhar, *Sanskrit Drama*, 148; Raghavan, "Sanskrit Drama and Performance," 25.
64. Vinay Dharwadker, "Rasa and Bhāva," in *RCP-RCN-EL*, 573.
65. Dharwadker, "Rasa and Bhāva," 575.
66. Quoted in Else, *Origin and Early Form*, 82.
67. Homer, *The Odyssey*, trans. Robert Fagles (Penguin Books, 1996), 78–79, 87, 113, 141, 262–63, and 474.
68. Peter Burian, "Myth into *Muthos*: The Shaping of the Tragic Plot," in *CCGT*, 184, 185.
69. Vernant and Vidal-Naquet, *Myth and Tragedy*, 24–25.
70. Manohar Laxman Varadpande, *History of Indian Theatre: Classical Theatre* (Shakti Malik, Abhinav Publications, 2005), 44.
71. A. C. Woolner and Lakshman Sarup, trans. *Thirteen Trivandrum Plays Attributed to Bhāsa*, 2 vols. (Oxford University Press, 1930), vol. 1, 106, 155.
72. Romila Thapar, *Śakuntalā: Texts, Readings, Histories* (Anthem Press, 1999), 44–45, 56.
73. Raghavan, "Sanskrit Drama and Performance," 18–19.
74. Csapo and Slater, *Context of Ancient Drama*, 167.

4 Silences and Successes

1. Ronald J. Leprohon, "Ritual Drama in Ancient Egypt," in *OTAGB*, 259.
2. Leprohon, "Ritual Drama in Ancient Egypt," 272.
3. Christina Geisen, *A Commemoration Ritual for Senwosret I: P. BM EA 10610.1—5/P. Ramesseum B (Ramesseum Dramatic Papyrus)* (Yale Egyptological Institute, 2018), 26.
4. Geisen, *Commemoration Ritual*, 47, 48. One example of the disconnection between ritual and mythological elements is in scene 6: The ritual action is placing emmer (a grain) on the threshing floor, while the mythology is Osiris talking about one of his eyes; the pun is untranslatable (290).
5. Geisen, *Commemoration Ritual*, 59.
6. H. W. Fairman, *The Triumph of Horus: An Ancient Egyptian Sacred Drama* (University of California Press, 1974).
7. Fairman, *Triumph of Horus*, 33.
8. Fairman, *Triumph of Horus*, 33, 35.
9. Fairman, *Triumph of Horus*, 26, 50.
10. Whether any Egyptian texts count as drama or theatre depends largely on definitions. Ronald J. Leprohon defines "pure theatre" as "a scripted performance played in front of an audience for the purpose of entertainment," which at least partially accounts for his hesitation over the Egyptian texts. "Ritual Drama in Ancient Egypt," 259.
11. John Baines, "Literacy and Ancient Egyptian Society," *Man (New Series)* 18, no. 3 (September 1983): 572–99, 584, 575, 588.

12. See *Ancient Egyptian Literature*, ed. Miriam Lichtheim (University of California Press, 2019). Miriam Lichtheim suggests that two narrative poems from the New Kingdom period (telling of victories at war) might be considered "epics" (312), but they are no more than a few hundred lines each.
13. Victor H. Mair, "Language and Script," in *CHCL*, 50.
14. William Dolby, *A History of Chinese Drama* (Paul Elek, 1976), 1–3.
15. Tao-Ching Hsü, *The Chinese Conception of the Theatre* (University of Washington Press, 1985), 201–205.
16. William Dolby, "Early Chinese Plays and Theater," in *CT:OPD*, 12.
17. Liu Yu, "Prohibit Popular Entertainment," in *CTTP*, 27.
18. Dolby, "Early Chinese Plays," 14.
19. Quoted in Dolby, "Early Chinese Plays," 13.
20. Mair, "Language and Script," 51.
21. Mair, "Language and Script," 51.
22. For the impact of *chuanqi* and other popular fiction, see William H. Nienhauser, Jr., "T'ang Tales," in *CHCL*, 579–94.
23. Eric Csapo and William J. Slater, *The Context of Ancient Drama* (University of Michigan Press, 1995), 3.
24. Alan H. Sommerstein, "Greek Comedy and Its Reception, c. 500–323 BC," in *HRGD*, 33.
25. Oliver Taplin, "How Was Athenian Tragedy Played in the Greek West?," in *Theater Outside Athens: Drama in Greek Sicily and South Italy*, ed. Kathryn Bosher (Cambridge University Press, 2012), 236.
26. Sarah Miles, "Greek Drama in the Hellenistic World," in *HRGD*, 46, 47.
27. P. E. Easterling, "From Repertoire to Canon," in *CCGT*, 225.
28. Peter Brown, "Greek Comedy at Rome," in *HRGD*, 72.
29. Gesine Manuwald, "Roman Tragedy," in *HRGD*, 80–85, 87–88, 85.
30. Richard C. Beacham, *Spectacle Entertainments of Early Imperial Rome* (Yale University Press, 1999), 9.
31. Beacham, *Spectacle Entertainments*, 143.
32. Frank Sear, *Roman Theatres: An Architectural Study* (Oxford University Press, 2006): Italy (including Sicily), 97; Britain, 98, Gaul, 98; Germany, 101; Spain, 101; North Africa (including Crete), 102–105; Levant, 106; Asia Minor (including Cyprus), 110; Balkans, 110; Greece, 113.
33. Carol Symes, "Ancient Drama in the Medieval World," in *HRGD*, 99.
34. Beacham, *Spectacle Entertainments*, 93.
35. Beacham, *Spectacle Entertainments*, 195.
36. Beacham, *Spectacle Entertainments*, 198.
37. Beacham, *Spectacle Entertainments*, 192–93.
38. Chris Wickham, *The Inheritance of Rome: Illuminating the Dark Ages, 400–1000* (Viking, 2009), 95, 75, 95.
39. Wickham, *Inheritance of Rome*, 256–59.
40. Symes, "Ancient Drama in the Medieval World," 108.
41. Andrew Walker White, *Performing Orthodox Ritual in Byzantium* (Cambridge University Press, 2015), 7.
42. Symes, "Ancient Drama in the Medieval World," 110–11.

43. White, *Performing Orthodox Ritual*, 7–8.
44. Aparna Dharwadker, "Representing India's Pasts: Time, Culture, and the Problems of Performance Historiography," in *RtP*, 173.
45. Harry Falk, "The Tidal Waves of History: Between the Empires," in *Between the Empires: Society in India 300 BCE to 400 CE*, ed. Patrick Olivelle (Oxford University Press, 2006), 145.
46. J. A. B. Van Buitenen, "Introduction," in *Two Plays of Ancient India*, trans. J. A. B. Van Buitenen (Columbia University Press, 1968), 39.
47. Bruce L. Sullivan, "Bhasa," in *EAT*, vol. 1, 57.
48. Stanley Wolpert, *A New History of India*, 4th ed. (Oxford University Press, 1993), 93–94.
49. Wolpert, *New History of India*, 94.
50. Brajadulal Chattopadhyaya, *The Making of Early Medieval India* (Oxford University Press, 1994), 18.
51. Chattopadhyaya, *Making of Early Medieval India*, 12.
52. Arthur Berriedale Keith, *The Sanskrit Drama in Its Origin, Development, Theory & Practice*, 1st Indian ed. (Motilal Banarsidass, 1998), 170–71.
53. Farley P. Richmond, "Characteristics of Sanskrit Theatre and Drama," in *IT:TP*, 63.
54. Richard Smith, "Trade and Commerce across Afro-Eurasia," in *CWH5*, 243.
55. This account of "context" draws from Steve Tillis, *The Challenge of World Theatre History* (Palgrave Macmillan, 2020), 101–103, 181–88.
56. Willmar Sauter, "Cyclical Perseverance and Linear Mobility of Theatrical Events," in *RtP*, 119.

Part III The Eurasian Convergence (starting c. 900 CE)

1. David Northrup, "Globalization and the Great Convergence: Rethinking World History in the Long Term," *Journal of World History* 16, no. 3 (September 2005): 249–67, 251.
2. For Bentley, see Ross E. Dunn, introduction to Part Seven, "Periodizing World History," in *NWH:TC*, 362; William H. McNeill, *Mythistory and Other Essays* (University of Chicago Press, 1986), 62.
3. Björn Wittrock, "The Age of Trans-regional Reorientations: Cultural Crystallization and Transformation in the Tenth to Thirteenth Centuries," in *CWH5*, 212.
4. Janet L. Abu-Lughod, *Before European Hegemony: The World System A.D. 1250–1350* (Oxford University Press, 1989), 3.
5. Michal Biran, "The Mongol Empire and Inter-civilizational Exchange," in *CWH5*, 534, 535.
6. Abu-Lughod, *Before European Hegemony*, 4.
7. Björn Wittrock, "Cultural Crystallizations and World History: The Age of Ecumenical Renaissances," in *Eurasian Transformations: Tenth to Thirteenth Centuries*, eds. Johann P. Arnason and Björn Wittrock (Brill, 2004), 58–59.

8. Wittrock, "Cultural Crystallizations and World History," 212.
9. Tao-Ching Hsü, *The Chinese Conception of the Theatre* (University of Washington Press, 1985), 201–205; William Dolby, "Early Chinese Plays and Theatre," in *CT:OPD*, 12–14.
10. Marvin Carlson, *Theatre and Islam* (Macmillan International, 2019), 10.
11. Carol Symes, *A Common Stage: Theater and Public Life in Medieval Arras* (Cornell University Press, 2007), 84.

5   The Engine of Convergence

1. Richard Smith, "Trade and Commerce across Afro-Eurasia," in *CWH5*, 233.
2. Quoted in David Northrup, "Globalization and the Great Convergence: Rethinking World History in the Long Term," *Journal of World History* 16, no. 3 (September 2005): 249–67, 258.
3. Valerie Hansen, *The Year 1000: When Explorers Connected the World – and Globalization Began* (Scribner, 2020), 199.
4. Jacques Gernet, *A History of Chinese Civilization*, 2nd ed., trans. J. R. Foster and Charles Hartman (Cambridge University Press, 1996), 320.
5. Janet L. Abu-Lughod, *Before European Hegemony: The World System A.D. 1250–1350* (Oxford University Press, 1989), 319.
6. John Brooke, "Material Life: Bronze Age Crisis to the Black Death," in *The Oxford Illustrated History of the World*, ed. Felipe Fernández-Armesto (Oxford University Press, 2019), 160–61.
7. Gernet, *History of Chinese Civilization*, 320, 321, 322.
8. Brooke, "Material Life," 165.
9. Richard von Glahn, "State Formation in China from the Sui through the Song Dynasties," in *CWH5*, 525.
10. Gernet, *History of Chinese Civilization*, 300.
11. Peter Burke, "Patterns of Urbanization, 1400 to 1800," in *CWH6.1*, 115.
12. Edwin O. Reischauer and John K. Fairbank, *East Asia: The Great Tradition* (Houghton Mifflin Company, 1958), 213.
13. I refer to "middling classes" because the more familiar term "middle class" carries distinct (and misleading) contemporary connotations. Middling classes are made up of a wide range of urban dwellers who are neither elite (whether by heritage or wealth) nor peasant.
14. Gernet, *History of Chinese Civilization*, 332.
15. William Dolby, *A History of Chinese Drama* (Paul Elek, 1976), 15–16.
16. William Dolby, "Early Chinese Plays and Theater," in *CT:OPD*, 21.
17. Dolby, *History of Chinese Drama*, 16.
18. Dolby, *History of Chinese Drama*, 17, 18.
19. Dolby, "Early Chinese Plays and Theater," 19.
20. Mei Sun, "Performances of *Nanxi*," *Asian Theatre Journal* 13, no. 2 (Fall 1996): 141–66, 141.
21. William Dolby, "Yuan Drama," in *CT:OPD*, 32, 33.

Notes to pages 96–100

22. Morris Rossabi, *A History of China* (Wiley Blackwell, 2014), 203, 202, 206.
23. Sun, "Performances of *Nanxi*," 141.
24. Dolby, *History of Chinese Drama*, 27.
25. Harold M. Tanner, *China: A History, Vol. 1: From Neolithic Cultures through the Great Qing Empire, 10,000 BCE–1799 CE* (Hackett Publishing, 2010), 210–11.
26. Jürgen Osterhammel, *The Transformation of the World: A Global History of the Nineteenth Century*, trans. Patrick Camiller (Princeton University Press, 2014), 251.
27. Colin Mackerras, *Chinese Drama: A Historical Survey* (New World Press, 1990), 49.
28. Dolby, "Yuan Drama," 34, 67.
29. Dolby, *History of Chinese Drama*, 54, 53, 54.
30. Dolby, *History of Chinese Drama*, 54–58.
31. Richard F. S. Yang, "The Social Background of the Yüan Drama," *Monumenta Serica* 17 (1958): 331–52, 331–32, 333.
32. Yang, "Social Background of the Yüan Drama," 338–39.
33. Wilt C. Idema, "Traditional Dramatic Literature," in *CHCL*, 794.
34. Tao-Ching Hsü, *The Chinese Conception of the Theatre* (University of Washington Press, 1985), 71.
35. Jiaqi Wu, "A Preliminary Exploration of Buddhist Culture in Tang Legends," *Proceedings of 3rd International Conference on Interdisciplinary Humanities and Communication Studies*, 31. https://doi.org/10.54254/2753-7064/47/20242406.
36. Hsü, *Chinese Conception of the Theatre*, 228.
37. Mei Sun, "*Nanxi*: The Earliest Form of *Xiqu* (Traditional Chinese Theatre)" (Dissertation, University of Hawaii, 1995), 83, 87.
38. Dolby, "Yuan Drama," 45.
39. Wai-Yee Li, "Full-Length Vernacular Fiction," in *CHCL*, 626, 632; George A. Hayden, *Crime and Punishment in Medieval Chinese Drama: Three Judge Pao Plays* (Council on East Asian Studies, Harvard University, 1978), 2.
40. Hsü, *Chinese Conception of the Theatre*, 117.
41. Tian Mansha, "Xiqu Hangdang," trans. Liza Bielby and Yan Ma, in *RCP-RCN-EL*, 134.
42. Dolby, *History of Chinese Theatre*, 8.
43. Tian, "Xiqu Hangdang," 141.
44. Tian, "Xiqu Hangdang," 136.
45. Sun, "Performances of *Nanxi*," 151; Dolby, *History of Chinese Theatre*, 60.
46. Tian, "Xiqu Hangdang," 136.
47. Sun, "*Nanxi*," 158.
48. Dolby, *History of Chinese Drama*, 60, 61–63.
49. Sun, "Performances of *Nanxi*," 141.
50. Sun, "Performances of *Nanxi*," 146; Dolby, *History of Chinese Theatre*, 74.
51. Sun, "Performances of *Nanxi*," 148.
52. Quoted in Dolby, *History of Chinese Theatre*, 74.

6 Along the Sea Route

1. Janet L. Abu-Lughod, *Before European Hegemony: The World System A.D. 1250–1350* (Oxford University Press, 1989), 356.
2. Victor Lieberman, *Strange Parallels: Southeast Asia in Global Context, c. 800–1830, Vol. 2: Mainland Mirrors: Europe, Japan, China, South Asia, and the Islands* (Cambridge University Press, 2009), 15.
3. Craig A. Lockard, *Southeast Asia in World History* (Oxford University Press, 2009), 35.
4. Anthony Reid, *A History of Southeast Asia: Critical Crossroads* (Wiley Blackwell, 2015), 14.
5. Reid, *History of Southeast Asia*, 39.
6. Lieberman, *Strange Parallels, Vol. 2*, 763, n. 1.
7. Reid, *History of Southeast Asia*, 2–3.
8. Lieberman, *Strange Parallels, Vol. 2*, 893.
9. Reid, *History of Southeast Asia*, 43.
10. James R. Brandon, *On Thrones of Gold: Three Javanese Shadow Plays* (Harvard University Press, 1970), 2–3.
11. Ghulam-Sarwar Yousof, *Dictionary of Traditional South-East Asian Theatre* (Oxford University Press, 1994), 291.
12. Fan Pen Chen, "Shadow Theaters of the World," *Asian Folklore Studies* 62 (2003): 25–64, 35.
13. Ghulam-Sarwar, *Dictionary of Traditional South-East Asian Theatre*, 276.
14. James R. Brandon, *Theatre in Southeast Asia* (Harvard University Press, 1967), 42.
15. Brandon, *On Thrones of Gold*, 1.
16. Brandon, *Theatre in Southeast Asia*, 43, 44.
17. Brandon, *On Thrones of Gold*, 33.
18. Ghulam-Sarwar, *Dictionary of Traditional South-East Asian Theatre*, 276–314.
19. Beth Osnes, *The Shadow Puppet Theatre of Malaysia: A Study of Wayang Kulit with Performance Scripts and Puppet Designs* (McFarland, 2010), 25.
20. Osnes, *Shadow Puppet Theatre of Malaysia*, 26; Chen, "Shadow Theaters of the World," 36.
21. A. E. Green, "Commedia dell'arte," in *CGAT*, 236.
22. Chen, "Shadow Theaters of the World," 36.
23. Ghulam-Sarwar, *Dictionary of Traditional South-East Asian Theatre*, 118; Eileen Blumenthal, "Robam Kbach Boran," in *EAT*, vol. 2, 623.
24. Brandon, *Theatre in Southeast Asia*, 58.
25. Osnes, *Shadow Puppet Theatre of Malaysia*, 24.
26. Brandon, *Theatre in Southeast Asia*, 73.
27. Trinh Nguyen, "Vietnam" section in Pawit Mahasarinand, Ty Bamla, Jennifer Goodlander, Khuon Chanreaksmey, Siyuan Liu, and Trinh Nguyen, "Modern Theatre in Mainland Southeast Asia: Thailand, Burma (Myanmar), Laos, Cambodia and Vietnam," in *RHAT*, 364.

28. A. R. Philpott, *Dictionary of Puppetry* (Plays, Inc., 1969), 277.
29. Nguyen, "Modern Theatre in Mainland Southeast Asia," 364.
30. Brandon, *Theatre in Southeast Asia*, 73.
31. Colin Mackerras, "Theatre in Vietnam," *Asian Theatre Journal* 4, no. 1 (Spring 1987): 1–28, 4.
32. Quoted in Mackerras, "Theatre in Vietnam," 6.
33. Abu-Lughod, *Before European Hegemony*, 273.
34. Abu-Lughod, *Before European Hegemony*, 261.
35. Johann P. Arnason, "State Formation and Empire Building," in *CWH5*, 502.
36. Victor Lieberman, *Strange Parallels: Southeast Asia in Global Context, c. 800–1830, Vol. 1: Integration on the Mainland* (Cambridge University Press, 2009), 661.
37. Stanley Wolpert, *A New History of India*, 4th ed. (Oxford University Press, 1993), 107.
38. John Keay, *India: A History* (Grove Press, 2000), 242.
39. Farley P. Richmond, "Characteristics of Sanskrit Drama and Theatre," in *IT:TP*, 83.
40. Indū Shekhar, *Sanskrit Drama: Its Origin and Decline*, 2nd ed. (Munshiram Manoharlal Publishers Pvt. Ltd, 1977), 153.
41. Shekhar, *Sanskrit Drama*, 153.
42. Shekhar, *Sanskrit Drama*, 155, 159, 164.
43. Govardhan Panchal, *Bhavāī and Its Typical Ahāryā: Costumes, Make-up and Props in Bhavāī* (Darpana Academy of Performing Arts, 1983), 7.
44. Panchal, *Bhavāī and Its Typical Ahāryā*, 7, 11, 9–11.
45. Kapila Vatsyayan, *Traditional Indian Theatre: Multiple Streams* (National Book Trust, India, 1980), 13.
46. Romila Thapar, *The Penguin History of Early India: From the Origins to AD 1300* (Penguin Books, 2015), 368, 369.
47. Farley P. Richmond, "*Kūtiyāttam*," in *IT:TP*, 94.
48. Bruce L. Sullivan, "Bhasa," in *EAT*, vol. 1, 57.
49. Vatsyayan, *Traditional Indian Theatre*, 18.
50. Vatsyayan, *Traditional Indian Theatre*, 20.
51. Vatsyayan, *Traditional Indian Theatre*, 16.
52. Richmond, "*Kūtiyāttam*," 103.
53. Richmond, "*Kūtiyāttam*," 93.
54. Richmond, "*Kūtiyāttam*," 87.
55. Vatsyayan, *Traditional Indian Theatre*, 21, 22.
56. Richard Smith, "Trade and Commerce across Afro-Eurasia," in *CWH5*, 236.
57. John Darwin, *After Tamerlane: The Global History of Empire since 1405* (Bloomsbury Press, 2008), 38–39. These "legal instruments" would eventually be employed by Italian merchants and become critical to the development of modern capitalism.
58. André Raymond, *Cairo*, trans. Willard Wood (Harvard University Press, 2000), 60, 61.
59. J. R. McNeill, "Biological Exchanges in World History," in *OHWH*, 330.

60. Raymond, *Cairo*, 118; Abu-Lughod, *Before European Hegemony*, 228.
61. Shmuel Moreh, *Live Theatre and Dramatic Literature in the Medieval Arab World* (New York University Press, 1992), 104.
62. Quoted in Moreh, *Live Theatre and Dramatic Literature*, 95, 96.
63. Cairo was not the only center of puppetry in Islamdom. In this same period, a nonliterary form of puppet theatre called *kheimeh shab bazi* emerged in Iran, of which a twelfth-century poet wrote: "Time starts the puppet play again / The beginning of the play is the hour of creation. / The Divine Puppet Master contemplates / The story he will present on the screen." Quoted in Shiva Massoudi, "'*Kheimeh Shab Bazi*': Iranian Traditional Marionette Theatre," *Asian Theatre Journal* 26, no. 2 (Fall 2009): 260–80, 262.
64. Shmuel Moreh, "The Shadow Play ('Khayāl al-Zill') in the Light of Arabic Literature," *Journal of Arabic Literature* 18 (1987): 46–61, 47.
65. Li Guo, *The Performing Arts in Medieval Islam: Shadow Play and Popular Poetry in Ibn Dāniyāl's Mamluk Cairo* (Brill, 2012), 112–13.
66. Marvin Carlson, *Theatre and Islam* (Macmillan International, 2019), 11. Marvin Carlson is presumably comparing the plays to the theatre of Europe at the time, for it seems evident that the contemporaneous *nanxi*, Yuan *zaju*, and *kutiyattam* were no less "ambitious."
67. Quoted in M. M. Badawi, *Early Arabic Drama* (Cambridge University Press, 1988), 83.
68. Badawi, *Early Arabic Drama*, 13–14.
69. Quoted in Guo, *Performing Arts in Medieval Islam*, 94.
70. Marvin Carlson, "Microhistory in the Middle East: The Case of Ibn Dāniyāl," *Theatre Survey* 55, no. 1 (January 2014): 81–95, 87.
71. Carlson, "Microhistory in the Middle East," 88, 89.
72. Marvin Carlson, "The Arab Aristophanes," *Comparative Drama* 47, no. 2 (Summer 2013): 151–66, 155, 162–63.
73. Guo, *Performing Arts in Medieval Islam*, 95, 93, 94.
74. Guo, *Performing Arts in Medieval Islam*, 97.
75. Raymond, *Cairo*, 138, 140.
76. Badawi, *Early Arabic Drama*, 24.
77. Badawi, *Early Arabic Drama*, 25.

7 On the Margins of Eurasia

1. Charles F. Pazdernik, "Late Antiquity in Europe c. 300–900 CE," in *CWH4*, 379.
2. William H. McNeill, *The Rise of the West: A History of the Human Community* (University of Chicago Press, 1963), 452.
3. Dagmar Schäfer and Marcus Popplow, "Technology and Innovation within Expanding Webs of Exchange," in *CWH5*, 315.
4. Victor Lieberman, *Strange Parallels: Southeast Asia in Global Context, c. 800–1830, Vol. 2: Mainland Mirrors: Europe, Japan, China, South Asia, and the Islands* (Cambridge University Press, 2009), 163.

5. McNeill, *Rise of the West*, 452, 453.
6. McNeill, *Rise of the West*, 453.
7. Norman Davies, *Europe: A History* (HarperPerennial, 1998), 311, 313.
8. McNeill, *Rise of the West*, 456.
9. Davies, *Europe*, 368.
10. Björn Wittrock, "The Age of Trans-regional Reorientations: Cultural Crystallization and Transformation in the Tenth to Thirteenth Centuries," in *CWH5*, 224.
11. Robert Bartlett, *The Making of Europe: Conquest, Colonization, and Cultural Change* (Princeton University Press, 1993), 292.
12. These reforms were initiated by Pope Gregory VII (c. 1020–1085).
13. Norman F. Cantor, *The Civilization of the Middle Ages* (HarperPerennial, 1994), 245.
14. Bartlett, *Making of Europe*, 23.
15. Diarmaid MacCulloch, *A History of Christianity: The First Three Thousand Years* (Viking, 2009), 369.
16. Carol Symes, *A Common Stage: Theater and Public Life in Medieval Arras* (Cornell University Press, 2007), 4, 1.
17. William Tydeman, *The Theatre in the Middle Ages: Western European Stage Conditions, c. 800–1576* (Cambridge University Press, 1978), 46.
18. V. A. Kolve, *The Play Called Corpus Christi* (Stanford University Press, 1966), 8.
19. Barbara K. Gold, "Hrotswitha Writes Herself: *Clamor Validus Gandeshemensis*," in *Sex and Gender in Medieval and Renaissance Texts: The Latin Tradition*, eds. Barbara K. Gold, Paul Allen Miller, and Charles Platter (State University of New York Press, 1997), 41.
20. Quoted in Gold, "Hrotswitha Writes Herself," 48.
21. Grace Frank, *The Medieval French Drama* (Oxford University Press, 1954), 9.
22. Eckehard Simon, "Preface," in *TME*, xiii.
23. These performers are variously also called *mimi, histriones, scenici*, and *joculatores*. Their contemporaries (including in 791, 950, the eleventh century, 1159, the late twelfth century, 1215, and early fourteenth century) attempted to sort out the terminology, but with little consistency. Tydeman, *Theatre in the Middle Ages*, 26, 184–88.
24. Tydeman, *Theatre in the Middle Ages*, 27.
25. Frank, *Medieval French Drama*, 5.
26. Tydeman, *Theatre in the Middle Ages*, 35.
27. David Wiles, "Medieval, Renaissance and Early Modern Theatre," in *CCTH*, 57.
28. Tydeman, *Theatre in the Middle Ages*, 39, 40.
29. Nils Holger Petersen, "Representation in European Devotional Rituals: The Question of the Origin of Medieval Drama in Medieval Liturgy," in *OTAGB*, 347. Nils Holger Peterson sees "what is happening" not as an "imitation of a biblical scene" but as an "analogy" of it (346). This seems a distinction without a difference since Peterson recognizes that the performers are "representing" characters in an action that everyone present understands is not taking place at the time of the performance.

30. Kolve, *Play Called Corpus Christi*, 42.
31. Cantor, *Civilization of the Middle Ages*, 243.
32. Janet L. Abu-Lughod, *Before European Hegemony: The World System A.D. 1250–1350* (Oxford University Press, 1989), 47.
33. Richard Smith, "Trade and Commerce across Afro-Eurasia," in *CWH5*, 243–44.
34. Symes, *Common Stage*, 1.
35. Frank, *Medieval French Drama*, 95, 212, 231; note that de la Halle is also known by the name Adam le Bossu.
36. Scholars disagree over whether to call the English theatre form "Corpus Christi plays," "cycle plays," or "mystery plays," with additional debate over whether the "mystery" is religious in nature or refers to the secret knowledge of the trade guilds that performed the plays.
37. Hansjürgen Linke, "Germany and German-Speaking Central Europe," trans. Eckehard Simon, in *TME*, 208; Frank, *Medieval French Drama*, 126. In England, the Feast of Corpus Christi was established in 1318. V. A. Kolve writes that a bible picture book (c. 1326–1331) "seems to have been influenced by drama traditions," being structured in a way that "resembles the mature English cycles" and seemingly showing "how the medieval drama, with its costumes, settings, and devices, might have looked in performance." And yet the first clear mention of Corpus Christi plays (in York) dates from 1376. Kolve tentatively suggests that the mid-century bubonic plague retarded the development of the emerging form, which seems plausible. *Play Called Corpus Christi*, 38, 37.
38. Tydeman, *Theatre in the Middle Ages*, 131–32.
39. Stanley J. Kahrl, "The Staging of Medieval English Plays," in *TME*, 134; see also Kolve, *Play Called Corpus Christi*, 50.
40. Fire was an especially popular effect: "Human performers ejected flames from various parts of their anatomies," including their buttocks, while "serpents and dragons belched forth fire." Other popular effects, such as hangings, beheadings, mutilations, burnings, and drownings, were created either with a special apparatus or the use of dummies. Tydeman, *Theatre in the Middle Ages*, 173, 176–77.
41. For an account of Japan's cultural borrowing from China, see G. B. Sansom, *Japan: A Short Cultural History* (Stanford University Press, 1978), 63–107.
42. Wittrock, "Age of Trans-regional Reorientations," 221.
43. Noel John Pinnington, *A New History of Medieval Japanese Theatre: Noh and Kyōgen from 1300 to 1600* (Palgrave Macmillan, 2019), 17.
44. Mikeal S. Adolphson, "Social Change and Contained Transformations: Warriors and Merchants in Japan, 1000–1300," in *Eurasian Transformations, Tenth to Thirteenth Centuries: Crystallizations, Divergences, Renaissances*, eds. Johann P. Arnason and Björn Wittrock (Brill, 2004), 317–18.
45. Adolphson, "Social Change and Contained Transformations," 310–11.
46. Kozo Yamamura, "The Growth of Commerce in Medieval Japan," in *The Cambridge History of Japan*, Vol. 3: *Medieval Japan*, ed. Kozo Yamamura (Cambridge University Press, 1990), 358.

47. Yamamura, "Growth of Commerce," 355; H. Paul Varley, "Cultural Life in Medieval Japan," in *The Cambridge History of Japan*, Vol. *3: Medieval Japan*, ed. Kozo Yamamura (Cambridge University Press, 1990), 460.
48. Benito Ortolani, *The Japanese Theatre: From Shamanistic Ritual to Contemporary Pluralism*, rev. ed. (Princeton University Press, 1995), 55.
49. William Lee, "Kagura and the Heavenly Rock-Cave," in *HJT*, 11.
50. Ortolani, *Japanese Theatre*, 14–15.
51. Ortolani, *Japanese Theatre*, 15; James R. Brandon, "Japan," in *CGAT*, 144.
52. Terauchi Naoko, "Ancient and Early Medieval Performing Arts," in *HJT*, 5.
53. Terauchi, "Ancient and Early Medieval Performing Arts," 7.
54. Ortolani, *Japanese Theatre*, 37, 44.
55. Ortolani, *Japanese Theatre*, 56–57. Note that Terauchi Naoko differs from Benito Ortolani by listing *sangaku* as a form that originated in China. "Ancient and Early Medieval Performing Arts," 6.
56. *Sarugaku* might mean something like "monkey entertainments," but it is unclear "why the [written] character for monkey was used to write the new word." Ortolani, *Japanese Theatre*, 57.
57. Pinnington, *New History of Medieval Japanese Theatre*, 26.
58. Ortolani, *Japanese Theatre*, 59.
59. Terauchi, "Ancient and Early Medieval Performing Arts," 15.
60. Ortolani, *Japanese Theatre*, 73–74.
61. Ortolani, *Japanese Theatre*, 85–92.
62. Noel John Pinnington observes that "because the works of Zeami and his pupils survive, we know more about them and groups close to them than we do about others. But that does not mean his group of actors were, in their time, the most important nor that his tradition was dominant." *New History of Medieval Japanese Theatre*, 83.
63. Varley, "Cultural Life in Medieval Japan," 462, 463.
64. Pinnington notes, "The shogun Yoshimitsu had an enthusiastic taste for beautiful young boys throughout his life" and that "such relationships were common, indeed, fashionable, at the time." *New History of Medieval Japanese Theatre*, 105.
65. Ortolani, *Japanese Theatre*, 94.
66. Donald Keene, *Nō and Bunraku: Two Forms of Japanese Theatre* (Columbia University Press, 1990), 32.
67. J. Thomas Rimer, "The Background of Zeami's Treatises," in *On the Art of Nō Drama: The Major Treatises of Zeami*, trans. J. Thomas Rimer and Yamazaki Masakazu (Princeton University Press, 1984), xxvii.
68. Shelley Fenno Quinn, "Zeami: Noh's Founding Genius," in *HJT*, 39.
69. Varley, "Cultural Life in Medieval Japan," 465.
70. Pinnington, *New History of Medieval Japanese Theatre*, 65.
71. Keene, *Nō and Bunraku*, 22–23.
72. William Lee, "Premodern Practitioner Principles," in *HJT*, 443.
73. J. Thomas Rimer and Yamazaki Masakazu, "Glossaries," in Zeami, *On the Art of Nō Drama: The Major Treatises of Zeami*, trans. J. Thomas Rimer and Yamazaki Masakazu (Princeton University Press, 1984), 262.

74. Zeami, *On the Art of Nō Drama: The Major Treatises of Zeami*, trans. J. Thomas Rimer and Yamazaki Masakazu (Princeton University Press, 1984), 92.
75. Ortolani, *Japanese Theatre*, 134.
76. Rimer and Yamazaki, "Glossaries," 265, 264, 266.
77. Ortolani, *Japanese Theatre*, 135.
78. Keene, *Nō and Bunraku*, 22.
79. Pinnington notes that "by the middle of the fourteenth century, scripts were being written" for *sarugaku* but does not give the sense that this was the norm. *New History of Medieval Japanese Theatre*, 113.
80. Varley, "Cultural Life in Medieval Japan," 449, 450.
81. Keene, *Nō and Bunraku*, 50.
82. Janet Goff, *Noh Drama and the Tale of Genji: The Art of Allusion in Fifteen Classical Plays* (Princeton University Press, 1991), 16–17.
83. Goff, *Noh Drama*, 60, 61.
84. Goff, *Noh Drama*, 46, 49.
85. Steven T. Brown, *Theatricalities of Power: The Cultural Politics of Noh* (Stanford University Press, 2001), 11.
86. Varley, "Cultural Life in Medieval Japan," 458.
87. Varley, "Cultural Life in Medieval Japan," 464, 465.
88. Keene, *Nō and Bunraku*, 28.
89. Quoted in Shinko Kagaya and Miura Hiroko, "Noh and Muromachi Culture," in *HJT*, 45; brackets in the original.
90. Kagaya and Miura, "Noh and Muromachi Culture," 52.
91. Pinnington, *New History of Medieval Japanese Theatre*, 193.
92. M. Cody Poulton, "Monomane and Riaru," in *RCP-RCN-EL*, 461–62.
93. Jonah Salz, "Kyogen: Classic Comedy," in *HJT*, 79, 68.
94. Keene, *Nō and Bunraku*, 21.
95. This account of "theatre regions" draws from Steve Tillis, *The Challenge of World Theatre History* (Palgrave Macmillan, 2020), 138–50.
96. Marshall G. S. Hodgson, *Rethinking World History: Essays on Europe, Islam, and World History*, ed. Edmund Burke III (Cambridge University Press, 1993), 279.
97. Martin W. Lewis and Kären E. Wigen, *The Myth of Continents: A Critique of Metageography* (University of California Press, 1997), 14, italics in the original.

Part IV The Eurasian Resurgence (starting c. 1500 CE)

1. James Belich, "The Black Death and the Spread of Europe," in *PGH*, 95–96.
2. James L. A. Webb, Jr., "Globalization of Disease, 1300 to 1900," in *CWH6.1*, 61.
3. Monica H. Green, "The Four Black Deaths," *American Historical Review* 125, no. 5 (December 2020): 1601–31, 1630.
4. Richard Smith, "Trade and Commerce across Afro-Eurasia," in *CWH5*, 249.
5. Janet L. Abu-Lughod, *Before European Hegemony: The World System A.D. 1250–1350* (Oxford University Press, 1989), 359.
6. Green, "Four Black Deaths," 1628–29.

7. Smith, "Trade and Commerce across Afro-Eurasia," 247.
8. Abu-Lughod, *Before European Hegemony*, 359–60.
9. Scott C. Levi, "Objects in Motion," in *CtWH*, 328.
10. Smith, "Trade and Commerce across Afro-Eurasia," 249.
11. David Christian, *Maps of Time: An Introduction to Big History* (University of California Press, 2011), 344–45.
12. Peter Frankopan, *The Earth Transformed: An Untold Story* (Alfred A. Knopf, 2023), 314.
13. Jack A. Goldstone, "Political Trajectories Compared," in *CWH6.1*, 460.
14. Charles H. Parker, "Entrepreneurs, Families, and Companies," in *CWH6.2*, 193.
15. Abu-Lughod, *Before European Hegemony*, 361.
16. Alfred W. Crosby, *The Columbian Exchange; Biological and Cultural Consequences of 1492* (Greenwood Press, 1972).
17. Ian Morris, *Why the West Rules – for Now: The Patterns of History and What They Reveal about the Future* (Farrar, Straus, Giroux, 2010), 435.
18. Robert B. Marks, "Exhausting the Earth: Environment and History in the Early Modern World," in *CWH6.1*, 38.
19. Andre Gundar Frank, *ReORIENT: Global Economy in the Asian Age* (University of California Press, 1998), 277.

8   Okuni's Crucifix

1. Samuel L. Leiter, *New Kabuki Encyclopedia: A Revised Adaptation of* Kabuki Jiten (Greenwood Press, 1997), 231.
2. Laurence R. Kominz, *The Stars Who Created Kabuki: Their Lives, Loves and Legacy* (Kodansha International, 1997), 18. Benito Ortolani writes of the *kabukimono*: "They would roam the streets and oftentimes engage in acts of violence and riots, flaunting their revolt against all conventions and decency, by performing such acts as playing the flute with one's anus." *The Japanese Theatre: From Shamanistic Ritual to Contemporary Pluralism*. Rev. ed. (Princeton University Press, 1995), 164.
3. Julie A. Iezzi, "Kabuki: Superheroes and *Femmes Fatales*," in *HJT* 111.
4. Andrew T. Tsubaki, "The Performing Arts of Sixteenth-Century Japan: A Prelude to *Kabuki*," in *A Kabuki Reader: History and Performance*, ed. Samuel L. Leiter (M. E. Sharpe, 2002), 11–12.
5. Kominz, *Stars Who Created Kabuki*, 19.
6. Kominz, *Stars Who Created Kabuki*, 19.
7. Iezzi, "Kabuki," 113.
8. Quoted in Donald H. Shively, "*Bakufu* versus *Kabuki*," in *A Kabuki Reader: History and Performance*, ed. Samuel L. Leiter (M. E. Sharpe, 2002), 34, 35.
9. Tsubaki, "Performing Arts of Sixteenth-Century Japan," 11.
10. Iezzi, "Kabuki," 111–12.
11. Marius B. Jansen, *The Making of Modern Japan* (Harvard University Press, 2000), 4, 5.
12. Jansen, *Making of Modern Japan*, 5, 7.

13. Jansen, *Making of Modern Japan*, 12–13, 15.
14. Jansen, *Making of Modern Japan*, 18, 22–23.
15. Jansen, *Making of Modern Japan*, 29.
16. Tsubaki, "Performing Arts of Sixteenth-Century Japan," 5.
17. G. B. Sansom, *Japan: A Short Cultural History* (Stanford University Press, 1978), 417.
18. Sansom, *Japan*, 420.
19. Sansom, *Japan*, 422, 423.
20. Dennis O. Flynn, "Silver in a Global Context, 1400–1800," in *CWH6.2*, 216.
21. Peter Perdue, "Empires and Frontiers in Continental Eurasia," in *E&E*, 165–66.
22. Peter Burke, "Patterns of Urbanization, 1400 to 1800," in *CWH6.1*, 109.
23. Burke, "Patterns of Urbanization," 109–10, 111.
24. Jansen, *Making of Modern Japan*, 167.
25. Jansen, *Making of Modern Japan*, 168–69, 169.
26. Sansom, *Japan*, 469.
27. Burke, "Patterns of Urbanization," 112.
28. Nishiyama Matsunosuke, *Edo Culture: Daily Life and Diversions in Urban Japan, 1600–1868*, trans. Gerald Groemer (University of Hawaii Press, 1997), 28–29.
29. Burke, "Patterns of Urbanization," 112–13.
30. Burke, "Patterns of Urbanization," 113. *Ukiyo* was originally "a Buddhist term for the transience of all worldly things," but it had acquired "hedonist overtones" with the meaning of "living for the moment" (113).
31. Shively, "*Bakufu* versus *Kabuki*," 34.
32. Ortolani, *Japanese Theatre*, 167, 168.
33. Donald H. Shively, "The Social Environment of Tokugawa Kabuki," in *Studies in Kabuki: Its Acting, Music, and Historical Context*, eds. James R. Brandon et al. (University of Hawaii Press, 1978), 7.
34. Shively, "*Bakufu* versus *Kabuki*," 41.
35. Shively, "*Bakufu* versus *Kabuki*," 39, 40.
36. Kominz, *Stars Who Created Kabuki*, 27.
37. Kominz, *Stars Who Created Kabuki*, 72.
38. Kominz, *Stars Who Created Kabuki*, 155.
39. Stanca Scholz-Cionca and Nanako Nakajima, "Introduction" [to Japanese concepts], in *RCP-RCN-EL*, 414.
40. The word *bunraku* derives from the name of a famous eighteenth-century puppeteer, Uemura Bunraku-ken. Ortolani, *Japanese Theatre*, 208.
41. Donald Keene, *Nō and Bunraku: Two Forms of Japanese Theatre* (Columbia University Press, 1990), 130.
42. Keene, *Nō and Bunraku*, 133.
43. Keene, *Nō and Bunraku*, 136.
44. Keene, *Nō and Bunraku*, 137.
45. Tsubaki, "Performing Arts of Sixteenth-Century Japan," 9.
46. Keene, "Introduction," in *Four Major Plays of Chikamatsu* (Columbia University Press, 1961), 33–35.

47. James R. Brandon, "Kabuki and Shakespeare: Balancing Yin and Yang," *TDR: The Drama Review* 43, no. 2 (Summer 1999): 15–53, 20.
48. Brandon, "Kabuki and Shakespeare," 48.
49. Keene, *Nō and Bunraku*, 138, 140.
50. Gotō Shizuo, "Bunraku: Puppet Theatre," trans. and adp. Alan Cumming, in *HJT*, 173–76.

9 Islamic Empires

1. John Darwin, *After Tamerlane: The Global History of Empire since 1405* (Bloomsbury Press, 2008), 5.
2. Ayşe Zarakol, *Before the West: The Rise and Fall of Eastern World Orders* (Cambridge University Press, 2022), 127.
3. Giancarlo Casale, "The Islamic Empires of the Early Modern World," in *CWH6.1*, 338.
4. Marshall G. S. Hodgson, *The Venture of Islam: Conscience and History in a World Civilization, Vol. 3: The Gunpowder Empires and Modern Times* (University of Chicago Press, 1974), 25.
5. Jerry H. Bentley, *Old World Encounters: Cross-Cultural Contacts and Exchanges in Pre-modern Times* (Oxford University Press, 1993), 122.
6. William H. McNeill, *The Rise of the West: A History of the Human Community* (University of Chicago Press, 1963), 518.
7. Marshall G. S. Hodgson, *The Venture of Islam: Conscience and History in a World Civilization, Vol. 2: The Expansion of Islam in the Middle Periods* (University of Chicago Press, 1974), 559.
8. Thomas Asbridge, *The Crusades: The Authoritative History of the War for the Holy Land* (HarperCollins, 2010), 528–32.
9. John Freely, *Istanbul: The Imperial City* (Penguin Books, 1998), 173.
10. Hodgson, *Venture of Islam*, vol. 2, 61.
11. Freely, *Istanbul*, 177.
12. Lord Kinross, *The Ottoman Centuries: The Rise and Fall of The Turkish Empire* (William Morrow, 1977), 111.
13. Kinross, *Ottoman Centuries*, 116–17.
14. This discussion of *karagöz* draws from Steve Tillis, *Rethinking Folk Drama* (Greenwood Press, 1999), 147–51.
15. Metin And, *A History of Theatre and Popular Entertainments in Turkey* (Dost Yayinlari, 1963–1964), 44–45; see also Sabri Esat Siyavusgil, *Karagöz: Its History, Its Characters, Its Mystic and Satiric Spirit* (Turkish Press, Broadcasting and Tourist Department, 1955), 18–20.
16. And, *History of Theatre and Popular Entertainments*, 45–46; see also Siyavusgil, *Karagöz*, 20–23.
17. And, *History of Theatre and Popular Entertainments*, 46–48; see also Aekaterini Mistakidou, "Comparison of Turkish and Greek Shadow Theatre" (Dissertation, New York University, 1978), 111–22.
18. Siyavusgil, *Karagöz*, 9.

19. John E. Wills, *The World from 1450 to 1700* (Oxford University Press, 2009), 16.
20. Siyavusgil, *Karagöz*, 1–3.
21. And, *History of Theatre and Popular Entertainments*, 36.
22. Siyavusgil, *Karagöz*, 16.
23. Metin And, *Karagöz: Turkish Shadow Theatre*, 3rd ed. (Dost Yayinlari, 1987), 25.
24. And, *Karagöz*, 34, 40.
25. Linda S. Myrsiades and Kostas Myrsiades, *Karagiozis: Culture and Comedy in Greek Puppet Theatre* (University of Kentucky Press, 1992), 39.
26. Linda Myrsiades, "The Karagiozis Performance in Nineteenth-Century Greece," *Byzantine and Modern Greek Studies* 2 (1976): 83–99, 95–97.
27. Fan Pen Chen, "Shadow Theaters of the World," *Asian Folklore Studies* 62 (2003): 25–64, 39. For the Egyptian *aragoz*, see Nashaat Hussein, "The Revitalisation of the *Aragoz* Puppet in Egypt: Some Reflections," *Popular Entertainment Studies* 3, no. 1 (2012): 57–70.
28. And, *History of Theatre and Popular Entertainments*, 39, 49, 44.
29. And, *History of Theatre and Popular Entertainments*, 11, 45, 40.
30. Quoted in Henryk Jurkowski, *Aspects of Puppet Theatre*, ed. Penny Francis (Puppetry Centre Trust, 1988), 2.
31. Hodgson, *The Venture of Islam*, vol. 2, 491–92.
32. H. R. Roemer, "The Safavid Period," in *The Cambridge History of Iran, Vol. 6: The Timurid and Safavid Periods*, eds. Peter Jackson and Lawrence Lockhart (Cambridge University Press, 1986), 210.
33. Roemer, "The Safavid Period," 345.
34. Roemer, "The Safavid Period," 269–70.
35. Hodgson, *The Venture of Islam*, vol. 3, 40–41.
36. Roemer, "The Safavid Period," 189.
37. This discussion of *ta'ziyeh* draws from Tillis, *Rethinking Folk Drama*, 162–67.
38. Jamshid Malekpour, *The Islamic Drama* (Frank Cass, 2004), 27.
39. Malekpour, *Islamic Drama*, 38–51.
40. Ehsan Yarshater, "*Ta'ziyeh* and Pre-Islamic Mourning Rites in Iran," in *Ta'ziyeh: Ritual and Drama in Iran*, ed. Peter Chelkowski (New York University Press, 1979), 90.
41. Willem Floor, *The History of Theatre in Iran* (Mage Publishers, 2005), 87.
42. Yarshater, "*Ta'ziyeh* and Pre-Islamic Mourning Rites," 90.
43. Yarshater, "*Ta'ziyeh* and Pre-Islamic Mourning Rites," 93.
44. Malekpour, *Islamic Drama*, 54, 55, 64.
45. Malekpour, *Islamic Drama*, 52.
46. Floor, *History of Theatre in Iran*, 129.
47. Malekpour, *Islamic Drama*, 57.
48. Floor, *History of Theatre in Iran*, 132.
49. Floor, *History of Theatre in Iran*, 130.
50. Floor, *History of Theatre in Iran*, 170.
51. Milla C. Riggio, "Ta'ziyeh in Exile: Transformations of a Persian Tradition, *Comparative Drama* 28, no. 1 (Spring 1994): 115–40, 127, 121.

52. Floor, *History of Theatre in Iran*, 170.
53. William O. Beeman, "A Full Arena: The Development and Meaning of Popular Performance Traditions in Iran," in *Modern Iran: The Dialectics of Continuity and Change*, eds. Michael Bonine and Nikki R. Keddie (State University of New York Press, 1981), 370.
54. Beeman, "Full Arena," 370, 371, 379. Note, though, that Willem Floor refers to *taqlid* as "danced mime" and distinguishes it from *tamasha* (*History of Theatre in Iran*, 41). The disagreement over terminology likely results from limitations of available evidence and the looseness with which the terms might have originally been used.
55. Beeman, "Full Arena," 372.
56. Beeman, "Full Arena," 379.
57. William O. Beeman, "Mimesis and Travesty in Iranian Traditional Theatre," in *Gender in Performance: The Presentation of Difference in the Performing Arts*, ed. Laurence Senelick (University Press of New England, 1992), 21, 18. Earlier *taqlid* and *tamasha* seem to have also included female dancers, though these women apparently performed only in private, where their services also included prostitution. Floor, *History of Theatre in Iran*, 42–43.
58. Floor, *History of Theatre in Iran*, 57.
59. Beeman, "Full Arena," 377.
60. And, *History of Theatre and Popular Entertainments*, 40, 39.
61. Hafizullah Baghban, "The Context and Concept of Humor in Magadi Theater" (Dissertation, Indiana University, 1976), 65–66, 146, 177.
62. Baghban, "Context and Concept of Humor," 158.
63. Baghban, "Context and Concept of Humor," 146, 149.
64. Baghban, "Context and Concept of Humor," 66, n. 5.
65. This discussion of South Asia draws from Steve Tillis, *The Challenge of World Theatre History* (Palgrave Macmillan, 2020), 282–87.
66. John Keay, *India: A History* (Grove Press, 2000), 294.
67. Keay, *India*, 274.
68. Keay, *India*, 289–92. Note that the word "Mughal" is the Indo-Persian form of "Mongol."
69. Darwin, *After Tamerlane*, 84.
70. André Wink, "South Asia and Southeast Asia," in *OHWH*, 430.
71. Victor Lieberman, *Strange Parallels: Southeast Asia in Global Context, c. 800–1830, Vol. 2: Mainland Mirrors: Europe, Japan, China, South Asia, and the Islands* (Cambridge University Press, 2009), 694.
72. John Stratton Hawley, *A Storm of Songs: India and the Bhakti Movement* (Harvard University Press, 2015), 2.
73. Catherine B. Asher and Cynthia Talbot, *India before Europe* (Cambridge University Press, 2007), 108–10.
74. Hodgson, *Venture of Islam*, vol. 3, 71, 72.
75. Hodgson, *Venture of Islam*, vol. 3, 60.
76. Farley P. Richmond, Darius L. Swann, and Phillip B. Zarrilli, "Introduction," in *IT:TP*, 8.

77. Richmond, Swann, and Zarrilli, "Introduction," 10. Although some scholars might refer to the forms in the "folk-popular sphere" as either "folk" or "popular," these authors suggest that neither term accurately describes forms that "are grounded in a specific local context" but have broad appeal in both urban and rural areas (10, n. 2).
78. Kathryn Hansen, *Grounds for Play: The Nautanki Theatre of North India* (University of California Press, 1992), 61.
79. Pamela Lothspeich, "Introduction: The Field of Ramlila," *Asian Theatre Journal* 37, no. 1 (Spring 2020): 3–33, 5. Note that Urdu and Hindi are mutually comprehensible but that Hindi is written in an Indic alphabet, whereas Urdu is written in a modified Arabic one.
80. Farley P. Richmond, "India," in *CGAT*, 82.
81. Devendra Sharma, "Community, Artistry, and Storytelling in the Cultural Confluence of Nautanki and Ramlila," *Asian Theatre Journal* 37, no. 1 (Spring 2020): 107–32, 108.
82. Govardhan Panchal, *Bhavāī and Its Typical Ahāryā: Costumes, Make-up and Props in Bhavāī* (Darpana Academy of the Performing Arts, 1983), 11.
83. David Mason, "Ankiya Nat," in *EAT*, vol. 1, 35.
84. Panchal, *Bhavāī and Its Typical Ahāryā*, 14.
85. Kapila Vatsyayan, *Traditional Indian Theatre: Multiple Streams* (National Book Trust, India, 1980), Appendix II.
86. Javaid Iqbal Bhat, "Loss of a Syncretic Theatre Form," *Folklore (Estonia)* 34 (2006): 39–56, 41. https://doi.org/10.7592/FEJF2006.34.bhat.
87. Moti Lal Kemmu, "The Bhānd Theatre of Kashmir," trans. Shashi Shekhar Tashkani, *Sangeet Natak* XLV, nos. 3–4 (2011): 33–70, 33; J. C. Mathur, *Drama in Rural India* (Asia Publishing House, 1964), 57; Richmond, "India," 81.
88. Kemmu, "Bhānd Theatre of Kashmir," 38; Balwant Gargi, *Folk Theatre in India* (Rupa and Company, 1991), 186.
89. Bhat, "Loss of a Syncretic Theatre Form," 42.
90. Tevia Abrams, "Tamāshā," in *IT:TP*, 169.
91. Abrams, "Tamāshā," 278.
92. Lieberman, *Strange Parallels*, vol. 2, 648.
93. Phillip B. Zarrilli, "Kathakali," in *EAT*, vol. 1, 317. In an earlier text, Phillip B. Zarrilli dated its emergence to the "late seventeenth to the late eighteenth century." *Kathakali Dance Drama: Where Gods and Demons Come to Play* (Routledge, 2000), 17.
94. Phillip B. Zarrilli, "Kathakali," in *IT:TP*, 315; Zarrilli, "Kathakali," in *EAT*, vol. 1, 317.
95. Zarrilli, "Kathakali," in *IT:TP*, 340.
96. Zarrilli, "Kathakali," in *IT:TP*, 326.
97. Richmond, "India," 92.
98. Zarrilli, "Kathakali," in *IT:TP*, 340, 329.
99. The *bhakti* movement, it will be recalled, was established in southern India well before the tenth century CE and only later rose to prominence in the north.

100. Richmond, "India," 94.
101. Martha Aston-Sikora, "Krishnattam," in *EAT*, vol. 1, 349.
102. Richmond, "India," 95.
103. Zarrilli, "Kathakali," in *IT:TP*, 317; Zarrilli, *Kathakali Dance Drama*, 4.
104. Richmond, "India," 85, 86.
105. Darius L. Swann, "Introduction to Part 4: The Folk-Popular Traditions," in *IT:TP*, 245.
106. Richmond, "India," 85.
107. Richmond, "India," 86; Richard A. Frasca, "Cavittu Natakam," in *EAT*, vol. 1, 80.

10 Across the South China Sea

1. Harold M. Tanner, *China: A History, Vol. 1: From Neolithic Cultures through the Great Qing Empire* (Hackett, 2010), 269, 270; italics in the original.
2. Tanner, *China*, 285.
3. Edwin O. Reischauer and John K. Fairbank, *East Asia: The Great Tradition* (Houghton Mifflin Company, 1960), 304.
4. Richard von Glahn, "State Formation in China from the Sui through the Song Dynasties," in *CWH5*, 532.
5. Jacques Gernet, *A History of Chinese Civilization*, 2nd ed., trans. J. R. Foster and Charles Hartman (Cambridge University Press, 1996), 429.
6. Jack A. Goldstone, "Political Trajectories Compared," in *CWH6.1*, 259.
7. Gernet, *History of Chinese Civilization*, 426.
8. Victor Lieberman, *Strange Parallels: Southeast Asia in Global Context, c. 800–1830, Vol. 2: Mainland Mirrors: Europe, Japan, China, South Asia, and the Islands* (Cambridge University Press, 2009), 559–60.
9. Peter Perdue, "Empires and Frontiers in Continental Eurasia," in *E&E*, 72–73.
10. Dennis O. Flynn, "Silver in a Global Context, 1400–1800," in *CWH6.2*, 215.
11. Gernet, *History of Chinese Civilization*, 429.
12. John Hu, "Ming Dynasty Drama," in *CT:OPD*, 77.
13. William Dolby, *A History of Chinese Drama* (Paul Elek, 1976), 113.
14. Dolby, *History of Chinese Drama*, 89.
15. Quoted in Hu, "Ming Dynasty Drama," 82.
16. Colin Mackerras, "China," in *CGAT*, 30.
17. The term *chuanqi* had earlier been used for a genre of fiction in the Tang era; its literal meaning is "the transmission of the marvelous." Hu, "Ming Dynasty Drama," 62.
18. Hu, "Ming Dynasty Drama," 62, 66, 65.
19. Grant Guangren Shen, *Elite Theatre in Ming China, 1368–1644* (Routledge, 2005), 4–5.
20. Mei Sun, "*Nanxi*: The Earliest Form of *Xiqu* (Traditional Chinese Theatre)" (Dissertation, University of Hawaii, 1995), 171.
21. Hu, "Ming Dynasty Drama," 66.

22. Cyril Birch, *Scenes for Mandarins: The Elite Theater of the Ming* (Columbia University Press, 1995), 35.
23. Colin Mackerras and Elizabeth Wichmann, "Introduction," in *CT:OPD*, 1.
24. Dolby, *History of Chinese Drama*, 90.
25. Wing Chung Ng, *The Rise of Cantonese Opera* (University of Illinois Press, 2015), 12; Dolby, *History of Chinese Drama*, 90–91.
26. Ng, *Rise of Cantonese Opera*, 12.
27. Colin Mackerras suggests that "some 330 styles of regional theatre … ranging from simple folk styles to highly sophisticated and widely spread forms" emerged during the Ming and Qing dynasties. "China," in *EAT*, vol. 1, 110.
28. Victor H. Mair, "Language and Script," in *CHCL*, 23. In contrast to China's many spoken languages, the written language is largely the same throughout China, which is likely why some people assume that "Chinese" is also a uniform spoken language.
29. Hu, "Ming Dynasty Drama," 71.
30. Shen, *Elite Theatre in Ming China*, 7.
31. Shen, *Elite Theatre in Ming China*, 9.
32. Dolby, *History of Chinese Drama*, 104.
33. Shen, *Elite Theatre in Ming China*, 22.
34. Li Ruru, *The Soul of Beijing Opera: Theatrical Creativity and Continuity in the Changing World* (Hong Kong University Press, 2010), 15.
35. Hu, "Ming Dynasty Drama," 74; Colin Mackerras, "The Drama of the Qing Dynasty," in *CT:OPD*, 92–93.
36. Ng, *Rise of Cantonese Opera*, 12.
37. Dolby, *History of Chinese Drama*, 91.
38. Mackerras, "China," in *CGAT*, 32; Colin Mackerras, *Chinese Drama: A Historical Survey* (New World Press, 1990), 55.
39. Li, *Soul of Beijing Opera*, 17.
40. Mackerras, *Chinese Drama*, 36, 55.
41. Ng, *Rise of Cantonese Opera*, 13.
42. Birch, *Scenes for Mandarins*, 6.
43. Perdue, "Empires and Frontiers in Continental Eurasia," 98.
44. Mackerras, "Drama of the Qing Dynasty," 92.
45. Perdue, "Empires and Frontiers in Continental Eurasia," 107.
46. Anthony Reid, *A History of Southeast Asia: Critical Crossroads* (Wiley Blackwell, 2015), 54, 54, 55.
47. Reid, *History of Southeast Asia*, 74.
48. Reid, *History of Southeast Asia*, 74. Note that the name of the city and the strait are the same but are conventionally transliterated differently.
49. Craig A. Lockard, *Southeast Asia in World History* (Oxford University Press, 2009), 52, 68, 67.
50. Reid, *History of Southeast Asia*, 99.
51. Lockard, *Southeast Asia in World History*, 52.
52. Ghulam-Sarwar Yousof, *Dictionary of Traditional South-East Asian Theatre* (Oxford University Press, 1994), 223.

53. Ghulam-Sarwar, *Dictionary of Traditional South-East Asian Theatre*, 99–100.
54. James R. Brandon, *Theatre in Southeast Asia* (Harvard University Press, 1967), 65.
55. Brandon, *Theatre in Southeast Asia*, 65; Kathy Foley, "Thailand," in *CGAT*, 237.
56. Pornrat Damrhung, "Khon," in *EAT*, vol. 1, 327.
57. Foley, "Thailand," 237; Brandon, *Theatre in Southeast Asia*, 63.
58. Foley, "Thailand," 237.
59. Beth Osnes, *The Shadow Puppet Theatre of Malaysia: A Study of Wayang Kulit with Performance Scripts and Puppet Designs* (McFarland, 2011), 189.
60. Brandon, *Theatre in Southeast Asia*, 64. Mattani Mojdara Rutnin specifies that the form's development largely took place in the sixteenth and seventeenth centuries. *Dance, Drama, and Theatre in Thailand: The Process of Development and Modernization* (Silkworm Books, 1996), 3.
61. Brandon, *Theatre in Southeast Asia*, 62; Foley, "Thailand," 236. The confusion seems to arise because the word *nok* means both "southern" and "outside." Brandon, *Theatre in Southeast Asia*, 62.
62. Surapone Virulrak, "Systems of Documenting Thai Traditional Dance and Dance Drama," *SPAFA Digest* 4, no. 2 (1983): 13–21, 18. www.spafajournal.org/index.php/spafadigest/issue/view/15
63. Brandon, *Theatre in Southeast Asia*, 62.
64. Sukanya Sompiboon, "The Reinvention of Thai Traditional-Popular Theatre: Contemporary *Likay* Praxis" (Dissertation, University of Exeter, 2012), 47.
65. Sompiboon, "Reinvention of Thai Traditional-Popular Theatre," 48.
66. Lockard, *Southeast Asia in World History*, 50.
67. Lockard, *Southeast Asia in World History*, 69.
68. Reid, *History of Southeast Asia*, 133.
69. James R. Brandon, *On Thrones of Gold: Three Javanese Shadow Plays* (Harvard University Press, 1970), 6.
70. Brandon, *On Thrones of Gold*, 7.
71. Ghulam-Sarwar Yousof, "Islamic Elements in Traditional Indonesian and Malay Theatre," *Kajian Malaysia* 28, no. 1 (2010): 83–101, 87. Note, though, that James R. Brandon insists that "the essentially Hindu-Javanese nature" of the form "was too firmly set to be penetrated, except occasionally, by Islamic thought." *On Thrones of Gold*, 7.
72. Ghulam-Sarwar, "Islamic Elements," 89–90.
73. Reid, *History of Southeast Asia*, 131.
74. Lockard, *Southeast Asia in World History*, 77; Reid, *History of Southeast Asia*, 121.
75. Reid, *History of Southeast Asia*, 123, 124.
76. Lieberman, *Strange Parallels*, vol. 2, 831.
77. Reid, *History of Southeast Asia*, 121.
78. Lockard, *Southeast Asia in World History*, 80–81.
79. Max Harris, "Muhammad and the Virgin: Folk Dramatizations of Battles between the Moors and Christians of Modern Sapin," *The Drama Review* 38, no. 1 (Spring 1994): 45–62.

80. Nicanor G. Tiongson, "Mexican-Philippine Relations in Traditional Folk Theater," *Philippine Studies* 46, no. 2 (Second Quarter 1998): 135–50, 146–47.
81. Tiongson, "Mexican-Philippine Relations," 145.
82. Isaac J. Donoso, "The Hispanic Moros y Cristianos and the Philippine Komedya," *Philippine Humanities Review* 11/12 (2009/2010): 87–120, 101–102; Tiongson, "Mexican-Philippine Relations," 145.
83. Nicanor G. Tiongson, *Philippine Theatre: History and Anthology, Vol. 2: Komedya* (University of Philippines Press, 1999), 35.
84. Tiongson, *Philippine Theatre*, vol. 2, 35.
85. Donoso, "Hispanic Moros y Cristianos," 110.
86. Tiongson, "Mexican-Philippine Relations," 147.
87. Brandon, *Theatre in Southeast Asia*, 113.

11 Erasmus's Prophecy

1. This discussion of European theatre draws from Steve Tillis, *The Challenge of World Theatre History* (Palgrave Macmillan, 2020), 278–82.
2. Desiderius Erasmus, "Letter to a Friend on Present Conditions," https://shorturl.at/8aI3T.
3. James Belich, "The Black Death and the Spread of Europe," in *PGH*, 96.
4. Wolfgang Reinhard, "Europe and the Atlantic World," in *E&E*, 787.
5. Peter Burke, "Patterns of Urbanization, 1400 to 1800," in *CWH6.1*, 120.
6. Peter Hall, *Cities in Civilization* (Pantheon, 1998), 115.
7. Hall, *Cities in Civilization*, 121.
8. Jerry H. Bentley, *Old World Encounters: Cross-Cultural Contacts and Exchanges in Pre-modern Times* (Oxford University Press, 1993), 183.
9. William H. McNeill, *The Rise of the West: A History of the Human Community* (University of Chicago Press, 1963), 530, n. 97.
10. William H. McNeill, *The Shape of European History* (Oxford University Press, 1974), 108.
11. Richard Smith, "Trade and Commerce across Afro-Eurasia," in *CWH5*, 253.
12. Fernand Braudel, *Out of Italy: 1450–1650*, trans. Siân Reynolds (Flammarion, 1991), 12.
13. Alan E. Knight, "France," in *TME*, 158.
14. Eckhard Simon, "German Medieval Theatre: Tenth Century to 1600," in *HGT*, 18–21.
15. Pamela M. King, "Morality Plays," in *The Cambridge Companion to Medieval English Theatre*, ed. Richard Beadle (Cambridge University Press, 1994), 240.
16. John Wesley Harris, *Medieval Theatre in Context: An Introduction* (Routledge, 1992), 160.
17. Alexandra F. Johnston, "All the World Was a Stage: Records of Early English Drama," in *TME*, 118–19.

18. Robert N. Watson, "Tragedy," in *The Cambridge Companion to English Renaissance Drama*, eds. A. R. Braunmuller and Michael Hattaway (Cambridge University Press, 1990), 334.
19. Braudel, *Out of Italy*, 46.
20. John Hale, *The Civilization of Europe in the Renaissance* (Simon & Schuster, 1993), 325–26.
21. Deno John Geanakoplos, *Constantinople and the West: Essays on the Late Byzantine (Palaeologan) and Italian Renaissances and the Byzantine and Roman Churches* (University of Wisconsin Press, 1989), 61, 5.
22. Geanakoplos, *Constantinople and the West*, 39.
23. Richard Andrews, "The Renaissance Stage," in *HIT*, 31.
24. Peter Brand, "Ariosto and Ferrara," in *HIT*, 47.
25. Pavel Drábek, "Circulation: Aristocratic, Commercial, Religious and Artistic Networks," in *CHTEMA*, 105.
26. Hale, *Civilization of Europe in the Renaissance*, 195.
27. Olly Crick, "The Coming Together," in *The Routledge Companion to Commedia dell'Arte*, eds. Judith Chaffee and Olly Crick (Routledge, 2015), 222.
28. Note that *commedia dell'arte* is an anachronistic name for the form, first used in the eighteenth century. Earlier names included *commedia all'improvviso*, *commedia mercenaria*, and (as the troupes toured beyond Italy) *commedia all'italiano*. Daniele Vianello, "Introduction: Commedia dell'Arte: History, Myth, Reception," in *Commedia dell'Arte in Context*, eds. Christopher B. Balme, Piermario Vescovo, and Danile Vianello (Cambridge University Press, 2018), 4.
29. Kenneth Richards and Laura Richards, "*Commedia dell'Arte*," in *HIT*, 105.
30. Richards and Richards, "*Commedia dell'Arte*," 106.
31. Ferdinando Taviani, "Knots and Doubleness: The Engine of the Commedia dell'Arte," in *Commedia dell'Arte in Context*, eds. Christopher B. Balme, Piermario Vescovo, and Danile Vianello (Cambridge University Press, 2018), 25–28.
32. Crick, "Coming Together," 222.
33. Richards and Richards, "*Commedia dell'Arte*," 115.
34. Taviani, "Knots and Doubleness," 29, 31.
35. Braudel, *Out of Italy*, 147.
36. Richards and Richards, "*Commedia dell'Arte*," 104.
37. Richards and Richards, "*Commedia dell'Arte*," 104.
38. Taviani, "Knots and Doubleness," 31.
39. Henryk Ziomek, *A History of Spanish Golden Age Drama* (University Press of Kentucky, 1984), 33. Additional entertainments in the program included an introductory *loa* ("a monologue or dialogue" calling for "the good will of the audience") and *entremeses* ("farces in verse") that were performed between the acts of the play (33).
40. Burke, "Patterns of Urbanization," 123.
41. Melveena McKendrick, *Theatre in Spain: 1490–1700* (Cambridge University Press, 1989), 72, 193.

42. Hall, *Cities in Civilization*, 116, 125.
43. Georges Mongrédien, *Daily Life in the French Theatre: At the Time of Molière*, trans. Claire Eliane Engel (George Allen and Unwin, 1969), 45.
44. Mongrédien, *Daily Life in the French Theatre*, 28; John Lough, *Paris Theatre Audiences in the Seventeenth and Eighteenth Centuries* (Oxford University Press, 1957), 43.
45. Jean-Noël Biraben and Blanchet Didier, "Essay on the Population of Paris and Its Vicinity since the Sixteenth Century," *Population, an English Selection* 11, no. 1 (1999): 155–88, 183–84. www.persee.fr/doc/pop_0032-4663_1999_hos_11_1_6984
46. Lough, *Paris Theatre Audiences*, 81, 80.
47. Ziomek, *History of Spanish Golden Age Drama*, 35.
48. Andrew Gurr, *The Shakespearean Stage*, 3rd ed. (Cambridge University Press, 1992), 103.
49. John Lough, *Seventeenth-Century French Drama: The Background* (Oxford University Press, 1979), 33.
50. McKendrick, *Theatre in Spain*, 74.
51. Ziomek, *History of Spanish Golden Age Drama*, 41–42.
52. Friedmann Kreuder, "Repertoire and Genres," in *CHTEMA*, 153, 154.
53. Marvin Carlson, *Theories of the Theatre: A Historical and Critical Survey, from the Greeks to the Present* (Cornell University Press, 1984), 93.
54. Lough, *Seventeenth-Century French Drama*, 118.
55. Stephan Orgel, *Impersonations: The Performance of Gender in Shakespeare's England* (Cambridge University Press, 1996), 4–5; Hugo Albert Rennert, *The Spanish Stage in the Time of Lope de Vega* (Dover Publications, 1963), 137–38.
56. Rennert, *Spanish Stage*, 142–44.
57. McKendrick, *Theatre in Spain*, 186.
58. Lough, *Seventeenth-Century French Drama*, 12.
59. Orgel, *Impersonations*, 2.
60. Robert Henke, "Introduction: Culture, Cultural History, and Early Modern Theatre," in *CHTEMA*, 13–14.
61. Orgel, *Impersonations*, 3, 49.
62. Laurence Senelick, *The Changing Room: Sex, Drag, and Theatre* (Routledge, 2000), 150, 133.
63. The "University Wits" included playwrights Christopher Marlowe, Robert Greene, Thomas Nashe, John Lyly, and George Peele.
64. W. R. Streitberger, "Personnel and Professionalization," in *A New History of Early English Drama*, eds. John D. Cox and David Scott Kasten (Columbia University Press, 1997), 350.
65. Streitberger, "Personnel and Professionalization," 350.
66. Senelick, *Changing Room*, 142.
67. Quoted in Peter Burian, "Tragedy Adapted for Stages and Screens: The Renaissance to the Present," in *CCGT*, 262.
68. David Kimball, *Italian Opera* (Cambridge University Press, 1991), 55.

69. Fiona Macintosh, "Tragedy in Performance: Nineteenth- and Twentieth-Century Productions," in *CCGT*, 285.
70. Ruth Katz, "Collective 'Problem-Solving' in the History of Music: The Case of the Camerata," *Journal of the History of Ideas* 45, no. 3 (July–September 1984): 361–77, 367.
71. Ellen Rosand, *Opera in Seventeenth-Century Venice: The Creation of a Genre* (University of California Press, 1990), 4.
72. Donald Jay Grout and Hermine Weigel Williams, *A Short History of Opera*, 4th ed. (Columbia University Press, 2003), 44–45.
73. Sara Elise Stangalino, "Aria, Recitative, and Chorus in Italian Opera," in *The Cambridge Companion to Seventeenth Century Opera*, ed. Jacqueline Waeber (Cambridge University Press, 2022), 47.
74. Burian, "Tragedy Adapted for Stages and Screens," 263.
75. Rosand, *Opera in Seventeenth-Century Venice*, 2, 3, 15.
76. Jennifer Homans, *Apollo's Angels: A History of Ballet* (Random House, 2010), 4.
77. Braudel, *Out of Italy*, 150.
78. Homans, *Apollo's Angels*, 7–8, quotation on 7.
79. Martin Butler, "Private and Occasional Drama," in *The Cambridge Companion to English Renaissance Drama*, eds. A. R. Braunmuller and Michael Hattaway (Cambridge University Press, 1990), 133, 136.
80. Mary Clarke and Clement Crisp, *Ballet: An Illustrated History* (Universe Books, 1973), 27; Stephen Orgel, *The Illusion of Power: Political Theater in the English Renaissance* (University of California Press, 1975), 40–41.
81. Graham Parry, "Entertainments at Court," in *A New History of Early English Drama*, eds. John D. Cox and David Scott Kastan (Columbia University Press, 1997), 210.
82. William N. West, "Communities of Production: Lives in and out of the Theatre," in *CHTEMA*, 128.
83. Fernand Braudel, *The Mediterranean and the Mediterranean World in the Age of Philip II*, trans. Siân Reynolds (Harper & Row, 1972), vol. 2, 1243–44.
84. Michael Adas, "Bringing Ideas and Agency Back In: Representation and the Comparative Approach to World History," in *World History: Ideologies, Structures, and Identities*, eds. Philip Pomper, Richard H. Elphick, and Richard T. Vann (Blackwell, 1998), 87.
85. For an overview of the debate, see Andre Gundar Frank, *ReORIENT: Global Economy in the Asian Age* (University of California Press, 1998), 230–48.

Part V The Global Transformation (starting c. 1800 CE)

1. This introduction draws from Steve Tillis, *The Challenge of World Theatre History* (Palgrave Macmillan, 2022), 287–89.
2. Jürgen Osterhammel, "Hierarchies and Connections: Aspects of a Global Social History," in *AEW*, 670–71.

3. Sebastian Conrad, "A Cultural History of Global Transformation," in *AEW*, 447.
4. R. Bin Wong, "Possibilities of Plenty and the Persistence of Poverty: Industrialization and International Trade," in *AEW*, 276.
5. Jürgen Osterhammel, *The Transformation of the World: A Global History of the Nineteenth Century*, trans. Patrick Camiller (Princeton University Press, 2014), 728.
6. Osterhammel, *Transformation of the World*, 638.
7. John Darwin, *After Tamerlane: The Global History of Empire since 1405* (Bloomsbury Press, 2008), 300.
8. Darwin, *After Tamerlane*, 299.
9. Conrad, "Cultural History of Global Transformation," 417–18, 418, 422.
10. Conrad, "Cultural History of Global Transformation," 423.
11. Patrick Manning, "Migration in Human History," in *CWH1*, 304.
12. Nile Green, *How Asia Found Herself: A Story of Intercultural Understanding* (Yale University Press, 2022), 24.
13. Kaoru Sugihara, "Global Industrialization: A Multipolar Perspective," in *CWH7.1*, 108.
14. Charles Bright and Michael Geyer, "Benchmarks of Globalization: The Global Condition, 1850–2010," in *CtWH*, 293.

12 The Dynamo of Transformation

1. Norman Davies, *Europe: A History* (Oxford University Press, 1996), 759.
2. Jürgen Osterhammel, *The Transformation of the World: A Global History of the Nineteenth Century*, trans. Patrick Camiller (Princeton University Press, 2014), 675.
3. Osterhammel, *Transformation of the World*, 331.
4. Osterhammel, *Transformation of the World*, 761; italics in the original.
5. Peter W. Marx, "Interpretations: The Interpretation of Theatre," in *CHTAEmp*, 135.
6. Jim Davis, "Social Functions: The Social Function of Theatre," in *CHTAEmp*, 51.
7. Stephen Prickett, "General Introduction: Of Fragments, Monsters and Translations," in *European Romanticism: A Reader*, eds. Stephen Prickett and Simon Haines (Bloomsbury, 2010), 15; the embedded quotation comes from Christophe Bode; italics in the original.
8. Jacques Barzun, *From Dawn to Decadence: 500 Years of Western Cultural Life, 1500 to the Present* (HarperCollins, 2000), 466, 468, 473.
9. Barzun, *From Dawn to Decadence*, 470.
10. Osterhammel, *Transformation of the World*, 18; italics in the original.
11. Bertolt Brecht, *Brecht on Theatre*, ed. and trans. John Willett (Hill & Wang, 1964), 109.
12. This is roughly how Émile Zola writes of naturalism. Marvin Carlson, *Theories of the Theatre: A Historical and Critical Survey, from the Greeks to the Present* (Cornell University Press, 1984), 275.

13. Jennifer Homans, *Apollo's Angels: A History of Ballet* (Random House, 2010), 122.
14. Ivor Guest, *The Romantic Ballet in Paris*, 2nd rev. ed. (Dance Books Ltd., 1980), 5, 106.
15. Homans, *Apollo's Angels*, 309, 312, 310.
16. Vlado Kotnik, "The Adaptability of Opera: When Different Social Agents Come to Common Ground," *International Review of the Aesthetics and Sociology of Music* 44, no. 2 (December 2013): 303–42, 321.
17. Kotnik, "Adaptability of Opera," 318, 313.
18. Stephen Wilmer, "Nationalism and Its Effects on the German Theatre," in *HGT*, 230.
19. Christopher Innes, "The Rise of the Director, 1850–1939," in *HGT*, 180. Richard Wagner also designed the *Festspielhaus* (Festival Playhouse) in Bayrueth, Germany, as a permanent home for his operas.
20. Nicola Savarese, *Eurasian Theatre: Drama and Performance between East and West from Classical Antiquity to the Present*, trans. Richard Fowler, rev. and ed. Vicki Ann Cremona (Routledge, 2010), 446.
21. Alan Mallach, *The Autumn of Italian Opera: From Verismo to Modernism, 1890–1915* (Northeastern University Press, 2007), 43.
22. Quoted in Robert Donnington, *Opera and Its Symbols: The Unity of Words, Music, and Staging* (Yale University Press, 1990), 151.
23. Zoltán Imre, "Representing a Nation through Popular Theatre: The Vienna-Budapest Operetta," in *CHTAEmp*, 172.
24. Cristopher Webber, *The Zarzuela Companion* (Scarecrow Press, 2002), 4.
25. Quoted in Eric Bentley, *The Life of the Drama* (Atheneum, 1983), 210.
26. Simon Shepherd and Peter Womack, *English Drama: A Cultural History* (Blackwell Publishers, 1996), 201; italics in the original.
27. Jim Davis, "Melodrama on and off the Stage," in *The Oxford Handbook of Victorian Literary Culture*, ed. Juliet John (Oxford University Press, 2016), 690.
28. Jim Davis, "Theatres and Their Audiences," in *The Cambridge Companion to English Melodrama*, ed. Carolyn Williams (Cambridge University Press, 2018), 78.
29. Quoted in Juliet John, "Melodrama and Its Criticism: An Essay in Memory of Sally Ledger," *19: Interdisciplinary Studies in the Long Nineteenth Century* 8 (2009): 1–20, 2. http://doi.org/10.16995/ntn.496.
30. Matthew Buckley, "Early English Melodrama," in *The Cambridge Companion to English Melodrama*, ed. Carolyn Williams (Cambridge University Press, 2018), 21–22, 22.
31. Martha Vicinus, "'Helpless and Unfriended': Nineteenth-Century Domestic Melodrama," in *When They Weren't Doing Shakespeare: Essays on Nineteenth-Century British and American Theatre*, eds. Judith L. Fisher and Stephen Watt (The University of Georgia Press, 1989), 179–80.
32. Bentley, *Life of the Drama*, 205.
33. Quoted in John, "Melodrama and Its Criticism," 3.
34. Simon Williams, "The Romantic Spirit in the German Theatre, 1790–1910," in *HGT*, 123.

35. Erika Fischer-Lichte, *History of European Drama and Theatre*, trans. Jo Riley (Routledge, 2002), 204, 219.
36. John Russell Taylor, *The Rise and Fall of the Well-Made Play* (Hill and Wang, 1967), 12.
37. Quoted in Stephen S. Stanton, "Introduction," in *Camille and Other Plays*, ed. Stephen S. Stanton (Hill and Wang, 1957), vii, note 2.
38. Bentley, *Life of the Drama*, 23.
39. Stanton, "Introduction," vii.
40. Stanton, "Introduction," xxix.
41. Quoted in Eric Bentley, *The Playwright as Thinker* (Harcourt, Brace & World, 1967), 7.
42. Quoted in Frederick J. Marker and Lisa-Lone Marker, *A History of Scandinavian Theatre* (Cambridge University Press, 1996), 199.
43. Maurice Valency, *The Breaking String: The Plays of Anton Chekhov* (Schocken Books, 1983), 184.
44. Marx, "Interpretations," 145.
45. Bentley, *Playwright as Thinker*, 6.
46. Christopher Innes, *Avant Garde Theatre: 1892–1992* (Routledge, 1993), 23, 25.
47. Stefan Hulfeld, "Modernist Theatre," in *CCTH*, 22.
48. Hulfeld, "Modernist Theatre," 30.
49. Min Tian, *The Poetics of Difference and Displacement: Twentieth-Century Chinese-Western Intercultural Theatre* (Hong Kong University Press, 2008), 11.
50. Savarese, *Eurasian Theatre*, 518, 517; italics in the original.
51. Rustom Bharucha, *Theatre and the World: Performance and the Politics of Culture* (Routledge, 1993), 14, 15.
52. Antonin Artaud, *The Theatre and Its Double*, trans. Mary Caroline Richards (Grove Press, 1958), 53.
53. Innes, *Avant Garde Theatre*, 11.
54. Brecht, *Brecht on Theatre*, 138.
55. Brecht, *Brecht on Theatre*, 143–46.
56. Tian, *Poetics of Difference and Displacement*, 57.
57. Innes, *Avant Garde Theatre*, 92.
58. Christopher B. Balme, *Decolonizing the Stage: Theatrical Syncretism and Postcolonial Theatre* (Clarendon Press, 1999), 17. The internal quotation comes from Joachim Fiebach.

13 The Neo-Europes

1. Alfred. W. Crosby, *Ecological Imperialism: The Biological Expansion of Europe, 900–1900*, 2nd ed. (Cambridge University Press, 2015), 5–7, 36.
2. Patrick Manning, *Slavery and African Life: Occidental, Oriental, and African Slave Trades* (Cambridge University Press, 1990), 104. Some 43 percent of all slaves were sent to the Caribbean islands, while 38.2 percent went to Brazil. The rest were divided between elsewhere in South America (11.8 percent),

North America (4.5 percent), and Central America (2.4 percent). William J. Bernstein, *A Splendid Exchange: How Trade Shaped the World* (Grove Press, 2008), 277.
3. Martin W. Lewis and Kären E. Wigen, *The Myth of Continents: A Critique of Metageography* (University of California Press, 1997), 182.
4. Dirk Hoerder, "Migrations," in *CWH7.2*, 12.
5. Note that "settler colony theory" has focused primarily on British colonization. Its application to Latin America is very much under contention. See Lucy Taylor and Geraldine Lublin, "Settler Colonial Studies and Latin America," *Settler Colonial Studies* 11, no. 3 (2021), 259–70.
6. Wolfgang Reinhard, "Europe and the Atlantic World," in *E&E*, 892.
7. Philippa Brown Yin, "Overview of Latin American Theatre," in *ELAT*, xvii.
8. Susan Castillo, *Colonial Encounters in New World Writing, 1500–1786: Performing America* (Routledge, 2006), 9.
9. Dennis Tedlock, ed. and trans., *Rabinal Achi: A Mayan Drama of War and Sacrifice*, trans. (Oxford University Press, 2003), 2.
10. Felicia Hardison Londré and Daniel J. Watermeier, *The History of North American Theatre: The United States, Canada, and Mexico: From Pre-Columbian Times to the Present* (Continuum, 1998), 29, 30.
11. Judith A. Weiss, et al., *Latin American Popular Theatre: The First Five Centuries* (University of New Mexico Press, 1993), 41.
12. Castillo, *Colonial Encounters in New World Writing*, 44–45.
13. Max Harris, *Aztecs, Moors, and Christians: Festivals of Reconquest in Mexico and Spain* (University of Texas Press, 2000), 123–31, 132–47.
14. Castillo, *Colonial Encounters in New World Writing*, 49.
15. Harris, *Aztecs, Moors, and Christians*, 139.
16. Weiss et al., *Latin American Popular Theatre*, 4.
17. Castillo, *Colonial Encounters in New World Writing*, 190, 191.
18. Yin, "Overview of Latin American Theatre," xix.
19. Castillo, *Colonial Encounters in New World Writing*, 199.
20. E. J. Westlake, *World Theatre: The Basics* (Routledge, 2017), 134.
21. Weiss et al., *Latin American Popular Theatre*, 65.
22. Yin, "Overview of Latin American Theatre," xx.
23. Fernando Peixoto, with Susana Epstein and Richard Schechner, "Brazilian Theatre and National Identity," *TDR: The Drama Review* 34, no. 1 (Spring 1990): 60–69, 61.
24. Londré and Watermeier, *History of North American Theatre*, 148.
25. Londré and Watermeier, *History of North American Theatre*, 98.
26. Yin, "Overview of Latin American Theatre," xxi–xxii.
27. Quoted in Laurence Senelick, "Musical Theatre as a Paradigm of Translocation," *Journal of Global Theatre History* 2, no. 1 (2017): 22–36, 28.
28. Londré and Watermeier, *History of North American Theatre*, 231–32; Yin, "Overview of Latin American Theatre," xxii, xxiv; Mirta Barrea-Marlys, "Argentina," in *ELAT*, 4.
29. Yin, "Overview of Latin American Theatre," xxv.

30. Victoria Lynn Garrett, *Performing Everyday Life in Argentine Popular Theater, 1890–1934* (Palgrave Macmillan, 2018), 16.
31. Dennis Kennedy, ed., *The Oxford Encyclopedia of Theatre and Performance*, Vol. 2 (Oxford University Press, 2003), 1174.
32. Weiss et al., *Latin American Popular Theatre*, 97–98.
33. Yin, "Overview of Latin American Theatre," xxv.
34. Londré and Watermeier, *History of North American Theatre*, 336, 337–42.
35. Weiss et al., *Latin American Popular Theatre*, 5.
36. Jürgen Osterhammel, *The Transformation of the World: A Global History of the Nineteenth Century*, trans. Patrick Camiller (Princeton University Press, 2014), 132.
37. Kole Omotoso, *The Theatrical into Theatre: A Study of the Drama and Theatre of the English-Speaking Caribbean* (New Beacon Books, 1982), 46–47.
38. Errol Hill, "Introduction to the English-Speaking Caribbean," in *CGACT*, 146.
39. Londré and Watermeier, *History of North American Theatre*, 63.
40. John Thornton, "The Slave Trade and the African Diaspora," in *CWH6.2*, 150. Enslaved Africans in the United States had a similar "cultural diversity." Enslaved Africans in Brazil, however, were mostly from the Portuguese colony in Angola (150).
41. Osita Okagbue, *Culture and Identity in African and Caribbean Theatre* (Adonis & Abbey Publishers, 2009), 143, 193.
42. Thornton, "Slave Trade and the African Diaspora," 152–53.
43. Peter Reed, "'There Was No Resisting John Canoe': Circum-Atlantic Transracial Performance," *Theatre History Studies* 27 (2007): 65–85, 65, 67, 69.
44. Reed, "'There Was No Resisting John Canoe,'" 70–71.
45. Reed, "'There Was No Resisting John Canoe,'" 67, 69, 75.
46. Errol Hill, "Perspectives in Caribbean Theatre: Ritual, Festival, and Drama," *Caribbean Quarterly* 46, no. 3/4 (September–December 2000): 1–11, 5–6.
47. Londré and Watermeier, *History of North American Theatre*, 158, 239, 240.
48. Errol Hill, *The Jamaican Stage 1655–1900: Profile of a Colonial Theatre* (University of Massachusetts Press, 1992), 28.
49. Hill, "Perspectives in Caribbean Theatre," 6.
50. David Mason, "Ritual and Theatrical Performance in Ramdilla," *Asian Theatre Journal* 37, no. 1 (Spring 2020): 179–99, 182.
51. Mason, "Ritual and Theatrical Performance in Ramdilla," 191, 193.
52. For an extended first-person account, see Guha Shankar, "Imagining India(ns): Cultural Performances and Diaspora Politics in Jamaica" (Dissertation, University of Texas at Austin, 2003).
53. Frank Korom, "Reconciling the Local and the Global: The Ritual Space of Shi'i Islam in Trinidad," *Journal of Ritual Studies* 13, no. 1 (Summer 1999): 21–36, 26.
54. Omotoso, *Theatrical into Theatre*, 29.
55. Jeffrey Huntsman, "Native American Theatre," in *American Indian Theater in Performance: A Reader*, eds. Hanay Geiogamah and Jaye T. Darby (UCLA American Indian Studies Center, 2000), 81, 83, 85–86.

56. Brian Eugenio Herrera, "To Imagine a Nuevomexicano Theatre History," in *Theatre and Cartographies of Power: Repositioning the Latina/o Americas*, eds. Jimmy A. Noriega and Analola Santana (Southern Illinois University Press, 2018), 83; see also 94, n. 1.
57. Londré and Watermeier, *History of North American Theatre*, 132.
58. David Emmett Gardner, "An Analytic History of the Theatre in Canada: The European Beginnings to 1760" (Dissertation, University of Toronto, 1982), 182.
59. Eugene Benson and L. W. Conolly, *The Oxford Companion to Canadian Theatre* (Oxford University Press, 1989), 150, 153.
60. John O'Brien, "Institutional Frameworks: The State, the Market and the People in the Age of Enlightenment," in *CHTAEnl*, 21.
61. Andrew B. Harris, *Broadway Theatre* (Routledge, 1994), 4.
62. Daniel C. Gerould, "The Americanization of Melodrama," in *American Melodrama*, ed. Daniel C. Gerould (PAJ Publications, 1983), 7.
63. William Coyle and Harvey G. Damaser, "Introduction," in *Six Early American Plays: 1798–1890*, eds. William Coyle and Harvey G. Damaser (Charles E. Merrill, 1968), vii.
64. Gardner, "Analytic History of the Theatre in Canada," 388.
65. Ira Berlin, *The Making of African America: The Four Great Migrations* (Penguin Books, 2010), 29.
66. Bernstein, *Splendid Exchange*, 278.
67. Berlin, *Making of African America*, 219.
68. Reed, "'There Was No Resisting John Canoe,'" 65.
69. Joseph R. Roach, "Deep Skin: Reconstructing Congo Square," in *African American Performance and Theater History: A Critical Reader*, eds. Harry J. Elam, Jr., and David Krasner (Oxford University Press, 2001), 103, 107.
70. Kellen Hoxworth, "The Jim Crow Global South," *Theatre Journal* 72, no. 4 (December 2020): 443–67, 450.
71. Don B. Wilmeth and Tice L. Miller, *Cambridge Guide to American Theatre* (Cambridge University Press, 1996), 262.
72. Robert B. Winans, "Early Minstrel Show Music, 1843–1852," in *IMM*, 160–61.
73. Eric Lott, *Love and Theft: Blackface Minstrelsy and the American Working Class* (Oxford University Press, 2013), 41.
74. Alexander Saxton, "Blackface Minstrelsy," in *IMM*, 79.
75. Hoxworth, "Jim Crow Global South," 456, 446, 453.
76. Gerould, "Americanization of Melodrama," 14.
77. Judith Williams, "Uncle Tom's Women," in *African American Performance and Theater History: A Critical Reader*, eds. Harry J. Elam, Jr., and David Krasner (Oxford University Press, 2001), 20.
78. Gerould, "Americanization of Melodrama," 14–15, 17.
79. Douglas Jones, "'The Black Below': Minstrelsy, Satire, and the Threat of Vernacularity," *Theatre Journal* 73, no. 2 (June 2021): 129–46, 136.
80. Jones, "'The Black Below,'" 132, 129.
81. Osterhammel, *Transformation of the World*, 156.

82. Daphne Lei, "The Production and Consumption of Chinese Theatre in Nineteenth-Century California," *Theatre Research International* 28, no. 3 (October 2003): 289–302, 292.
83. Robert Toll, "Social Commentary in Late Nineteenth-Century White Minstrelsy," in *IMM*, 86, 98.
84. Larry Stempel, *Showtime: A History of the Broadway Musical Theatre* (W. W. Norton, 2010), 47, 49.
85. Stempel, *Showtime*, 68, 70. Along the same lines, Jospeh Weber and Lew Fields created a series of variety-like musical shows around a pair of "Dutch" (i.e., German) characters (79–84).
86. Allen Woll, *Black Musical Theatre: From Coontown to Dreamgirls* (Louisiana University Press), 1989, 32–33.
87. Stempel, *Showtime*, 89.
88. Gerald Bordman, *American Musical Theatre: A Chronicle*, expanded ed. (Oxford University Press, 1986), 190–91; Stempel, *Showtime*, 90–91.
89. Stempel, *Showtime*, 135.
90. George Hauger, "Musical Comedy," *CGT*, 770.
91. Stempel, *Showtime*, 174–80.
92. Joseph P Swain, *The Broadway Musical: A Critical and Musical Survey* (Oxford University Press, 1990), 19–27.
93. Stempel, *Showtime*, 194.
94. Bordman, *American Musical Theatre*, 435.
95. Osterhammel, *Transformation of the World*, 135, 118.
96. Jim Davis, "Social Functions of Theatre," in *CHTAEmp*, 71, 72.
97. Margaret Williams, "Australia," in *CGT*, 58.
98. Howard McNaughton, "New Zealand," in *CGT*, 789.
99. Maryrose Casey, *Telling Stories: Aboriginal Australian and Torres Strait Islander Performance* (Australian Scholarly, 2012), 20.
100. Casey, *Telling Stories*, 23, 38, 23.
101. Casey, *Telling Stories*, 8.
102. Maryrose Casey, "Theatre or Corroboree, What's in a Name? Framing Indigenous Australian 19th-Century Commercial Performance Practices," in *Creating White Australia*, eds. Jane Carey and Claire McLisky (Sydney University Press, 2009), 139.
103. Ronald M. Berndt and Catherine H. Berndt, *The World of the First Australians: Aboriginal Traditional Life: Past and Present*, 5th ed. (Aboriginal Studies Press, 1999), 381.
104. Casey, "Theatre or Corroboree," 125, 123.

14 Colonial Experiences

1. John Darwin, *After Tamerlane: The Global History of Empire since 1405* (Bloomsbury Press, 2008), 304–305.
2. David Kerr, *African Popular Theatre: From Pre-colonial Times to the Present Day* (James Currey, 1995), 41.

3. Kathryn Hansen, "Parsi Theatrical Networks in Southeast Asia: The Contrary Case of Burma." *Journal of Southeast Asian Studies* 49, no. 1 (February 2018): 4–33, 4.
4. Andrew P. Killick, "Jockeying for Tradition: The Checkered History of Korean Ch'anggŭk Opera," *Asian Theatre Journal* 20, no. 1 (Spring 2003): 43–70, 51. Andrew P. Killick credits Hanne de Bruin for coining the term "hybrid-fusion."
5. Patrick Manning, *Slavery and African Life: Occidental, Oriental, and African Slave Trades* (Cambridge University Press, 1990), 16.
6. Frederick Cooper, "Africa in World History," in *CWH7.1*, 562.
7. Darwin, *After Tamerlane*, 305, 316.
8. Osita Okagbue, *African Theatres and Performances* (Routledge, 2007), 4–5.
9. Biodun Jeyifo, "The Reinvention of Theatrical Tradition," in *Modern African Drama*, ed. Biodun Jeyifo (W. W. Norton, 2002), 465; italics in the original.
10. Martin Banham, Errol Hill, and George Woodyard, "Masquerades in Africa" in *CGACT*, 4–5.
11. Okagbue, *African Theatres and Performances*, 14.
12. Walter E. A. van Beek and Harrie M. Leyten, *Masquerades in African Society: Gender, Power, and Identity* (Boydell & Brester, 2023), 13.
13. Walter E. A. van Beek, "Masks versus Cattle: The Ecology of an African Art Form," *Human Ecology* 52 (2024): 851–65, 854; https://doi.org/10.1007/s10745-024-00484-7. This distribution closely aligns with a mapping of forty masquerade traditions that was published in Steve Tillis, *The Challenge of World Theatre History* (Palgrave Macmillan, 2020), figure 5.3.
14. Van Beek and Leyten, *Masquerades in African Society*, 22.
15. Van Beek and Leyten, *Masquerades in African Society*, 23.
16. Van Beek and Leyten, *Masquerades in African Society*, 40. The absence of masking in what is sometimes called "the Akan Gap" (between zones 1 and 2) is ascribed largely to the "unique political structure" of the Ashanti that owes in part to the availability of gold as a means of heritable wealth (247).
17. David Reich, *Who We Are and How We Got Here: Ancient DNA and the New Science of the Human Past* (Vintage Books, 2018), 214.
18. Raphael Chijioke Njoku, *West African Masking Traditions and Diaspora Masquerade Carnivals: History, Memory, and Transnationalism* (University of Rochester Press, 2020), 11–12. Note, though, that Walter E. A. van Beek and Harrie M. Leyten think it "almost impossible to derive a monogenetic hypothesis." *Masquerades in African Society*, 342.
19. Susan Elizabeth Gagliardi, "Art and the Individual in African Masquerades: Introduction," *Africa* 88, no. 4 (2018): 702–17, 703. https://doi.org/10.1017/S0001972018000438.
20. Okagbue, *African Theatres and Performances*, 10, 12.
21. Okagbue, *African Theatres and Performances*, 12, 75.
22. Biodun Jeyifo, "Preface," in *Modern African Drama*, ed. Biodun Jeyifo (W. W. Norton, 2002), vii–viii.

23. Joel Adedeji, "Alarinjo: The Traditional Yoruba Travelling Theatre," in *Drama and Theatre in Nigeria: A Critical Source Book*, ed. Yemi Ogunbiyi (Nigeria Magazine, 1981), 221–23.
24. Jeyifo, "Preface," xii.
25. Adedeji, "Alarinjo," 224–27; Kacke Götrick, *Apidán Theatre and Modern Drama: A Study in Traditional Yoruba Theatre and Its Influence on Modern Drama by Yoruba Playwrights* (Almqvist and Wiskell International, 1984), 39.
26. Götrick, *Apidán Theatre and Modern Drama*, 98.
27. Okagbue, *African Theatres and Performances*, 273.
28. Okagbue, *African Theatres and Performances*, 274–76.
29. Chris Dunton, "Nigeria," in *CGACT*, 70.
30. For an observer's account of developments in the form over its first thirty years, see Peggy Harper, "The Kwag-hir of the People of Tiv: A Note on Dramatized History Telling and Constructions of Nature among the Tiv of Southern Nigeria," *Environment and History* 3, no. 3 (October 1997): 371–76. www.environmentandsociety.org/node/2949.
31. Karin Barber, John Collins, and Alain Ricard, *West African Popular Theatre* (Indiana University Press, 1997), 14; Catherine M. Cole, *Ghana's Concert Party Theatre* (Indiana University Press, 2001), 76–77.
32. Cole, *Ghana's Concert Party Theatre*, 1, 8.
33. Cole, *Ghana's Concert Party Theatre*, 26, 20.
34. Barber, Collins, and Ricard, *West African Popular Theatre*, 2, 3.
35. Barber, Collins, and Ricard, *West African Popular Theatre*, 38, 39.
36. Barber, Collins, and Ricard, *West African Popular Theatre*, 39–40; Biodun Jeyifo, *The Yoruba Popular Travelling Theatre of Nigeria* (Nigeria Magazine, 1984), 70–73.
37. John Conteh-Morgan, "Francophone Africa South of the Sahara," in *A History of Theatre in Africa*, ed. Martin Banham (Cambridge University Press, 2004), 114, 115, 117.
38. Conteh-Morgan, "Francophone Africa South of the Sahara," 121, 122, 86.
39. Mineke Schipper, *Theatre and Society in Africa*, trans. Ampie Coetzee (Raven Press, 1982), 154–55.
40. Christopher B. Balme, *Decolonizing the Stage: Theatrical Syncretism and Postcolonial Theatre* (Clarendon Press, 1999), 108–109, 114.
41. Ngugu Wa Thiong'o, "The Language of African Literature," in *The Postcolonial Studies Reader*, eds. Bill Ashcroft, Gareth Griffins, and Helen Tiffin (Routledge, 1995), 290.
42. Conteh-Morgan, "Francophone Africa South of the Sahara," 125, 128.
43. Osita Okagbue, *Culture and Identity in African and Caribbean Theatre* (Adonis & Abbey Publishers, 2009), 198.
44. Stanley Wolpert, *A New History of India*, 4th ed. (Oxford University Press, 1993), 173.
45. John Keay, *India: A History* (Grove Press, 2000), 377–401.
46. Keay, *India*, 371–72.

47. Jürgen Osterhammel, *The Transformation of the World: A Global History of the Nineteenth Century*, trans. Patrick Camiller (Princeton University Press, 2014), 551.
48. Keay, *India*, 437.
49. Osterhammel, *Transformation of the World*, 553.
50. Keay, *India*, 445.
51. Quoted in Victor Lieberman, *Strange Parallels: Southeast Asia in Global Context, c. 800–1830, Vol. 2: Mainland Mirrors: Europe, Japan, China, South Asia, and the Islands* (Cambridge University Press, 2009), 759.
52. Osterhammel, *Transformation of the World*, 52, 57.
53. Aparna Dharwadker, "Modern Indian Theatre," in *RHAT*, 245.
54. Darius L. Swann, "Rām Līlā," in *IT:TP*, 222, 218.
55. Pamela Lothspeich, "Introduction: The Field of Ramlila," *Asian Theatre Journal* 37, no. 1 (Spring 2020): 3–33, 10.
56. Lothspeich, "Introduction," 10, 7.
57. Tevia Abrams, "Folk Theatre in Maharashtrian Social Development Programs," *Educational Theatre Journal* 27, no. 3 (October 1975): 395–407, 396, 397.
58. Darius L. Swann, "Nautankī," in *IT:TP*, 250–51.
59. Kathryn Hansen, *Grounds for Play: The Nautanki Theatre of North India* (University of California Press, 1992), 13–14.
60. Hansen, *Grounds for Play*, 40.
61. Balwant Gargi, *Folk Theatre in India* (Rupa and Company, 1991), 43–46; Swann, "*Nautankī*," 264.
62. Gargi, *Folk Theatre in India*, 44.
63. Hansen, *Grounds for Play*, 40.
64. Kedar A. Kulkarni, "Introduction" [to Indian Languages concepts], in *RCP-RCN-EL*, 501.
65. Hansen, "Parsi Theatrical Networks," 9.
66. Kathryn Hansen, "Mapping Melodrama: Global Theatrical Circuits, Parsi Theater, and the Rise of the Social," *BioScope: South Asian Screen Studies* 7, no. 1 (June 2016): 1–30, 2.
67. Hansen, "Mapping Melodrama," 23.
68. Hansen, *Grounds for Play*, 81.
69. Hansen, "Mapping Melodrama," 15.
70. Hansen, "Parsi Theatrical Networks," 9.
71. Hansen, "Parsi Theatrical Networks," 6.
72. Kevin Wetmore, Jr., Siyuan Liu, and Erin B. Mee, *Modern Asian Theatre and Performance: 1900–2000* (Bloomsbury, 2014), 169–70, 178.
73. Farley P. Richmond, "Characteristics of the Modern Theatre," in *IT:TP*, 388.
74. Dharwadker, "Modern Indian Theatre," 244.
75. Dharwadker, "Modern Indian Theatre," 263.
76. Wetmore, Liu, and Mee, *Modern Asian Theatre and Performance*, 196, 208. *Yakshagana* is a sixteenth-century theatre form from Kerala.
77. Wetmore, Liu, and Mee, *Modern Asian Theatre and Performance*, 207, 208; italics in the original.

78. Rustom Bharucha, *Theatre and the World: Performance and the Politics of Culture* (Routledge, 1993), 7.
79. Anthony Reid, *A History of Southeast Asia: Critical Crossroads* (Wiley Blackwell, 2015), 211, 212.
80. Reid, *History of Southeast Asia*, 251.
81. Reid, *History of Southeast Asia*, 217.
82. Reid, *History of Southeast Asia*, 265, 290.
83. Reid, *History of Southeast Asia*, 265.
84. Sadiah Boonstra, "Negotiating Heritage: Wayang Puppet Theatre and the Dynamics of Heritage Formation," in *The Heritage Theatre: Globalisation and Cultural Heritage*, eds. M. Halbertsma, A. Van Stipriaan, and P. Van Ulzen (Cambridge Scholars Publishing, 2011), 33, 42.
85. Boonstra, "Negotiating Heritage," 42.
86. Jennifer Goodlander, "Southeast Asia" section in Arya Madhavan, Jonah Salz, Min Tian, CedarBough T. Saeji, and Jennifer Goodlander, "Traditional Asian Performance in Modern and Contemporary Times," in *RHAT*, 499.
87. Ma Thanegi, "Zat Pwe," in *EAT*, vol. 2, 878. The form's name probably derives from the Sanskrit word *jataka*, the stories of which were sometimes source material for the form. Ghulam-Sarwar Yousof, *Dictionary of Traditional South-East Asian Theatre* (Oxford University Press, 1994), 327.
88. Hansen, "Parsi Theatrical Networks," 29–30, 32, 31.
89. Mattani Mojdara Rutnin, *Dance, Drama, and Theatre in Thailand: The Process of Development and Modernization* (Silkworm Books, 1996), 103, 105.
90. Rutnin, *Dance, Drama, and Theatre in Thailand*, 144, 253.
91. Sukanya Sompiboon, "The Reinvention of Thai Traditional-Popular Theatre: Contemporary *Likay* Praxis" (Dissertation, University of Exeter, 2012), 74.
92. Sompiboon, "Reinvention of Thai Traditional-Popular Theatre," 137.
93. Gary Bryden Carkin, "Likay: The Thai Popular Theatre Form and Its Function within Thai Society" (Dissertation, Michigan State University, 1984), 216–17.
94. Carkin, "Likay," 48–49, 49.
95. This discussion of *bangsawan* draws from Tillis, *Challenge of World Theatre History*, 237–39.
96. The word *bangsawan* means "noble," but there is no evidence the form was a court theatre; it might have that name because of the royal or noble lineages of its typical characters. Madiha Ramlan and M. A. Quayum, "Mapping the History of Malaysian Theatre: An Interview with Ghulam-Sarwar Yousof," *Asiatic* 4, no. 2 (December 2010): 155–68, 160.
97. Tan Sooi Beng, *Bangsawan: A Social and Stylistic History of Popular Malay Opera* (Oxford University Press, 1993), vii.
98. Tan, *Bangsawan*, 191.
99. Mohd. Effindi Samsuddin and Rahmah Bujang, "Bangsawan: Creative Patterns in Production," *Asian Theatre Journal* 30, no. 1 (Spring 2013): 122–44, 126.

100. Ghulam-Sarwar, *Dictionary of Traditional South-East Asian Theatre*, 16.
101. Samsuddin and Bujang, "Bangsawan," 123.
102. Tan, *Bangsawan*, 189.
103. Tan, *Bangsawan*, 191.
104. Reid, *History of Southeast Asia*, 302, 305.
105. Wetmore, Liu, and Mee, *Modern Asian Theatre and Performance*, 243, 246, 242, 255.
106. Rutnin, *Dance, Drama, and Theatre in Thailand*, 151.
107. Wetmore, Liu, and Mee, *Modern Asian Theatre and Performance*, 246, 253, 243.
108. Michael Bodden, "Modern Theatre in Maritime Southeast Asia: Indonesia, Malaysia, the Philippines and Singapore," in *RHAT*, 370.
109. James R. Brandon, *Theatre in Southeast Asia* (Harvard University Press, 1967), 57–58.
110. Brandon, *Theatre in Southeast Asia*, 49.

15 Pacific Lands

1. Morris Rossabi, *A History of China* (Wiley Blackwell, 2014), 283.
2. Robert Kong Chan, *Korea-China Relations in History and Contemporary Implications* (Palgrave Macmillan, 2018), 127.
3. See Patrick Karl O'Brien, "The Deconstruction of Myths and Reconstruction of Metanarratives in Global Histories of Material Progress," in *Writing World History: 1800–2000*, eds. Benedickt Stuchtey and Eckhardt Fuchs (Oxford University Press, 2003), 67–89; and Gale Stokes, "The Fates of Human Societies: A Review of Recent Macrohistories," *American Historical Review* 106, no. 2 (April 2001): 508–25.
4. R. Bin Wong, *China Transformed: Historical Change and the Limits of European Experience* (Cornell University Press, 1997), 4.
5. Kenneth Pomeranz, *The Great Divergence: China, Europe, and the Making of the Modern World Economy* (Princeton University Press, 2000), 17.
6. R. Bin Wong, "Possibilities of Plenty and the Persistence of Poverty: Industrialization and International Trade," in *AEW*, 309.
7. Marius B. Jansen, *The Making of Modern Japan* (Harvard University Press, 2000), 277; Ian Morris, *Why the West Rules – for Now: The Patterns of History and What They Reveal about the Future* (Farrar, Straus, Giroux, 2010), 517.
8. Morris, *Why the West Rules*, 517–18.
9. Jansen, *Making of Modern Japan*, 312.
10. Jürgen Osterhammel, *The Transformation of the World: A Global History of the Nineteenth Century*, trans. Patrick Camiller (Princeton University Press, 2014), 416.
11. Quoted in Jansen, *Making of Modern Japan*, 456–57.
12. Kaoru Sugihara, "Global Industrialization: A Multipolar Perspective," in *CWH7.1*, 117.
13. John K. Gillespie, "Modern Japanese Theatre," in *RHAT*, 290.

14. Jonah Salz, "Japan" section in Arya Madhavan, Jonah Salz, Min Tian, CedarBough T. Saeji, and Jennifer Goodlander, "Traditional Asian Performance in Modern and Contemporary Times," in *RHAT*, 486.
15. Benito Ortolani, *The Japanese Theatre: From Shamanistic Ritual to Contemporary Pluralism*, rev. ed. (Princeton University Press, 1995), 106–107.
16. Donald Keene, *Nō and Bunraku: Two Forms of Japanese Theatre* (Columbia University Press, 1990), 43.
17. Gillespie, "Modern Japanese Theatre," 291.
18. Keene, *Nō and Bunraku*, 43–44, 45.
19. Thomas Leims, "Kabuki Goes to Hollywood: Reforms and 'Revues' in the 1980s," in *The Dramatic Touch of Difference: Theatre, Own and Foreign*, eds. Erika Fischer-Lichte, Josephine Riley, and Michael Gissenwehrer (Gunter Narr Verlag, 1990), 109, 111.
20. Karen Brazell, "Japanese Theater: A Living Tradition," in *Traditional Japanese Theater: An Anthology of Plays*, ed. Karen Brazell (Columbia University Press, 1998), 20.
21. Ortolani, *Japanese Theatre*, 186.
22. James R. Brandon, *Kabuki's Forgotten War: 1931–1945* (University of Hawaii, 2008), 4. The plays received their name "because, like hastily pickled radishes, scripts were rushed to the stage within days or weeks of a breaking new event" (4).
23. Brandon, *Kabuki's Forgotten War*, 5.
24. Kevin Wetmore, Jr., Siyuan Liu, and Erin B. Mee, *Modern Asian Theatre and Performance: 1900–2000* (Bloomsbury, 2014), 25, 26.
25. Gillespie, "Modern Japanese Theatre," 294, 291.
26. Ortolani, *Japanese Theatre*, 233.
27. Ortolani, *Japanese Theatre*, 239, 234.
28. Gillespie, "Modern Japanese Theatre," 293.
29. Mitsuya Mori, "Relevant Figures at the Early Stages of the Modernization of Japanese Theatre," in *MAT:PT*, 19.
30. Brian Powell, "Birth of Modern Theatre: Shimpa and Shingeki," in *HJT*, 207.
31. Ortolani, *Japanese Theatre*, 243.
32. Carol Fisher Sorgenfrei, "Japan" section in Anita Singh, Carol Fisher Sorgenfrei, Siyuan Liu, Jan Creutzenberg, and Kathy Foley, "Modern Asian Theatre and Indigenous Performance," in *RHAT*, 460.
33. Senda Akihiko, "The Rebirth of Shakespeare in Japan: From the 1960s to the 1990s," trans. Ryuta Minami, in *Shakespeare and the Japanese Stage*, eds. Takashi Sasyama, J. R. Mulryne, and Margaret Shewring (Cambridge University Press, 1998), 16.
34. Wetmore, Liu, and Mee, *Modern Asian Theatre and Performance*, 39–40.
35. Ortolani, *Japanese Theatre*, 245–48.
36. Ortolani, *Japanese Theatre*, 237.
37. Gillespie, "Modern Japanese Theatre," 307.
38. Edwin O. Reischauer and John K. Fairbank, *East Asia: The Great Tradition* (Houghton Mifflin Company, 1958), 447–48.

39. Wong, "Possibilities of Plenty," 367, 368.
40. For descriptions of, and texts from, six of these forms, see Oh-kon Cho, *Traditional Korean Theatre* (Asian Humanities Press, 1988).
41. Oh-kon Cho, "Korea," in *CGAT*, 181.
42. Andrew P. Killick, "Jockeying for Tradition: The Checkered History of Korean Ch'anggŭk Opera," *Asian Theatre Journal* 20, no. 1 (Spring 2003): 43–70, 45.
43. Oh-kon Cho, "Korea," in *EAT*, vol. 1, 344.
44. Killick, "Jockeying for Tradition," 45.
45. *Encyclopedia Brittanica*, "Seoul," www.britannica.com/place/Seoul.
46. Killick, "Jockeying for Tradition," 47.
47. Meewon Lee, "The Modernization of Korean Theatre through the Reception of Western Realism," in *MAT:PT*, 23–40, 25.
48. Killick, "Jockeying for Tradition," 46.
49. Lee, "Modernization of Korean Theatre," 25.
50. Hong Seunyong, "Theatre in Korea under Colonization," in *HJT*, 255.
51. Wetmore, Liu, and Mee, *Modern Asian Theatre and Performance*, 144.
52. Cho, "Korea," in *CGAT*, 184.
53. Lee, "Modernization of Korean Theatre," 27.
54. Hong, "Theatre in Korea under Colonization," 255.
55. Lee, "Modernization of Korean Theatre," 29.
56. Jinhee Kim, "On Making Things Korean: Western Drama and Local Tradition in Yi Man-hû's *Please Turn Out the Lights*," in *East of West: Cross-Cultural Performance and the Staging of Difference*, eds. Claire Sponsler and Xiaomei Chen (Palgrave Macmillan, 2000), 94.
57. Li Ruru, *The Soul of Beijing Opera: Theatrical Creativity and Continuity in the Changing World* (Hong Kong University Press, 2010), 36.
58. Li, *Soul of Beijing Opera*, 18–19.
59. Morris Rossabi, *A History of China* (Wiley Blackwell, 2014), 293, 294–95.
60. Rossabi, *History of China*, 295.
61. Rossabi, *History of China*, 303–307.
62. Li, *Soul of Beijing Opera*, 23, 24.
63. Fu Jin, *A History of Chinese Theatre in the 20th Century I*, trans. Zhang Qiang (Routledge, 2020), 13.
64. Li, *Soul of Beijing Opera*, 19. Note that the precise relationships between these forms and musical systems are a still a matter of scholarly debate (10).
65. Li, *Soul of Beijing Opera*, 20.
66. Li, *Soul of Beijing Opera*, 40.
67. Jin, *History of Chinese Theatre*, 24.
68. Li, *Soul of Beijing Opera*, 42.
69. Li, *Soul of Beijing Opera*, 53.
70. Siyuan Liu, *Performing Hybridity in Colonial-Modern China* (Palgrave Macmillan, 2013), 33.
71. Liu, *Performing Hybridity*, 45, 47, 48.
72. Liu, *Performing Hybridity*, 49; Wetmore, Liu, and Mee, *Modern Asian Theatre and Performance*, 77.

73. Gilbert Fong and Shelby K. Y. Chan, "Staging Reality: Premodern Drama in China at the Turn of the Twentieth Century," in *MAT:PT*, 72.
74. Quoted in Liu, *Performing Hybridity*, 64.
75. Liu, *Performing Hybridity*, 94.
76. Liu, *Performing Hybridity*, 3.
77. William Dolby, *A History of Chinese Drama* (Paul Elek, 1976), 205.
78. Fong and Chan, "Staging Reality," 75–76, 77–79.
79. Dolby, *History of Chinese Drama*, 208.
80. Wetmore, Liu, and Mee, *Modern Asian Theatre and Performance*, 96.
81. Dolby, *History of Chinese Drama*, 235.
82. Liu, *Performing Hybridity*, 182.
83. This discussion of *yangge* draws from Steve Tillis, *Rethinking Folk Drama* (Greenwood Press, 1999), 1–11. The original meaning of the form's name was possibly "rice-planting songs." David Holm, "Folk Art as Propaganda: The *Yangge* Movement in Yan'an," in *Popular Chinese Literature and the Performing Arts: In the People's Republic of China, 1949–1979*, ed. Bonnie McDougal (University of California Press, 1984), 16.
84. Holm, "Folk Art as Propaganda," 18–20; Sidney D. Gamble, *Chinese Village Plays from the Ting Hsien Region (Yang Ke Hsüan): A Collection of Forty-Eight Chinese Rural Plays as Staged by Villagers from Ting Hsien in Northern China* (Philo Press, 1970), xxv–xxvi.
85. Gamble, *Chinese Village Plays*.
86. Holm, "Folk Art as Propaganda," 13–14.
87. Holm, "Folk Art as Propaganda," 35.
88. Jonathan P. Stock, *Huju: Traditional Opera in Modern Shanghai* (Oxford University Press, 2003), 39, 40, 41.
89. Stock, *Huju*, 8, 30.
90. Stock, *Huju*, 59.
91. Wetmore, Liu, and Mee, *Modern Asian Theatre and Performance*, 8.
92. Erika Fischer-Lichte, *The Show and the Gaze of Theatre: A European Perspective* (University of Iowa Press, 1997), 153.
93. Wetmore, Liu, and Mee, *Modern Asian Theatre and Performance*, 265.
94. Liu, *Performing Hybridity*, 145.
95. Wetmore, Liu, and Mee, *Modern Asian Theatre and Performance*, 10.

Conclusion

1. This account of "trends" draws from Steve Tillis, *The Challenge of World Theatre History* (Palgrave Macmillan, 2020), 189–201.
2. This account of theatrical "syncretism" draws from Tillis, *Challenge of World Theatre History*, 235–42.
3. William H. McNeill, "Passing Strange: The Convergence of Evolutionary Science with Scientific History," *History and Theory* 40 (February 2001): 1–15, 12.

4. Erich Hatala Matthes, "Cultural Appropriation without Cultural Essentialism?," *Social Theory and Practice* 42, no. 2 (April 2016): 343–66, 347.
5. Quoted in Roger Williams School of Law, Library Blog, "What Is Cultural Misappropriation and Why Does It Matter?," https://law.rwu.edu/library/blog/what-cultural-misappropriation-and-why-does-it-matter.
6. Kwame Anthony Appiah, *The Lies That Bind: Rethinking Identity, Creed, Country, Class, Culture* (Liveright, 2018), 208.
7. For one account of the controversy, see Gautam Dasgupta, "*The Mahabharata*: Peter Brook's 'Orientalism,'" in *Interculturalism and Performance: Writings from PAJ*, eds. Bonnie Maranca and Gautam Dasgupta (PAJ, 1991), 75–82.
8. Appiah, *Lies That Bind*, 208–209.
9. Tobin Nellhaus, *Theatre, Communication, Critical Realism* (Palgrave Macmillan, 2010), 188.

Index

Page numbers in *italics* refers to Figures

Abbas I, Shah, 150
Aboriginal Australians, 14, 53, 224
Abydos Passion Play, 74–75
Addison, Joseph, 217
Aeschylus, 68, 70–73
Afghanistan, 153–55
Age of Warring States. *See* Sengoku
agency, human, 24, 189–90
Akbar, Emperor, 155–57, 159
alarinjo, 234, 236
Alexander the Great, 62, 79
Amir Hamza, 105, 173
analogy, concept of, 10–11
Anatolia, 146
Anhui, 260, 262
ankiya nat, 157
apidán. See alarinjo
aragoto, 142
Aristophanes, 51, 64, 73, 113
Aristotle, 61, 63
Arras, 117, 120
Artaud, Antonin, 205–6, 235
Assam, 157
Athens, 59, 66–67
audience-actor communications, 41–43
autos sacramentales, 210–11
avant-garde theatre, 6, 203–6, 213
Averroës (Abu'l-Walid Ibn Rushd), 27–28, 31, 112
Aztecs, 14, 209–10

Babur, Emperor, 155
ballet, 187–88, 197–99, *198*
Ballet Comique de la Reine (Balthasar de Beaujoyeulx), 187
Ballet Russes, 199
Bamana, 14, 52, 230
Bangkok, 246
bangsawan, 247–49, *248*
bangzi musical system, 165, 167–68, 262
Batavia. *See* Jakarta
Battles of Coxinga, The (Chikamatsu), 144

Beijing, 96, 260, 262
Beijing opera. *See jingju*
Berlin, Irving, 223
bhagat, 240
bhakti movement, 155–57, 160
bhand jashna, 159
bhand pather. See bhand jashna
Bharata, 13–14, 61
Bhasa, 60, 72, 83
bhava. See rasa theory
Bhavabhuti, 84
bhavai, 37, 157, 159
Black Crook, The (anon.), 222
Black Slave's Cry to Heaven, The (Zeng Xiaogu), 263–64
Bodel, Jehan, 120
Bombay, 239, 241
Borges, Jorge Luis, 27
Boxer Rebellion, 263
Boy and the Blind Man, The (anon.), 120
Boy Companies (English), 185
Brecht, Bertolt, 52, 197, 205–6, 235
British Raj, 238–39, 246
Brook, Peter, 206, 275
bubonic plague, 133–34, 138, 176
bufos habaneros, 216
bugaku, 123
bunraku, 13, 137, 143–44, 253
Byron, Lord, 202
Byzantine Empire. *See* Roman Empire, Eastern Empire

Cairo, 111–14
Calcutta, 239
Calderón de la Barca, Pedro, 188
Camerata de' Bardi, 186
Camille. See La Dame aux Camélias (Dumas)
canjun xi, 77
cantata, church, 236
Canton, 260
Cao Yu, 265

Capture of Miletus, The (Phyrnicus), 72
Caribbean Sea, 207, 214
cavittu natakam, 161
celebration, theatre and, 53
Central Asia, 154
ch'anggŭk, 257–58, *259*
Chandragupta II, Emperor, 59–60, 83
Charles II, King, 186
Chekhov, Anton, 203
cheo. See hat cheo
Chera Kingdom, 109
Chikamatsu Monzaemon, 144
Chinggis Khan, 90
Chŏngjo, King, 251
Chosŏn Dynasty, 251, 257–58
Christmas Morning Concerts, 216
chuanqi (literature), 78, 98
chuanqi (theatre form), 164–66
Chulalongkorn, King, 246
Chūshingura (Takeda Izumo, Miyoshi Shōraku, and Namiki Senryū), 52
City (or Great) Dionysia festival, 59, 67
Civil War, American, 219–20
Civil War, English, 185, 188
Clapperton, Hugh, 234
Clouds, The (Aristophanes), 51
Cohan, George M., 223
Coleridge, Samuel Taylor, 202
Columbian Exchange, the, 136, 177
Columbus, Christopher, 136
comedy, Roman, 10, 79
commedia dell'arte, 180–83, *181*
commedia erudita, 179–80, 182–83
commemoration, theatre and, 53–54
Communist Revolution, Chinese, 265
Concert Party theatre, 10, 235–36
Conquest of Jerusalem, The (anon.), 210
Conquest of Rhodes, The (anon.), 210
Constantinople, 82, 146–47, 179
context (societal, theatrical, and formal), concept of, 84–87
Corpus Christi cycle plays, 120–21, 178
corroboree, 225
costumbrismo, 212
court masques, 188
Crusades, the, 120, 146
Cruz, Sor Juana Ines de la, 210
cultural appropriation, 274–76
Cultural Revolution, Chinese, 53

da Gama, Vasco, 135–36
Dadu. See Beijing
Dafne (Jacopo Corsi and Jacopo Peri), 186
Dakar, 237
de la Halle, Adam, 120

Death and the King's Horseman (Soyinka), 238
Delhi Sultanate, 154–55
dengaku, 123–24
devotion, theatre and, 51
Dias, Bartholomew, 135–36
dithyramb, 59, 61
Divine Narcissus, The (Cruz), 211
Doctor Faustus (Marlowe), 178
Doll's House, A (Ibsen), 203
drama moden, 249
Dumas, Alexandre, *fils*, 202, 263
Dying Cato, The (Addison), 217

East India Company, British (EIC), 238–39, 260–61
East India Company, Dutch (VOC), 173
East–West dichotomy, 4–5
Edo. See Tokyo
egungun, 234
Ekong comic plays, 14
El Güegüence, o El Macho Ratón (anon.), 211
electronic media, drama via, 276–77
Elizabeth I, Queen, 184, 187
entertainment, theatre and, 49
Erasmus, Desiderius, 176, 178
erhuang musical system, 260, 262
Euridice (Jacopo Peri and Giulio Caccini), 186
Euripides, 52, 68, 71
Eurocentrism, 3–4, 191–92
evolution, cultural, 46–47
evolution, Darwinian, 32–33, 40–41, 43–44

fabula praetexta, 80
fabula togata, 79
Fall of Adam and Eve, The (anon.), 210
Father, The (Strindberg), 203
Fatimid Dynasty, 112
Ferdowsi, 152
Five Nights (Bhasa), 72
Friml, Rudolf, 223
Frogs, The (Aristophanes), 73

Gandersheim Abbey, 118
Gao Ming, 164
genero chico, 200
Ghosts (Ibsen), 203
gigaku, 123
The Girl Washing Silk, The (Liang), 166
Grant, Ulysses S., 253–54
Gregorian Reforms, 116–17
Gryphius, Andreas, 188
Guan Hanqing, 96
Gujarat, 109, 157, 159
Gupta Empire, 68, 83
Gutenberg, Johannes, 177

Hahoe, 257
haipai, 263
haiyan musical system, 165
hakāya, 112
hangdang, 95, 99–100, *100*
Hangzhou, 95–96
Hardy, Alexandre, 184
Harrigan, Edward, 222
Harsha, King, 83
Hart, Tony, 222
hat bôi, 106
hat cheo, 105
Hathras, 240–41
Havana, 214
Hellenistic Empire, 79
Hernani (Hugo), 202
Hideyoshi. *See* Toyotomi Hideyoshi
Homer, 70
homology, concept of, 10
horn-butting game, the, 77
hosay, 216–17
Hrotsvitha, 117–18
huaju, 264–65
Hubei, 262
Hugo, Victor, 202
huidiao, 260
huju, 266
humanism, 176, 178–80
humanist plays, 178–80, 182–83
Huns, 83
Husain, Imam, 51, 151–52
hybrid-popular theatre, concept of, 227

Ibibio, 14
Ibn Dāniyāl, Muhammad, 112–13
Ibsen, Henrik, 203
Ichikawa Danjūrō IX, 255
Ieyasu. *See* Tokugawa Ieyasu
Iliad, The (Homer), 70, 86
In Dahomey (Williams and Walker), 222
Incas, 209
Incidents in the Life of a Slave Girl (Jacobs), 219
Industrial Revolution, 136, 192
Innsbruck, 178
interludes, 178
Isfahan, 150
Ismail I, Shah, 150–51
Istanbul, 147–48
Iwakura Tomomi, 253–54

Jacobs, Harriet, 219
Jakarta, 173
James I, King, 177
Jarry, Alfred, 203–5
Jataka tales, 170–71

Java, 103, 105, 171, 173, 250, 275
Jayavarman II, King, 105
Jesuits, 140, 161
Ji Junxiang, 4
Jiangxi, 163
Jin Dynasty, 95
jingju, *261*
  emergence of, 260, 262–63
  reform of, 263
jingpai, 263
jingxi. *See jingju*
jo-ha-kyū compositional structure, 123, 125–26
Johnson, Bob, 235
jongleurs, 91, 118–19
jonkonnu, 215, 219

kabuki, *139*, 144
  in the 19th and 20th centuries, 254–55
  emergence of, 137–38, 141–43
kabukimono, 137–38
kagura, 123
Kalidasa, 4, 59–60, 72, 83
Kan'ami, 124, 126
Kanpur, 240–41
karaghiózis, 149
karagöz, 147–50, 153
Karbala, Battle of, 51, 151
Kashmir, 159
kathakali, 37, 160–61, 244
Kerala. *See* Malabar coast
khayāl al-zill, 112–14, 149
Khmer Empire, 105
khon, 170
kich nôi, 249
komedya, 174–75
Kong Shangren, 166
kote-tlon, 14, 52, 230
krishnattam, 160–61
kunqu, 166, *167*, 260
Kunshan, 165
kutiyattam, 109–11, *110*, 160, 244
kwagh-hir, 234–35
Kyd, Thomas, 188
kyōgen, 128
Kyoto, 127, 137, 141

La bohème (Puccini), 200
La Dame aux Camélias (Dumas), 202–3, 263
La Sylphide (Filippo Taglioni), 198
lakhon vao, 249
lakon kabach boran, 105
lakon nai, 170–71, 246
lakon nok, 171
lakon phut, 249
Le Théâtre de Neptune (anon.), 217

Leopoldville, 237
Liang Chenyu, 166
likay, 247
literacy
    in ancent India, 64–65
    in ancient China, 76–78
    in ancient Egypt, 76
    in ancient Greece, 63–64
literary theatre, concept of, 58
Little Ice Age, 134
liturgical theatre, Christian, 50, 119
loa, 210–11
London, 177–78, 182–85
Love Suicides at Amijima, The (Chikamatsu), 144
Lucerne, 178
Lysistrata (Aristophanes), 64

Macbeth (Shakespeare), 6, 201
Madrid, 176, 182
Magadi theatre, 153–54, 159
Mahabharata, The (epic) (Vyasa), 62, 64, 72
Mahabharata, The (play) (Brook), 275
Maharashtra, 159, 240
Mahmud of Ghazni, 107
Makah, 14
Malabar coast, 83, 109, 160–61
Malay Peninsula, 250
Mamluk Dynasty, 112
Manilla, 174
Marlowe, Christopher, 178, 188
Marx, Karl, 252
masquerades, African, 10, 14, 215, 230–34, *231*, *232*
Maurya Empire, 60, 68
Mayans, 14, 209
Medici, Catherine de, 187
Medieval Climate Anomaly, 94, 115
Mehmed II, Sultan, 147
Meiji Restoration, 252–54
Melaka, 169, 171, 173
melodrama, 218, 224
    in Asian regions, 241, 259, 264
    in Europe, 200–1
Menander, 79
metanarrative, 2, 15–16
Mexico City, 212
mime, Roman, 80, 118
Ming Dynasty, 162–66
minstrel shows, 10, 219–22
Miss Julie (Strindberg), 203
Mnouchkine, Ariane, 16, 206
modernity, conceptual frameworks of, 192–93
Molière, 51, 178
Mongol Empire, 90, 96, 133–34
monomane, 125, 128
Monteverdi, Claudio, 6, 187

morality plays, 178
Moros y Cristianos, Mexican, 210
Moros y Cristianos, Spanish, 53, 174, 210
Mr. Huang of the Eastern Ocean (anon.), 77
muá rôi nuoc, 106, *106*
Mughal Empire, 155–56, 238
Mummers' Play, British, 39, 46
musical comedy, British, 222
musical comedy, ethnic, 222
musical theatre, Black, 222
musical, Broadway, 7, 222–23

nang yai, 170
nanxi, 95–101, 164
nationhood, 7–8
Natyasastra (Bharata), 5, 69–70
nautanki, 240–41, *241*, 243
neo-Confucianism, 165, 168
Neo-Europes, concept of, 207–8
New Comedy, Greek, 73, 79
New York, 222
Ngugi Wa Thiong'o, 237
niches, concept of, 65–66
Nijinsky, Vaslav, 199
ningyō-jōruri. See bunraku
nō, 10, 123, 126–28, *127*
    in the 19th and 20th centuries, 253–54
    emergence of, 124–26
    in Tokugawa era, 140
noh. See nō

Oda Nobunaga, 139–40
Odyssey, The (Homer), 70, 86
Oedipus (Sophocles), 4
Offenbach, Jacques, 212
Ogunde, Hubert, 236
Oklahoma! (Richard Rodgers and Oscar Hammerstein II), 223
Okuni, Izumo no, 137–38, 140–41
Old Comedy, Greek, 73, 79
onnagata, 143
Ontario, 220
opera, European, 6–7, 39, 42, 188
    in the 19th and 20th centuries, 199–200
    emergence of, 186–87
operetta, 200, 212, 223
Opium Wars, 260–62
Oresteia trilogy (Aeschylus), 70–71
Orfeo (Monteverdi), 6, 187
Orphan of Zhou, The (Ji), 4
Orpheus in the Underworld (Offenbach), 212
orta-oyunu, 149–50, 153–54, 159
Orthodox Church, 82
Osaka, 141

Othello (Shakespeare), 201
Ottoman Empire, 146–49

p'ansori, 257–58
Panini, 62, 64
pantomime, Roman, 80
pantomime (panto), British, 216
Paris, 183, 197, 199
Parsi theatre, 241–43, 246
Passion plays (mainland Europe), 120–21
pastores, 210
Patanjali, 62, 64
Peach Blossom Fan, The (Kong), 166
pedagogy, theatre and, 52–53
Peking opera. *See jingju*
Peloponnesian War, 52, 79
Performance Studies, 55
periodicity, 8, 19–22
Perry, Matthew, 252
Persian War, 67
Persians, The (Aeschylus), 68, 70, 72–73
Philip II, King, 177
Phoenician Women, The (Phyrnicus), 72
Phyrnicus, 72–73
pièce bien faite. *See* well-made play
pihuang musical system, 262
Pires, Tomé, 169
Pixérécourt, Guilbert de, 201
Plautus, 79
Play of Robin and Marion, The (de la Halle), 120
Play of Saint Nicholas, The (Bodel), 120
Poetics, The (Aristotle), 61, 184
pretend play, childhood, 31–40, 43
progressivist thesis1, 5–7
Puccini, Giacomo, 200
pusong, 175
pya zat, 249
pyŏlsin-gut, 50–51, 257

Qianlong Emperor, 251, 260
Qing Dynasty, 168, 251, 263
Quem queritis trope. *See* liturgical theatre, Christian

Rabinal Achí (anon.), 209–10
Ramacharitmanas (Tulsidas), 155
Ramakien, The (anon.), 170
Ramayana, The (Valmiki), 62, 64, 72, 170
ramdilla, 216–17
Ramesseum Dramatic Papyrus, 75
ramlila, 157, *158*, 216, 239–40, 242
Ramnagar, 239
Rangoon, 246
rasa. *See rasa* theory
rasa theory, 62, 70, *71*

raslila, 157
realism, concept of, 196–97
Recruiting Officer, The (George Farquhar), 223
Revolution, French, 188
Rice, Thomas Dartmouth, 219
Richard III (Shakespeare), 201
Rig Veda (anon.), 61, 86
Rinuccini, Ottavio, 186
Rio de Janeiro, 212
ritual, theatre and, 5–6, 28–30, 48, 50–51
role categories. *See hangdang*
Roman Empire
  Eastern Empire, 82, 113, 146–47
  Western Empire, 80–84
Romance of the Three Kingdoms (Luo Guanzhong), 98
romanticism, concept of, 196
Romberg, Sigmund, 223
Rome, 79, 81
Rotimi, Ola, 237
Rudradaman I, King, 68
ru-howzi, 153–54, 159

Safavid Empire, 150–51, 153
sainete, 211–12
sainete criollo, 212–13, *213*
Sakas, 62, 68–69
Sakuntala and the Ring of Recognition (Kalidasa), 4, 72
Samarkand, 145
San Francisco, 221
sandiwara, 249
sangaku, 123
Sanskrit theatre, 57, 85–86
  decline of, 107–8
  Gupta and post-Gupta expansion, 82–84, 107
  historical context, 59–62
  influence on South Asian theatre, 50, 109–10, 160
  relationship with Greek theatre, 62–63
  societal conditions, 64–65, 68–69, 73
sarugaku, 123–25, 138
satyr plays, 59, 62
satyr-like mimetic plays, 61
scale, temporal and spatial, 11–12, 189
Schiller, Friedrich, 53
Scribe, Eugène, 202
Sea of Japan, 251–52
Seagull, The (Chekhov), 203
Selim I, Sultan, 148–49
Seneca, 80
Sengoku, 138–40, 143
Seoul, 258
Seville, 177, 182
Shaan-Gan-Ning border region, 266

Shāhnāmeh, The (Ferdowsi), 152
Shakespeare, William, 52, 188
Shanghai, 261, 263–64, 266
Shelley, Percy Bysshe, 202
Shiism, 150–51, 153, 216
shimpa. See *shinpa*
shingeki, 255–56
shingŭk, 258–60
shinp'agŭk. See *shinp'a*
shinpa, 255–56, 258, 263
shinp'a, 258–60
Show Boat (Kern and Hammerstein II), 223
Siege of Gibraltar, The (Charles Dibden), 54
Singapore, 250
Sino-Japanese War, 254
Siyavush, 151–52
social commentary, theatre and, 51–52
Song Dynasty, 93
Sophocles, 68, 71
South China Sea, 162
Southern Song Dynasty, 95
Soyinka, Wole, 238
spoken theatre, 37
   in Africa, 236–38
   in the Americas, 210–12, 218
   in East Asia, 264–65
   in Europe, 16th – 17th centuries, 182–86
   in Europe, 18th – 20th centuries, 203, *204*
   in Japan, 255–56
   in South Asia, 242–44
   in Southeast Asia, 249–50
   transference of, 10, 267–69
Statue Play (Bhasa), 72
Story of the Lute, The (Gao), 164
storytelling, 36, 43, 257
   in Africa and Southwest Asia, 14–15
   in East Asia, 98
   in Iran, 152
   in Japan, 143
   relationship with dramatic theatre, 13
Stowe, Harriet Beecher, 220
Strait of Malacca, 103, 162, 169
Strindberg, August, 203
Sturm und Drang movement, 201
Sumbawa, 173
sutradhara, 109
swang, 157, 240
Sydney, 223
syncretism, concept of, 60, 273

Taiping Revolution, 262
Taiwan, 263
Takarazuka theatre companies, 39
Taking Tiger Mountain by Strategy (Anon.), 53
Tale in Twelve Episodes of Jōruri, The (anon.), 143

Tale of Genji, The (Murasaki Shikibu), 126
Tale of the Heike, The (anon.), 126
tamasha, Indian, 159, 240, 242
tamasha, Iranian, 153, 159
Tamerlane, 145–46, 154–55
Tang Xianzu, 14
taqlid, 153
Tartuffe (Molière), 51
tayao niang, 77
ta'ziyeh, 37, 51, *151*, 151–53, 216
Terence, 79, 118
theatre form, concept of the, 16–17
theatre of roots (TOR), 243–44
theatre regions, concept of, 78, 129–30, *194*
Thespis, 45, 59
Thingspiele, 52
Tiv, 234
Tokugawa Dynasty, 139, 251–52
Tokugawa Ienari, 251
Tokugawa Ieyasu, 139, 141
Tokyo, 138, 141, 144, 256
Tom shows, 220, *221*
Top Graduate Zhang Xie (anon.), 96
Toyotomi Hideyoshi, 139–40
traditional-modern dichotomy, 226–27
tragedy, Greek, 10, 57
   expansion beyond Athens, 78–79
   historical context, 59–61
   influence on European opera, 186
   relationship with Sanskrit theatre, 62–63
   societal conditions, 66–68, 70–73
transformation texts, Buddhist, 98
Treaty of Nanjing, 261
Treaty of Tordesillas, 208
Triumph of Horus, The, 75–76
Trojan Women, The (Euripides), 52
Tulsidas, 155
tuông. See *hat bôi*
Twelfth Night (Shakespeare), 185

Ubu Roi (Jarry), 203–5
Ujjain, 59–60, 68–69, 72
ukiyo, 141
Uncle Tom's Cabin (novel) (Stowe), 220
Uncle Tom's Cabin (play), 264
Uncle Vanya (Chekhov), 203
University Wits, 185

Vacarezza, Alberto, 212
vaudeville, American, 222
Vega, Lope de, 188
Venice, 187
verfremdungseffekt, 206
verismo opera, 199–200
vidusaka, 109, 161

Vietnamese water puppetry. *See muá rôi nuoc*
Vikramaditya, King, 60
Visakhadatta, 83
Visitation Exchange. *See* liturgical theatre, Christian
Vondel, Joost van den, 188

Wagner, Richard, 199
wagoto, 143
Walker, George, 222
War of Independence, Mexican, 212
Washington, George, 217
Water Margin (Shi Nai'an), 98
wayang golek Menak, 173
wayang kulit Menak, 173
wayang kulit purwa, 10, 172, *172*
  in the 20th century, 245–46
  emergence and development, 104
  Islamic influence on, 171–72
  transmission through Southeast Asia, 104–5
Weber, Max, 252
Wei Liangfu, 166
well-made play, 202–3, 218
wenmingxi, 263–65, 268
Wenzhou, 95
Wilhelm Tell (Schiller), 53
Williams, Bert, 222

World War, First, 191
World War, Second, 236, 254

xipi musical system, 262
xiqu, 100

yakshagana, 244
Yalley, "Teacher," 235
yangge, 265–66
Yeats, William Butler, 206
yiyang musical system, 165, 167–68, 260
Yōrō (Zeami), 127
Yoruba, 234
Yoruba Travelling (or Popular) Theatre, 236
Yoshimitsu, 124, 127
Yuan Dynasty, 95, 134, 162
Yuan *zaju*. *See zaju*, Yuan era
yuanben, 95
yūgen, 125, 128
yuyao musical system, 165

zaju
  Ming era, 164
  Song era, 95
  Yuan era, 96–101
zarzuela, 200, 212, 216
zat pwe, 246
Zeami, 13, 124–27
Zola, Émile, 200

For EU product safety concerns, contact us at Calle de José Abascal, 56–1°,
28003 Madrid, Spain or eugpsr@cambridge.org.

www.ingramcontent.com/pod-product-compliance
Ingram Content Group UK Ltd.
Pitfield, Milton Keynes, MK11 3LW, UK
UKHW022234220226
468302UK00017B/274